Care(ful) Relat

Between Mothers and the Caregivers They Hire

Edited by Katie B. Garner and Andrea O'Reilly

DEMETER

Care(ful) Relationships Between Mothers and The Caregivers They Hire
Edited by Katie Bodendorfer Garner and Andrea O'Reilly

Demeter Press
PO Box 197
Coe Hill, Ontario
Canada
K0L 1P0
Tel: 289-383-0134
Email: info@demeterpress.org
Website: www.demeterpress.org

Demeter Press logo based on the sculpture "Demeter" by Maria-Luise Bodirsky www.keramik-atelier.bodirsky.de

Printed and Bound in Canada

Cover design and typesetting: Michelle Pirovich
Proof reading: Casey O'Reilly-Conlin

Tracy Royce's "Untitled Tanka" first appeared in *Ribbons* 2009

Library and Archives Canada Cataloguing in Publication
Title: Care(ful) relationships between mothers and the caregivers they hire / edited by Katie Bodendorfer Garner and Andrea O'Reilly.
Names: Garner, Katie B., editor. | O'Reilly, Andrea, 1961- editor.
Description: Includes bibliographical references.
Identifiers: Canadiana 20230572421 | ISBN 9781772584660 (softcover)
Subjects: LCSH: Child care workers. | LCSH: Child care. | LCSH: Child care workers, Social conditions. | LCSH: Mothers.
Classification: LCC HQ778.5 .C37 2024 | DDC 649/.1—dc23

Funded by the Government of Canada

Canadä

The publisher gratefully acknowledges the support of the Government of Canada

For all the women who care to make the world
a better place, and my children, who always make
the world a place I love.
—Katie B. Garner

For the Demeter team—Michelle, Casey, and Jesse
for their care in the creation of this collection
and to our contributors for their caring research.
—Andrea O'Reilly

Table of Contents

8.

Family Exchange Norms and Mother-Nanny Relationships
in Leila Slimani's *The Perfect Nanny* and Kiley Reid's *Such a Fun Age*
Jill Goad

9.

Seeing Beyond Black and White in the Mother-Nanny Novel:
Problematics, Purpose, and Possibilities of Empathy
Katie B. Garner

10.

"I'm Quitting Your Service; I've Had Quite Enough":
Representations of Caregivers' Subjectivity in Tamara Mose Brown's
Raising Brooklyn and Victoria Brown's *Minding Ben*
Elizabeth Podnieks

Section III
Care(ful) Relationships around the Globe: Sociological and
Anthropological Analyses

11.

Between Cosmopolitan Mothering and the Global Care Chain:
Japanese Mothers, Intra-Asian Migration, and Everyday Struggles
of "the Nanny Question"
Aya Kitamura

12.

Paradoxes of Power in Carework
Laura Bunyan and Barret Katuna

Introduction

Mothers and the Caregivers They Hire: Problematics and Possibilities

Katie B. Garner

As I write this in summer 2023, it is hard not to consider the truths revealed to us during the pandemic and the ensuing letdown that "normal" has returned without noticeable political or cultural changes to how we configure and value care. Too many businesses and governments remain determined to avoid addressing the unsustainability of contemporary carework, parenting, mothering, and waged work. During the pandemic, most governments quickly deemed carework essential. Nurses, doctors, psychologists, childcare workers, and more were recognized for the critical work that they were doing. Caregivers, often mothers, held the hands of those in need of company, assessed physical and psychological risk, helped with online schooling, comforted fears, made meals, tended the sick, and carried the heavy load of work that is almost always deeply under-remunerated if it is paid at all. All this work occurred long before the pandemic and will continue into the foreseeable future, yet the rhetoric of "essential work" has largely disappeared from politicians' speeches, mass media, and daily conversation. Although it is impossible to ignore the ways the bloodlines of carework revealed the profound anemia within our care infrastructure, we continue to wait for the change both mother-employers[1] and childcare providers (who are often mothers themselves) so desperately need.

The work in this anthology examines the fissures that strain the fabric of care in North America and beyond. This work follows in the footsteps of Patricia Hill Collins, Nancy Folbre, Evelyn Nakano Glenn, Pierrette Hondagneu-Sotelo, Cameron Macdonald, Rhacel Parrañas, Mary Romero, Joan Tronto, and so many other brilliant feminist scholars and activists who have spotlighted the inequities of carework and mothering. The article that launched my own research on this topic was Tronto's "The Nanny Question in Feminism," which draws forth the inherent tension between a feminist agenda that encourages women to participate in waged work and the inequitable system of carework that has filled the gaps of labour in the home primarily by Black and brown women as well as those who are poor and have recently immigrated. As a woman raised in the "women can have it all" era of choice feminism, her work helped me name the ways that this form of trickle-down feminism is unethical. I continue to grapple with the questions Tronto poses nearly two decades later.

In its broadest sense, "care is our individual and common ability to provide the political, social, material, and emotional conditions that allow the vast majority of people and living creatures on this planet to thrive" (Care Collective 6). One of the goals of this anthology is to examine a subset of carework, specifically the problems and possibilities for reform via the relationships that form between mother-employers and the childcare workers they hire.[2] Equality studies scholar Kathleen Lynch writes, "Although the nurturing values that underpin care relations are generally politically domesticated and silenced, naming and claiming them can help reinvigorate resistance to neoliberalism" (4). This silencing benefits no one, and the authors in this collection actively push back against it.

This anthology aims to examine the relationships that develop between mother-employers and the women they hire from an interdisciplinary approach. Storytelling and autoethnography lead to explication of fictional depictions of these relationships in novels and dramatic presentations, which then feed into studies that offer an international examination from primarily sociological and anthropological approaches. What connects these chapters are issues of power, privilege, unmet need, love, altruism, problematics, and possibilities. The introduction itself aims to provide a cursory overview of the problems and possibilities endemic to outsourced childcare in North America while also providing context to and an overview of the interdisciplinary material in this anthology.

The Problems with Many Names

The problems that plague waged childcare work often impact both the mother-employer and the childcare provider, a point that I will address again in the section covering possibilities. While mother-employers nearly always experience more social and financial privilege, they remain part of, and perpetuate, a broken system that is currently unsustainable, unequal, and unfair.[3] This does not mean that they are reprehensible, since they, too, are often navigating broken systems that offer few good options. By most accounts, those who are tasked with completing outsourced childcare work are the ones that are most in need of our efforts to revamp care circuits, and we should begin by listening to them. It is also important to note that carework is complex not only as an activity but the ways that it is classed, raced, and gendered. While many issues could be addressed in this section, I will limit the scope to three primary issues that seem most pertinent to the work in this anthology: 1) our ubiquitous undervaluing of childcare work and mothering; 2) gendered, classed, and raced notions of childcare work and mothering; and 3) contradictory and irreconcilable messages regarding women, carework, and waged work. The limited space of this introduction does not permit me to do justice to the myriad interconnected issues that are embedded in outsourced childcare, and I encourage you to read the work of the many brilliant foremothers of this subdiscipline (as well as the work herein of course!).

Our Ubiquitous Undervaluing of Carework in Capitalist Societies

When childcare is done in the home by the mother, it is seldom remunerated. In *Care and Capitalism*, Lynch writes:

> "To justify making care cheap it had first to be defined as worthless, part of nature rather than society. This was achieved through the equation of care labour with femininity and women.... Like water, trees and clean air, care was defined as freely available from the nature of women, regarded as being produced without effort or work" (41-42).

This work is a necessity, but it is not viewed as productive in an economic sense. A key feature of former President Bill Clinton's Personal Responsibility and Work Opportunity Reconciliation Act of 1996 (PRWORA), also known as the Welfare Reform Act, was to decrease participation in federal welfare programs by having women, including mothers, engage in waged work outside the home, even when that work, which was sometimes low-wage, required mothers to secure childcare from another woman, who was likely earning minimum wage (or less) herself.

Childcare work within family units can be paid or it can be offered for free, albeit "free" is a misnomer both in regard to the labour that is shared and the sense of obligation that can be entangled in family dynamics (see Wiggins, chapter 13). While money is not always exchanged, kinship norms and notions of reciprocity remain in play. Carework completed by those outside of families is nearly always paid and the work can be completed in the employer's home, the childcare provider's home, or neither (typically at a daycare). While nearly all feminized work is under-remunerated, carework stands out as one of the most egregious examples, with the average childcare worker in the United States earning a paltry $11/hour, well under the $20/hour that economists say is required to keep pace with productivity and inflation (Baker). Most experts believe wage data is inflated since domestic work is often performed as part of the informal labour market, thereby permitting those not providing a living wage the means to conceal their transgressions.

Too often a childcare provider's salary is linked solely to a mother's income rather than a family income, particularly if her salary is considered secondary. Some mothers, particularly those who are solo mothering, have little choice but to leave waged work or pay their childcare provider less than they themselves earn, creating a drought-stricken version of trickle-down economics or, as Arlie Hochschild calls it, "the nanny chain". Interestingly, unlike other types of waged work, there is a pernicious belief that "free" care is purer and less sullied by the stigma of capitalism (Folbre 45).

Regardless of whether reproductive labour, carework, and childcare are remunerated, they remain part of the economy of all countries and serve as the backbone of capitalism as we experience it globally and locally. Oxfam estimates that unpaid reproductive labour adds eleven trillion dollars to the world economy every year, but it has yet to be factored into the GDP in any meaningful way, with scholar Catherine Rottenberg positing: "As an economic order, neoliberalism relies on reproduction and care work in order to reproduce and maintain human capital," yet "as a political rationality, neoliberalism has no lexicon that can recognize let alone value reproduction and care work" (16). She later explains that "reproduction and the care work it entails" are "outsourced to other women deemed 'disposable,' since they are neither considered 'strivers' nor properly 'responsibilized'" (84). Philosopher Nancy Fraser similarly writes: "Ironically, then, carework produces the labor that [capitalism] calls 'productive' but is itself deemed 'unproductive'" (56). This inherent contradiction will not be resolved easily and will require a shift in cultural norms and legal policy.

Classed and Raced Notions of Childcare Work and Mothering

The relationship between a mother-employer and the caregiver she hires is nearly always fraught. Our values and social placement in relation to mothering, feminism, gender and sexuality, immigration, class, race, religion, neoliberalism, legal policy, and social norms all shape access, beliefs, and overall equity. Notably, while these markers are discussed separately at times, the "matrix of domination," as feminist Hill Collins calls it, functions in a way that allows for cumulative oppressions to be enacted simultaneously. Gender, class, and race in particular define both who gets to be cared for and who is charged with doing carework. Those with money receive more care—and often better care—than those without it. This is true in schools, medical systems (particularly in the United States), and our homes. Romero warns that middle- and upper-middle-class feminists who hire women to clean or care for their children run the risk of claiming rights to sisterhood based on the "brute fact that all women share the burden of housework," but these women fail to recognize that they simultaneously continue to "enjoy class privilege in their ability to shift that burden to another woman" (*Maid* 195). Mother-employers in many contexts "other" those outside the dominant culture to fulfill menial or under-remunerated domestic work, which ultimately serves to maintain patriarchal and racist modes of motherhood.

While childcare work is ubiquitously under-remunerated, childcare work that closely aligns with the intensive mothering practices described by sociologist Sharon Hays is more costly and is therefore restricted to the economically elite. Nannies who belong to a privileged social class and who have increased social capital often garner more lucrative and desirable positions that involve fewer children, more independence, and better benefits (see Wood and O'Donnell, chapter two; Kitamura, chapter eleven; Mahanty, chapter fourteen). This segment of the childcare labour market often receives the most robust salaries as well as substantial perks and may include paid vacation, sick leave, health insurance, and/or use of a vehicle as well as a general higher degree of status within the family. These women are more likely to receive "work that does not differ in kind from that taken on by the parents" (Wrigley 66). As discussed in Madeline Wood's and Rachel O'Donnell's chapter, families who have the financial resources to be the most selective often seek a nanny who most closely resembles their own ethnic, religious, and economic background (i.e., nannies who are accustomed to the mores of the middle- or upper-middle-class and who can instill in the children of the family the same values that the mother would were she a full-time stay-at-home mother). In a time when intensive mothering is growing even more entrenched in the quest to arm children with the intellectual and socio-emotional skills required to work in a neoliberal, global economy, many families vie for the nanny who can help support this development, which, by its nature, requires copious time and money as well as physical and emotional investment—just as intensive mothering would.

Like class, race should not be predictive of the contours of childcare, but it is. The history of enslavement in the United States (US) influences policies in effect today and continues to shape the employment protections and opportunities of Black (and brown) people. Many Black women in the US were coerced into low-wage domestic work well into the twentieth century, since other fields were not open to them. Sociologist Mignon Duffy notes that this coerced extraction of carework was not limited to Black women, with Indigenous, Asian, and immigrant women all being pushed into domestic work that demanded long hours, offered little pay, and presented almost no chance of promotion. Indigenous people and Latina/Hispanic women were often employed, with varying degrees of pay and agency, in the southwest US. Similarly, immigrants from Asia (both men and women) were recruited for domestic labour on the West Coast. Many of these women were mothers themselves and/or were removed from their families under the guise of providing opportunity for themselves and their families. This pattern of extracting care from those with less social capital or who are racially marginalized remains in place throughout the world today.

Notably, some employers purposely seek out cultural difference to enhance their own social standing as well as the knowledge and cultural access of their children—traits that are increasingly valuable in a globalized economy (see Garner, chapter nine). Race and ethnicity mark an individual seeking a childcare position, but it is a marker that can be either an advantage or a disadvantage based on the market, the individual seeking employment, or trends in racial preference.[4] This profiling can also occur by caregivers seeking employment (Hondagneu-Sotelo 57-60). While there are limited advantages for women who meet race-based employment trends, it is impossible to place this in the ensuing section, which cover possibilities for progress, for two primary reasons. First, while some women may benefit financially from preconceived ideas of race and ethnicity, any advantages—even when financially crucial to an individual woman's or family's success— are rooted in unfounded bias. Second, while there may be important short-term gains for some childcare workers, this is not sustainable or a system we would ever want to replicate. Not only are those involved left hoping that mercurial beliefs regarding race, ethnicity, sex, and gender might sway in their favour, but even when they do, this form of unfunded, unlegislated, and unequal childcare is not one that leaves room for respect, growth, love, or stability.

Like racial-ethnic markers, insecure immigration status can be used by some employers to extract additional labour for reduced pay. For some women with tentative legal status, particularly those who lack strong language skills and have limited formal education, childcare is one of the few positions they can secure that permits them to contribute much-needed funds to their families. Many women who pursue work in the Global North must leave their families, including their children, in order to earn a wage. Some migrant mothers who emigrate for care-work positions see their income as more valuable to their families than the mothering they could offer if they stayed (Abrego; Hondagneu-Sotelo; Marrun).

Nannies' immigration status and the strength of the nation-states that export their human capital can play large roles in the degree of exploitation that nannies may experience. Actions taken by the World Trade Organization (and other similar organizations) along with the overall ability of more women to travel outside of their homeland has led to an influx of cheap labour. The US and some other economically developed countries seem unwilling to establish and/or enforce immigration/labour policies that would support domestic workers and caregivers due to the economic boon that this labour provides materially comfortable citizens (Chang). Sociologists have examined the ways in which neoliberalism, structural adjustment programs (SAPs), and immigration have altered migration patterns, particularly by focusing on the women who emigrate, the husbands who are asked to adapt to different gender expectations, the children whose mothers have left in order to provide them with material items and educational opportunities, and the ways in which the immigration of such a vast pool of cheap, feminized labour has impacted the US economy and family life therein (Anderson; Chang; Ehrenreich; Glenn; Guevarra; Hochschild; Hondagneu-Sotelo; Macdonald; Misra; Parreñas; Romero; Uttal; Wrigley). Meanwhile, many developing countries rely heavily on the remittances women send back to their families and are reluctant to protect their citizens when they are abroad (Anderson; Guevarra; Parreñas). Even if the desire to assist were present, it is unlikely these besieged governments would have the political power required to create fundamental change. As a result, importing countries must do better.

Square Pegs and Round Holes: Women, Childcare, and Waged Work

Carework—both physical and emotional—is synonymous with women's work. Women and mothers carry the lion's share of unwaged care labour around the world. More than 90 per cent of waged careworkers are women. This commonality should not be interpreted as an equalizer among women, however. Sociologist Bridget Anderson claims: "Feminists have tended to regard domestic work as the great leveler, a common burden imposed on women by patriarchy and lazy husbands," but when one group of women can outsource this work to another, we can no longer consider this labour to be an equalizer (1). Like carework more broadly, the work of mothers is seldom regarded as high-status labour in the Global North, even while our cultural imagination is fed with romanticized, commodified, and manufactured notions of the people doing this work. Many women do experience emotional, spiritual, and psychic rewards that are rooted in their subjectivity as mothers, but this cannot be unspooled from the spindle of carework that has been co-opted and formed into the current institution by patriarchal forces that undermine women's means of mothering (Rich).

While mothers may find their labour fulfilling to varying degrees, many remain uneasy with classifying this labour as work. Sociologist

Pierette Hondagneu-Sotelo shows this when she describes her challenges with the constant and unpredictable demands of being a mother while completing *Domestica: Immigrant Workers Cleaning and Caring in the Shadows of Affluence*. Despite hiring a Salvadoran cleaning woman, Hondagneu-Sotelo confesses that the "ironic rub" of her situation is that "I argue that cleaning houses and taking care of children is 'real work,' yet in the ways I live my life, I still define my real work as my teaching, research, and writing, not the varied activities involved in taking care of my children and home" (*xxi*). Complicating this is the fact that while we tend to rely on a rhetoric of choice when it comes to motherhood and work, few women are truly "opting in" or "opting out" (Stone). One woman may not earn enough to make outsourcing care feasible while another may want to be at home but cannot sacrifice the additional wages that employment can provide.

Mothering often takes place in addition to women's waged work—both for the mother-employer and the childcare provider. Social anthropologist Melinda Vandenbeld Giles argues, "Mothers must be neoliberal self-optimizing economic agents in the 'public' realm and maternalist self-sacrificing mothers in the 'private' realm" (4). As employment numbers from the pandemic showed, mothers are "allowed" to work as long as they care of their children first—or find a suitable female replacement—despite a changing economic landscape that all but requires most families to have two incomes to thrive. In 2021, women did three times the amount of carework as men (Bloomberg), with women self-reporting that they were doing more than 80 per cent of homeschooling during the pandemic lockdowns (Miller). During these lockdowns, mothers who remained in waged work struggled, as they were less likely to carve out separate workspaces (Subramanian), reduced their work hours four to five times more than fathers (Collins, "Covid"), and faced profound challenges tied to the dearth of childcare, which continues today (DePillis). In 2023, women are participating in waged work at rates similar to pre-pandemic times, but it remains unclear what long-term financial impact women will incur.

In response to this, journalist Anne Helen Petersen has commented: "Other countries have social safety nets. The US has women." These women are mothers, grandmothers, aunts, other-mothers, childcare providers, nannies, and babysitters. The US is certainly not the only country to rely heavily on the free and under-remunerated labour of women to keep their economy and families afloat, but the US is remarkable in its refusal to financially support paid leave or subsidize childcare. Unfortunately, regardless of the country, when a government does not provide infrastructure and oversight, do-it-yourself solutions take their place. Many middle-class, predominantly white US women feel they have few options than to outsource care (and other home responsibilities) to other women, typically women who identify as belonging to an historically marginalized community, have immigrated, are financially impoverished, or are otherwise disenfranchised. Too often, these markers overlap, creating a constellation of vulnerability that can be and is exploited by employers who face little to no legal oversight.

Ironically, when families most needed help during the pandemic, many childcare workers were terminated as a result of lockdowns, leaving these workers unable to provide for themselves and their families. By March 2020 in the US, nearly 90 per cent of domestic workers, including childcare providers, were fired, most without pay (NDWA). Domestic workers in other countries experienced similar situations. These women often faced additional hardships, since they could not qualify for government subsidies directed at workers displaced due to COVID-19, and many careworkers faced complications with immigration and work status. Like the mother-employers who hired them, many childcare workers had their own children at home, and if they acquiesced to work it increased COVID-19 exposure for themselves and their families.

Looking for Spaces of Possibility of Progress

The problems that exist within the matrixes of carework are clear to most, but finding solutions remains difficult. There is little agreement even among experts. If this work is outsourced, to whom should this work be assigned and who should manage it? Women with biological ties to the individual(s) needing care tend to oversee the work being outsourced, in effect never fully being relieved of these duties. To break this chain, Tronto sees a role for government; however, some feminists highlight the ways that government overreach has destroyed families in historically marginalized communities (Hill Collins; Harp and Bunting; Nakagawa; Smith and Reeves; Swinth). "Social protections," according to Fraser, "are often vehicles of domination, aimed at entrenching hierarchies and at excluding 'outsiders'" (15). Groups such as the National Domestic Workers Association (NDWA) focus their advocacy on public education and the adoption of policies that offer more robust protections to domestic workers, who in the US are often excluded from most laws designed to protect employees. However, as sociologist Tamara Mose Brown argues, some of the work done by this organization is out of step with careworkers' resistance to public protest, which they believe could result in termination of employment (154) (Bapat).

Despite profound challenges, however, there has been remarkable progress. Gender scholar Jennifer N. Fish writes:

> No longer are domestic workers completely isolated in their employers' "backyards"; they are WhatsApp-ing solidarity messages to their sisters throughout the world, texting union announcements, and organizing across wide geographic divides. In this larger constellation of forces, women workers' organizations have engaged with international governance to demand global recognition and tangible protections. (9)

In my thinking and writing (and indeed my life), I aim to look forward, focusing on the pressure points that can be manipulated for progressive change. We have to believe that we can do better, and this requires isolating the soft softs in hard systems. In this section, I highlight four places of optimism and reform.

1. The Interdependent Nature of Care

First, as covered above, norms rooted in class, race, gender, religion, culture, and more all impact how we view carework. Embedded within what is often a complex web of scarcity and oppression are glimmers of possibility. Lynch writes: "The neediness of the human condition leads to interdependencies that generate feelings of belonging, appreciation, intimacy, and joy, but also feelings of ambivalence and anxiety, tension and fear" (17). In other words, there can be benefits to our mutual vulnerability. Culture columnist Hanna Rosin illustrates this point in an anecdote in which her nanny, who had cared for her children for nearly a decade, accidentally substantially damaged Rosin's house. While her nanny immediately presumed Rosin would fire her, Rosin claims she could "honestly say that the thought never crossed [her] mind" because a "pile of bricks" was worth much less than a "decade's worth of love" for her children ("New Nanny Fiction"). Both women felt a sense of powerlessness due to their need for the other. Lynet Uttal highlights a similar, albeit less rosy, point about power when she writes:

> The political economy of the childcare market, which privatizes the care and devalues the labour, and the outdated ideological context, which questions mothers who transfer the care of their children to others, combine with the structural organization of daily care to complicate matters, because neither childcare providers nor mothers feel they have much power in the arrangement. (111)

Sociologist Judith Rollins posits that the relationship between a female employer and the domestic worker she hires is "extraordinarily complex" and contains elements of "love, economic exploitation, respect and disrespect, mutual dependency, intense self-interest, intimacy without genuine communication, [and] mutual protection" (178). Macdonald, in *Shadow Mothers: Nannies, Au Pairs, and the Micropolitics of Mothering*, adds: "The relationship [between a mother and the caregiver she hires] is in many ways more intense—more vexing, more rewarding, more vital, more fraught—than a marriage" (71). My own interviews with women who employ nannies have confirmed this via participants' frequent use of verbiage that mirrors romantic relationships. I have argued elsewhere that a portion of the unpaid labour nannies perform is as a mother-proxy and/or spouse (albeit typically platonic) (Garner).

These scholars draw our attention to the ways in which the mother-employer/caregiver relationship is not entirely top-down. To be clear: childcare workers do not have copious power, particularly those who have little social and financial privilege to begin with, but there is room here, an opening that we can continue to pry apart.

2. Recognition

Most people involved in a transactional care relationship can easily name the ways that the system is broken, including in terms of access, affordability, quality, turnover rates, and salary. While power differences exist, many mother-employers I interviewed were clear they wished they could pay their childcare provider more. Unfortunately, verbal recognition, while appreciated, does not replace a living wage, healthcare, and paid leave—a point Kiley Reid astutely highlights in her novel *Such a Fun*

Age. Economist Julie A. Nelson and sociologist Paula England deftly highlight that few if no care relationships can avoid aspects of hierarchy entirely while advocating against a bluntly binaristic stance in which all labour that is commodified is debasing. They also stress that if we agree there are times and ways in which waged work, including carework, is fulfilling, dignified, and useful, then the "question shifts to *how* relations, including market relations ... could be structured and lived in order to increase the possibility of mutual recognition and fair distribution, and decrease the likelihood of oppression, domination and poverty" (11). In other words, it is important to not only name the ways that carework systems are not meeting people's needs but also radically re-imagine what respected carework would look and feel like. From there, we can develop a plan that could get us closer to achieving more equitable care relationships.

3. Good Work Is Being Done

The NDWA has achieved tremendous gains for US domestic workers by strengthening legal protections and supporting their work to directly help domestic workers. Ten states plus the District of Columbia have codified laws that protect domestic workers. Their sister organization Hand in Hand offers important resources to those who are underprepared to be an employer of a carework professional. Similarly aligned organizations exist around the world. The Fair Play Institute, led by Eve Rodsky, has made it a priority to have reproductive labour be included in the US's GDP and focusses on having more men be involved in raising their children and doing housework. Fish in particular highlights not only the critical work done by individuals around the globe but cites the International Labour Union (ILO) as being instrumental in establishing a framework that centres human rights, social justice, and gendered labour. We must continue to support the work that these groups are doing and pressure our representatives to engage with their demands.

4. Change Is Happening

Although cisgender men, particularly those who are white, do not do their fair share of reproductive labour, the gap is shrinking. As more men are involved in the hard labour of childcare, it seems likely that more men will be using their social privilege to advocate for change alongside the women who are already doing this work. While the pandemic did not bring about the radical change many of us were hoping would happen, with the defeat of the Build Back Better bill being particularly wrenching, more employers, parents, and others did witness firsthand the ways carework and the economy are intertwined. Fish tracks the impressive change in her book, *Domestic Workers of the World Unite!: A Global Movement for Dignity and Human Rights*, writing that the "model of transnational activism [centering domestic work and workers]—in the face of the predominant social, political, and economic forces of globalization—stands as one of the most promising human rights victories of the 21st century" (9). We should very much celebrate these wins even as we recognize that much more work needs to be done.

None of these silver linings is enough to upend the history of oppression or the present state of undervalued, extracted care; however, there are seeds in the soil that we can nurture together. This anthology is evidence of writers who are doing the work to evaluate current practices, advocate for change, and craft a more equitable world. The following chapters bring an interdisciplinary examination of waged childcare work from diverse authors.

Chapter Overview

This anthology is eclectic in approach, with multiple disciplines and modes of inquiry employed. While the majority of carework studies has been housed under sociology, this collection draws on autoethnography and memoir; drama, film, and literary studies; as well as qualitative and quantitative sociology. We hear from authors from various disciplines, countries of origin, ages, and years of expertise. This collection speaks not only to the universality of carework but sheds light on the ways carework is in turn shaped by mothers' and caregivers' specific lived experiences. We hope readers can locate points of interconnection and divergence while they question why both exist.

This book is divided into three primary sections: (Re-)Telling One's Story: Autoethnography, Drama, and Poetry; Contemporary Representations of Nannies in Literature and Film; and Care(ful) Relationships around the Globe: Sociological and Anthropological Analyses. The first section begins with a poem by Tracy Royce. Following that, Elizabeth

Cummins Muñoz's chapter, "Helpers: A Personal Reflection on the History and Language of Domestic Service," offers an intimate look at the attachments that form between a caregiver and her charge, and between a nanny and her employer, as well as at the vocabulary that has developed to describe them. She finds that the language of servitude permeates these relationships and complicates a persistent desire to name the emotional authenticity of the bonds and to acknowledge the shame engendered by the occupation's history of gendered, racial, and class-based injustice. In the end, this very personal meditation offers one possible response: to name the silences that the language conceals.

The second chapter is a testimonio—"Mothering for Pay: The Perspective of a White, College-educated Nanny" by Madeline Wood and her co-author Rachel O'Donnell. This work details the experiences of a nanny in a busy household in New York State, both honouring the reproductive labour nannies perform and highlighting the personal experiences of a nanny. They ask, "How can caregivers participate in maternal narratives and reframe their role in the nuclear family?" This type of testimonio can allow us to track the intensification of paid and unpaid mothering labour as part of the larger cultural conversation about caregiving work, especially from caregivers themselves.

Chapter Three, "Mothering in the Balance: Rewriting the Mother Code to Serve the Whole Family" by Gertrude Lyons, is a description of Lyons's conceptual framework—the mother code—as applied to the complex relationship between employing mothers and nannies. In it, she argues that rather than seeing this relationship in reductionist, transactional terms, the mothering done by both parties can become an act of solidarity in which mothers work together for the successful development of not just children but also one another. Rewriting the mother code is introduced as a methodology that prioritizes development and explodes myths that limit the opportunities of mothers to achieve true personal fulfillment while engaging in the essential carework of raising children.

Chrissie Andrea Maroulli's chapter, "Murky Milks: Outsourcing Breastmilk and Maternal Failure in the Early Modern Ballad 'Lamkin,'" explores the problematic relationship between a biological mother and a wet-nurse in the early modern English ballad *Lamkin*. Maroulli historically contextualizes the ballad to argue that both of these women are equally responsible for the death of the wet-nursling, even though it seems at first that the one at fault is the corrupt wet-nurse. The ballad is a cautionary tale against wet-nursing and demonstrates how a woman's failure to meet the patriarchal structures of the era results in her demise.

In the next chapter, "(Care)Give and (Care)Take: Boundaries, Differences, and Choice in Dramas about Undocumented Care," Lynn Deboeck uses Judith Butler's concept of "a grievable life" to examine themes of exploitation presented in two plays (*Living Out* by Lisa Loomer and *One House Over* by Catherine Trieschmann) through an intersectional feminist lens—looking at how multiple facets of a person's identity intersect to create their lived reality. Butler's theory particularly targets how society values life (or does not), and this chapter investigates how that valuing interacts with the experiences of undocumented care workers in the US. Deboeck argues that it is precisely because we do not value the lives of women care workers as lives that our care system has resulted in a cycle of abuse that is maintained through establishing boundaries, weaponizing difference, and limiting choice. This chapter serves as a bridge to the following section.

The second section, "Contemporary Representations of Nannies in Literature and Film," opens with Jane Griffith's chapter, "Mrs. Banks and Mary Poppins: Tensions of the Maternal Nanny." Griffith analyzes perhaps one of the most famous fictional nannies, Mary Poppins, arguing that both the source texts by PL Travers and the 1964 Disney film feature an antagonism between Mrs. Banks and Mary Poppins. The source for the tension in the texts is the threat of Mary Poppins overtaking the role of mother; in the film, which elides Mary Poppins's maternality entirely, the antagonism instead stems from Mrs. Banks's first-wave feminist desires to escape her role as mother.

In chapter seven, "'The Damage Done and May This Madness Be Over': Exposing and Eradicating Matrophobia through a Reading of the Nanny Trope in the Psychological Thrillers *The Nanny* and *Nanny Dearest*," Andrea O'Reilly explores how these two psychological thrillers use the tropes of this genre to unmask the disruption and distortion of empowered mother-daughter bonding theorized by Adrienne Rich in her concept of matrophobia. In each novel, the nanny figure becomes an agent of patriarchy who seeks to divide and disempower mothers and daughters and who must be slayed to restore mother and daughter connection. More specifically, Hannah in *The Nanny* seeks to estrange the daughter from the mother to claim the husband/father and the patriarchal power he represents, whereas Anneliese in *Nanny Dearest* seeks to estrange the daughter from the mother to become the perfect mother of idealized patriarchal motherhood. This chapter explores how each novel through the tropes of the psychological thriller—psychological dread, shocks, and surprise endings—exposes, confronts, and eventually eradicates the matrophobia of patriarchal culture as enacted and symbolized by the nanny trope.

Jill Goad's "Family Exchange Norms and Mother-Nanny Relationships in Leila Slimani's *The Perfect Nanny* and Kiley Reid's *Such a Fun Age*" applies concepts of family exchange norms and paranormal management to a reading of nannies Louise and Emira and their relationships with mother-employers to make claims about the current nature of carework. Specifically, the chapter argues that analyzing the nannies in these novels gives insight into race as a determinant in nanny hiring, the nanny as "shadow mother," socioeconomic disparity between employee and employer in the care work system, and the nanny's tenuous "one of the family" status.

Chapter nine, "Seeing Beyond Black and White in the Mother/Nanny Novel: Problematics, Purpose, and Possibilities of Empathy," by Katie B. Garner, examines how three novels (*Substitute Me* by Lori Tharps, *Minding Ben* by Victoria Brown, and *Such a Fun Age* by Kiley Reid) expose the limitations and possibilities of empathic reading and ultimately social change. Garner provides a brief history of nanny novels that centre Black nannies working in white families before moving into an analysis of how white readers' empathy might be shaped by the act of reading. The chapter questions if white mother-employers who read empathically are engaging in antiracist work and whether novelists should be tasked with producing pro-social texts.

Elizabeth Podnieks's chapter, "'I'm Quitting Your Service, I've Had Quite Enough'": Representations of Caregivers' Subjectivity in Tamara Mose Brown's *Raising Brooklyn* and Victoria Brown's *Minding Ben*" is designed to serve as a bridge to the third section and positions Brown's novel *Minding Ben* in relation to Mose Brown's ethnography *Raising Brooklyn*, showcasing intersecting representations of migrant women from the West Indies working as caregivers in New York. Classifying these texts as iterations of the genre of matroethnography (matifocal autoethnography), Podnieks illuminates how Brown and Mose Brown, as participant-observers, render caregiving subjectivities that are individual, communal, and collaborative. In so doing, Podnieks argues that these two texts evidence how contemporary mothering unfolds within the geopolitical contexts of globalization informed by ethnicity, race, and class as well as within the dynamics of power, labour, and love.

The final section, titled "Care(ful) Relationships around the Globe: Sociological and Anthropological Analyses," begins with Aya Kitamura's chapter, "Between Cosmopolitan Mothering and the Global Care Chain: Japanese Mothers, Intra-Asian Migration, and Everyday Struggles of 'the Nanny Question,'" which uses original interview data to examine Japanese mothers in Singapore, women who become part of the global care chain in an intra-Asian context. Kitamura focuses on the increase of third-shift labour—namely, emotional management of family members and live-in domestic workers—and the ways the gendered division of labour at home is sustained and, in some cases, strengthened. Readers will benefit from this analysis of the interconnectivity between personal experiences and sociopolitical hierarchies and disparities in the Asian global city.

Chapter twelve, "Paradoxes of Power in Carework" by Laura Bunyan and Barret Katuna examines nanny-employer dynamics when nannies are of privileged status (i.e., white and educated). This research examines the difficulties nannies experience when they share social markers and social statuses with their employers. They also address whether nannies gain power in nanny work via these shared markers.

Yolanda Wiggins's chapter "Kin Care Versus Paid Care: How Black College Women Navigate Dual Roles and Work to Earn a Degree" examines the experiences of Black undergraduate women who act as paid and unpaid caregivers during college. She finds that these college women must alternate between college, work, and family and often feel pulled in multiple directions due to competing demands. Interestingly, many of these college women who care for elders or small children also consider their client's family to be extensions of their own. This chapter emphasizes the nuances of caregiving and the academic, emotional, and economic toll it poses for financially disadvantaged students of colour.

Chapter fourteen, "Friending with the Caregivers in a Bengali Household: An Autoethnographic Study of a Bengali Household" by Medhashri Mahanty talks about the ineffable moments between caregivers and their employers in the domestic space. It specifically argues that while caregivers form a faux kinship with the employer's family, they enter into a semi-abusive relationship with the employers because of their caste, class, and the kind of work they are hired to do. While Raka Ray and Seemin Qayum study the manoeuvres in this relationship using the "rhetoric of love" to suggest the naturalness with which employers deal with different emotions, such as guilt to bind the employees to them, Mahanty uses a more destabilizing notion of friending to study the tactics employed in the constantly shifting relationship. Friending, this essay argues, is a political stance that is mostly used by employees to question the unjust tones masked by the love rhetoric and negotiate the touch barriers, yet it manages to continue the relationship without an assurance that comes with friendship/rhetoric of love. Friending is unlike the love rhetoric trope, which can be identified in the narratives of employers (and reproduced in their employees) but is rather visible in moments and gestures. To that end, this essay uses autoethnography to understand the unfixed becomings and their constantly fluctuating limits in domestic spaces.

The anthology closes with chapter fifteen, Safwan Amir's "Temporary Sisterhoods: Thinking Ethics through Postnatal Care among South Asian Muslims," which ethnographically explores the grammars of Muslim maternal worlds in South India. Here, it is not only the carer and mother who come to form a relationship but the baby's grandmother, the mother's relatives, as well as friends and neighbours; they all partake in a range of special and everyday events revolving around maternity. Specifically, the chapter argues for possibilities in sisterhoods that Muslim women form through informal networks of care and practices of healing. While these networks are temporary, they still manage to have a deep ethical impact on the women who participate in them and allow for nurturing sisterhoods that aspire a better future in the afterlife.

Conclusion

It is important to note that much of the work included herein has been produced by women thinking and doing and working and caring during a time in which most people's lives were overturned by a lack of critical carework infrastructure. Both mother-employers who relied on caregivers to tend to their loved ones and caregivers who relied on the income this work provides them and their families were profoundly impacted.

By virtue of my academic focus and place of residence, I enter this analysis as a white, cisgender, heterosexual woman who is a United States citizen and resides therein. I have relied on multiple women to help with childcare so that I could pursue professional and personal goals. My worldview cannot help but be influenced by my status in a nation that has profited from carework extracted from those who were enslaved legally and culturally. Shame about this past is not sufficient, particularly since our neoliberal approach to government and community support continues to extract resources from those who are most vulnerable so that the privileged among us can have more.

As I have attempted to think through how to shape this introduction, I have felt stymied by how little I know about carework histories in other countries. That said, regardless of location, it is critical that we never lose sight of the ways class, race, gender, religion, ableism, education, and citizenship status impact who receives care and who is expected to provide care. As Wrigley points out, it is not uncommon for employers to "ask more from the caregiver than would be expected in ordinary business relationships" even though "they are not sure they want to transcend their own roles as employers" (89). The aim of this collection is to create space for reflecting on, contextualizing, reframing, discussing, inciting, and facilitating an exploration of the relationship between mothers and the caregivers they hire. Throughout this anthology, the authors think through many of the problems inherent in carework relationships and possibilities for reform. This collection offers a broad range of voices and experiences, insights, and observations as it interrogates the many meanings and practices within the mother and caregiver relationship. We hope that you find this work to be as important as we do and continue to explore the nuances of the care(ful) relationships between mothers and the caregivers they hire.

Endnotes

1. Throughout this introduction, I use the terms "mother" and "women" as female-identifying people, as they are the ones most often tasked with carework. More than 90 per cent of waged careworkers are women: mothers, grandmothers, daughters, granddaughters, sisters, aunts, nieces, as well as nurses, teachers, therapists, and more. These are the same people who experienced the greatest fallout from

COVID-19 professionally and personally. The use of these terms should not be interpreted as a belief that men are not caregivers or that men cannot mother/parent. I look forward to a time when sex and/or gender differences do not impact parenting and caregiving in the ways they do currently, and, like Sara Ruddick, I advocate actively for an inclusive sense of the term "mothering."

2. There are times throughout this introduction when I will reference carework and reproductive labour more broadly (rather than child-care specifically) particularly if the data available does not permit more specific categorization. On a similar note concerning semantics, there is little agreement on what differentiates a nanny from a baby-sitter, with some using the former for full-time work done under a contract and the latter being used for more temporary, sporadic, or part-time work. Unless an author specifically uses one of those two terms, I default to the more general term "childcare worker" or "childcare provider." Additionally, while "childcare worker" can be expansive, in the context of this book, it will primarily be applied to women doing waged childcare work in the home of the mother -employer.

3. Not surprisingly, little research addresses father-employers and nannies, although some are involved in nannies' hiring and oversight. Media and literary depictions generally portray father-employers as philandering. That women are blamed specifically and solely for their positionality as neoliberal subjects who exploit women is worth further examination.

Works Cited

Abrego, Leisy, and Ralph LaRossa. "Economic Well-Being in Salvadoran Transnational Families: How Gender Affects Remittance Practices." *Journal of Marriage and Family*, vol. 71, no. 4, 2009, pp. 1070-85.

Anderson, Bridget. *Doing the Dirty Work? The Global Politics of Domestic Labor.* Zed, 2000.

Baker, Dean. "This Is What Minimum Wage Would Be If It Kept Pace with Productivity." *Center for Economic Policy and Research*, 21 Jan. 2020, https://cepr.net/this-is-what-minimum-wage-would-be-if-it-kept-pace-with-productivity/. Accessed 25 Sept. 2023.

Bapat, Sheila. *Part of the Family? Nannies, Housekeepers, Caregivers and the Battle for Domestic Workers' Rights*. Ig, 2014.

Gabriella Boston. "New Class of Nannies." *Washington Times*. 30 Sept 2009, https://www.washingtontimes.com/news/2009/sep/30/new-class-of-nannies/. Accessed 25 Sept. 2023.

Brown, Tamara Mose. *Raising Brooklyn: Nannies, Childcare, and Caribbeans Creating Community*. New York: New York UP, 2011.

Care Collective. *The Care Manifesto: The Politics of Interdependence*. Verso, 2020.

Chang, Grace. *Disposable Domestics: Immigrant Women Workers in the Global Economy*. Cambridge, Mass: South End, 2000.

Collins, C, et al. "COVID-19 and the Gender Gap in Work Hours." *Gender Work Organ*, 2020, vol. 28, no. S1, 2020, pp. 549-60.

Collins, Patricia Hill. *Black Feminist Thought*. Routledge, 2000.

DePillis, Lydia, Jeanna Smialik and Ben Casselman. "Jobs Aplenty, but Shortage of Care Keeps Many Women from Benefiting." *New York Times*. 7 July 2022, https://www.nytimes.com/2022/07/07/business/economy/women-labor-caregiving.html. Accessed 25 Sept. 2023.

Duffy, Mignon. "Doing the Dirty Work: Gender, Race and Reproductive Labor in Historical Perspective." *Gender and Society*, vol. 21, no. 3, June 2007, pp. 313-36.

Fish, Jennifer N. *Domestic Workers of the World Unite!: A Global Movement for Dignity and Human Rights*. New York University Press, 2017.

Flanagan, Caitlin. "How Serfdom Saved the Women's Movement: Dispatches from the Nanny Wars." *The Atlantic*. March 2004, https://www.theatlantic.com/magazine/archive/2004/03/how-serfdom-saved-the-women-s-movement/302892/. Accessed June 12, 2023.

Folbre, Nancy. *The Managed Heart: Economics and Family Values*. New York Press, 2001.

Friedan, Betty. *The Feminine Mystique*. New York, 1963.

Garner, Katie B. "Mirroring a Mother's Love: A Chodorowian Analysis of the Complicated Relationship Between Mothers and Nannies." *Nancy Chodorow and The Reproduction of Mothering: Forty Years On*. Ed. Petra Bueskens. USA: Palgrave Macmillian, 2020.

Glenn, Evelyn Nakano. "From Servitude to Service Work: Historical

Continuities of the Racial Division of Paid Reproductive Labor." *Signs*, vol. 18, no. 1, 1992, pp. 1-43.

Gonzales, Matt. "Nearly 2 Million Fewer Women in Labor Force." *Society for HR Management*, 17 Feb, 2022, https://www.shrm.org/resourcesandtools/hr-topics/behavioral-competencies/global-and-cultural-effectiveness/pages/over-1-million-fewer-women-in-labor-force.aspx. Accessed 25 Sept. 2023.

Guevarra, Anna Romina. *Marketing Dreams, Manufacturing Heroes: The Transnational Labor Brokering of Filipino Workers*. Rutgers, 2010.

Harp, K.L.H., and A.M. Bunting. "The Racialized Nature of Child Welfare Policies and the Social Control of Black Bodies." *Soc Polit.*, vol. 27, no. 2, 2020, pp. 258-81.

Hays, Sharon. *The Cultural Contradictions of Motherhood*. Yale University Press, 1998.

Hirshman, Linda R. *Get to Work: A Manifesto for Women of the World*. Viking, 2006.

Hondagneu-Sotelo, Pierrette. *Doméstica: Immigrant Workers Cleaning and Caring in the Shadows of Affluence*. California University Press, 2001.

Hondagneu-Sotelo, Pierrette, and Ernestine Avila. "'I'm Here, but I'm There': The Meanings of Latina Transnational Motherhood." *Gender and Society*, vol. 11, no. 5, 1997, pp. 548-71.

Kantor, Jodi. "Nanny Hunt Can Be a 'Slap in the Face' for Blacks." *The New York Times*, 26 Dec. 2006, https://www.nytimes.com/2006/12/26/us/26nannies.html. Accessed 25 Oct. 2023.

Lynch, Kathleen. *Care and Capitalism: Why Affective Equality Matters for Social Justice*. Polity, 2022.

Marrun, Norma A. "Queering La Familia: A Redefinition of Mothering, Immigration, and Education." *Chicana/Latina Studies*, vol. 15, no. 2, 2016, pp. 64-95.

Macdonald, Cameron Lynne. *Shadow Mothers: Nannies, Au Pairs, and the Micropolitics of Mothering*. California University Press, 2010.

Miller, Claire Cain. "Nearly Half of Men Say They Do Most of the Home Schooling. 3 Percent of Women Agree." *New York Times*. 6 May 2020, https://www.nytimes.com/2020/05/06/upshot/pandemic-chores-homeschooling-gender.html. Accessed 25 Sept. 2023.

Misra, Joya et al. "The Globalization of Care Work: Neoliberal Economic Restructuring and Migration Policy." *Globalizations*, vol. 3, no. 3, 2006, pp. 317-331.

Nakagawa, Shihoko. "Single Mothers' Activism against Poverty Governance in the U.S. Child Welfare System." *Motherhood and Single-Lone Parenting: A Twenty-First Century Perspective*, edited by Maki Motapanyane. Demeter, 2016, pp. 337-68.

Nelson, Julie A., and Paula England. "Feminist Philosophies of Love and Work." *Hypatia*, vol. 17, no. 2, 2002, pp. 1-18.

Parreñas, Rhacel Salazar. *Servants of Globalization: Women, Migration, and Domestic Work*. Stanford University Press, 2001.

Petersen, Anne Helen. "Other Countries Have Social Safety Nets. The U.S. Has Women." *Anne Helen*, 11 Nov. 2020, https://annehelen. substack.com/p/other-countries-have-social-safety. Accessed 25 Oct. 2023.

Rich, Adrienne. *Of Woman Born: Motherhood as Experience and Institution*. New York, 1976.

Rollins, Judith. *Between Women: Domestics and Their Employers*. Temple University Press, 1985.

Romero, Mary. *Maid in the U.S.A.* Routledge, 2002.

Ruddick, Sara. *Maternal Thinking: Towards a Politics of Peace*. Ballantine, 1989.

Stone, Pamela. *Opting Out?: Why Women Really Quit Careers and Head Home*. Berkeley: University of California Press, 2007.

Subramanian, Divya. "The Pandemic Reminded Us that Most Women Still Don't have a Room of Their Own." *Atlantic*. 2 May 2022, https://www.theatlantic.com/books/archive/2022/05/feminist-architecture-matrix-making-space-review/629713/. Accessed 25 Sept. 2023.

Tronto, Joan. "The 'Nanny' Question in Feminism." *Hypatia* 17, no. 2, 2002, pp. 34-51.

Slaughter, Anne-Marie. *Unfinished Business*. Random House, 2015.

Stone, Pamela. *Opting Out?: Why Women Really Quit Careers and Head Home*. California University Press, 2007.

Uttal, Lynet. *Making Care Work: Employed Mothers in the New Childcare Market*. Rutgers University Press, 2002.

Wrigley, Julia. *Other People's Children: An Intimate Account of the Dilemmas Facing Middle-Class Parents and the Women They Hire to Raise Their Children*. Basic Books, 1995.

Zoepf, Katherine. "Wanted: Tibetan Nannies." *New York Observer*, 17 July. 2007, www.newyorkobserver.com. Accessed 25 Sept. 2023.

Untitled Tanka

Tracy Royce

fired
for caring too much
the nanny packs
a photograph
of someone else's children

Section I

(Re)Telling One's Story:
Autoethnography, Drama, and Poetry

Chapter 1

Helpers: A Personal Reflection on the History and Language of Domestic Service

Elizabeth Cummins Muñoz

The relationships that form between families and the caregivers they hire unfold across a thorny moral landscape of economic imperatives, historical injustice, and intense emotional bonds. Such complexity demands a nuanced vocabulary, but the language of servitude that accompanies domestic service cannot account for the entangled dimensions of its power-infused intimacy. In the pages that follow, I examine my personal experience of relationships with caregivers through a critical framework informed by histories of domestic service in the United States (US). As a privileged white woman from the American South, my understanding of this dynamic has been shaped by my relationships with two women: E, the middle-aged Black woman who cared for me as a child; and L, the young Guatemalan woman who cared for my own young children when I became a mother. With E, I learned that words like "maid" and "housekeeper" have power. With L, I confronted unspoken conflicts wrapped up in the role of employer and "señora." When I reflect on these lessons and consider the occupation's histories of power, I find that the only way to name these relationships honestly is to employ a language that sustains their inherent contradictions—to name the shame and hold the love.

Maids and Housekeepers

"I'm not your maid." That's how I remember E's words. I think I had been on the phone with a school friend. Bronzed and bored in the lazy days of my childhood summer when school was out and the days stretched long, I'd invited a playmate over and said something like, "It's okay. My maid's here." I don't remember where I was standing or even what E looked like when she responded. Was she looking at me hard with her deep brown eyes? Was she busy at a laundry basket or winding up the cord of the thirty-pound Hoover? "I'm not your maid," she told me. "You call me a 'housekeeper.'" These were probably her words, the best I can recall. Perhaps in a different order, perhaps embedded in some other mandate, certainly shot through with the authority she held over me. What I remember clearly about that afternoon was the lesson she imparted: Words matter, and "maid" is an insult.

The failures of memory haunt me. I struggle to retrieve E's exact words or the light in that midday kitchen. Other things escape me, too, like the lines of her daughter's face—the little girl who sometimes came to play. She was older than I was. I remember her pigtails and a sense of grace about her movements. I remember the excitement of her arrival and feeling starry-eyed in her presence, but I can't recall her face. It has receded along with other memories lost. When did E stop coming to our house every day? Had there been a goodbye, some formal marking of the transition? There were other goodbyes, I know, graduations, farewell parties, special dinners before summer camp, but I don't recall any moment when we stopped and gathered to say to E, to each other, "Well, this time we've shared together; it will be a thing of the past now."

We visited throughout my adulthood. She called from time to time, and her voice would transport me back to those bronzed summer days and early afternoon naptimes when I would not sleep—could not sleep—and so I'd jump from one twin bed to another until I heard her call my name in a voice that felt safe and strong and carried all the summers and mid-week afternoons of our relationship. Years later, on visits and calls, her voice touched a place in me outside of words and I softened to who we two had been. I had learned at a young age that E was not "maid," but neither did "housekeeper" capture the tenderness in her aging voice or its effect on me. Only "E" felt right to me as a girl, and it took some time to realize that she was the only adult whom I was taught to address by her first name.

The last time I saw E was the first time I learned that she had cancer. She was smaller and older but still strong, still herself as she entered my sister's home to join our family's Thanksgiving holiday celebration. Her daughter, R, was there beside her, and as much as I tried, I could not find the pig-tailed girl I remembered in that woman's frame. Instead, I saw an imposing line in her spine and shoulders. She stood long, tall, and guarded, it seemed to me, against everything that space held within it—the china and the wine, the sports coats and the loafers, and all the markers of social class and privilege that, in some way, included the mother and daughter who stepped across the threshold.

History, language, relationship. "Maid," "housekeeper," "E." In time, I would learn to trace the complicated forces that shaped my relationship with the woman who cared for me as a child. I would understand her presence in my home and the bond we shared as the products of two phenomena—on the one hand, a historical legacy of gendered, racialized domestic service; on the other, the peculiar nature of the carework it engenders. I would learn about my own place in the society we shared, and something of E's, and my memories of her would become heavy with a sense of confused guilt and unclear responsibility. Even so, I would never find the right word to name our relationship, and I would always struggle to recall the particular lines of her daughter's face, the girl I had admired so.

In teaching "housekeeper" over "maid," E distanced herself from a legacy of servitude that begins with institutionalized slavery. Judith Rollins writes that wherever slavery has existed in the world, slaves have been tasked with the domestic duties of women (21-22), although it would take time for "maid" to acquire its uniquely feminine vulnerability and derogatory cadence. The idea of "maid" as domestic servant begins in the preindustrial aristocratic households of Europe, where the ranks of cleaners and cooks and laundresses were distinguished from the more prestigious "housekeeper," who managed and supervised the chambermaids and the housemaids, the laundry maids and the dairy maids, and the lowly scullery maid (Rollins 26). "Housekeeper" lingered in this preindustrial space, privileged among servants, while "maid" moved towards the nineteenth century, soaking up associations.

In the new middle-class homes of industrialized Europe, the elaborate staff of the wealthy gave way to a "maid-of-all-work," or simply "maid"—overworked, toiling in closer quarters with her employers, and supervised directly by a mistress likely new to middle-class status. It became important to mark distinctions: liveried uniforms were required, "servants" were summoned, and training manuals were published (Rollins 35). Across the pond, though, this process looked different. The egalitarian spirit that reigned in the newly independent United States lived on in the "hired girls" model of paid domestic labour that characterized the preindustrial North. These young women— daughters of neighbors or friends—laboured and ate alongside the families for whom they worked. They dressed as their employers did and often worked seasonally or as needed (Duffy 21-22).

The hired girls were "help" to these families, not servants (Rollins 50); but in the tumultuous social reordering that resulted from nineteenth-century industrialization and urbanization—with its anonymous cities and its waves of Irish and other European immigrants— a different model emerged (Duffy 22-23). In its return to the language of servitude, in its uniforms and back door entrances and separate eating spaces, this model reflected the country's enduring tension between a rhetoric of egalitarian values and a socially stratified reality (Rollins 52, Romero Maid 77).

This tension is inevitable in an occupation defined by the master-servant relationship, a dynamic that has historically been shaped and reinforced by such shows of deference as uniforms and physical separation. In the southern US, where the ninety per cent of domestic servants labouring in slavery continued to serve after the Civil War, such deference was baked into the social order reproduced in private homes. In those homes, future masters and mistresses learned that maids are called by their first names no matter how grown-up, that they are "girls" no matter how old, and that they stand apart, do not sit, and never talk back (Rollins 158-72).

In those homes, domestic servants worked and lived in the intimate contours of a space divided between the ones who were "Ma'am" and the others who were "girl." Such markers of who people are to one another signify not only different social classes and unequal power but a category of relationship that inserts power and difference into the vulnerable spaces of family. The fiercely patriarchal household of feudal Europe, in which servants were infantilized, protected, cared for, and morally guided in exchange for lifelong loyalty and submission found its legacy in the homes of the new middle classes, where servants continued to be seen as less than full and capable adults. From Lord and Father to Mistress and Ma'am, the maternalism that has marked the mistress -maid relationship in the American South since the late nineteenth century generates a confusing mix of affection and disrespect (Rollins; Romero, *Maid*).

By the time E was scolding me for jumping on the bed and instructing me in the language of our relationship, "maid" had become heavy with the weight of this disrespect, even as the relationship retained its confusing intimacy. Around that time, Judith Rollins interviewed several women working as "domestics" in the American South. One of her interviewees reflects, "There was a lot of possession and belonging. But there was love too, you know?" (178). Rollins explains the possession as a kind of psychological domination, so much so that the language that turns grown women into children is reproduced uncritically: "I don't know, I always say 'girl,'" another woman explains. "Everybody says that" (160). "My girl," the Southern mistress might casually say, no matter her employee's age—or the daughter for whom she is "Mother." Growing up in the seventies and eighties, E's daughter may not have heard her mother called "girl," but she's sure to have known that some, like me, called her "my maid." Where words shift, the language of infantilized possession endures.

In her 2011 study of adult children of domestic workers, Mary Romero finds that children first learn that their mothers are considered somebody else's "girl" when employers call the home in the evening. "For many," she writes, "the phone calls were the first time they had heard their mothers treated as inferior or disrespectfully" (*Daughter* 37). Among the Hispanic domestic workers in the US who have largely replaced Black women like E in the last forty years, "girl" has its direct equivalent in "muchacha," which itself reflects a parallel history of powerlessness and infantilized paternalism.[1] Children of Hispanic domestics might be further struck when the voice on the phone asks for their mothers in an unfamiliar name. As Romero explains, the first names of Hispanic domestic servants have often been changed by their American employers— "Rose" to a tongue that trips over "Rosario," or if an Americanized version isn't readily found, simply "María" (*Daughter* 38).

The meanings of "maid" that may have moved E to teach me her lesson are not exclusive to the southern legacy of slavery. They reflect an ideology of domestic labour that since its emergence in the nineteenth century has relied on associating paid domestic work with inferior social status. Here, a twin evolution of material practice and ideological justification unfolded across these centuries, tracking women of colour into the low-status, low-wage occupation, while simultaneously justifying the disrespect and poor conditions in a framework of racial inferiority.

The first "Marías" in the US were young Mexican women living in the newly annexed territories of the Southwest. As Anglo dominance took hold in the second half of the nineteenth century, training for domestic service became an ideological exercise in the morality of assimilation, even as it addressed the practical problems of domestic dirty work and social control. "When trained," a 1917 discourse on Mexicans in the Southwest reads, "there is no better servant than the gentle, quiet Mexicana girl" (Romero, qtd. in Nakano Glenn, "Servitude" 12).[2] Just as early twentieth-century "Mexican" girls in the Southwest were taught to clean and launder in lieu of reading and writing,[3] Black women, too, were forced into the occupation by limited options in a changing economy that had opened up opportunities to the daughters of European immigrants but held the doors firmly closed to women of colour. In the Southwest, Mexicana and Chicana women trained and scrubbed. In the far west, the Chinese and Japanese male servants of the previous century gave their places to newly-immigrated Japanese women, and in Hawaii Japanese and Chinese women served their men's plantation employers (Nakano Glenn, "Servitude"; Romero, *Maid*). By mid-twentieth century, American domestic service had taken on a universal palette: Dark-skinned women serving in light-skinned homes. By the time the civil rights era and women's movement came along to threaten the model and confuse my childhood observations, this country had established a standing racialized servant class maintained by racist social structures and targeted policies.

These policies have been enacted by public institutions. Segregated school systems like the ones in the Southwest have historically trained Black and Mexican girls to domestic service. Depression-era work programs placed Black and Mexicana women exclusively in private household service positions (Nakano Glenn, "Servitude"; Romero, *Maid*). A decade later, Japanese women in the west were pressured to service by a rhetoric of patriotism and forced into live-in positions after release from internment (Nakano Glenn, "Servitude" 13). Later developments would use welfare and immigration policy to maintain a steady supply of "employable mothers" (Chang; Nakano Glenn, *Forced*).

As a result of this conscious design, it felt natural to my child's eye that maids were Black and brown people. "Natural," given the ubiquity of the practice and the deference embedded in its cultural forms. Subtle, how natural it appeared that those who were called "nanny" were fair and often European, while those who were dark were always "the maid." In the late 1970s and 80s of my childhood, I simmered in these social structures, immersed but unaware of labour systems buoyed up by an ideology of race and gender that would make of me both victim and aggressor, both privileged and oppressed. My education took the form of first names and Mrs., tracing a social map across our home in indelible ink and defining the lines between unexamined constructions of "us" and "them."

As a child immersed, I used "housekeeper" in dutiful obedience, but when I became a woman steeped in the ambivalence of keeping house, the term became fraught with gendered complications. "Homemaker," "housewife," "mistress," a twenty-first century "señora" bewildered by the burden and the complicity, the privilege and the need.

Señoras and Helpers

By the time I became a domestic employer myself, memories of E and her daughter had receded into my childhood mythology, and I found myself presiding over a demanding domain: Two very small children, two very small paychecks, a husband moved by circumstance to work long days and weekends, and a stubborn will to study and write that left me exhausted. Along with the tenderness and the love, the laughter and the devotion, I experienced a growing sense of betrayal at a social education that had inculcated in me the rhetoric of liberation even as it shamed me into accepting a very different reality. This project of home turned out to be my burden to bear alone. This making of babies and living rooms and dinners and salaries. This giving of breast and womb and arms and touch. This relinquishing of time and emotion and energy and self.

"You need help," my mother told me. She sat on our hand-me-down loveseat holding my newborn second child and looked at me with concern. In her eyes, I saw reflected a mother's love, a mother's worry, and generations of feminine domesticity shaped around the shadowed presence of "helpers" who would lighten the load. "You need help," she'd said, by which she meant, "you need a maid."

A housekeeper's pay was not in our budget, but childcare for the hours I spent teaching classes and attending seminars was a must. I found L through a neighborhood connection. She was a few years younger than me, Guatemalan, pretty, and as new to the domestic project as I was. Here is what I felt when L arrived to take my place:

To leave my babies was to break my heart.

To leave my studies would have been to erase my identity.

To find money to pay her was physically painful.

To be a mistress hiring a maid, a patrona counting out bills for the muchacha, was to force a reckoning.

At first, I was only hiring a "babysitter" for a few hours a week. "Babysitter" didn't question my values. It conjured images of teenage girls and familiar neighbours with shared social backgrounds and did not threaten the illusion of a home untainted by class and race divisions. "Babysitters" don't cross thresholds into intimate spaces and stand testament to the privilege of those who inhabit those spaces—and babysitters don't clean. On this point I insisted: No cleaning. But child-care is messy, diapers are dirty, and L quickly saw what I wouldn't—that the work of care and cleaning go hand in hand. So, one day when I got home, L announced: "Vamos a organizarnos," let's get organized, and we began to redefine the terms of the work.

Historically, the dirty work of keeping house—the soiled diapers and bathroom floors and grease-caked pans—has been delegated to the darker of the paid domestics. Similar to the governess and scullery maids of hierarchies of old, a dual labour and wage system emerged early in America along racial lines (Romero, *Maid*; Rollins). But in the landscape of my own twenty-first century mothering, such categories had largely collapsed. Cleaners were almost invariably Central American or Mexican, and Hispanic nannies almost invariably cleaned.[4]

This shift reflects the changing landscape of domestic work in late twentieth-century America. When L made her way into my home from her native Guatemala, she followed paths established by refugees fleeing military violence of the 1980s. In conjunction with the Mexican economic crisis and American boom years of the same period, Mexican and Central American women flooded the market for cheap domestic labour, filling spaces left by Black women who had moved away from the occupation in the wake of the civil rights era. At the same time, the advance of globalization generated a dramatically expanded service sector, and the increased number of women in the professional workforce created a higher demand for domestic workers. These forces combined so that by the time I found myself surrounded by syllabi and dirty diapers somewhere in the early 2000s, the work of house and home had become "the domain of disenfranchised immigrant women of color" (Hondagneu-Sotelo xii). Given the historical patterns and contemporary labour supply, it felt as natural for me to hire a Central American woman to care for my children as it had for my mother to hire a Black woman to care for me.

Whether L was the "babysitter," the "nanny," or the "*muchacha*," her work was wrapped up in the histories of housecleaners and maids, just as my role was inescapably related to the legacy of the mistress and the señora. The titles reflect the privilege. While the Black women Rollins interviewed understood that "Ma'am" signaled a ritual deference to maintain the power of the mistress, women like L employ the more innocuous "Señora." But this term, and its more precise alternative, "patrona," carry their own historical weight.[5] The idea that L might call me "Señora" elicited a discomfort that was difficult to name. That she might treat me with the formal "usted," when I so naturally addressed her in the informal "tú," made me uneasy, threatened by the rhetorical deference embedded in our relationship. "Vamos a organizarnos, señora."

Discomfort, unease, let's call it the domestic employer's "liberal guilt"—a phenomenon of the late twentieth century that has only been exacerbated by the inescapable reality that, where inequality deepens, the employment of domestic servants grows in direct proportion (Milkman). Liberal guilt—the uneasiness that enlightened employers feel in the presence of their domestic employees, the discomfort that arises in the close quarters of an American home where the señora's privilege is outlined in bold strokes by the woman who's come to sanitize the surfaces and sweep away the dirt. To avoid the discomfort, we keep our distance. We leave the house so as not to witness the work. Aware of the emotional labour demanded by our unenlightened foremothers, we avoid personal relationships. We think of ourselves as consumers. We call them "babysitters" instead of "maids" and shut in the dirty work of domesticity on our way out, leaving the drudgery behind in an imagined prefeminist past.

L and I quickly moved from "usted" to "tú," from "Señora" to "Elizabeth." We were young and conversation was easy. L took on the diapers, laundered the children's clothes, and completed dinner prep tasks. She smiled at my apologies for the dishes and disarray when she arrived, put it all in order before she left. I was grateful, she was practical, and our relationship responded to the immediacy of domestic demands. Still, as the borders between babysitter and maid shifted and blurred, neither felt true to what L's role was in our home.

Not "sitter" or "housekeeper," not full-time enough to be "nanny," in the end, what L was in relation to me was a "helper." She was my helper. She and I both understood this, as my mother had, as the kids did, and my husband. All of us understood that the project of domestic management—the cleaning and laundering and cooking, the grocery buying and childminding and sippy cup procuring—was mine alone to manage. And as my employer guilt dulled, a deeper conflict took shape, protesting that this burden should fall to me, that it should be so substantial and demanding that I needed help, and at the same time so dismissed, ridiculed, and denigrated, that the job of helping was the domain of underprivileged women, disenfranchised and publicly invisible.

The history of L's public invisibility is tied up in the changing ideas of home and womanhood that emerged in the nineteenth century. As the rise of capitalism shifted the home from a place of production to a place of consumption, the work of women became relegated to the extra-economic imagination. Where men made money, the new thinking went, women kept house. The "housewife" thus found her identity transformed from an economic asset to a dependent, while the cult of domesticity elevated her to an angel presiding over a domestic haven, an unstained vessel of moral virtue and selfless love (Crittenden).

But the cultural logic that made the housewife both a moral angel and a financial burden was founded on the invisibility of women like E and L. The ideal required women to make a haven of the home through grace and devotion, not sweat and muscle. Words like "menial, "dirt," and "drudgery" defined themselves in opposition to the purity and spirituality of the domestic haven (Duffy 38). To remain unstained, someone else was needed to do the dirty work (Romero, *Maid* 57-60). As a result, by the dawn of the twentieth century, a white, middle-class woman's calling required, on the one hand, that she employ someone else, who would then be denied her own "true womanhood," and on the other, that she rely on her husband's income to purchase the goods and services necessary to maintain her domestic haven. The power of the mistress, the powerlessness of the woman.

In an interview with John Langston Gwaltney published in 1980, interviewee Nancy White recalls: "My mother used to say that the black woman is the white man's mule and the white woman is his dog" (qtd. in Nakano Glenn, "Servitude" 17). This peculiar dynamic gives a specific shape to the relationship between domestic employees and the women they work for. Rollins observes that the domestics she studies fulfill a social role as "an extension of [their employer's] most menial self" (183). She argues that from within the housewife's patriarchal subordination, the mistress buoys up the racist ideology that empowers her by denying her employees' right to fulfill the ideals of womanhood, of motherhood (203).

In my own twenty-first century home, I was empowered in my relationship and acutely aware of L's shared humanity, but I nonetheless felt beaten down by a patriarchal system that had chained me to a certain kind of labour and simultaneously told me that my "woman's work" was shameful and without value. I felt betrayed by a culture that promised me gender liberation, then slapped me in the face when I sought fulfillment outside of my motherhood. And I was sinking under a budget that would label me privileged but felt like a cruel indictment of two undervalued educators. Perhaps this is why, when I looked for an alternative to "señora," "boss" didn't feel right either. Bosses belong to a world of money and public economy, outside of domestic havens and "women's work." What we do here, in this private space of home, this is supposed to be a labour of love.

Love and Labour

It's late in the afternoon, closing in on dinner time. I'm standing on a ramp just outside the door of a small building on campus, where I've excused myself from a seminar in order to make a call. The baby won't stop crying, L tells me. We think he might have an ear infection. No need to come home, she insists; she knows how to comfort him. I call the paediatrician's office. "When did the crying start?" the nurse asks. "What are his symptoms?" "What have we given him?" These are easy questions. Their answers live inside my head, competing for space with seminar notes, tomorrow's lesson plans, and tonight's dinner menu. "Is he pulling on his ear?" "What is the cry like?" "How did he nap today?" These are harder. These answers don't belong to me.

"I'm going to have to get the babysitter on the other line," I say. "Why don't you patch her in?" the nurse suggests. So, we conduct a spontaneous conference call there outside my classroom—employer and employee, mother and othermother—while on the other end of the line, I hear my baby cry in L's arms. I am overwhelmed with conflicting emotions: a powerful impulse to hold him tight to my chest, the confused guilt of a working mother, a familiar frustration for the lecture that I'm missing on the other side of the door, and running through it all: bitter-sweet gratitude. I am so glad he loves her. I am so sad he loves her.

This work of caring is a labour that begets the love, and a love that demands the labour. In a financial arrangement that trades care for wages, where do we locate the feelings that emerge? Does the relationship serve as the substitute we hope it will be, holding true and authentic within the temporal bounds of the work arrangement? Or does it spill out of waged hours and breed some deeper union? I don't know if my baby boy grew out of his love for L; if, when we see her now, he feels what I do, the easy nostalgia, the quiet loss. It's an emotion I associate with a certain once upon a time—their very young childhood, my young motherhood, afternoons when L would arrive, fresh and friendly. She feels like a friend from another stage of life. But "friend" seems wrong here because L was something else, too.

Those who have considered the nature of relationship in contemporary private domestic labour explain that the home breeds a dynamic unlike other workplaces. It is a space ruled by the emotional logic of the family (Tronto 36-37), a "zone of trust" founded in intimacy and informed by the expectation of "long-term reciprocity" (Zelizer 290-91). It is a space in which emotion is currency, is work, is labour, and power is rarely named. In this landscape of blurred boundaries, a caregiver's charge—"my child" as West Indian sitters often call them (Brown)—can become "emotional anchors" that keep them in place (Hondagneau-Sotelo 152). They may find themselves working not to feel or working to perform the feeling required.[6] That this work of emotions is theirs to manage reflects their relative power. That the work is necessary at all reflects a thornier dynamic—the moral boundary work we all do around love and money.

Sociologist Viviana Zelizer studies the intersections of economics and morality. She finds that intimacy and economic transaction are two deeply embedded realms. When money changes hands within intimate ties or when intimacy is bred from an economic arrangement, those involved engage in relationship work designed to define the moral limits of transaction. A lover receives an allowance labelled "gift." The nanny is invited to the child's birthday party but not to Sunday dinner. The child is encouraged to love her nanny but instructed never to call her "mommy." To do so would be to violate a cultural ideal that defines "mother" by virtue of her selfless devotion and her exclusive social role and biological claim. The possibility that the bond shared between child and nanny might be of the same category reveals a different reality lurking beneath the status and security of "mother." But the child lives there in that murky underneath, seeking a name that explains the labour and the love. Where "Miss" or "Auntie" or Sunday dinners are unavailable, the child finds only a deep and empty silence.

Within that silence, a more insidious understanding begins to take root. The child feels the devotion, comes to expect it. At the same time, she perceives the difference in naming and soaks up the unequal respect as natural. She learns to tolerate the imbalance and to sort it according to certain generalities—dark, feminine faces whom we call "L" and "E" exist to serve and offer up to us this caring love. Mary Romero warns of such a dynamic. She speaks of it in terms of consumption, invoking the stain of money and transaction that so challenges our notion of caring labour as born from authentic emotion. She tells us that children who grow up with full-time nannies in the context of class and race segregation "are likely to learn a sense of entitlement to receive affection from people of color that is detached from their own actions"; they will learn to be "consumers of care" (*Daughter* 23).

The day I listened on the phone as L comforted my baby, I did not consider the privilege that he was learning, only that he might love L in a way that should only be for me. As a child, I had known that real and abiding bond, and I had felt that I should be able to claim the rights of relationship with E, although I never found the words. Had I been a casualty of silenced experience, then, or merely an entitled child? Was I the protagonist of an unacknowledged love, or simply a "consumer of care"? And if I was somehow both, which of the two hurt E's daughter more?

Language and memory conspire to erase the girl, E's daughter summoned from my childhood mythology. Although our games were few, I remember vividly the anticipation of her presence. "R is coming to play today!" I'd shout. But our encounters fade in the unpractised recollection of those visits, and the feeling of knowing each other weaves in and out of other testimonies, snippets of research carrying voices from the other side. Edward Miller, the adult child of a domestic worker, recalls his encounters with white playmates at his mother's workplace:

> No, we didn't speak. It was, like, we wanted to. It was like we just didn't know what to say, or we knew that if we did, we would be crossing some invisible boundary that we weren't supposed to ... we just kind of stared at each other, and that was it, you know: no expression, no smile, no ugly faces. Nothing. Just a kind of look like we were both aliens from another planet. And we could see each other, but we couldn't understand each other. (qtd. in Romero, *Daughter* 34-35)

Did R see an alien where I worshipped an older girl in pigtails? In her reserved stare, tucked into the side of her busy mother, did she carry the legacy of daughters before her? Women like the former domestic who tells her interviewer that, in the segregated South, "If you worked for a family, your daughter was expected to, too" (qtd. in Nakano Glenn, "Servitude" 10).

Across imperfect memories, a clear line emerges: R as a stoic, straight-backed woman helping her mother across the threshold towards a Thanksgiving gathering of family that was not hers but was—in some confusing way—her mother's. A year or so later, that same long spine, that same reserved strength greeting mourners on the church steps at E's funeral. We filed past, my parents, siblings, and I, said our quiet hellos and found a pew tucked away into the back. There, we shared a pack of tissues and listened to E's loved ones celebrate her life. There, I traced my fingers along the funeral program and followed the cursive font beneath "E's Story," where mourners read about her birth and her schooling, her marriage and her children, her death and those she left behind; where they found testament to a work history that began, in those lines, after she left us. "She retired after she gave fourteen years to [a local school district]," it begins. "She then worked as a health care provider for a number of elderly people, who," we learn, "grew to love and accept E as their family and dear friend." No mention of the years she worked for us, only the empty space before these lines, silence inscribed.

In those missing lines, tear-stained now in the program that lays open beside me as I write, I read all the silences that E's first lesson contained. They come together to form an unspoken history of domestic work and the relationships it engenders. In its opposition to "maid," E's "housekeeper" acknowledged and denounced the racist foundations of the institution and its historically continuous practices of racial tracking. It denounced a cultural value system that denigrated the woman and the work in a dynamic of oppression that has dehumanized women and denied them the full acknowledgment of their motherhood.

In educating me away from "maid," "housekeeper" also carried the silence of a long line of resistance to the humiliation, abuse, and devaluation associated with the occupation. Resist by slowdowns and pushbacks and replacing one mistress with another (Hondagneau-Sotelo, Romero *Maid* 43). Resist by caring and cleaning in institutions rather than private homes so as to cast off the air of servitude (Nakano Glenn, "Servitude"). Resist by instructing the ones entrusted to their care in the ways of respect, in the language of dignity. In her lesson, E imparted to me the silent histories of injustice, of resistance, and of the relationships that spill out of the bounds of language.

What does it mean to love those who serve us? What does it mean to be shaped by their service? When I reflect on my childhood with E, I am struck by notes of shame and tenderness. I struggle to reconcile the affection that felt so real with the context in which it unfolded: the privileged child who learned to consume care and the worker limited by material need and ritual deference. In these pages, I've tried to name the shame—the privilege, the power, the intimate injustices of race, class, and gender; while also giving voice to the relationship—this confused thing that is love bound by injustice, injustice struck through with love. To name the shame and hold the love even so.

Recently, I searched for R on Facebook and found her staring out at me from photographs posted over the years. At times, she remembers her mother, longs for her, and reaches out on difficult days: "Miss you mom. Happy heavenly birthday." She posts her mother's picture, and E is lifted up to me once more, smiling into a camera from inside a full and unfamiliar life. She is beautiful, and she is happy, and I loved her. To see her takes my breath away. I expected emotion when I found the photos, but not to be breathless before E's familiar smile, eyes warm on the camera. I expected to recognize R somehow, this childhood playmate delivered to me through a confusing haze of tainted legacy, but nothing in the pictures triggered my memory. Then, I came upon a photo montage of R's own child: "Happy twenty-fifth to this beautiful daughter." In the centre, an image of R's daughter as a young girl, smiling brightly in pigtails. She's the spitting image of her mother. I know she is because I remember that face.

In this long history of language that shies away from confronting the shame—"help," "babysitter"—and falls short of acknowledging the bond—"maid," "housekeeper"—there are truths to be revealed. When we give voice to the intimate experience of an occupation shot through with both power and love, we can begin to confront the injustices inherent in its entangled histories. Perhaps then, like the lost memory of R's face, the silences, too, can be recovered.

Endnotes

1. The term "muchacha" evokes a legacy of vulnerable, exploited domésticas in Latin America, largely sourced from once-colonized Indigenous communities. These domestic workers have historically been so ubiquitous in the region that Argentina delayed creating a system of mail delivery for years because every family had a muchacha to fetch the post (Rollins 39).

2. On the relationship between domestic service and narratives of assimilation, see Romero's *The Maid's Daughter*. On the use of domestic service training in the context of American imperialism, see Nakano Glenn *Forced to Care*, pp.81-84.

3. In this reflection on language, it's worth noting that the term "Mexican" has undergone a complicated resignification in the American Southwest and beyond, as it has progressively lost its exclusive association with the category of nation and has come to identify racial difference among American citizens both native and naturalized.

4. Hondagneau-Sotelo offers the term "housekeeper-nanny" for this work. Mignon Duffy notes that while the language of "nannies" and "housekeepers" has replaced the language of servitude in contem-

porary practice (30), the model persists, as does the diffuse nature of the work (33).

5. "Patrona," the feminine form of "patrón," is the most common term for domestic employers in Latin America. The word refers to the defender and protector of a certain domain, as well as "one who is served by a maid." In this last exception, "patrona" is equal to "señora," a more common term among Spanish-speaking domestic workers, which holds the additional meaning of "one who reigns in a certain environment." In other words, the lady of the house (*Diccionario de la Lengua Española,* my translations).

6. Some nannies describe engaging in the difficult emotion work of closing themselves off to affection. Those who do not develop real feelings for their charges and the families they work for are additionally burdened with the emotional labour of fronting an inauthentic affection (Cummins Muñoz).

Works Cited

Brown, Tamara Rose. *Raising Brooklyn: Nannies, Childcare, and Caribbeans Creating Community.* New York University Press, 2011.

Chang, Grace. "Undocumented Latinas: The New Employable Mother." *Mothering: Ideology, Experience, and Agency,* edited by Evelyn Nakano Glenn, Grace Chang, and Linda Rennie Forcey, Routledge, 1994, pp. 259-86.

Crittenden, Ann. *The Price of Motherhood: Why the Most Important Job in the World Is Still the Least Valued.* Metropolitan Books, 2001.

Cummins Muñoz, Elizabeth. "*Madre/Moneda*: The Moral Value of Motherwork in Immigrant Nanny Personal Narratives." *Mothers, Mothering and Globalization,* edited by Dorsía Smith Silva, Abigail Palko, and Laila Malik, Demeter Press, 2017, pp. 34-51.

Duffy, Mignon. *Making Care Count: A Century of Gender, Race, and Paid Care Work.* Rutgers University Press, 2011.

Hondagneau-Sotelo, Pierrette. *Doméstica: Immigrant Workers Cleaning and Caring in the Shadows of Affluence.* University of California Press, 2001.

Milkman, Ruth. "The Macrosociology of Paid Domestic Labor," *Work and Occupations,* vol. 25, no. 4, 1998, pp. 489-510.

Nakano Glenn, Evelyn. "From Servitude to Service Work: Historical Continuities in the Racial Division of Paid Reproductive Labor." *Signs,* vol. 18, no. 1, 1992, pp. 1-43.

Nakano Glenn, Evelyn. *Forced to Care: Coercion and Caregiving in America.* Harvard University Press, 2010.

Rollins, Judith. *Between Women: Domestics and their Employers.* Temple University Press, 1985.

Romero, Mary. *Maid in the U.S.A.* Routledge, 1992.

Romero, Mary. *The Maid's Daughter: Living inside and outside of the American Dream.* New York University Press, 2011.

Tronto, Joan. C. "The 'Nanny' Question in Feminism." *Hypatia,* vol. 17, no. 2, 2002, pp. 34-51.

Zelizer, Viviana. *The Purchase of Intimacy.* Princeton University Press, 2005.

Chapter 2

Mothering for Pay: The Perspective of a White, College-Educated Nanny

Rachel O'Donnell and Madeline Wood

Most parents rely on some form of paid childcare. Individual expectations in this relationship can reveal a deeply held set of cultural opinions around caregiving and mothering, including how caregivers and their work relate to broader assumptions about race, gender, as well as social and economic class position. In this chapter, we consider the direct experience of the nanny role to offer increased visibility to caregivers and to pay attention to the combined caregiving labour being done in families. We aim to improve open, accessible, and friendly conversations among all members of the household. This can be a difficult conversation to navigate, especially for parents who may feel guilty that they cannot manage everything a family demands, including the intensive caregiving that often accompanies middle-class family life. We argue that looking at the role of an individual nanny can help us understand the intensification of carework, socially reproductive labour, mothering and, that caregivers' participation in maternal narratives can reframe our understanding of their roles in the nuclear family.

This chapter offers a reading of the role of the nanny in the nuclear family and her complicated role as coparent, both honouring the reproductive labour performed and highlighting the personal experiences of a nanny working for a family in New York State. Looking at a nanny's work directly allows us to track the contemporary intensification of mothering work for an individual household when it requires more than two parents to perform the caregiving labour. We recognize, however, that a nanny's narrative highlights a subset of a class of families. Only the most economically privileged can hire nannies, as it requires paying a full-time labourer from outside of their family for mothering work that individual family members (typically the mother) have historically performed for free.

In this piece, one nanny, Maddy, makes visible the invisible labour that comes with performing outsourced mothering work. Like testimonios and other stories that counter a mainstream narrative, the story she shares is a "crucial means of bearing witness and inscribing into history those lived realities that would otherwise succumb to the alchemy of erasure" (Latina Feminist Collective 2). We use Maddy's direct quotes and her story to "remove a mask previously used as a survival strategy" and urge others to enact social and systemic change around who is responsible for this work (Reyes and Rodríguez 527).

Maddy has worked both as a babysitter and a full-time nanny for multiple families in a mostly white suburb of Rochester, New York. Most recently, Maddy was employed by one upper-middle-class family of local business owners who have three young children. This family employed Maddy, who is white and a college graduate, full-time for a period of three years, including during the COVID-19 lockdown and the year and a half when the children were not attending full-time school. In this role, Maddy acted as not only caregiver and household manager but also as a teacher for the school-age children when they were at home.

As we know from research on nannies, including pieces in this collection, the dependence on family characteristics of middle-class social mobility often depends on the labour of domestic workers, not only the work of a young, white, college-educated nanny. Maddy offers something particular for the many white, middle-class families she has worked for: Her embodiment may be more comfortable in a white household for a family who feel they should not have a nanny. Maddy has noted this discomfort when she is called a babysitter in public and a nanny at home. For a nanny who is both white and college educated, she may be a more idealized form of nonmigrating domestic worker, one who chooses domestic work as a break before a career or her own motherhood. Of course, the housewife narrative (or the future housewife narrative, in this case) does not apply to all women, especially women of colour (Ferguson 108-9). For professional working mothers in partic- ular, these younger versions of themselves (white women) maintain a home that allows them to take on work with increased time and inten- sity. In the absence of federal support, precarious work (including un- regulated childcare) has continued to fill the gap, with the result being that not all families can access childcare (Ferguson 118).

Maddy's narrative therefore considers the dual role of a nanny as both a paid labourer and a member of the family. We argue that the specific role of the nanny in a mostly white and middle-class United States suburb implies that the work is particularly suited for young, white, college-educated women and that these identities serve to natu- ralize the work relationship between the nanny and her employer. Maddy explores her role as a nanny in a busy household with a focus on two specific pieces of her work: the additional unpaid work expectation (love) and the location (at home) that further complicate and intensify her role. We recognize that this represents much of the day-to-day domestic work that usually falls on mothers, who, if they can afford it, pay other women to do this work. No matter who performs this "inti- mate labour" (Boris and Parrenas) that signals a "closeness with dirt and bodies" (Jaffee 61), which other workers can avoid, this work remains low paid, with low job security, and low prestige.

Maddy's Story: The Work of a "Good" Nanny at Home

The Job of the Good Nanny

As a nanny, Maddy works as a household organizer, performing tasks for running the household, such as weekly linens washing and grocery shopping, running errands, maintaining a list of household items or children's clothing that needs to be replaced, managing extracurricular activities, overseeing day-to-day scheduling and last-minute changes, including arranging transport to a child's activity if another is napping, and more. This labour can be intense, and Maddy notes the "mental gymnastics" of the family schedule are often the most exhausting part of the work and consistently include exerting emotional labour on behalf of the household. Maddy ponders her role: "I ask myself questions that most parents are familiar with: How are the kids doing emotionally? Are their friendships okay? Are they too overwhelmed? Are they having tantrums because they have gymnastics practice right after school, and it's too much?"

Maddy has noted that the affluent, white families she has worked for often prefer to hire a white nanny from a similar class background. Some families have articulated that they like her because she has "some connection to the community," meaning Maddy was raised in the same affluent suburb in which she now works. She suspects that this may reflect the discomfort some families in the white suburb experience when it comes to allowing outsiders into their homes, although there are of course many class-based and race-based layers to this. Maddy imagines that for mothers who feel guilty they are not performing this work themselves, they may be tempted to consciously or unconsciously look for someone "like them" to perform mothering labour. Maddy has noted that many mothers in the affluent suburb where she works have told her that she reminds them of a younger version of themselves, perhaps signalling implicit messaging around class or race or discomfort with dependence on a nanny's labour. Either way, this discomfort begins to signal her role both inside and outside of the family.

About her insider role, Maddy states the following:

> By working in the same community in which I grew up, I feel comfortable and at ease in the role of the nanny because I am familiar with the geographical area. I remember the places that I loved to go growing up, and the things that most children in the area like to do. In a way this means that I can excel in my field, because I am able to provide children with a variety of experiences outside of the home, which often pleases and impresses parents. Although I differ from nearly all of the families I work for because growing up, my family did not have the finances for a nanny. In fact, we did not have the finances for a regular babysitter as well, and my parents depended upon my older brother to watch me, babysit, when they would work late or have the occasional outing. My parents never hired a babysitter or a nanny, and I was never cared for by an outsider. I was cared for only by my immediate family, and therefore found it difficult to establish my role in the household initially, since I had no idea what a nanny was supposed to be other than what I had seen in media. I was not afforded many of the privileges that the children I work with are, in terms of socioeconomic status.

As the COVID-19 shutdown only further intensified her work, Maddy went from having to care for a toddler full-time and a six-year-old half the day to homeschooling two school-age children and caring for the toddler. She had to be comfortable with the risk of additional COVID-19 exposure and had to make decisions regarding not to see her own parents and family or friends for many months to reduce risk. This is a good example of the uncomfortable blend between work and personal life that many nannies are expected to endure for the good of the children.

"My job is to protect those kids and keep them safe," Maddy said at one point during the COVID-19 lockdown. "I know I could make more in another job, but if you're a good nanny, you're not just going to switch for money." The "goodness" of the nanny role is important here and is an extension of the good mother role; it thus also allows mothers who outsource care to display (by proxy) their own goodness and dedication to their mothering. The hiring of a so-called good nanny by a working mother can fulfill the "good mother" ideal when the mother herself is unable to perform this role to her own expectations.

The cultural expectation of the good nanny may become blurred by a white nanny's relative privilege, working, and perhaps living in an upper middle-class or affluent household for what is considered a good wage. Still, the nanny must often sacrifice job security, employment status, a personal life, other opportunities for work experience or resume building, benefits, and paid time off. The work expectations are also for the children, meaning that a nanny works as an extension of the parents and is expected to respond as a parent would. Maddy remembers that she once got a call from a child at 10:15 p.m. and was asked to resolve a problem with bedtime. She was off the clock from her daytime nanny role, but when the employment relationship becomes a personal relationship with children she knows and cares for, the nanny may feel like she must respond at all hours, as a parent would. Maddy reports that as a nanny, the relationship with the children is more important than the relationship with the parent-employers, and when the nanny starts doing the mothering work, it intensifies the work relationship as she is expected to voluntarily work outside of the accepted role.

Nannies are often expected to love the children they care for and have a passion for their work. Advertisements for nannies on Care.com often request a "loving" nanny, leading us to think that parents are aware that they are outsourcing some of the love work, and that nannies are expected to love children unconditionally, as a parent would. Maddy reports that to be a good nanny, one must love the children, and that this love extends far beyond work hours, and is in fact woven into the most personal parts of her life, many of which occur during off hours. "I'm twenty-four [years old] and sometimes unable to enjoy the pleasures that young people seek. I think, 'Should I go on that super fun rock-climbing trip with my friends? Maybe not, if something happens to me, the children would be devastated.'" Friends who ask her to go out late at night and suggest she call in sick tomorrow do not understand her role. Maddy worries about the children's schoolwork and frets if a child has a spelling test the next day, wondering if the parents will help them prepare. She is often moved by the children's love, reporting that they tell her how much they enjoy their time with her. Maddy often responds positively to children's requests for her time on weekends, to attend gymnastics meets or soccer games, because she imagines how much this means to them, but this type of "good nanny" dedication can mean sacrificing free time.

Maddy explains:

> A good nanny doesn't say, "I'm not working that day, sorry" because that implies I'm only interested when money is involved, but of course that's not true. I'm always interested. I am thrilled the oldest has perfected her routine, and the middle has become somewhat of an expert in seven-year-old dribbling. And I am so proud because I love them. Because while it's my job to love them, it's also become part of my being. So, while the parents may think that these added things on the weekend are not work and it will be fun and I am "part of the family," I also know that I will be handed the toddler in the middle of the gymnastics meet when she gets cranky or be asked to run back to their house as the soccer game begins because a child has forgotten her cleats.

Maddy also reflects on how this makes her feel:

> It's the most fulfilling job I can imagine, and it feels good, every single day. But it also feels heavy, every single day. To know how much I can help these families means a lot, but the relationships between myself and the children are what makes me feel so

proud and humbled by the work that I do. But they give me something as well: a family. By needing to be part of the family to really fill the good nanny role, you quite literally become part of the family. You go to dinners and spend holidays and birthdays together. And for me, I've always wanted a family, and it has filled a major void I always felt growing up, coming from a more unstable family/home life. I am actively being the person I yearned for when I was growing up. And in some way, being that for these children fills that void for me. So, there's a lot of gratitude to be a part of this family, but the weight of my role is never lost on me. I know how much I'm depended upon. Physically, I have tasks to do and errands to run, but I also have hugs to give and cuts to bandage. Mentally, I have to remember everyone's schedules and activities, but I also have to think about the children and how they're doing and feeling. I know that my relationship with the children is one of the most important in their lives, and as a twenty-four-year-old childfree woman, that's a huge responsibility. I feel so full of love, and I feel so much pressure and exhaustion. In short, I feel like a mom.

Children often see the nanny as a natural extension of their family, and this line becomes further blurred when parents can hire out the goodness of their role to a good nanny. Maddy has found that the worse the parents are in terms of managing the children, the better the nanny must be to make up for that, but this disciplining becomes complicated as a nanny who lacks parental authority over many important decisions that heavily impact the children. Maddy found herself having to carry out decisions or punishments for the children in her care in ways she disagreed with and potentially found hurtful forms of discipline. She often felt she had to compromise her own values and beliefs for children she genuinely loved because it was her job. Most labour requires a person to occasionally go along with decisions they may not agree with, but in Maddy's case, these decisions affected young children she loved and respected deeply and felt that she was helping to raise, making it hard for her to stomach. She explains:

Having to follow through on "punishments" or "consequences" that I didn't believe were correct was extremely difficult. Because while I could say to the children, "I'm sorry honey, but this is what mom and dad decided," it's still coming from my mouth. I am the messenger of the bad news and therefore the person who is first in line to deal with the resulting emotions, which were often strong and heavy. I found it hard to comfort a child upset by a decision when I too did not support the decision. Part of my work is being a united front with the parents, and I would never want to undermine them to their children in any way, and this often meant that I had to justify their choices to their children, even when I didn't agree with them. It's difficult to love children as your own but have less of a say in the way that they are treated or raised.

In addition to recognizing her lack of parental control in the family, Maddy also felt like a mother could hire a nanny to highlight her family's class position. In what ways is an affluent mother attempting to outsource her in-home labour to another woman to achieve a standing as a good mother? Certainly, parents get credit for the raising of children, and the nanny who does the work may be discounted. Maddy, who has experience as a Montessori teacher, remembers well that when she taught the toddler she worked with to do certain tasks to create independence, she would hear from others about how incredible the mother was. Maddy explains:

And while the mother was incredible in many ways, I spent so much time and effort into guiding the children and teaching them how to do certain things. And while it doesn't matter who taught them what, it's frustrating to not be seen for my labour. People view nannies in a lot of lights, but it's rare that we are ever acknowledged for our part in raising the child. There is a narrative around nannies "caring" for children, which is absolutely part of the job. But when we use "caring" rather than "raising," it sounds like we are a placeholder for the parents; someone who is there to ensure the basic needs are met until the parents are home to do the real parenting job. Most of this is probably because of the difficulty admitting that someone else, an outsider, had a major influence in the way your children were raised. The caring is the easy part, the raising is hard. Raising children is labour, and it is often not viewed as part of the nanny's role, when inevitably it is.

Feminist researchers (e.g., Boris; Ferguson; Rosenbaum) have shown that well-performed housework and childcare are often connected to one's identity as a mother, but this can get more complicated when that work is done by a nanny. Good caregiving can often be extended to a good mother who finds a good nanny. The mother can outsource the "goodness" to another woman who can love and care for her child(ren), but this is not without some discomfort, especially when the children show a preference for the nanny's attention or company. Maddy has noted that mothers are particularly uncomfortable when the children call her "mommy," although this often comes easily to small children, especially when in public with other mother-child pairs. Here, the relationship between the nanny and the family blurs the relationship between work and kinship: The worker works at home and maintains a "good relationship with the family," meaning the family is provided with love, not merely work, and may mean that the nanny cannot expect job security or a limited working relationship at all. Furthermore, the nanny may recognize the children's misunderstanding about her role as well as those who are not told that she is a paid employee.

Indeed, this reproductive labour can be crucial to achieving affluence, as these families depend on their nannies to maintain their careers. Having a white, college-educated nanny can also become a status marker. Sociologist Susanna Rosenbaum notes in her study of domestic workers in Los Angeles that motherhood for upper-middle-class women has become a "predicament" (85), in which the working mother in particular feels exhausted, deficient, and guilty for not having enough time and energy to be the kind of mother she imagines (86). The social privilege of being an upper-middle-class working mother comes with expectations about the type of house one has and what one provides for the children (e.g., lessons or private schools or quality childcare) and does for oneself (take time to exercise or socialize). Maddy notes that for many of these mothers, this social privilege has also come to depend on employing a so-called good nanny, as mothers often report about their nannies, and Maddy has heard many times: "We just couldn't get along without her."

The Nanny's Work in the Family's Home

Household labour is often seen as separate from other forms of work, and this lack of understanding that the home is a work environment presents itself in the nanny's day-to-day work. Maddy also found that she would arrive to work in the morning and find a messy house or a pile of dishes had been left before her shift, leading her to say, "I often can't do my work until I've finished theirs." She was the only one to ensure that the work environment and children's living space was cared for. This lack of consideration for other labourers in the home often comes about because of discomfort surrounding discussion of labour in the home as "not really labour." In Maddy's case, the family she worked for adopted an untrained puppy without consulting her. Since Maddy was at the house during most of the daytime hours, this meant the responsibility of training the puppy, feeding it, and walking it fell mostly to her. The parents, of course, viewed the puppy's adoption as a decision for their family rather than added labour for the nanny.

Any conflict between the nanny and mother-employers often feels more intense because of the work performed in a private home. While Maddy reports that working for a family who makes a nanny feel included and loved is wonderful, and something that most individuals in the field look for, it can become problematic for the worker, as it blurs the work-family relationship and makes it more difficult to discuss standard labour expectations. For example, Maddy felt that she was expected to work without a guaranteed contract or any form of job security. When the mother of the family Maddy worked for decided to return to part-time work, she gave Maddy only two-weeks' notice regarding a significant reduction of hours and pay cut. For Maddy, she felt she was expected to continue to care for the family on a part-time basis because it would be difficult for the children if she were to leave. The mother-employer seemed to not understand the impact that the pay would have on Maddy's ability to support herself and save for school. Maddy also felt she was often asked to work around the employer's schedule, whatever it may be, because she is young, and domestic labour is not seen as real work.

The hiring of the nanny for busy professional women may be an escape from the subordinate labour a mother does in a family, the same way the hiring of a house cleaner may remove this labour from those in the household, but it can involve less obvious components. A clean house is easier to see than emotional labour done to care for children, manage the household, and remember appointments, practices, homework, and playdates. Maddy heard, for example, "I want to work out today; can you please grocery shop and get a gift for the children's father?" A professional woman who hires a nanny may find it difficult to understand the powerlessness of her hired domestic worker because of the paid role for work that many mothers do for free. Maddy's labour meant her employers were able to finish a busy workday and come home to a clean home, fed children, a stocked kitchen, with additional parenting tasks— such as bathing the children, coordinating playdates, or checking on homework—being taken care of for them, too. This meant the mother was able to perform paid labour outside of the home during daytime hours and could relax with her family without added concerns of household labour in the evenings, much like some fathers could when the mother of his children did not work outside the home. In a way, a working mother with a full-time nanny is paying for her free time and peace of mind. Once Maddy left the position, and much of the household labour was no longer being taken care of while she was working, the mother quickly found that she was exhausted by performing the home labour in addition to her day job, and even later reported this to Maddy.

Conclusion: What a Nanny Wants Us to Know

Working for wealthier families exacerbates a class divide between a young nanny who is in college, repaying college loans, or beginning a career and a dual-income, busy, upper middle-class family in need of help. For the nanny, then, a typical day is a long day, as it typically begins before and ends after the parents' work hours. The line between work and family as well as between employment and free time can get blurred and intensifies the household labour in ways that are not easily identified. A nanny who is expected to work "like one of the family" removes our clear understanding about the nature of domestic work and its relation to mothering work. Under COVID-19 restrictions, many nannies like Maddy were suddenly forced to become homeschool teachers without warning, often with little to no additional compensation. This form of work made further inroads into nannies' free time, as it limited their personal lives to care for their employers and their children more fully. At times, this meant the nannies' own families, other work, or social activities suffered. When an upper-middle-class family's preference is for a worker who matches them in terms of race and class, the relationship between family and nanny can be complicated. Childcare, which is difficult work, requires loving and caring work for children without question, much of it for free or in hours that are unpaid. In some cases, this work occurs in an affluent family's home, making it a workplace as well as a home.

Because we often view full-time, home-based mothering work as a woman's deliberate decision to leave the labour force, and because this mothering work is often deemed unproductive labour, being a nanny can likewise be considered not a real job or career. The childcare experience Maddy gained while nannying helped her move into a professional assistant teacher job at a Montessori school, and she has found that in a school setting, the removal of the home-based intimacy made the work expectations at school less intense. While she is still responsible for the well-being of the children in her care, Maddy has found that there is much more separation between work and home. While nannying, much of the labour Maddy performed during the day involved tasks such as errands, laundry, grocery shopping, and house cleaning, which then had to be repeated at her own household in the evening, making her own home labour that much more exhausting. What Maddy has termed a "Groundhog Day effect" quickly led to fatigue and burn-out in a mothering role where one is expected to be always on: happy, loving, and emotionally available. The burnout itself is difficult for all those doing mothering labour to manage, but with the added stress of trying to maintain a pleasant mood and appearance for one's employers and care for a home that is not one's own, the emotional exhaustion for a nanny can skyrocket, and it certainly did for Maddy.

Instead of increased care for children in society more broadly, college-educated nannies working in such households are increasingly making up for much of what is lacking in society and its microcosm at the household level—close, personal attention to children and consistent emotional care. If we are serious about recognizing the invisible mothering work being done by all caregivers, we must revisit how we discuss labour at home and include the nanny's role as an important piece of the mothering work being done. The structural components and the difficult relationships in both the household and the broader community make it difficult or perhaps impossible for all those doing mothering labour to feel successful. Subtle forms of discrimination and the invisibility of household and mothering labour are difficult to recognize and change. If we want change to happen, we need to welcome nanny stories differently. A nanny of any race and class is often intimidated in her role; being nervous about managing the terms of employment while being available and loving for children in a home that is not hers does not help. We need to make discussions of home-based labour more open, accessible, and friendly for mothers and their families to become comfortable talking to one another about who is doing the labour necessary and about the guilt all family members feel when they cannot manage everything, especially the intensive mothering that a contemporary middle-class family often engages in.

Works Cited

Boris, Eileen, and Rhacel Salazar Parreñas, editors. *Intimate Labors: Cultures, Technologies, and the Politics of Care.* Stanford Social Sciences, 2010.

Care. "Find Trusted Caregivers for Every Need." *https://www.care.com/.* Accessed 30 April 2022.

Ferguson, Susan J. *Women and Work: Feminism, Labour, and Social Reproduction.* Pluto Press, 2020.

Jaffe, Sarah. *Work Won't Love You Back: How Devotion to Our Jobs Keeps Us Exploited, Exhausted, and Alone.* Bold Type Books, 2021.

Latina Feminist Collective. *Telling to Live: Latina Feminist Testimonios.* Duke University Press, 2001.

Reyes, K. B., and J.E. Rodríguez Curry. "Testimonio: Origins, terms, and resources." *Equity and Excellence in Education*, vol. 45, no. 3, 2012, pp. 525-38.

Rosenbaum, Susanna. *Domestic Economies: Women, Work, and the American Dream in Los Angeles.* Duke University Press, 2017.

Chapter 3

Mothering in the Balance: Rewriting the Mother Code to Serve the Whole Family

Gertrude Lyons

Introduction

Across societies and eras, nannies have been an invisible part of the process of raising children; they have been critical to many families but are too often treated as though they were "shadow workers" and marginalized participants in a child's upbringing (Sekeráková Búriková; Macdonald). For some, it is easier to frame this aspect of modern living as merely transactional than to attempt to address the myriad implications of delegating parenting responsibilities to others (Epp and Velagaleti). The myths that have been promulgated in our society and directed especially at women further drive the help that is available for mothers into the shadows, even as these myths set out unrealistic expectations. The modern mother living in Western culture requires relationships within a support network to function. Because these relationships are so important to members of the complex families they create, a sophisticated framework is needed not only to guide the understanding of those relationships but also to experience them as personal growth and development opportunities for both mother and nanny.

The mother code is such a framework, as it allows the act of mothering to be viewed as fluid and fecund, a role that can be and is played by many people in many ways over a childhood. Although much has been written about the broadening scope of mothering in recent years, the intellectual, emotional, and psychological mosaic of rules, assumptions, and habits of the heart associated with "mother" often avoids scrutiny, in part because they are so deeply embedded in our cultural matrix as to be essentially invisible. This alternate approach inventories the elements of that mosaic and interrogates the point of origin of each of them, with the intended effect of allowing, through illumination, the opportunity to remake those patterns of behaviour. I argue that rewriting the mother code (RMC)—which I coined and conceived based on original research (Lyons) and is the subject of numerous papers, interviews, podcasts, and other popular media—could be applied to the question of how to frame hired mothering in an inclusive family context.

Overview

To arrive at what could be possible for the mother and nanny in their respective psycho-social developments, a summary of how RMC came into being is needed. This is followed by an analysis of how the framework can be applied to both mother-employers and nannies. Next, the sources of the mother code are enumerated. Case studies, including some reflections on my own journey, are next, with a section tying all these topics together preceding the concluding section. I close with a vision for what is possible for not only the mother, nanny, and children but also the world, when we apply the concepts and process of RMC.

This chapter will make the case that the common narrative of mothering as an all-consuming investment in children at the sacrifice of any other meaningful experiences for mothers should give way to a focus on development for all parties, including both mothers and children. It further contends that the assumptions and social cues that drive contemporary practices that erase the humanity of mothers can be recognized, interrogated, and re-evaluated through an understanding of their origins and purpose. This, in short, is seeing and rewriting the mother code. While the approach of most scholars exploring mothering and nannies narrows the scope of their research to the relationship defined by one mother hiring another to serve as a mother to a limited extent in her stead, this perspective, which both centres and challenges our assumptions and practices surrounding mothering, can easily identify that there are two equally important poles intersecting the axis of care for children. And although their relationship to one another is most directly defined by the children related to the transaction which binds them, there are very often other children impacted by and exerting influence over that transaction.

Nannies are often either mothers themselves or people with a strong connection to mothering experiences. Increasingly in recent decades, a nanny working in the United States (US) is a mother with children in a distant country who has been compelled to travel to earn money for her family to survive (Baquedano-López; Pierette Hondagneu-Sotelo; Rhacel Salazar Parreñas). The cold logic of capitalism sends her hundreds or thousands of miles from the children for whom she has honed her mothering skills to earn money to keep them alive by being a mother to another woman's children. In families where nannies are employed to take care of children, a tension can arise between the parents and the nanny—and often specifically between the mother and the nanny (Sheftel; Macdonald; Armenta). A variety of factors contributes to that tension, but much of it is the result of seeing mothering as a zero-sum proposition in which a mother and nanny struggle over a perceived limited amount of love available for the children they are hired to watch over (Macdonald).

In this tension, one can see both the presence of the mother code and opportunity to remake it. Just as lines and lines of programming code collectively comprise operating systems, so too can one imagine the rules of mothering we take for granted to be an operating system, essential to the task of mothering but capable of being rewritten. Consequently, this chapter hypothesizes that the mother code offers a valuable perspective on the scholarship exploring these relationships, an oft-researched topic. By framing the psycho-social forces at play in our idea of mothering as both enumerable and malleable, RMC presents a perspective that affirms the essence of the idea of mothering and empowers mothers to adapt much of the idea of mothering to different contexts. In this way, it both upends traditional ideas of mothering and creates broad opportunities for personal growth rooted in mothers and mothering but extending benefits to the whole family. As a mother deepens their self-awareness and can draw upon new reservoirs of strength, the whole family is strengthened. Exploring the relationship between mothers and nannies will illustrate this benefit.

A robust literature exists surrounding what could be characterized as "the problem of the nanny." Many modern households in the West rely on childcare to provide a degree of freedom for parents that historically was denied to the mother in a family unit (Ayaydin; Cox). While this clearly translates into benefits for the parents, there are many interviews and surveys of parents expressing challenges in the nanny-caregivers relationship (Epp and Velagaleti; Cox). The freedom offered by childcare support, it seems, comes at a substantial cost in the form of interpersonal conflict (Garey, et al.). This is often characterized as a power struggle between the adults (Macdonald; Greenfield et al.). Consequently, nanny research often focuses on this conflict to understand its underlying causes. This tension is an obstacle to personal development for both the employer and the employee. Each is sacrificing some of their status as a mother by making decisions that are inconsistent with the myths of their society about how they should behave—the one leaving home each day for work or other personal engagement or simply becoming unavailable to the children even if she still remains in the house, the other who in many cases is travelling far from her own children and community out of economic necessity—and must confront the myths that question their legitimacy in order to free themselves from the accompanying guilt and barriers to fulfillment and growth.

This chapter contends that rewriting the mother code can reframe this dynamic in a way that considers the act of mothering as based in abundance rather than scarcity. By interrogating the core beliefs of mothering, one can posit that each additional person engaged in the act of mothering a child adds to the total mothering effect, a remaking of the code in which the mothering role is traditionally assigned to a single person. As Sara Ruddick has explained across her body of scholarship regarding motherhood, there are no limits in terms of who can mother beyond one's individual capacity to do so (29). Nevertheless, the idea of mothering, as opposed to a more generic conceit such as parenting, must be recognized as both specific in its meaning and historically as something that has been undertaken, in most cases, by women (Ruddick 41). In researching the dynamics between parents and nannies, then, one seeks out the complementary elements and the ways in which more than one approach can be reconciled to build a more nuanced and complex mothering experience rather than adjudicating the "right" and "wrong" way to mother. Where there are still concrete obstacles, they can be discerned outside of cultural, socioeconomic, or other biases.

The Emergence of the Mother Code

My credibility in framing the mother code construct was not born out of masterfully navigating the landscape of mothering and later imparting my sage wisdom on others. Rather, I got here by consciously engaging in an intensive, painful, rewarding, and spiritual process—not unlike giving birth. Reflecting on the years of mothering my two daughters, I came to terms with some painful truths. At the top of the list of regrets was the fact that even though I was already coaching other mothers and parents and immersed in a growth community, I explicitly avoided myself and my own personal growth potential for long stretches of time. It was like stalling in labour out of the fear of going into the terrifying next stage of pushing. Not until I embarked on my doctoral journey did I fully allow myself to feel the pain of all but giving up the opportunity of engaging in self-actualization as I mothered our children. I also realized that my regrets were not unproductive, and I could support other women to utilize this process in the hopes that we would begin to contradict the pervading culture of mothering as a limiting, self-sacrificing activity that takes us further from our core self and instead seize the growth opportunity through mothering. Despite my status as a middle-class, white woman in the US, I believe mothering can be a practice and a worldview that sets the stage for solidarity beyond these limiting qualities. Motherhood, when reimagined, holds out the possibility of uniting us in solidarity where socioeconomic factors divide us.

Mothering, more than any other role we perform, is where our unresolved emotional triggers will arise. Therefore, as research shows (Heffner; Arendell), it is also fertile soil for adult development. In fact, it is so important that how we think about mothering must be understood as completely as possible. As Andrea O'Reilly points out, we must insist on the value of development during the mothering process as a benefit to mothers as human beings, not simply to the extent it makes us better parents ("Outlaw[ing] Motherhood," 369). Mothering is more than a set of ideas or even a philosophy. We engage in mothering behaviours so swiftly that it is often described as an instinct, something that precedes rational thought (Benveniste). The truth is much more complex. I describe our relationship to mothering as existing within our consciousness in much the same way computer code is used to make technology operational (Lyons). It is invisible while you are typing or listening to music or calling your friend, but there is code written into all your interactions using a smartphone or computer. Likewise, all our mothering moments are made possible by a mother code, a set of assumptions and rules that began to be wired into us before our minds were even fully formed. Our relationship to the idea of mothering begins as we attach to our own mother at an early age as an object of love (Chodorow). This framework influences the entirety of the life of a mother, everything from work relationships to our friendships. Our primary paradigm for mothering is typically the way our mothers raised us and our reaction to it. Was your mom cold and distant? Was she warm and caring? Did she smother? Did she give you room to grow? How you interpret your childhood experience with your mother is typically the foundation for how you think about mothering today. Equally important is how you react to that experience. Regardless of one's overall impression of one's upbringing, that assessment drives a great deal of the paradigm we have developed for our own mothering—just one aspect of the study of the intergenerational transmissibility of family health. Reexamining the code in large part consists of replacing those unexamined reactions with a more fully realized relationship to the mothering experience.

Beyond childhood, there are myriad cultural cues that further complicate the rules we follow, many of which are millennia old. Beyond that, the idea of mothering in its most universal sense reverberates throughout culture, and we feel and are influenced by this presence as well. Judith Wright distills the categories of mothering, which stay constant and transcend cultural constraints, into three categories: 1) traditional mothering—raising and caring for children; 2) mothering others—nurturing people and projects; and 3) mothering self—developing an internal capacity to nurture oneself and take responsibility for one's own ongoing growth. This is a universal vantage point, and it is as applicable to the mother who is working for another person to raise their children as it is to the mother who hires a nanny. All these factors come into play as we make the decision to bring outside assistance into our family. Whether one is even capable of thinking of a nanny as a figure that will fulfill mothering duties within the family is questionable, so profound is our dependence on the code to frame our experience. Once a nanny does become part of the family's daily routine, positive relations depend in large part on whether one is able to reconsider the assumptions one was raised with, which are promulgated throughout society.

Likewise, nannies will have to take these factors into consideration as they come to terms with the economic realities that stretch and change what the act of mothering looks like when it means living far from one's own children to ensure their survival. In other words, making room for the nanny—and for the families who hire them—requires rewriting the mother code.

Nannies and the Mother Code

The narratives of motherhood this examination and transformation of the traditional mothering framework seek to transcend are not limited to those of the expectation for middle-class women. Their children are often cared for by women who have their own children in other countries who have made the heart-wrenching decision to leave their families to care for them (Baquedano-López). These women arrive in a country which simultaneously is responsible for the economic pressures that send them here and nevertheless stigmatizes them from the moment they arrive. Much like the "welfare queens" of the Black and brown communities of the US, nannies from other countries are labelled, as described by Katrina Bloch and Tiffany Taylor, as "'bad' mothers, fraudulent and lazy" (199). Although it is beyond the scope of this chapter to analyze the gamut of forces at work in these mischaracterizations, it is worthwhile to note that having women pigeonholed into these categories is deemed necessary by the structural forces at work, as necessary as the circumscribed identities of the "good" mothers they work for. The Mother Code, as conceived, is not limited to any one social order. In fact, it is presented as a consequence in part of myths that are as old as society itself (Lyons). This means that the cultural assumptions, social cues, and personal struggles that arise from the unique context of being a mother from another country and another culture working for a middle-class woman in the US must be a part of any comprehensive dissection of the components of the Mother Code.

This chapter seeks to introduce RMC rather than fully interrogate it, but there are critical observations to be made with respect to the position of nannies in American culture and the potential represented for them in the idea of the Mother Code. In some ways, the possibility of personal growth in a space defined by one's relationship to raising children is an even more urgent project for people who are forced by economic necessity to live hundreds or thousands of miles away from their children. That growth may not look the same as what a comfortable US citizen might be looking for, but it is no less significant or complex as a result. For them, transcending the messaging of the code will very likely include confronting their employers' own limitations. Employers of nannies are known to surveil them (Bern et al.), use their legal status to enforce some imagined superiority (Armenta), and even treat them as status symbols, not unlike an expensive car or an elaborate vacation (Ayaydin). Additional examples of the potential oppression nannies face abound. To contextualize rewriting the mother code for them very likely will mean confronting complex power dynamics and weighing their own dignity against the safety and well-being of their children.

One additional element must be observed to make this circuit complete. To transcend the limits set for oneself by the extant cultural programming for mothers who hire nannies or work as nannies, the relationship between the two mothers and their personal growth trajectories is inextricably linked. To some very real degree, the ability of each mother to transcend personal limitations is bound up in the extent to which both parties operate from this framework of rebuilding their idea of mothering. Much of the influence nannies hold can be related to the turning away from mother to father, which is a typical reaction of children to the omnipotence of mother (Chodorow). To the extent that this dynamic drives influence, power struggles are fundamental to the relationships in the family and must be addressed somehow to avoid counterproductive conflict. What is more, the intense and complicated relationship between these two mothers, the employer and the nanny, offers the possibility of a transformative space that could become a "place of possibility" (Garner 326) in which the traditional roles and power dynamics are called into question just as the traditional categories are also interrogated by mothers remaking their roles. As more overtly political discussions often observe, only when we see that, as was famously coined by a collective of aboriginal rights activists from Australia, our liberation is bound up in the liberation of others do we achieve real change.

Finally, the focus of this analysis on women employing women is a matter of convenience, as opposed to a limitation of the concept. In fact, a central theme of the author's broader scholarship is the universality of mothering (Lyons). Nevertheless, the idea of "mother" remains persistently female to many people and is too often limited to those who have given birth. To the extent that one can extrapolate from the experiences of biological mothers working together in a socio-economic context to other permutations of mothers interacting with mothers, the author enthusiastically hopes such adaptation will occur.

Sources of the Mother Code

Our own experiences and the cultural cues that are all around us combine to create a framework that many of us operate within uncritically. Our ideas about motherhood are a dramatic illustration of this. Between our childhood experiences and the relentless messaging about what a mother should be by mainstream culture, there is little room for one's own opinion. As Andrea O'Reilly observes, the "messy and muddled realities of motherhood are camouflaged—masked by the normative discourse of motherhood" (*Mother Matters* 14). By identifying these influences as the elements of a perspective we can deconstruct and evaluate, we begin the process of rewriting the mother code.

Personal Wiring Code: We are often unconscious of the impact our mothers (and to some extent our fathers) have had on us. We are wired from what we experienced growing up, and we usually parent reactively as a result. We may blindly do what we experienced, or, on the flip side, we default to going in the exact opposite direction (Daines et al.). Regardless of the mothering experience we had as a child and our reaction to it, the foundation of our own mothering experiences should be a product of reflection, not reaction, so we can be intentional about making our own choices. If we had a wonderful experience, we still want to question the choices our mothers made so we make the journey of mothering our own. And we want to learn from, rather than react to, the negative experiences of growing up.

Cultural Wiring Code: The cultural context of mothering is key to understanding the mother code. Without an understanding of its source, however, it becomes a kind of prison that limits a mother's ability to imagine what is possible. Mothering can seem like ten thousand questions for which nobody has provided useful answers. Contemporary culture often weaves a subtext of inadequacy, suffering, and judgment into these questions, beginning with the birth itself—and even before the birth. Children do not come with owner's manuals, but the cultural refrain is that mothers "just know" how to mother—and that good mothers are able to do it all themselves. Mothers are expected in this society to engage in "intensive mothering," a bottomless pit of emotional and physical expectations in terms of parenting (Hays). Meanwhile, women are under huge pressure to pursue successful professional careers. Nannies are employed at the very peak of this postpartum professional anxiety.

At its heart, the topic of nannies is connected to two questions: whether mothers should get help and whether that help should come from outside the family. Understanding the relationship between both of those questions and dominant cultural concerns is a precondition to being able to navigate a path forwards with respect to social attitudes towards nannies and mothering. Because the agenda of one's culture is rarely aligned with optimal human development for mothers, there is always tension between these two forces. Human ecologist Rima Apple, in *Perfect Motherhood: Science and Childrearing in America*, powerfully describes the tension of "scientific motherhood" (2) and outlines how women have come to expect "that medical and scientific experts and expertise should intervene in their daily lives, helping them in all areas of childcare" (10). Apple challenges mothers to assess the prevailing models and practices. Certainly, the selection process when hiring a nanny and the working relationship between mother and nanny require a similar sort of assessment and engagement outside of external metrics and cultural cues. Developmental psychologist Alison Gopnik brings our current culture into focus by challenging modern parents to understand that the now ubiquitous term "parenting" is a cultural construct that first came into existence in 1958 and was popularized in the 1970s. According to Gopnik, smaller families scattered around geographically and broke the norms from past generations. Moreover, the middle-class models for learning something new, just as is the case with mothering, are the same frameworks we use for schooling and our jobs where there is a regimented system with constructed measures for performance and "success." Gopnik continues: "There is a reason the [1958 cultural construct known as the] parenting model is popular. But it's a poor fit to the scientific reality" of the nature of a child's growth (22). In *The Myths of Motherhood: How Culture Reinvents the Good Mother*, psychologist Shari Thurer reviews the iterations of motherhood across the centuries and in different cultures. She argues that the prevailing ideas about motherhood have changed over time, but the one constant is that society always attempts to control the meaning of motherhood. Thurer comes close to describing a rewriting of the mother code when she posits, "If we can formulate a bottom-line basis of mothering behaviour, by which we may describe future incarnations, perhaps we can determine what is essential and good—for babies, mothers, and societies" (2). Within the context of RMC, we would add that the foundation would be a doorway to as many "right" versions of mothering as there are mothers. With that proviso in mind, this formulation can provide some clarity to the mother-nanny relationship.

Our current time has a specific set of myths that are hardwired into our idea of what mothering ought to be. In my research, I identified fourteen modern myths that bind a woman into a narrow definition of what it means to be a mother and curtail the breadth of transformation possible in motherhood. These myths occupy spaces that are, in many ways, like O'Reilly's eight characteristics or rules of the Western patriarchal motherhood ("Outlaw[ing] Motherhood," 369). Myths of motherhood begin with an imaginary version of mom in which she magically transforms into a fount of endless love and affirmation for her children and spouse or partner upon giving birth. A new source of intuition arrives with the baby that furnishes her with all necessary skills. According to these myths, experts, if they are needed, largely consist of other mothers in her own family and mainstream experts like professors and doctors. Mothers are expected to follow the rules and told that happiness will come from devoting one's life to raising her children. Sharon Hays captured the demands placed on the modern mother with the term "intensive mothering," which she describes as "a gendered model that advises mothers to expend a tremendous amount of time, energy, and money in raising their children" which is at odds with "a society where the logic of self-interested gain seems to guide behaviour in many spheres of life" (x). Hays calls this paradox the cultural contradiction of contemporary motherhood. Although these myths hold glimmers of truth, they create a false dichotomy in which it is easy for a mother to doubt herself. The dimensions of these myths are confounded by the presence of a nanny in a family. How does one identify an employee who adheres to all these behaviours? How can one reconcile the myth of putting kids first and still hire someone to watch them while a mother is at work and otherwise engaged? The use of hired support in raising children and the prevalent myths about motherhood today are often in direct conflict.

Through a reframing of what it is to be a mother by rewriting the mother code, one can distill the essence of truth in each myth and re-build the mothering construct to embrace the complex world we live in and to build a version of mothering that sees personal development as a priority for all family members. This is, fundamentally, what RMC is about: creating a vision of mothering that prioritizes human develop-ment for mothers but also in turn for the whole family. This in turn opens the possibility of a healthy, productive relationship with the nanny, who must be seen as a human being deserving of an enriching experience as well.

Application—Case Studies

The following are examples from women's lived experiences of applying the mother code framework. The first is taken from my life, the second is from a colleague who has been engaged in this process of interrogation and transformation throughout the raising of her children, and the third is from a client who is both a nanny and a mom-to-be. It is important for readers to see some of the blind spots I identify in my own story to gain an understanding of the context from which the RMC framework derives, both its insights and limitations.

Gertrude

After my first birth, I was asked to come back to work sooner than I anticipated. I had not made any childcare plans, as I thought I was going to have more time. I decided I would hire a nanny, and some of my earliest decisions about who to include and exclude in my search were based on broad stereotypes from my childhood and cultural wiring. I decided that I would not hire anyone European, especially Eastern European, because I merged all women from this geographic area into mistaken stereotypes of cold, serious, and harsh caregivers. Instead, I focused my efforts on women from Mexico, Central America, and South America because my unexamined belief was that they were warm moth-ers. From a childhood wiring perspective, I was unconsciously looking for the kind of mothering I did not receive. Had I recognized this at the time, I would have identified my lack of healthy early attachment and yearning for affection and sought out ways to give that to myself in the moment and going forwards. By not being conscious of this, I was setting both of us up for inevitable resentment and conflict.

Bridget

For Bridget, the thought of having a nanny or any kind of childcare support seemed indulgent. "That is what rich people do that don't love their kids," she said in my conversation with her. What was wired in her from childhood was the paradigm of mother as martyr-saint. Childrearing in her home was carried out by her mother (who also worked outside the home) with the support of siblings and grandparents—not by outsiders. Hiring someone challenged Bridget's belief that if she did not "do it all," then she was surely a failure as a mother. It was uncomfortable, but she knew if she wanted to keep working at a job she loved, she would have to challenge these beliefs and break the family rule of not hiring outside help.

Having hired many employees throughout her career, Bridget followed the same process, which resulted in a lot of interviews. They made an offer to a woman who was perfect on paper. She was a former teacher with lots of experience. She even had her own curriculum for early childhood learning. The candidate ended up turning them down. They stepped back and reevaluated their hiring criteria based on values.

This inquiry went deep for Bridget, as she explored more of her historical wiring that needed to be discovered and rewritten. Through one-on-one coaching, intensive group work where she immersed herself in assignments to expand her thinking, she realized she was valuing the "doing" aspects more than the "way of being" qualities. This opened two doors for her. The first door brought them the nanny they have employed for thirteen years. Yes, they felt she would be diligent, responsible, and hardworking, but it was her way of being, her listening skills, and her experience with her own colicky daughter that mattered most. It also allowed Bridget to address her own biases of valuing doing and external credentials over being and emotional accessibility.

Bridget also faced the common mother-nanny dilemma, "Will they love her [the nanny] more than me?" She remembers the first time she heard her toddler daughter call their nanny "mom." When this happened, she had gained the emotional intelligence skills to appear unbothered in the moment, but she internally acknowledged her hurt feelings. Bridget used the space of her personal and group coaching to say the unsayable and even let go of anger that had been broiling inside of her. Only then could she see the possibility that her daughter was articulating the expanded definition of mothering that included all her close caregivers.

Anna, the nanny who works for Bridget and had been a manicurist and hair stylist, would often do Nora's hair and make-up before recitals and theatre performances. One time, Anna was not available to do her daughter's hair and make-up before a recital. Nora was visibly disappointed, and she let her mother know. Bridget learned that despite the myth that mothers are not supposed to prioritize their own feelings over those of a child, it was not only appropriate but essential to be with her feelings when her child is disappointed in her lack of skill in a certain area.

It took a lot of introspection and rewiring on Bridget's part to come to believe she is valuable. There were skills and attributes of Bridget's that Anna could not do well, too. After rewiring mistaken beliefs, Bridget was able to celebrate her nanny and acknowledge how lucky she was to have her without dismissing her own hurt feelings. The mistaken belief that she was not good enough could have caused her to spiral, resulting in her finding a reason to fire Anna. With her daughter, she may have sought out affirmation by trying to make her feel guilty or by criticizing the nanny to her daughter for her other shortcomings to try and achieve balance. Bridget now feels that she, her husband, and nanny are truly raising their children together. Before rewriting her mother code, she had to continuously work internally around how she was embarrassed she needed a nanny. Now Bridget says at least six people are needed to do this job!

Sonia

Sonia immigrated to the US from Brazil with her twin sister when they were in their early twenties. She took a job as a nanny because she "liked kids" and thought "it would be fun." Sonia started her personal growth and adult development work because she "wanted answers" to life's big questions, and during her self-exploration experience, she began to realize that she could apply what she learned in real time with both the children she was caring for and the parents she interacted with.

An aspect of Sonia's development was reckoning with the truth that she hid her position as a nanny from others. She shared with me, "I was very embarrassed being a nanny, because I considered it a low-level job." She thought she should be doing "better than her mother" who worked her whole life as a domestic, taking care of a family's household in Brazil. Sonia thought she was very different from her mother, but she realized that her wiring was similar in that she would compare herself and feel inferior to her peers and friends who were lawyers, teachers, and successful business owners. People would tell her she was doing beautiful and important work, but it took considerable rewiring to move from the internal mistaken belief that she was somehow less than others to owning her value and contribution. She now proudly shares that her career is nannying, and while she has also started a business as a mother and nanny coach, her priority is as a nanny.

While Sonia was clear that her work as a nanny was a job, she started to notice a heaviness about it. By the end of a normal day where she was focused so intently on the children, she would leave and "take a deep breath." The responsibility started feeling like a burden. In the RMC framework, it is at these junctures of upset and upheaval that a person is most ripe for transformation. Rather than complain to the other nannies (she shared that this is a common way people try to deal with being upset), she brought these feelings into her coaching with the attitude that her current way of being was getting in the way of her showing up fully for the children, and, more importantly, it was impeding her own self-care and nourishment.

How to Rewrite the Mother Code

The first part of rewriting our own mothering code is to heal our family experiences so we are no longer trapped by our histories, and instead have these experiences become vehicles for our personal growth and transformation. In the examples above, each woman recognized where faulty wiring was blocking her path and then employed tools to achieve transformation. One is unable to sufficiently perceive the broader cultural forces at play, let alone confront them, without first achieving a substantial degree of mastery over one's personal framework.

What this means in practical terms is that we are constantly aware, on a moment-to-moment basis, of our mothering reactions. We can ask ourselves: Why is this triggering to me? Am I seeing myself and my old wounds in my child's experience or feelings right now? Or am I feeling myself reacting in the way my parents did? And as we answer these questions, we can take ourselves out of our past histories and be in the present moment—where we can not only function more optimally but also be more nourished and fulfilled. We can be more intentional about how we act—or do not—on the thoughts and feelings that are coming up for us—so we do not find ourselves parenting reactively. And we can protect ourselves from experiencing all too common mothering shame. Until our unconscious wiring around mothering is brought to the surface, our choices will be limited. Freud's metaphor of our unconscious as an iceberg is fitting here. Most of the decisions we think we are making are being driven by unconscious memories and experiences below the surface. When we plumb these depths, we bring to the surface material that can help us make more informed and discerned choices.

Becoming aware of one's existing mother code requires learning the language the code was written in. It is much easier to approach this vast web of meaning with some experience in the theory and practice of personal development. For my personal journey and the work I do with other women, an integrative and applied education system comprised of developmental psychology, humanistic psychology, existential philosophy, and neuroscience has been invaluable. Increasing our emotional intelligence is another key pathway to rewriting our codes. Contrary to popular opinion, emotions are non-dualistic and do not fit into a "good versus bad" framework. The five primary emotions—fear, hurt, anger, sadness, and joy—are purposive and serve important functions. Learning to identify and express emotions responsibly opens the possibility for more nourishing and authentic interactions; they are also imperative for our decision making and rational thinking (Damasio). This is especially relevant for mothers and nannies when it comes to managing intense emotional triggers that accompany childrearing.

The second step to rewriting our mothering code is to become aware of our cultural blocks. At the very heart of these messages is the idea of the "perfect mother," who sacrifices everything to raise her children. For women who choose to employ a nanny as additional support, this myth can cause tremendous harm. Just as the mother code can accommodate the capacity of everyone to mother, regardless of whether they have given birth, so, too, can mothering involve a whole network of support. Nannies perform critical mothering support that fosters strong bonds with the children they watch over and help raise. Mothering happens outside of biological mothers. Where traditional messaging prevents mothers from seeking help, it does not promote the nurturing of children, nor does it allow mothers to develop as complete human beings. Rewriting the mother code is necessary because conscious development is key to effective mothering, in addition to being the right of every mother.

Future Outlook

And finally, for this new paradigm of mothering, we must expand our definition so that everyone finds themselves on the mothering continuum. We must resist defining mothering as an act that transcends a single, womb-based life event. We must go beyond motherhood. All women mother. All women have access to the processes of conceiving, gestating, and birthing. Even if we do not have children, we conceive, create, and give birth to ideas, careers, and relationships. And the most overlooked and yet important person we need, and have an opportunity to mother, is ourselves. For when we mother ourselves, we take care of our physical needs, our emotional well-being, and we invest in building a core sense of self—before we endeavour to build anybody else's.

What happens when we take the expanded definition of mothering and apply it to the relationship dynamic of a mother and nanny? We go from territorial conflicts to a framework that allows for the possibility of a mutual co-voyage where the similarities in the values inherent in mothering are allowed to emerge through differences in approach and backgrounds—a promising if difficult potentiality. A "one-team" approach is born and cultivated. Rather than having "mother" and "nanny" set in conflict with one another by external forces, they are brought into a state of synergy and mutuality. I further assert that propagation of this dynamic has the power to move our world toward harmony and balance that bridges the current patriarchal and matriarchal division.

Conclusion

The US is so driven by its capitalist founding that money permeates every aspect of our society, but this does not prevent certain tropes and cultural myths from operating in contradiction to that reality. The economic relationship between an employing mother and a nanny is an almost inevitable consequence of the many pressures placed on middle-class mothers in the US. The question posed by this chapter is whether there can be more to that relationship than a transaction. I argue that viewed through the lens of RMC, there is ample opportunity to achieve mutual development and growth even while engaged in the shared labour of raising children. This argument by no means magically removes the power dynamic set up by the underlying economic context (and, in many cases, race-based oppression), but it does raise the possibility that just as we do in so many other areas of contemporary life, we might find meaning in shared mothering despite the complications of materialism and the freight of assumptions about what it means to be a mother in the modern world.

Works Cited

Apple, Rima. Perfect Motherhood: Science and Childrearing in America. Rutgers University Press, 2006.

Arendell, Terry "Conceiving and Investigating Motherhood: The Decade's Scholarship." Journal of Marriage and Family, vol. 62, no. 4, 2000, pp. 1192-1207.

Armenta, Amada. "Creating Community: Latina Nannies in a West Los Angeles Park." Qualitative Sociology, vol. 32, no. 3, 2009, pp. 279-92.

Ayaydin, Deniz Berfin. "Found a Nanny and Lived Happily Ever After: The Representations of Filipino Nannies on Human Resources Agency Websites in Turkey." Migration at Work: Aspirations, Imaginaries & Structures of Mobility, edited by Fiona-Katharina Seiger et al., Leuven University Press, 2020, pp. 171-90.

Baquedano-López, Patricia. "A Stop at the End of the Bus Line: Nannies, Children, and the Language of Care." Berkeley Collection of Working and Occasional Papers. Center for Working Families, University of California, Berkeley, 2002, accessed August 5, 2023, https://dlib.

bc.edu/islandora/object/bc-ir:100065/datastream/PDF/download/citation.pdf.

Benveniste, Daniel S. "Mother-Infant Observations: A View into the Wordless Social Instincts that Form the Foundation of Human Psychodynamics." Journal of the American Psychoanalytic Association, vol. 69, no. 1, 2021, pp. 33-50.

Bloch, Katrina, and Tiffany Taylor. "Welfare Queens and Anchor Babies: A Comparative Study of Stigmatized Mothers in the United States." Mothering in the Age of Neoliberalism, edited by Melinda Vandenbeld Giles, Demeter Press, 2014, pp. 199-210.

Búriková, Zuzana Sekeráková. "'Good Families' and the Shadows of Servitude: Au Pair Gossip and Norms of Au Pair Employment." Au Pairs' Lives in Global Context, edited by Rosie Cox, Palgrave Macmillan, 2015, pp. 36-52.

Busch, Nicky. "The Employment of Migrant Nannies in the UK: Negotiating Social Class in an Open Market for Commoditised in-Home Care." Social & Cultural Geography, vol. 14, no. 5, 2013, pp. 541-57.

Chodorow, Nancy. "The Psychodynamics of the Family." The Second Wave: A Reader in Feminist Theory, edited by Linda Nicholson, Psychology Press, 1997, pp. 181-97.

Cox, Rosie. "Competitive Mothering and Delegated Care: Class Relationships in Nanny and Au Pair Employment." Studies in the Maternal, vol. 3, no. 2, 2011, pp. 1-13.

Daines, Chantel L., et al. "Effects of Positive and Negative Childhood Experiences on Adult Family Health." BMC Public Health, vol. 21, no. 1, 2021, pp. 1-8.

Damasio, Antonio. The Feeling of What Happens: Body, Emotion, and the Making of Consciousness. Harcourt Brace, 1999.

Ehrenreich, Barbara, Arlie Russell Hochschild, and Shara Kay, editors. Global Woman: Nannies, Maids, and Sex Workers in the New Economy. Macmillan, 2003.

Epp, Amber M., and Sunaina R. Velagaleti. "Outsourcing Parenthood? How Families Manage Care Assemblages Using Paid Commercial Services." Journal of Consumer Research, vol. 41, no. 4, 2014, pp. 911-35.

Garey, Anita Ilta, et al. "Care and Kinship: An Introduction." Journal of Family Issues, vol. 23, no. 6, 2002, pp. 703-15.

Garner, Katie B. "Mirroring a Mother's Love: A Chodorowian Analysis of the Complicated Relationship Between Mothers and Nannies." Nancy Chodorow and The Reproduction of Mothering, edited by Petra Bueskens, Palgrave Macmillan, Cham, 2021, pp. 301-28.

Goleman, Dan. Emotional Intelligence: Why It Can Matter More Than IQ. Bantam, 1995.

Gopnik, Alison. The Gardener and the Carpenter. Farrar, Straus and Giroux, 2016.

Green, Christopher D. "Where Did Freud's Iceberg Metaphor of Mind Come From?" History of Psychology, vol. 22, no. 4, 2019, pp. 369-72.

Greenfield, Patricia M., et al. "What Happens When Parents and Nannies Come from Different Cultures? Comparing the Caregiving Belief Systems of Nannies and Their Employers." Journal of Applied Developmental Psychology, vol. 29, no. 4, 2008, pp. 326-36.

Hardin, Harry T., and Daniel H. Hardin. "On the Vicissitudes of Early Primary Surrogate Mothering II: Loss of the Surrogate Mother and Arrest of Mourning." Journal of the American Psychoanalytic Association, vol. 48, no. 4, 2000, pp. 1229-58.

Hays, Sharon. The Cultural Contradiction of Motherhood. Yale University Press, 1998.

Heffner, Elaine. Mothering: The Emotional Experience of Motherhood After Freud and Feminism. Doubleday Anchor, 1980.

Hondagneu-Sotelo, Pierrette, and Ernestine Avila. "The Meanings of Latina Transnational Motherhood." Gender Through the Prism of Difference, edited by Maxine Baca Zinn, Pierrette Hondagneu-Sotelo, and Michael A. Messner, Oxford University Press, 2016, p. 308.

Lyons, Gertrude. Expanding Mothering: Raising a Woman's Awareness of the Opportunities for Personal and Psychosocial Growth and Development in Mothering—A Curriculum Evaluation Study. 2017. Wright Graduate University, Ed.D. dissertation. Print.

Lyons, Gertrude. "Rewrite the Mother Code—Dr. Gertrude Lyons." Mindful Mama Mentor Hunter Clarke-Fields, 2 Nov. 2021, https://

www.mindfulmamamentor.com/blog/rewrite-the-mother-code-dr-gertrude-lyons-318/. Accessed 4 Oct. 2023.

Macdonald, Cameron Lynne. Shadow Mothers: Nannies: Au Pairs, and the Micropolitics of Mothering. University of California Press, 2011.

Martin, Lee, and Bo Shao. "Early Immersive Culture Mixing: The Key to Understanding Cognitive and Identity Differences among Multiculturals." Journal of Cross-Cultural Psychology, vol. 47, no. 10, 2016, pp. 1409-29.

O'Reilly, Andrea, editor. Twenty-first Century Motherhood: Experience, Identity, Policy, Agency. Columbia University Press, 2010.

O'Reilly, Andrea, editor. Mother Matters: Motherhood as Discourse and Practice: Essays from the Journal of the Association for Research on Mothering. Association for Research on Mothering, 2004.

Parreñas, Rhacel Salazar. "The Reproductive Labour of Migrant Workers." Global Networks, vol. 12, no. 2, 2012, pp. 269-75.

Ruddick, Sara. Maternal Thinking: Toward a Politics of Peace. Beacon Press, 1995.

Scheftel, Susan. "Why Aren't We Curious About Nannies?" The Psychoanalytic Study of the Child, vol. 66, no. 1, 2012, pp. 251-78.

Thrupkaew, Noy. "Are Au Pairs Cultural Ambassadors or Low-Wage Nannies? A Lawsuit Enters the Fray." Washington Post, 1 November 2016, https://www.washingtonpost.com/lifestyle/magazine/are-au-pairs-cultural-ambassadors-or-low-wage-nannies-a-lawsuit-enters-the-fray/2016/11/01/09e8a1ee-8f2e-11e6-9c85-ac42097b8cc0_story.html. Accessed 4 Oct. 2023.

Thurer, Shari L. The Myths of Motherhood: How Culture Reinvents the Good Mother. Penguin Books, 1994.

Walks, Michelle. "Introduction: Identifying an Anthropology of Mothering." An Anthropology of Mothering, edited by Michelle Walks and Naomi McPherson, Demeter Press, 2011, pp. 1-47.

Wright, Robert, and Judith Wright. Foundations of Lifelong Learning and Personal Transformation. Chicago: Evolating Press, 2012. Print.

Wright, Robert, and Judith Wright. Transformed! The Science of Spectacular Living. Turner, 2013.

Wright, Judith. Lecture at the Woman's Essential Experience Training, May 2016.

Wright, Judith. Living a Great Life: The Theory of Evolating. 2008. Fielding Graduate University, PhD dissertation.

Chapter 4

Murky Milks: Outsourcing Breastmilk and Maternal Failure in the Early Modern Ballad *Lamkin*

Chrissie Andrea Maroulli

Little is known about the functions of wet nursing in early modern
times but what we do know is that when a mother chose not to
breastfeed, her only option in a preformula era was to hire a lactating woman to nurse her child. Wet-nurses are generally depicted
unfavourably in early modern literature; the practice of wet-nursing was
frowned upon by respectable writers of the time, for whom ideal motherhood could only be achieved through breastfeeding their children. In
this chapter, I analyze the early modern ballad *Lamkin* (Child 93), in
which a wet-nurse participates in the murders of her lady and her
wet-nursling. The ballad demonstrates how straying from the societal
structures of the time results in tragedy. I argue that both the biological
mother and the wet-nurse are interchangeable in the demise of the family, for they both fail to fulfil their prescribed roles as defined by early
modern standards. The tale enforces the idea that outsourcing motherhood is problematic and embodies the anxieties found in the era's
writings, which divinify maternal breastfeeding.

Historically contextualizing the ballad reveals considerable anxieties
about motherhood that otherwise go unnoticed. The instrumental
presence of the corrupt nurse in the crimes and the lady's passiveness
are deliberate and monumental. *Lamkin* is not merely an entertaining

horror story of a blood-thirsty rogue with an ambivalent super objective; in fact, Lamkin is not the protagonist in the eponymous ballad. At the core of this moralizing narrative are the two women, a biological mother and a surrogate mother, both of whom fail to fulfill their prescribed roles because of each other's presence. *Lamkin*, a seemingly motiveless murder ballad, addresses the deeper issue of ideal motherhood as this was constructed and promoted by the patriarchal standards and writings of the era. In other words, the cautionary tale aims to moralize audiences by demonstrating the consequences of a nonpatriarchal model of motherhood.

Methodology

I historically contextualize the ballad *Lamkin* within early modern England by reading it comparatively with other primary sources, including diaries, sermons, and medical and midwifery manuals. I discuss the concept of ideal motherhood, the nonbreastfeeding elite, the commodification of motherhood, the disapproval of wet-nursling, and the class struggle between the upper and lower classes.

Lamkin (Child 93)

Lamkin is an early modern murder ballad of Anglo-Scottish origin from 1775. Francis James Child includes twenty-five versions in his monumental collection *The English and Scottish Popular Ballads*, all of which present the same narrative but offer substantial variations. The premise connecting the variations describes the revenge murders of a mother and her baby boy by a man named Lamkin and their wet-nurse. Lamkin is the mason who built the family's castle, but since the lord did not pay him for his services, he decides to take revenge. When the lord and servants are absent, Lamkin is allowed into the castle by the family's wet-nurse or breaks in through an unpinned window, depending on the version. Together, they plot to prick the baby that is under the nurse's care so that his screaming lures his mother downstairs into their trap. When the lady emerges to comfort the child, she is seized by Lamkin, who kills her despite her pleas. The lord returns home and discovers the gruesome crime scene. In the end, both Lamkin and the nurse receive death sentences for the crime and die by hanging, burning, or boiling.

Ballads are not esteemed for their historical accuracy. The reason we study them is that their content contributes to the reconstruction of early modern society in a unique way—as the literature of the lower classes. They give voice to the otherwise unheard, since most sources of the era represent only the elite, who were much more likely to be literate and were able to write poetry, plays, and novels as well as keep personal documents. *Lamkin* has drawn scholars' attention primarily because of the extreme violence; the images are particularly disturbing because the slain body belongs to an infant. The unsettling images include the nurse ramming bolts up the baby's nose, nipping or stabbing him in the heart several times with a silver bodkin or sharp penknife, and pricking him all over his body with a pin while blood runs from the cradle onto the floor or is collected into a basin. In one version, the mother unwittingly steps into her dead baby's blood. Scholars have been puzzled by the lack of a convincing motive for Lamkin's brutality. Being owed money is not analogous to the gruesomeness of the murders. Moreover, the captured noblewoman offers to pay Lamkin in gold to settle the debt, but he turns the proposal down, which shows that material reward is not his primary concern. Lamkin's reasons seem even more obscure in some versions because there is no background information at all; therefore, the killings appear to be entirely random. That is until one turns their attention to the two women.

An Ideal Mother

Wet-nursing was a practice early modern medical, conduct, and religious writers frowned upon and actively tried to abolish while they intensely promoted exclusive maternal breastfeeding. Based on classical, biblical, and medieval arguments, they declared that women, as the inferior sex, are naturally designed to care for the home and family and satisfy their children's stomachs and spirits. The ideal mother, they claimed, breast-feeds her children selflessly, piously, and tirelessly. As historian Marylynn Salmon writes: "A nursing mother represents selfless devotion to early modern men and women, for in feeding her child, she gave, quite literally, all of herself. Her milk was her own blood, her own life-sustaining fluid" (251-52).

The most influential prescriptive literature of the time included the conduct manuals, which provide long passages about the advantages of breastfeeding. Conduct book writers, who were primarily clergymen, firmly opposed the practice of wet-nursing. English Puritan clergyman and author William Gouge believed breastfeeding was a sacred maternal obligation that steeply increased the love between parent and child. The medical literature also celebrated mothers who breastfed their children, recognizing the burdensome nature of the task and the physical power of the female body. Women who opted not to breastfeed were harshly criticized, being called nonmothers: "In giving birth, women fulfilled only part of their duty as women ... only those women who undertook the office of breastfeeder were true mothers" (Salmon 255).

Early modern English midwife Jane Sharpe combines medical with religious advice, prompting mothers to breastfeed their children: "Every woman to Nurse her own Child, because Sarah, the wife to great a Man as Abraham was, nursed Isaac" (361). Sharpe also doubted a mother's ability to love her child if she did not nurse them: "And if the mother do not Nurse her own Child, it is a question whether she will ever love it so well as she doth that proves to Nurse it as well as Mother" (361). Such cultural norms and motherhood expectations are also articulated in ministerial representations, which frequently utilize the image of the breastfeeding mother as a symbol for divine love and weaning for spiritual loss. God and good mothering are strongly connected and appear very frequently in these texts, which evoked strong emotional responses in readers and affected them deeply.

One of the reasons mothers were encouraged to breastfeed is that it was practically free of charge; if the biological mother fed her own baby, then the family did not have to pay someone else to do so. Moreover, breastfeeding kept women at home, where patriarchy wanted them. Archbishop Tillotson firmly preached in his sermons that women should be confined in the domestic sphere feeding their babies instead of socializing or engaging in pleasurable activities: "The neglect of this duty ... is little better than the laying of a Child in the Streets" (523-24). Outsourcing breastfeeding enabled mothers to resume their social and sexual lives, empowering women but generating social anxiety.

Women writers generally agreed with the patriarchal theories promoting maternal breastfeeding but embellished them with personal experiences and anecdotes. The preachers' advice was followed by such puritan wives as Mrs. Josselin, who, according to her husband's diary, nursed all of her children for at least one year. English noblewoman and writer Elizabeth Clinton believed mothers should nurse their children because of its positive effect on their spiritual development. Lady Willoughby was also one who enjoyed breastfeeding her children. On August 3, 1637, she wrote: "I have some thoughts on weaning her, my own strength failing; but put it off day after day, it is hard to dismiss her from the food and warmth which have been hers by right so long, and break this first Bond of Companionship and Mutual Dependence" (42).

The nonbreastfeeding mother was heavily criticized for supposedly depriving her child of spiritual care and growth. Deemed ungodly and unmotherly, she was categorized as transgressive, along with shrews, wantons, and witches. In the modern sense, she was "mom shamed," much like today's nonbreastfeeding mothers who are made to feel worthless by campaigns like "breast is best." An example can be seen in the writings of early modern mother Elizabeth Clinton, who was moved to write by conscience. She was guilt ridden for not breastfeeding all of her children and advised women to breastfeed (Eales 42).

The lady in *Lamkin* departs from the description of the ideal mother; she embodies a nonmotherly figure that pays her way out. The secret to unlocking the ballad lies in this unfavourable representation of the leading lady, a victimized woman that receives great amounts of violence. As a young female murder target, she should have been archetypally depicted as innocent, virtuous, and idealized to align with the way the genre usually describes this type of character. But this particular ballad heroine is an exception to the rule.

The Nonbreastfeeding Elite

Noblewomen chose not to breastfeed for several reasons. For one, their mothers and friends discouraged it because it was unfashionable. Vanity was a huge factor: "Women said they did not nurse because they felt it would make them look old before their time, because their clothes would be soiled, and because their breasts would sag and be scarred" (Kolata 746). Richard Steele wrote in 1709: "My grandmother began a loud lecture upon the idleness of this age who for fear of their shapes, forbear suckling their own offspring" (127).

Several early modern writers wrote that husbands were to blame for their wives' attitude against breastfeeding. English writer, philosopher, and advocate of women's rights Mary Wollstonecraft wrote that noblemen often lacked caring emotions: "The man has been changed into an

artificial monster by the station in which he was born, and the conse-
quent homage that benumbed his faculties like the torpedo's touch" (19).
Because of the belief that semen corrupted breastmilk, couples had to
abstain from sex if the wife was breastfeeding. "Let the Nurse wholly
abstain from Venus, for it disturbs the Milk, draws the Bloud to the
Womb, whereby the Milk is spoiled, and the quantity of it abated,"
writes Théophile Bonet (Evans & Read). Hiring a wet-nurse preserved
their social standing in the upper-class circles, for wet-nursing was a
symbol of wealth and high rank. Therefore, some men of the higher
classes opted to hire wet-nurses despite the probreastfeeding propaganda
in the early modern writings.

Noble families also needed to produce male heirs. Many believed
lactation was a form of birth control and prevented ovulation. English
philosopher William Petty writes that prolonged breastfeeding is a
"hindrance to the speedier propagation of mankind" (194). The Duch-
ess of Devonshire wrote that her relatives were so impatient for her to
have a son that they discouraged her from nursing her daughter. These
attitudes towards breastfeeding and the frequency of wet-nursing among
the upper classes are possibly what inspired writers to write so passion-
ately about its dangers, for they wanted to make a change to the status
quo.

Noblewomen worried that breastfeeding would be harsh on their
bodies and health; this concern is understandable given the high mortality and lack of medical expertise of the era. Private collections of
medicinal recipes and published medical manuals often include thera-
pies, such as salves and poultices for breast ailments, such as cracked
nipples, plugged milk ducts, abscesses, fever, and infections. The frequency of such incidents in the literature proves they occurred regularly
and were potentially deadly before antibiotics had been invented. Women
suffered for weeks, and damage to the breast tissue and nipples could be
disfiguring and permanent. Valerie Fildes notes that breastfeeders
sometimes lost their nipples because of biting or infections. "The hesi-
tance of some mothers to breastfeed in the face of such dangers, and the
inability of others to do so despite their attempts, made those women
who did intensive nursing seem all the more nurturant, giving and
bountiful," writes Salmon (262). Under the light of breastfeeding's
lingering risks, the *Lamkin* nurse's frustration can be somewhat explained; in her eyes, the wealthy lady pays to retain her well-being,

while she is endangered to sustain another woman's child just because she was born poor.

Elite women were often unable to lactate properly, and they complained that they had no milk. "But whose breasts have this perpetual drought? Forsoothe it is like the goute, no beggars may have it, but citizens or Gentlewomen," writes Puritan writer Henry Smith (Paster 203). Smith makes a joke here, implying that noblewomen brought the lack of lactation upon themselves because of their material resources. This happened because noblewomen hired wet-nurses to nurse their babies until their own milk came in. Regretfully, this practice decreased their milk supply; there was no stimulation to help with milk production, and the baby did not learn to latch to the mother's breast. Moreover, until the middle of the eighteenth century, they believed colostrum was hurtful for the baby and the bloody discharge of the lochia corrupted the milk, so they waited a few days before putting the baby to the breast. Less privileged women had a much higher success rate in breastfeeding because they could not afford wet-nurses, so they had to put the baby to their breast much sooner.

The Commodification of Motherhood

Mothers who could not or chose not to breastfeed, despite the preachers' warnings and the circulating literature, did not have many options concerning their newborn's sustenance. Animal milk was considered unsuitable, and formula had not been developed yet. The only option was to hire a lactating woman. According to Fildes, the wet-nursing boom began around 1500, when the practice transitioned from necessity to fashion; this signalled the commodification of motherhood. Wet-nurses were hired by the upper classes not only to breastfeed but "to perform the duties of a mother to her offspring" (Davis 68).

Noble nurslings were often sent miles away to be cared for by a wet-nurse in her home in a small rural or suburban village. Babies had minimal interaction with their biological families; it was uncommon for the parents to visit frequently. By the time of their weaning and homecoming, they were around two years old, so it is reasonable to assume that their emotional connection to their biological family suffered. Jane Sharpe warns that "without doubt the child will be much alienated in his affections by sucking of strange Milk, and that may be one great cause of Childrens proving so undutiful to their Parents" (361). Sometimes, the wet-nurse moved into the family's home and cared for the baby around the clock, including the night feedings. Such is the case in *Lamkin*.

Early modern literature nurses are accused of being seductive, untrustworthy, or plotting; these traits clash with the motherly and caring nature a surrogate mother should have. A seductive nurse is unlikeable, but the epitome of nurses gone bad is the murderous wet-nurse in *Lamkin*, in whom surfaces an unparalleled oxymoron: a proxy mother hired to sustain life who takes life away. Favourable depictions of wet-nurses in contemporary literature are scarce. The reasons behind this relate to the enforcement of patriarchal motherhood, which frowns upon hiring someone to perform the duties of a mother.

Wet-Nursing Disapproved

Historically contextualizing the dynamics of the women's relationship in *Lamkin* reveals a patriarchal attempt to depict the harmfulness of breastfeeding as a financial arrangement to discourage its application by real-life people. The intense conflict between the wet-nurse and her lady is not accidental or unfortunate; it embodies the theoretical unnaturalness of wet-nursing, as this was explained in contemporary texts, such as Sharpe's midwifery manual. The moralizing pronatal/anti-wet-nurse agenda is communicated as an example for avoidance.

To understand the passionate propaganda against wet-nursing, one must keep in mind that men were gravely baffled by lactation and had severe anxieties about it. In Samuel Pepys' diary entry on March 22, 1664-65, Sir William Petty is said to have willed parts of his estate to him who "could discover truly the way of milk coming into the breasts of a woman." Needing to explain the absence of menstruation after childbirth, medical writers theorized that menstrual blood was transformed into breast milk. John Sadler writes that breastmilk was "nothing but the menstruous bloud made white in the breasts" (10), changed by nature to avoid the disturbing sight of infants being covered in blood. In 1657, French physician and surgeon Jean Riolan talked of two veins by which the breasts and womb were directly linked (a concept introduced by Leonardo Da Vinci). Since the uterus and breasts were believed to be parts of one mechanism, it was thought the humors from the uterus could affect the breast and, consequently, the quality of the milk. Therefore, the most appropriate breastmilk for a baby was thought to be the biological mother's.

Paramount issues pertaining to wet-nursing were possible neglect, abuse, or feeding issues that could remain undisclosed to the parents by the wet-nurse. Writers and balladry provided horrific anecdotes about babies dying because of "overly mercenary or bad wet-nurses who did not provide adequately for their charges" (Fissel 125). There is not enough evidence to support the idea that wet-nurses were dangerous or took advantage of their position, though. Fildes finds that the infant death rate was not notably higher among wet-nurslings.

An Ideal Wet-Nurse

Writers and physicians gave detailed instructions on wet-nurse selection, but pointed out that wet-nursing should be avoided as much as possible. Finding what writers described as a decent wet-nurse must have been quite challenging. Steele writes that his parents saw ten nurses before they chose one, who ended up being a "careless Jade eternally romping with the Footmen, and downright starved me" (127). Some of the traits Sharpe recommends include: the nurse should be between eighteen and forty; live where the air is clean (but not close to the sea); have given birth in the past two to ten months to a baby of the same sex as the employer's nursling; be well-bred and exercise (but not excessively); be a light sleeper; enjoy entertaining children; have handsome, average-sized, and well-proportioned breasts and nipples; and have such clear skin that her veins are visible. She adds: "Beware you choose not a woman that is crooked, or squint-eyed, nor with a misshapen Nose, or body, or with black ill-favoured Teeth or wit stinking breath, or with any notable depravation; for these are signs of ill manners that the child will partake by sucking" (363). Sharpe's long list of overly specific standards is nearly impossible to meet.

The stereotypical faults of a wet-nurse were alcohol consumption and sex, which were thought to corrupt her milk. Sharpe writes, "The Nurse must not company with Man so long as she gives suck to the child" (365). The nurse should be sexually abstinent. While it was somewhat tolerable for breastfeeding wives to lay with their husbands, wet-nurses were not allowed to be sexually active. The nurse should prioritize the wet-nursling, which often resulted in neglecting her own child.

English writer Alice Thornton writes that breastmilk gave her "principles of grace and religion" (2), but she also attests to the dangers of "neglects and brutishness of nurrses ... and evil milk" (4). She was convinced that her daughter Betty developed diseases and died because of the "ill milke at two nurses" (94). If the nurse were indecent or corrupt, the wet-nursling would assimilate these traits. The child was supposedly affected permanently because breastmilk was believed to have long-term effects. Wet-nurses were treated as scapegoats and blamed for any deficiencies with a child, whether that be a childhood illness or sudden death, as well as issues that arose in adulthood.

An inept wet-nurse highlights the parents' incapability to provide for their child, since guidance was available to them. A nurse of ill character only becomes an issue if someone invites her into their life. It seems, then, that partly at fault is the parent who misjudges her suitability and neglects to monitor her performance. In this respect, *Lamkin's* lady fails as a mother, for she trusts her baby's life to an inappropriate person.

A Mother's Failure

The lady in *Lamkin* fails as a mother on several levels. What immediately stands out is the repeated prompting she needs to run to her baby when he is being tortured. One should imagine how the infant must have cried, being pricked and stabbed, bleeding to death. Still, the mother does not go to him nor suspects the nurse's ill-doings; she yells from the top floor multiple times: "O still my bairn, nourice" (A), "O please my babie, nurse" (C). One expects a mother would run at the sound of her baby wailing in agony. In version F, she accuses the nurse of sleeping heavily, snoring, not doing her job:

> Oh nurse, how you sleep!
> Oh nurse, how you snore!
> And you leave my little son Johnstone
> to cry and to roar.

The wet-nurse's plan, which presumes the lady would respond, would fail if the lady does not come downstairs for Lamkin to capture her. Her failure to respond suggests she is not meeting the wet-nurse's expectations of good mothering. The nurse has to repeatedly plead with her, saying she tried suckling, entertaining, and feeding him to no effect. She begs the lady to come to rock the baby in her chair or hold him in her lap. Still, in most versions, the lady, awakened from a nap, engages in a lengthy negotiation with the nurse. She finds excuses to avoid caring for her child, claiming, for example, that it is too cold or dark to descend the stairs, all the while the baby is screaming, literally, bloody murder.

The lady also fails to protect the family from an expected intruder, even though her husband warns her of Lamkin's lurking. In most versions, "The lord said to his lady ... O beware of Balankin" (B) and instructs her to "Go bar all the windows / both outside and in" (D), and "Let the doors be all bolted / and the windows all pinned / and leave not a hole / for a mouse to creep in" (F). However, in some versions, the lady fails to secure the windows properly: "She has barred all the windows, both outside and in; But she left a window open" (D). This highlights her incapability to mother since her carelessness enables a villain to enter the home. In other versions, Lamkin is let in by the "false" wet-nurse instead. The interchangeability of the two caregivers shows how the women enabled the crime as one and the same, one failing her child and the other failing her employer.

Lastly, the lady demonstrates her maternal failure when she offers Lamkin her older daughter as a sexual prize or wife to save herself: "Oh spare me, Long Lankyn, / oh spare me one hour, / You shall have my daughter Betsy, / she is a sweet flower" (F) and "I'll g' ye my eldest daughter, Your wedded wife to be" (X). It must be kept in mind that in early modern times, virginity was highly valued and sought after by men. The maidenhead was an unsurpassed prize for its conqueror and the most glorious way to establish manhood. An invisible factor, such as the violent breaking of a hymen, furnished a man with authority to determine a woman's value and claim ownership—a vivid metaphor of patriarchal entitlement over the female body. Ballads typically present ballad heroines' virginity as treasures protected by their families. Untimely or parentally unapproved loss of virginity in balladry often results in suicide, infanticide, or murder. The lady in *Lamkin* is empowering a man by reinforcing his manhood instead of guarding her daughter's most prized possession. This is the epitome of her villainy.

Therefore, the lady, who should have been a virtuous victim, demonstrates highly unflattering character traits when contextualized historically. Her aforementioned faults contribute to the derogation of the nonbreastfeeder and, subsequently, the sanctification of the breastfeeder in perfect harmony with the corresponding socially constructed schemas. The lady has foolishly opened her home to a false wet-nurse; thus, not only did she fail in breastfeeding her own child, but she also similarly failed in properly selecting a surrogate caregiver. She also offered her older daughter's body to save herself.

The Class Struggle

In early modern times, it was a common belief that the nursling inherited the nurse's characteristics through her breastmilk; this gave rise to an inevitable class struggle. Noble wet-nurslings absorbing physiognomies from a plebeian nurse posed an alarming threat to societal balance. Elite babies being transformed into middle- or low-class folk was a serious matter for the elite. Sometimes they worried the nurse would swap her own baby with theirs, so it would live a life of riches or even inherit estates while their biological child would be raised in poverty.

Lamkin's wet-nurse's humble origin is self-evident, but the fact that she is singing, an activity considered unfitting for proper women, brings it to the forefront. Work songs were customary in the middle and lower strata, but nurses singing to babies was frowned upon by writers like Barthélemy Batt, who called these songs silly. In version Q, the ballad presents the word "sings" instead of "says." When the nurse speaks with Lamkin, she essentially sings her answers, highlighting her lowly origins. Her unladylike singing contrasts with the upper-class characteristics of her employers, such as "fine clothes" (A), "gold rings" (C), "silver mantles" (F), "bright diamonds" (O), "gold basin" (T), "red gold" (B) and "gold and silver" (U). Most importantly, the nurse sings to accompany the baby's murder: "Lamerlinkin did rock, / and the fause nurse did sing; / Ower the four-cornered cradle / the red blood did spring" (C), and "Lammikin nipped the bonie babe, / while loud fals nourice sings" (P). The acts of violence she commits while singing are unspeakable: "She rammed the silver bolt / up the baby's nose, / Till the blood it came trinkling / down the baby's fine clothes" (D). The fact that her singing is combined with the torturing of the baby showcases her ultimate failure as a surrogate mother. Instead of singing to soothe the baby, she sings as she is murdering him. Depicted as rotten to the bone, she lets Lamkin in and devises the idea of killing the baby. When Lamkin is hesitant to murder the little boy, the nurse encourages him: "'That would be a pity,' / said Lambert Linkin: / 'No pity, no pity,' / said the false nurse to him" (B). There is absolutely no hesitation or regret in her actions.

The nurse's feelings of inferiority motivate her to destroy her employers to punish them for living in abundance. Whereas the lady believes the nurse should be grateful for being employed, the nurse believes the lady owes her because she has resources. She expected to receive more than her salary: "I wanted not my meat, / I wanted not my fee, / But I wanted some bounties / That ladies can gie" (Y). Her bitterness is not entirely ungrounded, for she was endangering her health for the child of a woman who did not provide bonuses that were well within her means. The nurse also claims the lady did not treat her well. The lack of respect has intensified her feeling of subordination: "O kill her, kill her, Lamkin, / for she neer was good to me" (A).

The nurse's resentment towards her lady's status surfaces multiple times. She discourages Lamkin from collecting her lady's supposedly pure blood because: "What better is the heart's blood / o the rich than o the poor?'" (A) and suggests that they take over her employers' lives: "And ye'll be laird of the castle, / and I'll be ladie" (B). In version D, she says: "She's none of my comrades, / she's none of my kin; / Ram in the knife, Bold Rankin, / and gar the blood rin." She gleefully agrees with Lamkin when he says that the lady will not live to wear the "pearlings" her lord would bring her: "'Then she'll never wear them,' / said Lambert Linkin: / 'And that is nae pity,' / said the false nurse to him" (B). In several versions, Lamkin checks with the nurse before killing the lady, and it's with her permission that he does so in the end. The lady also views the nurse unfavourably, for she says, "My nurse is not my friend, / my nurse is my foe; / She'll hold the gold basin, / my heart's blood to flow" (T). One might wonder where the bond of sisterhood is in this equation. A woman tortures and kills another woman's baby and facilitates her own murder.

Conclusion

The two women in *Lamkin* demonstrate two different types of maternal failure: The lady fails as a mother, and the wet-nurse fails at her job as a surrogate mother. The noblewoman is enabled by the wet-nurse's presence to neglect her motherly duties, as these are prescribed by early modern standards, whereas the wet-nurse is jealous and shamed by the noblewoman; therefore, she destroys her. At the heart of this tale are the oppressive structures modelled by patriarchy that aimed at shaping ideal mothers to create their desired gender and class dynamics within society. The women's inadequacies demonstrate the prescribed mother-hood standards of the era, the disapproval of wet-nursing, and the in-evitable class conflict raised by the commodification of motherhood.

Works Cited

Archbishop Tillotson, John. *Sermons,* "Concerning the Education of Children." 1694. Unknown Publisher, 1720.

Batt Barthélemy, and William Lowth. *The Christian Mans Closet.* At the Three Cranes in the Vintree, 1581.

Bartlett, Jon, and Rika Ruebsaat. "Lamkin, 'The Terror of Countless Nurseries.'" *The Canadian Folk Music Bulletin,* vol. 36, no. 1, 2002, pp. 34-37.

"Child 93: Lamkin." *The Child Ballads: 93. Lamkin,* Internet Sacred Text Archive. sacred-texts.com/neu/eng/child/ch093.htm. Accessed 10 Oct. 2021.

Clifford, Anne. *The Diaries of Lady Anne Clifford,* edited by J. H. David and Alan Sutton, The History Press. 1992.

Davis J. H. "Child-Murder and Wet-Nursing." *BMJ,* vol. 1, no. 7, 1861, pp. 183-84.

Davies, Kathleen M. "The Sacred Condition of Equality How Original Were Puritan Doctrines of Marriage?" *Social History,* vol. 2, no. 5, 1977, pp. 563-80.

Delany, Paul. *British Autobiographies in the Seventeenth Century.* Routledge, 1969.

Eales, Jacqueline. *Women in Early Modern England: 1500-1700.* UCL Press, 1998.

Eckstorm, Fannie Hardy. "Two Maine Texts of 'Lamkin.'" *The Journal of American Folklore*, vol. 52, no. 203, 1939. p. 70.

Evans, Jennifer, and Sara Read. "'Blood Made White': The Relationship between Blood and Breastmilk in Early Modern England." *Hektoen International Journal*, vol. 12, no. 2, 2020, hekint.org/2019/11/04/blood-made-white-the-relationship-between-blood-and-breastmilk-in-early-modern-england. Accessed 13 Jan. 2022.

Fissell, Mary E. "Introduction: Women, Health, and Healing in Early Modern Europe." *Bulletin of the History of Medicine*, vol. 82, no. 1, 2008, pp. 1-17.

Josselin, Ralph. *The Diary of Ralph Josselin: 1616-1683*, edited by Alan Macfarlane, Oxford University Press for the British Academy. 1976.

Kolata, Gina. "Wet-Nursing Boom in England Explored." *Science*, vol. 235, no. 4790, 1987, pp. 745-47.

Kuznetsova, Anna, et al. "Breast Is Best? The Influence of Breast Feeding Campaigns on NICU Mothers who Exclusively Breastfeed Compared to Mothers Who Are Unable." *American Academy of Pediatrics*, vol. 164, no. 1, 2020, pp. 137-39.

Mclaren, Dorothy. "Fertility, Infant Mortality, and Breast Feeding in the Seventeenth Century." *Medical History*, vol. 22, no. 4, 1978, pp. 378-96.

Niles, John De. "Lamkin: The Motivation of Horror." *The Journal of American Folklore*, vol. 90, vol. 355, 1977, pp. 49-67.

Paster, Gail Kern. *The Body Embarrassed: Drama and the Disciplines of Shame in Early Modern England*. Cornell University Press, 1993.

Pepys, Samuel, and Richard Griffin Braybrooke. *The Diary of Samuel Pepys, from 1659 to 1669*. Frederick Warne, 1825.

Perry, Ruth. "Colonizing the Breast: Sexuality and Maternity in Eighteenth-Century England." *Journal of the History of Sexuality*, vol. 2, no. 2, 1991, pp. 204-34.

Pollock, Linda A. "Childbearing and Female Bonding in Early Modern England." *Social History*, vol. 22, no. 3, 1997, pp. 286-306.

Renwick, Roger deV. "The Servant Problem in Child Ballads." *The Flowering Thorn: International Ballad Studies*, edited by Thomas McKean, University Press Colorado, 2003, pp. 91-100.

Renwick, Roger deV. and Sigrid Rieuwerte, editors. *Ballad Mediations: Folksongs Recovered, Represented, and Reimagined. Ballads and Songs.* Wissenschaftlicher Verlag Trier, 2006.

Salmon, Marylynn. "The Cultural Significance of Breastfeeding and Infant Care in Early Modern England and America." *Journal of Social History*, vol. 28, no. 2, 1994, pp. 247-69.

Schucking, L. Levin. *The Puritan Family.* Routledge, 1969.

Sharp, Jane. *The Midwives Book.* 1671. Garland Publishing. 1985.

Skuse, A. "Wombs, Worms and Wolves: Constructing Cancer in Early Modern England." *Social History of Medicine*, vol. 27, no. 4, 2014, pp. 632-48.

Steele, Richard. *The Tatler: No. 1.* 1709. Oxford Scholarly Editions Online,2014. oxfordscholarlyeditions.com/display/10.1093/actrade/ 9780198124849.book.1/actrade-9780198124849-div1-15. Accessed 7 Aug. 2020.

Thornton, Alice. *The Autobiography of Mrs. Alice Thornton*, edited by Charles Jackson, Andrews and Co, 1875.

Wollstonecraft, Mary. *A Vindication of the Rights of Men.* Prometheus Books, 1996.

Chapter 5

(Care)Give and (Care)Take: Boundaries, Difference, and Choice in Dramas about Undocumented Care

Lynn Deboeck

The outsourcing of care in the United States (US) is a vestige of slavery and indentured servitude. It has been recreated today with an emphasis on exploitative practices that target immigrant populations. This chapter investigates the interaction between undocumented careworkers and their employers in stories told through two plays: *Living Out* by Lisa Loomer and *One House Over* by Catherine Trieschmann. Dramatic literature—and by extension live, performed theatre—has power, despite our heavily virtualized media landscape because the audience cannot pause, stop, or fast-forward the proceedings. Spectators must face societal commentary that often hits close to home and then walk away, forever changed by the experience. The plays analyzed here, while not as directly activist in nature, offer narratives about our current care labour market and display some of the complex burdens placed on undocumented care-workers, which audiences are expected to witness.[1] The harsh and sometimes life-or-death realities of undocumented care-workers are often obscured in real life due to the pseudo-feminist moves to allow for women to be upwardly mobile by outsourcing care (Rottenberg). This phenomenon not only inculpates our own participation in institutions that produce these realities but also highlights which lives hold value in our society. Using philosopher Judith Butler's concept of "a grievable life," I examine the themes of exploitation presented in these plays through an intersectional feminist lens—looking at how multiple facets of a person's identity intersect to create their lived reality. Butler's theory particularly targets how society values life (or does not), and this chapter investigates how that valuing interacts with the experiences of undocumented care workers in the US. I argue that it is precisely because we do not value the lives of women care workers as lives that our care system has resulted in the repetitive cycles of abuse. I demonstrate how the narratives reflect reality by highlighting their cyclical script: Through establishing boundaries, weaponizing difference, and limiting choice, these damaging cycles are maintained.

Method and Analysis: Butler's "Grievable Life" and Ngozi Adichie's "Single Story"

Through a close reading of the two plays addressed in this chapter, I apply feminist author Chimamanda Ngozi Adichie's warning not to reduce people to a "single story" while also using Butler's notion of the "grievable life" as a lens through which to understand these stories of caregivers and care receivers. While Butler presents her theory in connection with how wars initiated by the US have created distinctions around who is allowed to live or die, it is applicable here because the exploitation of undocumented care workers is a different type of war—a battle fought out in the shadows, leaving damaged lives in its wake. Butler also does not limit her theory to actual lives lost but extends it to include how hardship, labour, and strife of "less grievable lives" go unseen. The foundation of her claim is that the level of precarity for each human life is what grants beings' lives legitimacy, but it is those with less precarity who are able to lay claim to such legitimacy. The move to correct this, according to Butler, is to form allyships that will reveal truth (as these plays do) and enable those who fly under the radar to be apprehended as real, true, and valuable lives. I demonstrate that these plays, while depicting the too-often unequal relationship between undocumented labour and wealthy American citizens, offer opportunities to apprehend and recognize the lives behind the labour in the playwrights' handling of boundary, difference, and choice—three facets of how Butler asserts life is apprehended. More specifically, the playwrights show how their employer characters establish boundaries that restrict employees' ability to function, how the differences between employer and undocumented worker are painfully felt by the employee while celebrated or ignored by the employer, and how the employers retain the full power of choice in most situations.

Butler theorizes that one cannot grieve a life that one does not view *as* a life and that there are levels of "apprehending" a life. She explains that there are frames and norms that create the boundaries for apprehending and acknowledging a person who is granted rights and protections. If recognition of life does not happen, these rights and protections can be withheld. In addition, while all life is precarious, the differences in precariousness change how certain lives are seen, recognized, and valued.[2] For example, Butler asserts that one area where this happens is "the politics of immigration, according to which certain lives are perceived as lives while others, though apparently living, fail to assume perceptual form as such" (24). I focus on a type of outsourced labour, typically done by undocumented female immigrants, which is at once the most precious commodity, in that it involves the care of what matters most to us—our children, our elderly, our homes—and at the same time is dispensable. These "'disposable nannies' who may be dumped once babies become older or newer immigrants can be found who are willing to work for even lower wages" are not perceived as lives (Chang 58). This disposability reveals a significant lack of choice as workers and as people. Compounding this problem is the way they are perceived. As Ngozi Adichie reminds us, there is danger to the single story. We as a nation have established a single story about these undocumented immigrants who work in American households. More recently this story has included, as the plays in this study do, a peek into the danger, precariousness, and tragedy of these people's lives. But while this might grant US citizens what we see as a right to pity them, it does not allow for true, legitimate acknowledgement of their lives. Ngozi Adichie offers a personal account of how the single story limited her own view of Mexicans when she first visited Mexico because of the immigration crisis going on at the time (8:27-9:20). This blinded her to their humanity. The plays examined here complicate the single story we have established in the US about undocumented women caregivers. They also offer places from which to break the cycle and recognize lives in dire need of equitable treatment and protection. Giving stage time to stories that contain complexity and challenge the single story can be juxtaposed with normative narratives and create spaces where privilege is forced to see itself.

Lisa Loomer's *Living Out*

Late in Lisa Loomer's play, a character states, "Everyone's working and paying someone else to take care of their child—it's insane!" (62). The "insanity" of a mother paying another woman to care for her child is a large part of the social landscape of class and racial hierarchies in the US.[3] This current reality has roots in the nation's history of indentured servitude and slavery. The practice of outsourcing childcare in the US to private nannies is still primarily undertaken today by white parents, and caregivers continue to be mostly underpaid women of colour (who are often immigrants as well) and must neglect their own families to secure employment.

Living Out, a play published in 2003, is about Ana, an undocumented Salvadoran woman living in the US who takes a job as a nanny for Nancy, a white woman who is returning to her job as a lawyer after having a baby three months earlier. After repeatedly asking Ana to perform work beyond her job description, Ana is once again made to work late despite having plans to see her son Santi play a soccer game. She receives a panicked call from her husband that Santi had an asthma attack, and he tells her to rush to the hospital. Sadly, because of the distance between their neighbourhood and the nearest hospital, Santi dies before he is able to get medical attention. Although this heartbreaking story underscores inequity and realities society would prefer not to see, it is the very visibleness of documentation (and the legitimation it grants) that Loomer masterfully uses to shine a light on the exploitation of undocumented labour. The ability to access medical care, or indeed to even be available to care for your own children (or have them cared for), is an issue of equity in the US for marginalized communities, particularly undocumented persons. What makes it worse is that, per Butler's theory, when access and care are denied to such extremes, the news of it often goes unreported, further erasing the lives of people who live in the US but are seldom granted full acknowledgment, socially or legally, as human beings.

In the opening scene of *Living Out*, Ana endures three brief interviews for nanny positions—the first with Wallace, the second with Linda, and the third with Nancy. It takes Loomer only eleven lines to reveal a common micro-aggression; Wallace, a wealthy white mother looking for a caregiver for her children, asks where Ana is from. Ana responds: "Do you know Huntington Park?" but Wallace pushes, saying, "No, I meant, where are you—[Gestures] from?" (8). After learning Ana is from El Salvador originally, Wallace continues the interview with much more thinly veiled commentary on her assumption that Ana is not really qualified to be a nanny, despite having years of experience on her resume and having two sons of her own. The following interview with another white mom, Linda, depicts a person tone deaf to her own racism: "We've had a couple of nannies from El Salvador, they were wonderful, such hard workers..." (10). This type of compliment, backhanded as it may be, is an example of how Butler describes tolerance. Predicated on the necessity of differentiating oneself from another group, tolerance has the appearance of acknowledging a life, but behind the façade is the diminishment of an entire population to a stereotype (a single story) that only serves the individual's need (Butler 140). In other words, Butler's theory posits that acknowledging differences must happen in order to acknowledge a life (since all are defined against an "other"). But it is not merely difference that must be recognized. If another person or group is understood as only different, they become invisible in the system. The dominant in society can then dismiss what is different from them. The interconnectedness that similarity provides allows those on the margins, like Ana, to access the same privileges as those with social and economic power.

Boundaries—Who Is Allowed to Have Flexibility?

An example of privilege is the ability to create the boundaries one wants. Flexibility is a term used in *Living Out*, and it is wielded as a weapon by the privileged white women doing the hiring to create the boundaries they wish their employees to exist within. As Ana continues her first interview with Wallace, she politely asks whether she could keep regular hours (such as 8:00 a.m. to 5:00 p.m.) but is met with "No. I need someone who's flexible" (9). When Ana explains that she needs to pick up her son, Wallace becomes furious, indicating that she told the agency not to send any nannies who had young children themselves. Further underscoring Wallace's entitled behaviour is the fact that she does not work outside the home but wishes to have a nanny to watch her children during the day so she can have the flexibility to do what she wants with her time.

During Ana's second interview with Linda, Ana is expected to be flexible once again. After the interview, which both women scheduled into their days, Linda presses Ana to stay significantly longer. Linda wants Ana to meet her twin sons so she can see if they get along, but once again, Ana's own child makes her ability to get a job caring for others' children more difficult:

LINDA. Could you stick around for an hour or so? They're back from the doctor at noon.

ANA. They sick?

LINDA. [*Defensive.*] No, no, they're fine! [*Ana hesitates.*]

ANA. Maybe I could come back tomorrow? I said I would be someplace at twelve.

LINDA. Can't you make a call?

ANA. I'm sorry [*Beat; just admits it.*] I have to pick up my son from soccer.

LINDA. Oh. You have children?

ANA. Just one in this country. My other son is in El Salvador.

LINDA. [*Dying to make this work.*] Well, can't your husband pick up your child?

ANA. He's working.

LINDA. You don't have a—a mother or something?

ANA. She's in San Francisco.

LINDA. [*Still trying.*] How old is your child?

ANA. Six—

LINDA. Ouch. You know what, Ana? [*Distraught.*] We had a nanny with a young child—she got sick all the time... I just can't put myself through... I'm sorry, Ana. I need someone who can make my kids a priority. (11)

Beautifully illustrating the double standard and assumptions applied to marginalized communities, Loomer offers a microcosm of massive injustices that are rooted in class (and race) hierarchies. Linda feels entitled to demand unrealistic flexibility from Ana even while she does not offer flexibility in return. At Ana's third interview with Nancy, Ana lies and says both of her sons live in El Salvador, thus giving the appearance of flexibility in hopes of securing the position.

Difference—Difficult to See for the Privileged

Loomer displays scenes of both Ana's and Nancy's home life, which grants the audience a clearer understanding of both the similarities and differences that produce the conditions to apprehend their lives as separate, distinct, yet equally worthy. Their differences pointedly show how feminism and privilege play overt roles in the choices one makes. While Ana needs to work to get a green card and bring her eldest son from another country, Nancy needs to work to pay for a new mortgage and a good preschool. A dilemma lies in the fact that both situations can only be acknowledged together from the less-privileged position because privilege can blind people from seeing the disadvantage of others. In other words, Nancy's privilege, or what María Lugones would term her "world" and lack of "world travelling," shapes her understanding in such a way as to hinder her from realizing the disparities between Ana's and her own life challenges. As Butler contends, the problem of "how best to arrange political life so that recognition and representation can take place" is one constructed "through norms that produce the idea of the human who is worthy of recognition and representation at all" (138). In this situation, the norms that Nancy participates in do not produce Ana as a complete person—one who has important things she is working towards—but Ana's norms produce a reality where Nancy is already assumed to be complete. For example, Ana, by virtue of being an employee working in Nancy's home, cannot escape knowing Nancy's experience because she is immersed in it every day, and Nancy intentionally relates her reality to Ana on a regular basis. Nancy, in contrast, knows little of Ana's real, lived experience, except for the labour she executes while there in her home. To Nancy, Ana becomes "the labour" while Ana sees both herself and Nancy (and Nancy sees herself) as the person who lives, works, hires, pays, and mothers.

Several scenes in *Living Out* juxtapose groups, emphasizing difference on a community level as well. The groups are comprised of three white mothers who have hired nannies (Nancy, Wallace, and Linda) and the three Latina women who care for their kids (Ana, Zoila, and Sandra). In both groupings, the community instructs their new members. Nancy's new friends educate her on how to spy on her nanny to make sure she does not lie or steal. And Ana's comrades laugh at their employers largely because they do not agree with them about how to raise children.

Society's need for outsourced labour is underscored humorously in a conversation between the nannies:

> ANA. One day we should all stay home!
> SANDRA. Everybody! The waiters, the parking peoples, the cleaners—
> ZOILA. Los Americanos be driving around in their dirty clothes —starving. Can't go to a restaurant—there's nobody to wash the plate! You get home, the house is a mess—
> ANA. The plants is all dead—
> SANDRA. Nobody to deliver you pizza—
> ZOILA. And then you got to take care of your own kids! [*They all laugh.*] (Loomer 30)

Sadly, it is the humour that both reveals and grants distance from the reality of what we value. It may be true that middle- and upper-middle class US families depend on the services of the underpaid and exploited, but it is treated as a joke because the presumed audience cannot imagine it not always being true. The exchange above reveals differences in experience that are not often dwelt on given the dependence in the US on certain types of undervalued labour. And in the end, the nannies in the play do not stay home because they do not have the choice to do so.

Choice—Largely One Sided

The summary of *Living Out* from Dramatists Play Service asks, "How do we make someone 'the other?' What is the cost of doing so?" (Loomer, back cover). Stories like the ones in the play offer windows to view how the "other" who gives care is both different and the same as the one who receives care. Although the upper-middle-class white women in the play (in particular Wallace) are sometimes caricatures of white privilege, Nancy and Linda also show real concern for their nannies, and Loomer highlights that, at times, social forces out of the employers' control work to sustain power differentials. Still, the fact that one side of the employer-employee dyad has significantly more conventional agency is a disparity that often leads to exploitation. The lack of quality childcare is a crisis in the US. Often childcare is addressed at the private individual level (e.g., community based rather than government mandated), and unpalatable hiring practices can run rampant.[4] Caregivers like Ana are expected to sacrifice the scant resources and security they have in a home they cannot claim as their own in order to support and serve those who are ignorant and indifferent to problems outside their sphere of privilege. One way we make people into "others" is by not realizing—whether intentionally or not—that we all deserve care and choice. Butler's "grieveable life" theory proposes that it is in the interactions between marginalized people and people who have been systemically "othered" that reveals the value placed on certain lives over others. To give care and to take it means that care is a commodity—one that inherently should hold no bias but is unequally distributed. The labourers who carry most of this burden frequently have (by deliberate acts made by the employers or by circumstances outside their control) little choice.

One of scenes in *Living Out* has the three white mothers meeting in a park, discussing Nancy's job. Neither Wallace nor Linda work outside the home, and the scene offers a poignant look at the privileged expectation of choice. Loomer offers lines like, "Well, if you have to work, that must be an interesting job," and "Well. Guess I just have my hands full just being a mom." The women commiserate on how difficult it is to juggle everything (e.g., making Thanksgiving decorations, getting their roots done, doing yoga), but they also fervently state that they "just couldn't imagine not being there the first time one of [their kids] crawled, or walked, or said their first word" because "why else have kids?" (34). Couched in the white feminist language of women's "progressive" choice, Loomer depicts the lack of perspective some privileged people have. That a nanny could just walk away from her job does not register with the white employers, which reveals how they see (or rather, do not see) their hired nannies. Not expending the effort to understand lives outside their own, they assume that the women they hire *choose* for themselves, giving the white women free reign to exploit their workers. Another way to understand this is that these women employers are using a white feminist tactic that erases racial and class differences to create a level playing field, as though everyone is operating with the same level of choice and privilege. In the best light, and on only one level, the white women portrayed here are choosing to interpret their employees' actions through the lens of their own experience—as many people do. However, in other moments—for example, when talking together about how their nannies "are"—these three white women only see them as different from themselves, with the implication that the nannies are inherently worse. Loomer depicts these white women as only seeing difference when it puts them in the best light ("I pay my nanny top dollar.") or to paint their careworkers in the worst way ("They all steal.").

Disregarding (or just not seeing) the struggles Ana faces, Nancy seeks care and reassurance for herself as well as for her child, as depicted below.

> NANCY. But tell me the truth—because I'd quit in a minute—in a second if I thought...I mean, I'm her mother, I can fuck her up for life! [*Ana thinks. She decides, for a variety of reasons, but mostly for the sake of her own children...*]
> ANA. You're a good mother, Nancy. And Jenna is fine.
> NANCY. [*Utterly vulnerable.*] You think?
> ANA. I think Jenna is... a very lucky child. And—you *like* to work—
> NANCY. I *do* like to work! I like to work—*and* I love my child! Is that so horrible of me?
> ANA. You know what? I like to work too! [*Laughs.*] Ay, don't tell that to my husband. Because, in my country, all the women is supposed to love to stay home. I get depressed if I stay home all the time!
> NANCY. I know, I know!
> ANA. I tell you a secret, I want to go back to school—[*Quickly adds.*] When Jenna is older—
> NANCY. You should! You're a smart woman. (*Puts an arm around her.*) You should go to school and get a real job! (54)

Nancy's lack of awareness is humorous. She both requires unequivocal allegiance from Ana in what she esteems as the most important job—the care of her baby—while simultaneously acknowledging that the labour is not considered valuable by society.

In the second-to-last scene, after Ana rushes off to the hospital (with Jenna in tow because she could not reach Nancy, who had forgot her cell at home), the audience learns what happened via gossip from the other white mothers. Wallace is aghast that Ana would dare take Nancy's baby out of the house without permission, but Linda points out that they still do not even know the fate of Ana's son, who they refer to as "the child" (61). By referring to Santi as "the child," Loomer does rhetorically what the white characters do throughout the script, which is to diminish Santi to an abstract nonpresence one can view with little direct emotional attachment—a nonlife belonging to no one. Perceiving Ana as "the other" frees themselves from any guilt while Ana blames herself for her son's death: "If I'd picked him up.... If I'd been there. Like a mother. Like any mother" (64). The choices Ana made, which led to the travesty, show how constrained her choices are, and Loomer highlights that Nancy has had a hand in establishing artificially rigid boundaries in order to in-crease her own flexibility. When Nancy calls, not realizing that Santi died, and asks if he is better, Ana lies and says yes. It is the path of least resistance for her immediate life (with the little choice she is allotted), but it also tragically starts the cycle yet again. Despite their implicit roles in what led to Ana's distress, Nancy and her husband Richard free themselves from blame and console themselves that their child is okay. Nancy again exercises her increased agency by choosing to quit her job, deciding to stay at home with her baby (63). The story this play offers is a reflection of real, lived experience of marginalized communities whose losses and struggles are not felt or shared by the more privileged—either due to indifference or the boundaries set in place that distance them from their employees' hardships. In this way, we see Butler's concept of the grievable life as one that is typically usurped by the more privileged in the situation.

Catherine Trieschmann's *One House Over*

One House Over is a play about Joanne, a woman in her fifties, who hires a home healthcare person named Camila to care for her elderly father. Playwright Catherine Trieschmann notes in the casting list at the be-ginning of the script the generation of each character. Milos and Camila are first-generation immigrants (from the Czech Republic and Mexico, respectively), whereas Milos's daughter Joanne is second generation, and the neighbour, Patty, is third generation. These denotations, com-bined with the setting of an American suburban backyard, underscore the title's commentary that even though we may live only one house over, the length of time one has resided in the US is a part of what creates the "us versus them" dichotomy that informs how we draw boundaries that grant some lives legitimacy and erase others almost entirely.

Boundaries—Only Employer's Boundaries Matter

The play opens with Joanne showing Camila the house and yard since Camila will be living in Joanne's basement while employed. Joanne takes pains to establish a boundary of who belongs in this American home and who is the guest. She demarcates where Camila is allowed to be and how she wants things to work. She also states several times that she wants Camila to feel at home and to "make herself at home," although her necessary employer boundary-setting would seem to counter this. As the play is set in 2010, the political climate is of particular import. Joanne mentions President Obama frequently and claims "it's a good time to be from Chicago" (6). Throughout the play, she repeatedly tries to paint a picture of America as on the right, progressive path, distinctly different from how it used to be. This by itself erects boundaries, as Joanne determines the frame with which to view other people. In the frame she creates for herself, everyone is equal because she helped to elect a Black president, and her democratic efforts are cast as being for the good of all. This tactic effectively erases all experience outside her own by employing "rose-coloured glasses," which permit her to see only what she chooses. Joanne is similarly choosing what not see as well, which is the reality of many others, including her employee. Trieschmann counters this by putting a heavy focus on Camila's and her husband Rafa's experiences with being undocumented and the limited options they legally have to exercise their agency. After her own boundary making, Joanne is surprised when Camila has some boundaries of her own:

> CAMILA. I like to be clear about my job before I start.
> JOANNE. Have I not been clear? You'll take care of Daddy from ten to—
> CAMILA. I mean, other duties. I'll clean up after myself, but I'm a home healthcare provider not a maid.
> JOANNE. Understood. I would never take advantage. (8-9)

Later, we find this promise does not hold as Camila becomes more important to Milos, Joanne becomes jealous, and then starts making demands of Camila that are not a part of her job description.

Another instance of Joanne's imposition of boundaries happens one day when she asks Camila to put her shirt on while sunbathing because her yellow bikini top is distracting her thirteen-year-old violin student. This directly contradicts Joanne's frequent declarations about how things are to be shared ("I want us *both* to be comfortable" [7], and "this is *our* yard" [26]). Yet she interrupts Camila and Rafa kissing in the backyard, causing Camila to say—in a brilliant microcosm of the undocumented immigrant's constant paranoia (Miziara "Immigrants Suffer")—"I feel like someone is always watching us here. It's hard to get comfortable" (27). Indeed, the reality of being deported is all too real for Camila.[5] The audience learns that Camila's father was pulled over a few years before without a driver's license and subsequently deported. This stokes Camila's own fear of being deported and underscores how deportation is felt by different characters.

Difference = Diversity = Always Positive

Mirroring Ana's life in *Living Out*, Camila cares for another person's family member, while her own family member, in this case her father in Mexico who is diabetic, requires help. He needs money for insulin, and like Ana, Camila sends what money she can to her country of origin. Meanwhile, Milos tries to undermine Camila's position in the early days of her job by stressing that she is a different kind of immigrant:

> JOANNE. Daddy, you have no proof that Camilla is here illegally, and even if she is, who cares? It's not like I'm running for office any time soon.
> MILOS. They could arrest us for harboring criminals.
> JOANNE. It doesn't work that way.
> MILOS. How do you know?
> JOANNE. Because I read the paper? Because we live in a progressive state. Because President Obama supports amnesty. Trust me, it doesn't matter. And frankly, it's none of our business. (29-30)

Although the sentiment "it's none of our business" seems respectful of others' privacy, this is one of many examples of Joanne's privilege granting her the choice not to care because of the difference in privilege between herself and her employee. This same privilege creates blind spots for Joanne by blocking out other elements of difference between her and Camila or Rafa, such as the threat-level of being pulled over without a driver's license or official ID and the ability to maintain close proximity to loved ones in order to provide care for them.

Interestingly, by juxtaposing Joanne's father Milos—an immigrant who escaped the Nazis when he was nineteen—against contemporary Mexican immigrants like Camila and Rafa, Trieschmann shows how people use injustices and hardships they have experienced to erase those of people more marginalized than themselves. All that results from this exercise is, as Butler asserts, the lack of apprehending different lives by claiming the difference is not there or does not matter. As Milos claims, "white, black, brown, who cares? What matters is if a man has money in his pocket" (74). Yet he can only say (and believe) this because he is white and has money.

One night, Camila finds Milos drinking gin in the backyard. He will not listen to her pleas for him to come inside, so she finally gives up and joins him. The two exchange stories with Milos describing his escape from Czechoslovakia before Hitler came. Through this anecdote, he tries to show how it was worse for him than for Camila, claiming all she had to do was "wade across the Rio Grande" (86). Camila responds with her own harrowing story of crossing the river at night, being sexually molested, and having to travel for hours in a crowded frozen food truck: "Crossing was the easy part. I still don't have a golden ticket. I'm stuck. Always scared of making a mistake, or they'll deport me, or Rafa, or somebody else I love" (87). Milos, much like Joanne, disregards stories that are not his own. Since he has experienced emigrating, he feels he owns the entire experience of immigration. He excuses the fact that he was one of the very lucky refugees who actually were admitted into the US. (Most who wanted to emigrate were not permitted to enter due to the restrictive immigration laws at the time, although there were more generous policies for countries with predominantly white citizens who wished to bring in white or white-passing people ["Immigration"].) Milos ultimately claims the right to both the success of "making it" and the trauma of hardship faced in order to do so.

Another example of disregarding difference is when Joanne suggests to Rafa, after he expresses a wish to go to Italy, that he just save up and go. In response, he says he "lost his passport," by which he means he does not, and cannot, have one (39). She is embarrassed at her assumption, which is rooted in the privilege afforded her by her citizenship, and tries to apologize, leading to a revelation of how differently they are viewed politically:

RAFAEL. It's okay. I'm used to gringos stepping in it.

JOANNE. For the record, I think we should be offering paths to citizenship, work visas, driver's licenses. It's ridiculous. On behalf of my country, I apologize.

RAFAEL. Hey, at least you guys elected Obama this time round. That's an improvement.

JOANNE. Right? It's like America has finally turned a corner, thank God. The one good thing I can say about George W. Bush is that he killed off the old white Republican party for good. They're going to have to appeal to Hispanic voters if they ever want the Presidency again. Who knows, in another four years, both parties could be running on platforms of amnesty.

RAFAEL. It's the one political advantage brown people have over white. We make more babies (Trieschmann 40).

Racial difference creates the space for humour, but it also shows that regardless of how liberal minded Joanne claims to be, she still sees Hispanic voters—and by extension Camila and Rafa—as "others."

Joanne ends up hiring Rafa, who has lost his restaurant job, to be her own in-home healthcare support person when she is diagnosed with breast cancer. This causes strife between him and Camila because he feels freer to take risks, despite his status, such as driving Joanne's car alone without a license. Camila tries to reason with him about the fact that he and Joanne are not on the same level, saying, "You think because you've lived here most of your life, you're safe. *Pero es una ilusión*. It doesn't matter if you've gone to public school and paid taxes. They can take you away just like that" (69). Not only does this exchange highlight difference, but it shows that despite performing all the same actions, sameness is not accessible for some.

"Everyone Has Choice": A Progressive Assumption

In addition to the assumption Joanne holds that the decision to drive a car or not is a personal choice that is the same for everyone, she also seems blind to the lack of choice her employees have regarding bringing up their compensation. Later in the play, and after waiting several weeks, Camila reminds Joanne that she never paid her for twelve hours of overtime she worked after Joanne's mastectomy. Joanne says she forgot—which is entirely understandable, given her medical issues—but fails to acknowledge how her privilege permits this forgetfulness while

Camila's precarious position restricts her ability to demand prompt payment. After establishing the boundaries of the employer-employee relationship, Joanne breaks the rules of payment, further emphasizing that the rules were meant for Camila and Rafa, not her. More of the same rule breaking is seen as Rafa and Joanne start becoming close, and Camila tells him that he needs to respect boundaries. However, since Joanne is the one who sets the boundaries, Camila starts having less and less agency to change the situation. Eventually, Joanne makes sexual advances toward Rafa (though Rafa rebuffs her), which Camila secretly sees but is powerless to do anything about because she runs the risk of losing her job, her home, and her husband if she confronts either of them. While both she and Rafa are undocumented, they cling to each other for support and empathize with one another more easily via their shared experience and insight. Camila feels she cannot lose him, or she loses this support—essentially her only unconditional support network. But she also needs her job, which provides income, a place to live, and the ability to send money home to care for her own father, who is ill. Still at the mercy of Joanne remembering to pay her, Camila is left with no choice but to wait and hope.

A few days after these payment issues, Patty, the next-door neighbour, comes with a letter from the homeowner's association warning Joanne that she is not allowed to rent out her basement. She speaks to Camila, who is scared Patty is going to call the police. Patty responds: "The police have nothing to do with it, I promise. The letter is just a warning. That's all. Joanne will either turn in an application or not. Probably not. Then she'll be fined. That's all. That's the very worst that can happen. There's nothing to be upset about" (101). But of course, it is not the worst that can happen to Camila. Patty fails to acknowledge the precarity of Camila's life as a life, and Camila is given no assurances that she will be able to remain living in the home she has established.

The penultimate scene of the play takes place during Milos's ninetieth birthday party. After disparaging Joanne's birthday gift and relishing the one Camila gives him, Milos stirs up more trouble by telling Camila that he loves her like a daughter. Joanne orders Camila to pick up the wrapping paper on the ground, but Milos says he wants her to take him to the bathroom, which further aggravates Joanne:

JOANNE. Is it too much to ask the people I pay to pick up the trash? Or water the plants or help me put a simple tablecloth on the table? Is that really so terrible a thing to ask?

CAMILA. You don't pay me to pick up the trash. You pay me to take care of Milos.

JOANNE. That's right, to take care of him. Not to play house. I don't pay you to be his daughter. He is not your fucking father! He's MINE. (128)

Joanne sees Camila's affront of "playing house" with her father as an insult, believing Camila is doing it on purpose (i.e., choosing to overstep). But Camila can only ever "play" at living in an American home, since she can be uprooted at any point. A fight ensues, cake is thrown, and a hose is sprayed. In the struggle, Milos steps in between the two women and is accidentally knocked down by Rafa. Seeing Milos lying motionless on the ground, Joanne screams at them to call 911, but Camila and Rafa run away instead, "out of the yard, out of the neighbourhood, as far as [they] can go" (131).

Much like Nancy calling to check on Ana after the tragedy had happened, there is the inevitable white guilt. In Joanne's case, she realizes in the final scene that she was cruel to Camila, but it is too late. Patty suggests apologizing because "most fences can be mended," but there is a problem with their premise—they are using their own metrics to decide what they need to apologize for, and they do not know the whole story because they have never been invested in knowing about the lives in that story (134). Without acknowledging and understanding this difference, one cannot fully apprehend another's life. And it is this lack of understanding that blocks how much "mending" can happen. Patty suggests that an apology itself would be enough. Yet Camila and Rafa cannot live off of an apology, nor would one protect them from US Immigration and Customs Enforcement.

Conclusion

Butler addresses the adaptability of art to move through and mediate contexts with regard to war (9). As an artform, theatre continually exists within and produces new contexts with each performance. These two plays "brea[k] from itself" to form new ways of understanding the stories and people within them. It is precisely because, as Butler writes, "the frame that seeks to contain, convey, and determine what is seen (and sometimes, for a stretch, succeeds in doing precisely that) depends upon the conditions of reproducibility"—that plays wield such power (10). Often going unseen, the plight of immigrants (particularly women) who are trafficked or forced to work under terrible circumstances is reality for many. For some, their passports and visas are taken by their employers, essentially holding them hostage. For others, their pay is so little that there is no way they can escape. The representations of undocumented working domestics in these plays offer a glimpse of the everyday precarity of lives that continue to be invisible to those whose lives are less precarious.

While *Living Out* and *One House Over* provide only two examples of how power, agency, and subjectivity play out in the world of undocumented care labour, they highlight and validate a problem with how the US navigates labour use and misuse. Systemic issues, such as lack of universal healthcare, contribute to the position that so many are placed in and hinder people in their quest for autonomy. There is little choice when it comes to finding dependable and quality childcare or eldercare in this country. Yet there is even less choice for those in the system who are made dependent upon employers who can act without oversight. Since our social structure does not consistently acknowledge (in our cultural practice or legal system) the "them" from other countries to be legitimate lives, a cycle of exploitation (even sometimes unintentional) is sustained. US citizens, finding themselves in need of care service, hire undocumented workers because that is what is available. With no regulation around this process, the employers themselves establish the boundaries that will grant them the best service rendered but often limit the autonomy and agency of their employees in the process. In the best case, the differences between undocumented labourers and citizens are celebrated (although this limits the ability to understand marginalized life by restricting the lens to the privileged person's experience as the baseline). In the worst case, the difference is criminalized. What results is that the employer's choice to employ creates imposed rules for the most vulnerable in the situation, with no choice on their part but to follow them or risk losing job, home, family, or life. The relationships between mothers or family members and the caregivers they hire are fraught with these concerns, and part of the deeper problem is that the oppression is largely invisible. Telling stories through dramatic literature, such as the two pieces covered in this chapter, is a part of the work to make undocumented lives visible and reveal their value, which was there all along.

Endnotes

1. Other, more activist theatrical endeavours include groups, such as the East Side Arts Alliance, which produces Guerilla Theatre, a program that espouses resourcefulness in confronting injustice with performing arts. As Eden Silva Jequinto, the program creator, describes, this approach is "about having people—a person—who's willing to speak up and tell their story and challenge the oppressive systems we live in" (Eastside 1:25-1:32). In more recent years, this program has pushed for legislative protections for undocumented, immigrant, women careworkers in California.

2. A recent example of this was the disappearance of the Titan sub, for which hundreds of thousands of dollars were spent searching for it. The sub had, in fact, imploded, and the five people aboard were killed. This event is in contrast with the more than 300 Pakistani nationals whose lives were lost at sea when their overcrowded boat sank; however, the story received far less media attention.

3. In her investigation into the lives of immigrant women working as domestics, Grace Chang finds that "two-career, middle-class families employing so-called illegal immigrants to do child care and domestic work is so common that employment agencies routinely recommend undocumented immigrants to their clients" (55). By making the practice routine, agencies are complicit in the cycle of abuse felt by immigrant women and women of colour who are hired for carework.

4. One example of this that has been used as a model is the Association for Legalized Domestics that was organized in El Paso, Texas, in 1953 and characterized as "housewives calling for a program to facilitate hiring Mexican women to work for them as maids" (Chang 107). This eventually led to the Federal Commission on Immigration Reform creating the "Nanny Visa," or nonimmigrant, temporary worker visas, for labour sectors where the US was experiencing a shortage of workers. Unfortunately, much like those working with temporary agricultural worker visas, the caregiving industry has continued to exploit undocumented labourers with unsavoury expectations and practices.

5. The consequences of the border-control-enforcement post-9/11 were "seen in the number of work raids, criminal prosecution of immigrants and their families through new anti-immigration legislation at the state level, vilification of undocumented immigrants in the popular media, and an increase in hate crimes committed against Latinos" (Toro-Morn 39).

Works Cited

Alberto, Lourdes. "Nations, Nationalisms, and Indígenas: The 'Indian' in the Chicano Revolutionary Imaginary," *Critical Ethnic Studies*, vol. 2, no. 1, 2016, pp. 107-27.

Armenta, Amada. "Creating Community: Latina Nannies in a West Los Angeles Park," *Qualitative Sociology*, vol. 32, 2009, pp. 279-92.

Butler, Judith. *Frames of War: When is Life Grievable?* Verso Books, 2009.

Chang, Grace. *Disposable Domestics: Immigrant Women Workers in the Global Economy.* South End Press, 2000.

Eastside Arts Alliance. "Guerilla Theatre Documentary" *YouTube*. 24 Feb. 2013, https://www.youtube.com/watch?v=q56Ftqem_e8&t=93s Accessed 23 Oct.

Gonzales, Roberto, et al. "No Place to Belong: Contextualizing Concepts of Mental Health Among Undocumented Immigrant Youth in the United States," *American Behavioural Scientist*, vol. 57, no. 8, 2013, pp. 1174-99.

Loomer, Lisa. *Living Out.* Dramatists Play Service, 2003.

Miziara, Pedro Gabriel. "Immigrants Suffer Higher Rates of Psychosis—Here's How to Start Helping Them." *The Conversation*, 21 Apr. 2017, https://theconversation.com/immigrants-suffer-higher-rates-of-psychosis-heres-how-to-start-helping-them-73552 Accessed 27 Aug. 2023.

Ngozi Adichie, Chimamanda. "The Danger of a Single Story" *YouTube: TED Talks Channel*, 7 Oct. 2009, https://www.youtube.com/watch?v=D9Ihs241zeg Accessed 4 Aug. 2022.

Rottenberg, Catherine. *The Care Manifesto: The Politics of Interdependence.* Verso, 2020.

Toro-Morn, Maura. "Elvira Arellano and the Struggles of Low-Wage

Undocumented Latina Immigrant Women," *Immigrant Women Workers in the Neoliberal Age*, edited by Nilda Flores-González, et al., University of Illinois Press, 2013, pp. 38-55.

Trieschmann, Catherine. *One House Over.* Catherine Trieschmann, 2018.

Valentín-Cortés, Mislael, et al. "Application of the Minority Stress Theory: Understanding the Mental Health of Undocumented Latinx Immigrants." *Community Psychology*, vol. 66, no. 3-4, 2020, pp. 325 -36.

"Immigration to the United States 1933-41." *Holocaust Encyclopedia.* United States Holocaust Memorial Museum (USHMM), https:// encyclopedia.ushmm.org/content/en/article/immigration-to-the -united-states-1933-41 Accessed 23 Oct. 2023.

Section II

Contemporary Representations of Nannies in Literature and Film

Chapter 6

Mrs. Banks and Mary Poppins: Tensions of the Maternal Nanny

Jane Griffith

The 2013 film *Saving Mr. Banks* (Hancock) professes to depict the "true story" of Disney and PL Travers, the author of the *Mary Poppins* books. The film, starring Tom Hanks and Emma Thompson, features Travers wholly resistant to her literary nanny being Disneyfied on the grounds that animation, music, and dancing animals would destroy the Mary Poppins of Travers's books.

Travers's fears were not unfounded: Disney's 1964 film *Mary Poppins* (R. Stevenson) departs wildly from Travers's textual creations. Although Travers wrote eight books featuring the character Mary Poppins, Disney based the 1964 film on the first two of Travers's series: *Mary Poppins* (1934) and *Mary Poppins Comes Back* (1935). Disney sticks to the spirit of these texts in that Mary Poppins descends upon the Banks household with her terse speech, unsentimental ways, and journeys to magical worlds that invert order, never disclosing how or why.[1]

The Travers texts and the Disney film are also similar in that all main characters are white. As Makeda Silvera, Cameron Lynne Macdonald, and Rosie Cox argue in different contexts, race must be considered in analyzing female domestic work, both historically and today. All main characters in the text and film are white, and race factors into understandings of the texts of Mary Poppins. Both the books and the film have racist scenes. In the film, Mr. Banks praises colonialism—a railroad through Africa, tea plantations, dams on the Nile—and laments the falling of empire (Szumsky 102). The film features anti-Black scenes and language (Pollack-Pelzner). The books, too, feature anti-Indigenous and anti-Black language and a particularly racist chapter in the first text that Travers ended up revising twice: her chapter "Bad Tuesday" in *Mary Poppins* features a magical compass that takes the children around the world. In the 1967 revision, the people from the around the world whom Mary and the children meet have the racist depictions of dialect edited out; in the 1981 revision, the people are replaced by racist caricatures in the form of animals (Nel 69; 88-89).

Disney made many changes, as any adaptation requires: Travers's five children become two; the 1930s change to the Edwardian period; and Travers's episodic narrative transforms into a feature-length plot. And the nuance and complexity of Travers's Mary Poppins—her androgyny; her brashness and yet deep love for her charges; her communion with nature; her Gurdjieffian mysticism—become flattened, resulting in what education scholar Giorgia Grilli remarks as a "drain-[ing]" of Mary Poppins's "very essence" (xix).

Despite these major changes, what remains constant is a hostility between Mary Poppins and her employer, Mrs. Banks. Such hostility in literary and filmic depictions of nanny-mother relationships is common, often rooted in the blurring of class boundaries. As Katie B. Garner also notes, "the dependence and affection mother-employers experience *may* be a place of possibility, a tension that could de-center some of the established arguments regarding how power is allocated and used" (326) while still acknowledging the inherent power dynamics of the relationship. Nanny figures have traditionally been scrutinized for their liminality: As a mother figure but also a paid employee, nannies "challenge the customary hierarchy structuring the service relationship," effecting a "material link with a member of the household that [threatens] to confound distinctions of class and kinship" (O'Toole 329). Permitting such an intimate, bodily connection between a working-class nanny figure and an upper-class, non-biological child is riddled with concern because of the liminal space the nanny figure occupies. As literary scholar Anne McClintock writes, the nanny figure is at once "the repudiated, working class other" and, simultaneously, someone who performs maternal tasks (84–85). Others have labelled the nanny as both "family and not-family" (McLeer 84), as "half-parent, half-servant" (Gathorne-Hardy 77), and as "a threshold figure: existing between 'within the family' and 'outside the family'" (Gallop 146). In these understandings, the tension between employee and employer arises due to the threat to the role of the mother and the muddying of otherwise clear separations between family and outsider.

Psychoanalyst Susan Scheftel speculates on another understanding of this tension: "The nanny may function as a kind of personified embodiment of the darker side of the parent/child dyad, a concrete representation of the inevitable and often-unconscious ambivalence and conflict that children can and necessarily will produce in their primary caregivers" (255). For Scheftel, "the mother can displace or project hatred of the child onto a nanny whose role and position she can then devalue. Any nanny can become a target for the mother's feelings of hostility toward her child" (260). For Scheftel, the nanny receives the rage of the mother because the mother knows it is unacceptable to direct it at her own children.

Texts have always had ways of ensuring the nanny figure did not cross over the line of mother. At one extreme, the trope of the wicked or violent nanny (found in *The Turn of the Screw* as well as the film *The Hand That Rocks the Cradle*) warns against the contaminating threat of the lower-class nanny, who may too closely, and at times parasitically, mirror the role of the biological mother. In comedies such as *Mrs. Doubtfire, Mr. Nanny,* and *Daddy Day Care,* mothers are punished for working yet the films' homophobia and transphobia ensure the children's mothers will not be replaced. Although they feature incompetent parents and sincere relationships between nanny and child, texts such as *The Nanny Diaries* and *Uptown Girls* highlight the nanny's motivation of money, the ultimate power of the parent to hire and fire, and therefore the impermanence of the nanny in the children's lives.

In this paper, I argue that the Mary Poppins of Travers's texts crosses this line more than typical texts featuring a nanny, exhibiting a nanny far more maternal than is usually found. This maternality is, I argue, what underscores the particular hostility between nanny and mother. With the Disney adaptation, Mary Poppins's blurring of these lines is lessened, her maternality elided. The hostility between Mary Poppins and Mrs. Banks thus morphs into a relationship threatened not by the mothering role of the nanny but by the first-wave feminist agenda the film attempts to foreclose.

Mary Poppins and Maternality on the Page

Both of Travers's books *Mary Poppins* and *Mary Poppins Comes Back* display the at best uneasy and at worst hostile relationship between Mrs. Banks and Mary Poppins. The reader learns most clearly of Mrs. Banks's private thoughts towards her employee after Mary Poppins states that she "can manage anything" (212), igniting a reaction from Mrs. Banks of jealousy:

> "I sometimes wish [Poppins] wasn't [a treasure]!" Mrs. Banks remarked to her great-grandmother's portrait as she dusted the Drawing-room. "She makes me feel small and silly ... And I'm not! ... I'm a very important person and the Mother of five children. She [Mary Poppins] forgets that!" (P.L. Travers, *Mary Poppins Comes Back* 212)

Mrs. Banks reveals feelings of insignificance and displacement by Mary Poppins's adeptness at caring for her children. This scene is internalized, with the reader only learning of Mrs. Banks's thoughts through the omniscient narrator. Mrs. Banks shares them not with Mary Poppins, whom the remarks are about, but with a portrait of Mrs. Banks's great-grandmother, who of course cannot answer. Perhaps Mrs. Banks thinks her great-grandmother may understand these feelings if she, too, had had a nanny.

In another scene, Mrs. Banks is attacked by Mr. Banks and receives no support from Mary Poppins, who witnesses his onslaught. In a particularly cruel encounter, Mrs. Banks is forced to apologize for giving birth, which Mr. Banks describes as "very awkward indeed" (*Comes Back* 128). Mr. Banks does not accept his wife's apology: "You're not sorry, not a bit. In fact, you're very pleased and conceited. And there's no reason to be. It's a very small one" (128). This statement alone is symptomatic of the threat of maternal power. Before he leaves, Mr. Banks calls Mrs. Banks "a very stupid woman" (129). Instead of finding female solidarity with Mary Poppins, who understands something of the toil of childrearing save for literal birth, Mrs. Banks belittles Mary Poppins in a show of lateral violence. In this scene, class supersedes female solidarity. Mary Poppins is definitively not on Mrs. Banks's side when it comes to Mr. Banks's verbal abuse.

In these and other more mundane scenes, Mrs. Banks and Mary

Poppins have a fraught relationship. The narrator seldom reveals Mary Poppins's attitude towards Mrs. Banks, resulting in an impression of Mrs. Banks as the victim. Why, when Mrs. Banks holds the power (albeit constrained by the power of Mr. Banks) to fire Mary Poppins? When Mary Poppins's livelihood and identity as a nanny is contingent upon her employment in the Banks's household? When many other tales and real-life stories reveal the victimization instead of the nanny and not the employer?

I argue that in Travers's books, in which the maternality of Mary Poppins is repeatedly revealed, Mrs. Banks is threatened. Mary Poppins's maternality comes in part from a physical intimacy with her charges. Poppins undresses the children, "[tweaking] the bed-clothes from Jane's shoulders" (*Comes Back* 62). She also begins "to undress [the children]" (*Poppins* 12), and they notice that "buttons and hooks had needed all sorts of coaxing from Katie Nanna" (12), their previous nanny, but with Poppins, the children's clothes "[fly] apart almost at a look" (12). In Travers's books, everyone sleeps together in the nursery, with only "the sound of five people breathing very quietly" (*Comes Back* 27). Throughout the night, Jane and Michael "[creep] closer to [Poppins] and [lean] up against her sides" (*Poppins* 47). With Mrs. Banks or the previous nanny, Katie Nanna, we see no such scenes of intimacy.

The maternality of Mary Poppins in Travers's books is further evidenced by her relationship to milk. Milk circulates symbolically in the maternal nanny relation in the form of care. Mary Poppins is portrayed as a nanny in both film and text, not a wetnurse. There are many differences between Mary Poppins and a wetnurse: most notably, Travers never offers a scene in which Mary Poppins is feeding the Banks children milk from her breast or chest. As well, historical wetnursing scholarship indicates that wetnurses almost always had babies of their own, and readers receive no indication that Mary Poppins has or had her own children

Despite these differences, the reader encounters scenes in the books involving Mary Poppins and milk. Mary Poppins feeds Jane and Michael magical medicine that changes flavour according to who drinks it. When Mary Poppins administers the medicine to the babies, John and Barbara, the "substance in the spoon this time [is] milk," prompting John to "[lap] at it eagerly," and Barbara to "[gurgle] and [lick] the spoon twice" (*Mary Poppins* 12). Poppins also gives warm milk to Michael, though not a baby, when he is scared (99). As he drinks, Poppins waits "beside him ... without saying a word, watching the milk slowly disappear" (99). Michael attempts to prolong the milk-feeding session, "tasting every drop several times with his tongue, making it last as long as possible so that Mary Poppins should stay beside him" (99). Perhaps because of this experience, Michael concludes that the neighbourhood fishmonger's melancholy must be the effect of having a mother who "fed him entirely on bread and water when he was a baby" (112). When the children visit the zoo at night, and humans are locked up while animals patrol the grounds, Mary Poppins and the children throw "bottles of milk ... to the babies, who [make] soft little grabs with their hands and [clutch] them greedily" (158). Throughout, both texts highlight milk's importance, and Mary Poppins is the one administering it.

In terms of Travers's Mary Poppins and her relationship to milk, wetnurses were typically perceived as a threat, particularly regarding the potential for contagion (Sherwood; Thorley; Rhodes) and for interfering with the bond between mother and child (Baumgartel et al.). Virginia Thorley also notes "the jealousy some mothers felt towards a wet-nurse who was able to do what they could not do, or were deterred from doing, for their babies" (312). For Wolf, "mothers felt simultaneously superior to and jealous of the wet nurses who suckled their babies" (Wolf 102). Rather than surrogate mothers or family members, wetnurses were strictly viewed as employees (Thorley 316).

This intimacy extends beyond the walls of the nursery. In Travers's texts, Mary Poppins introduces the Banks children to mythological scenes of alignment, companionship, and union with cosmic entities and animals. Jane and Michael follow Mary Poppins to the zoo at night, where they witness an inversion: humans have been locked in cages, and the animals are free to join hands in a chain around Poppins (*Poppins* 166). Predator and prey classifications are not only nullified but also reversed, as "the small are free from the great and the great protect the small" (168). The Hamadryad snake, a ringleader of the inversion, preaches that "we are all made of the same stuff ... the same substance composes us ... we are all one" (170). This uncanny aspect of the maternal hooks into Freud's theory, as interpreted by Jessica Benjamin, that "the ego's earliest, primordial feelings are of oneness with the world— 'the oceanic feeling'—like that of the infant at the breast who does not yet distinguish the world from itself" (Benjamin 129). Mary Poppins is a reminder of the promiscuity of love that is not devoted to a single mother. Endowed with mystical powers, she threatens to embody the fantasy of the omnipotent mother all too literally. And, as Travers's texts display, Mary Poppins encountering mystical experiences of oneness with the cosmos, her maternality evokes the possibility of an alternative, occult grounding of religion and culture in primal relations with the mother, not with the father.[2]

Mary Poppins also invokes the mythological maternal world when she and the children meet Maia, part of the Pleiades star cluster and sister to Electra, Merope, Taygete, Alcyone, and Celaeno (*Poppins* 180-83). When Mary Poppins gives Maia a present, Maia kisses Mary Poppins and "a long look [passes] between" (187) them. Mary Poppins's feelings for Maia, and Maia's immersion in the world of sisters, evokes a mysticism that celebrates the maternal world. A similar scene occurs in Travers's second Poppins book. Jane and Michael visit a circus comprised of the constellations and Greek mythological figures (183-88). Poppins concludes the evening by dancing with the sun, who, "with great ceremony, carefully, lightly, swiftly" kisses Mary Poppins (204). In these scenes, Mary Poppins's identification with the maternal world underscores her maternal relationship with the Banks children—a relationship not visible in the texts between the children and their mother.

Travers further highlights Mary Poppins's maternality in relation to her female charge, Jane. Travers's texts endow Mary Poppins with the ability to "reproduce mothering" (Chodorow), meaning Mary Poppins in the books teaches Jane how to one day be a mother herself. Jane "[rushes] to cover the Twins with their perambulator rug" when she discovers they are cold (*Poppins* 87). When Poppins abruptly departs at the end of *Mary Poppins*, Jane tucks "[Michael] in just as Mary Poppins used to do" (202). Jane fantasizes about being a bird who has "just laid seven lovely white eggs and [is] sitting with [her] wings over them, brooding" (*Comes Back* 62). She later paints "a picture of herself, quite alone, brooding over her eggs" (71). She pleads to Mary Poppins that she would love to assist her (87), and Poppins allows Jane eventually to "help [her] push the pram" (169). Most notably, Jane is asked in the absence of her own mother to take over Poppins's roles when she departs: "'Jane! Take care of Michael and the Twins!' said Mary Poppins. And she lifted Jane's hand and put it gently on the handle of the perambulator" (*Comes Back* 286). Poppins's placement of Jane's hand symbolically passes the maternal torch even though Mrs. Banks is alive and seemingly able to reassume her role as mother in the home. Such maternal operations could not have been taught to Jane by her mother because Mrs. Banks never completes them; it is Mary Poppins, instead, who carries out the maternal tasks Jane mimics.

Not only does Travers's texts associate Mary Poppins with the maternal, but additionally other characters recognize Mary Poppins as maternal. *Mary Poppins Comes Back*, for instance, further displays the maternal nanny with the arrival of the Banks's new baby, Annabel. The baby recounts to the Starling the story of her vaginal birth. Annabel states she comes from "the Dark where all things have their beginnings" (133). The baby began with sleep and a dream, which proceeds when she "awoke and came swiftly," feeling "warm wings" around her as she "passed the beasts of the jungle and came through the dark, deep waters" in the "long journey" of her birth (134). The Starling states that "every silly human" (135) forgets the story of his or her birth but not Mary Poppins. According to the Starling, Mary Poppins is "Different, she's the Oddity, she's the Misfit" (135) because she is the only human not to forget the story of her birth—another instance of the maternal world to which Mary Poppins is privy. Besides the Starling, other characters recognize Mary Poppins as maternal. As she takes the children on a tour around the world, they meet a Hyacinth Macaw who broods over his wife's eggs (*Mary Poppins* 89). He asks Poppins to "take a turn" because he needs to sleep. The macaw's logic in asking her is that "if [Poppins] can look after all those creatures," implying the Banks children, she "can keep two small eggs warm" (90). Being a mother and a nanny figure are viewed as interchangeable to the macaw.

Travers's version of Mary Poppins, though maternal, has a brash side. She frequently punishes and scolds the children and is by all accounts acerbic in many places to various characters, including the children. While Mary Poppins's brashness and more punitive qualities in the texts may appear as the opposite of maternal, psychoanalysts such as D.W. Winnicott remind us that such qualities of aggression and even hatred towards children in fact run central to maternality, albeit outside of popular depictions. The reader does not view Mrs. Banks treating her children harshly in the Travers texts the way Mary Poppins does, but the reader seldom views Mrs. Banks with her children. Mary Poppins's terseness, while seemingly undercutting claims that she is maternal, in fact reveals an even greater show of her maternality especially when compared with Mrs. Banks.

In addition to Mary Poppins, Travers's texts display another maternal nanny figure: Mrs. Corry. This additional nanny figure featured by Travers works at a gingerbread shop with her daughters Fannie and Annie. Mrs. Corry literalizes the primary function of a wetnurse: She feeds the Banks babies part of her body. Mrs. Corry, hearing John and Barbara cry, breaks "off two of her fingers and [gives] one each to John and Barbara" (*Poppins* 118). Like breast milk, which replenishes itself, "in the space left by the broken-off fingers two new ones grew at once." Mrs. Corry explains that her fingers are "only Barley-Sugar," a substance that new mothers are instructed to eat while breastfeeding. Mrs. Corry's fingers are "splendid for the digestion," and Mary Poppins agrees that anything Mrs. Corry gives the babies "could only do them good."

Mrs. Corry also expresses qualities of a maternal nanny figure in that she can soothe John and Barbara. As soon as Mrs. Corry hears the babies crying, she runs "to the perambulator and [rocks] it gently, crooking her thin, twisted, old fingers" until the babies are pacified (117). The text makes clear, though, that Mrs. Corry is not a mother figure—she requires payment for services rendered. After talking to the Banks children, Mrs. Corry states, "Here am I running on and on and you not being served" (119). She entertains the Banks children and serves everyone gingerbread but reminds Mary Poppins that she is "not *giving* [the gingerbread] away," as she "must be paid" (121). In this scene, Mrs. Corry performs maternal functions but is still an employee.

Mrs. Corry also exhibits the characteristics of a nanny because she places the needs of her charges ahead of her own children's. Although Mrs. Corry has two daughters, she ignores their concerns when Mary Poppins and the children enter her shop. Mrs. Corry disregards her own daughters in favour of Jane, Michael, John, and Barbara—children she is being paid to feed. Mrs. Corry is kind to the Banks children but regards "her gigantic daughters furiously" and talks to them in a "fierce, terrifying voice" (*Poppins* 119). She shrieks at them, calling her daughter Annie a "cowardly custard ... cry-baby" while emitting a "harsh cackle of laughter" (120). With the same breath, Mrs. Corry cheerily addresses Jane and Michael, and she "[smiles] and [beckons] so sweetly to Jane and Michael that they [are] ashamed of having been frightened by [Mrs. Corry] and [feel] that she must be very nice after all" (121). Mrs. Corry, like Mrs. Banks, is a mother who is portrayed negatively throughout the Travers texts. Mrs. Corry is only portrayed as kind when operating in a nannylike role with the Banks children, but as a mother, similar to Mrs. Banks, the reader is left to understand her in a negative light. Travers's texts do not portray mothers positively, leaving this light for nanny figures such as Mary Poppins and Mrs. Corry.

In the 1964 Disney film version of Travers's texts, the relationship between Mrs. Banks and Mary Poppins is also strained, although more in a vein of indifference. In the film *Mary Poppins*, Mrs. Banks—seldom sharing the screen with Mary Poppins—is a much maligned, parody of a suffragette. Although Poppins does not outwardly condemn Mrs. Banks's involvement with the suffragettes, "her silence on the matter does not suggest feminist solidarity" (Cuomo 215). Her brand of first-wave feminism is treated as one of the problems with the Banks household, which Mary Poppins ultimately helps to remedy, culminating in the concluding scene when Mrs. Banks's suffragette ribbon is taken off from her dress and instead used to buoy a kite for the children. As historian Ana Stevenson notes, the film *Mary Poppins* "reproduces both pro-suffrage rhetoric and the misogynist humor of anti-suffrage films and postcards" (70), ultimately arguing that despite the inclusion of Mrs. Banks as a suffragette, the film parodies feminism through Mrs. Banks. As novelist Makeda Silvera writes in *Silenced* on racialized domestic workers in Canada, "the lived relations between the woman-as-mistress and the woman-as servant are complex and rarely mentioned even in contemporary writings on women and work" because such work "remains private, invisible, exempt from the feminist principle 'the personal is political'" (107). The film does not depict Mrs. Banks lending any support to Mary Poppins, even though the first wave of feminism and the suffragettes supported working women—which would include a female domestic worker such as Mary Poppins.

As philosopher Chris J. Cuomo states, the character of Mary Poppins in the 1964 film version is "not a bit maternal" (212)—a notable shift in emphasis from the figure of Travers's texts. We do not see Mary Poppins in the film giving milk to anyone, nor does she embrace the children or dress them as the Travers's texts depict. The philosophical leanings found in the literary texts are also edited out, presumably so Disney could avoid offering Gurdjieffian mysticism to Christian audiences. The 1964 film has overt Christian messages: Mary Poppins in the film has been read as a Christ figure (Reddick) as well as a Mother of Jesus figure (Rocchio). Such readings of Christianity would be challenging to argue in terms of Travers's books. With this omission in the film of Travers's focus on Greek mythology also went the maternal elements of *Mary Poppins* and *Mary Poppins Comes Back,* such as the evocation of a pre-Oedipal dependency on the mother.

Curiously, the 1964 film alludes to Mrs. Corry, the other nanny figure depicted in Travers's texts, twice but only in passing: at the beginning of the film, she is among the patrons of Bert's street performance. She is kind and silent, as her two tall and slim daughters stand supportively behind her. In another scene, Mary Poppins quietly tells herself that she must pick up some gingerbread from Mrs. Corry. Although the Disney film oddly still chose to include Mrs. Corry, her role is limited to asides rather than the centrality of her maternal qualities in the textual character.

The 1964 film contains the blurring of lines by editing out the maternality of Mary Poppins found in Travers's texts and also portraying Mary Poppins as the beautiful Julie Andrews. Travers's Mary Poppins is portrayed as "unfeminine." When Michael first spots Mary Poppins descending from the sky, he exclaims, "There he is!" (*Poppins* 5). Jane corrects him, explaining that the figure is "not Daddy" (5). Poppins is described as being "like a wooden Dutch doll" (6) with "large feet and hands, and small, rather peering blue eyes" (6). Her "nose [is] turned upwards like the nose of a Dutch doll" (*Comes Back* 16). A bird admits that Poppins is "not [special] in the matter of looks." Indeed, one of the bird's "own day-old chicks is handsomer than Mary P. ever was" (*Poppins* 138). Mrs. Brill, the family's cook, states that Poppins is "plain ... nothing much to look at" (*Poppins* 200). As McClintock insists, the "figure of the nurse in late Victorian culture is ... frequently invested with 'masculine' attributes and powers" (95), where working class women like the nanny are coded as "unsexed, manly, coarse, and rude" (95). Mary Poppins can be maternal and ugly, or non-maternal and beautiful: a beautiful and maternal Mary Poppins is too close to a mother's role. Disney's audience can thus distinguish between the mother and the nanny figure.

Travers's Mary Poppins (as well as Mrs. Corry) serves as a nanny intimately connected to her charges. Despite these lines, Travers's Mary Poppins feeds milk (and in the case of Mrs. Corry, her body) to children;

she undresses the children, undresses herself, and sleeps with the children; she recalls Freud's oceanic feeling in her oneness with the cosmos; she reproduces motherhood in her female charge, and she threatens the mother's role. Disney's *Mary Poppins* retains the figure of the nanny. However, her maternality is at the same time ousted when it gets too close, as is the case in the adaptation of Travers's works. At the conclusion of the film, the Banks family skips down the street holding hands and singing; Poppins watches them out of a window, and her talking umbrella comments that the Banks children think more of Mr. Banks than Poppins. She retorts that this is "as it should be"—Mrs. Banks does not factor in. Travers's two texts, in contrast, conclude with Mary Poppins abruptly leaving while the children panic, and Mrs. Banks erupts in anger over the departure.

Conclusion

PL Travers, itself one pseudonym of many she used, refused to identify herself as the creator of Mary Poppins. She mysteriously claimed that she "discovered" (Cott 195) or "came across" (196) the character, who "sort of appeared to" (207) Travers. Travers would characterize herself as "a mere intermediary, someone whom Mary Poppins brushed past, and who had the good luck and sense to catch the impression and put it down" (Demers 70). However, in a 1988 *Parabola* article entitled "The Interviewer," an eighty-eight-year-old Travers offered a very different history: Travers explains that she created the Poppins character to calm her younger siblings as their mother attempted to kill herself in a nearby pond (*What the Bee Knows* 204). Travers responds by snuggling with her siblings "on the hearth rug, the warm downy quilt around [them] like a bird's wing shielding a hatch of nestlings" (205). She proceeds to tell them a story featuring a proto-Mary Poppins. Travers's admission that Mary Poppins was in fact a surrogate mother helps in thinking about her texts and their layered maternal nanny figure.

Endnotes

1. The first three Mary Poppins texts feature the same pattern: arrival, multiple chapters of carnivalesque adventure, and abrupt departure; the fourth and fifth volumes depart from this pattern (Didicher 141).

2. Travers's interest in mythology and mysticism is demonstrated much more in her subsequent Mary Poppins's texts. After *Poppins* and *Comes Back* were written, Travers studied with AE, Gurdjieff, and a Zen roshi (Cott 203), encouraging her interest in mysticism and philosophy. *Saving Mr. Banks* subtly alludes to Travers's leanings with a Gurdjieff text on her desk in one scene.

Acknowledgement

Thanks to Sheila Rabillard, Janelle Jenstad, Lisa Farley, and all the families I used to nanny for.

Works Cited

Baumgartel, Kelley L., et al. "From Royal Wet Nurses to Facebook: The Evolution of Breastmilk Sharing." *Breastfeeding Review: Professional Publication of the Nursing Mothers' Association of Australia*, vol. 24, no. 3, Nov. 2016, pp. 25-32.

Benjamin, Jessica. "The Omnipotent Mother: A Psychoanalytic Study of Fantasy and Reality." *Representations of Motherhood*, edited by Donna Bassin et al., Yale Univ. Press, 1994, pp. 129-46.

Chodorow, Nancy. *The Reproduction of Mothering: Psychoanalysis and the Sociology of Gender.* University of California Press, 1999.

Cott, Jonathan. *Pipers at the Gates of Dawn: The Wisdom of Children's Literature.* University of Minnesota Press, 2020.

Cox, Rosie. *The Servant Problem: Domestic Employment in a Global Economy.* Palgrave, 2006.

Cuomo, Chris. "Spinsters in Sensible Shoes." *From Mouse to Mermaid: The Politics of Film, Gender, and Culture*, edited by Elizabeth Bell et al., Indiana University Press, 1995, pp. 212-23.

Demers, Patricia. *P.L. Travers.* Twayne, 1991.

Didicher, Nicole E. "The Children in the Story: Metafiction in Mary Poppins in the Park." *Children's Literature in Education*, vol. 28, no. 3, 1997, pp. 137-49.

Gallop, Jane. *Feminism and Psychoanalysis: The Daughter's Seduction.* Macmillan, 1982.

Garner, Katie B. "Mirroring a Mother's Love: A Chodorowian Analysis of the Complicated Relationship Between Mothers and Nannies." *Nancy Chodorow and The Reproduction of Mothering: Forty Years On*, edited by Petra Bueskens, 2021, pp. 301-28.

Gathorne-Hardy, Jonathan. *The Rise and Fall of the British Nanny*. Faber, 2014. *Open WorldCat*, http://www.myilibrary.com?id=780990.

Grilli, Giorgia. *Myth, Symbol, and Meaning in Mary Poppins: The Governess as Provocateur*. Translated by Jennifer Varney, Routledge, 2007.

Hancock, John Lee. *Saving Mr. Banks*. 2013.

Macdonald, Cameron Lynne. *Shadow Mothers: Nannies, Au Pairs, and the Micropolitics of Mothering*. University of California Press, 2011.

McClintock, Anne. *Imperial Leather: Race, Gender, and Sexuality in the Colonial Contest*. 1995.

McLeer, Anne. "Practical Perfection? The Nanny Negotiates Gender, Class, and Family Contradictions in 1960s Popular Culture." *National Women's Studies Association Journal*, vol. 14, no. 2, 2002, pp. 80-101.

Nel, Philip. *Was the Cat in the Hat Black? The Hidden Racism of Children's Literature, and the Need for Diverse Books*. 2019. *Open WorldCat*, https://www.vlebooks.com/vleweb/product/openreader?id=none&isbn=9780190635084. Accessed 2 Oct. 2023.

O'Toole, Tess. "The Servant's Body: The Victorian Wetnurse and George Moore's Esther Waters." *Women's Studies*, vol. 25, 1996, pp. 329-49.

Pollack-Pelzner, Daniel. "'Mary Poppins,' and a Nanny's Shameful Flirting with Blackface." *New York Times*, 28 Jan. 2019, https://www.nytimes.com/2019/01/28/movies/mary-poppins-returns-blackface.html. Accessed 2 Oct. 2023.

Reddick, Niles. "Feeding the Birds: Divine Intervention by Mary Poppins, a Female Christ Figure." *Journal of Popular Film and Television*, vol. 43, no. 3, July 2015, pp. 148-56, https://doi.org/10.1080/01956051.2015.1043233.

Rhodes, Marissa C. "Domestic Vulnerabilities: Reading Families and Bodies into Eighteenth-Century Anglo-Atlantic Wet Nurse Advertisements." *Journal of Family History*, vol. 40, no. 1, Jan. 2015, pp. 39-63, https://doi.org/10.1177/0363199014562551.

Rocchio, Vincent F. "*Mary Poppins* and the Dialogic Imagination of Christianity." *Culture and Religion*, vol. 11, no. 2, June 2010, pp. 109-

26, https://doi.org/10.1080/14755611003776301.

Scheftel, Susan. "Why Aren't We Curious About Nannies?" *The Psychoanalytic Study of the Child*, Yale University Press, 2012, pp. 251-78.

Sherwood, Joan. *Infection of the Innocents: Wet Nurses, Infants, and Syphilis in France, 1780-1900*. McGill-Queen's University Press, 2014.

Silvera, Makeda. *Silenced: Talks with Working Class West Indian Women about Their Lives and Struggles as Domestic Workers in Canada*. Williams-Wallace, 1986.

Stevenson, Ana. "Cast Off the Shackles of Yesterday." *Camera Obscura: Feminism, Culture, and Media Studies*, vol. 33, no. 2, 2018, pp. 69-103, https://doi.org/10.1215/02705346-6923118.

Stevenson, Robert. *Mary Poppins*. Buena Vista, 1964.

Szumsky, Brian E. "'All That Is Solid Melts into the Air': The Winds of Change and Other Analogues of Colonialism in Disney's Mary Poppins." *The Lion and the Unicorn*, vol. 24, 2000, pp. 97-109.

Thorley, Virginia. "A Mother, yet Not 'Mother': The Occupation of Wet-Nursing." *Journal of Family Studies*, vol. 21, no. 3, Sept. 2015, pp. 305–23. https://doi.org/10.1080/13229400.2015.1108993.

Travers, P. L. *Mary Poppins*. Harcourt, 1997.

Thorley, Virginia. *Mary Poppins Comes Back*. Harcourt, 1997.

Thorley, Virginia. *What the Bee Knows*. Aquarian, 1989.

Winnicott, D. W. "Hate in the Counter-Transference." *The International Journal of Psycho-Analysis*, vol. 30, no. 69, 1949, pp. 69-74.

Wolf, Jacqueline H. "'Mercenary Hirelings' or 'A Great Blessing'?: Doctors' and Mothers' Conflicted Perceptions of Wet Nurses and the Ramifications for Infant Feeding in Chicago, 1871-1961." *Journal of Social History*, vol. 33, no. 1, 1999, pp. 97-120.

Chapter 7

"The Damage Done and May This Madness Be Over": Exposing and Eradicating Matrophobia through a Reading of the Nanny Trope in the Psychological Thrillers *The Nanny* and *Nanny Dearest*

Andrea O'Reilly

In her article "Why Motherhood Is a Fertile Subject for Crime Fiction," Sarah Vaughan, author of *Little Disasters*, argues that "Motherhood is such a fertile area for exploration that psychological suspense mines it in at least four overlapping ways, [including] the use of a typically problematic surrogate, a nanny or stepmother; a toxic outsider who infiltrates the family and becomes a threat [to it]." Similarly, Emma Fraser argues in her article "The Nanny as Protector and Tormentor in Horror" that the nanny in the horror genre is often portrayed as an insidious force who exists in a space in between hired help and a member of the family, and in these conflicting parameters of outsider and insider, the nanny covers the spectrum between aggressor and victim. And although the nanny may be fiercely protective of the children, she also may elicit or provoke the insecurities of the mother figure, particularly in relation to the mother's attractiveness, sexuality, and competence in caring for her child. However, Fraser emphasizes that the nanny is rarely positioned as inherently monstrous but rather is driven to evil through a tragedy or loss of her own and/or brings out the evilness of the mother figure. Indeed, the nanny, as Fraser emphasizes, "can be a force for good, evil, or an ambiguous middle ground." Of interest to me in this chapter is the purpose and function of the ambiguity/duality of the nanny archetype in maternal narratives. The chapter considers how the nanny's positionality and perspective of insider/outsider, aggressor/victim, and protector/tormenter allow for new and perhaps unanticipated insights into mothers and mothering. I suggest that like the role of stepmothers in fairy tales, wherein the child's negative feelings towards the mother are transferred to the stepmother, the nanny figure in maternal psychological thrillers makes possible an exploration of fractured mother-daughter relationships, which leads to reconciliation between mother and daughter.

In the two contemporary psychological thrillers considered—*The Nanny* by Gilly MacMillan (2021) and *Nanny Dearest* by Flora Collins (2021)—the nanny, as the dual and ambiguous insider/outsider, estranges the daughter from her mother and seeks to become the mother to that daughter. In both psychological thrillers, the nanny is specifically a toxic and insidious threat to the mother-daughter relationship, as she seeks to claim and control the daughter and separate her from her mother. In this, the nanny trope, I argue, may be read as symbolizing and enacting what Adrienne Rich has defined as "matrophobia": the rupture of mother-daughter connection and attachment. Rich elaborates: "Matrophobia can be seen as a womanly splitting of the self in the desire to become purged once and for all of our mothers' bondage, to become individuated and free" (236). When a daughter performs this radical surgery, she severs her attachment to her mother. However, it is patriarchal culture that scripts the roles mothers and daughters are expected to play to position antagonism and animosity between daughters and mothers as normative, which in turn necessitates daughters distancing and differentiating themselves from their mothers. Hence, matrophobia thwarts understanding and intimacy as well as empathy and connection between mothers and daughters. Rich writes: "The loss of the daughter to the mother, the mother to the daughter is the essential female tragedy. We acknowledge Lear (father-daughter split), Hamlet (son and mother), and Oedipus (son and mother) as great embodiments of the human tragedy, but there is no presently enduring recognition of mother-daughter passion and rapture" (237). These two novels seek to recognize this mother-daughter passion and rapture and to move towards healing. Using the nanny trope, each maternal narrative explores how daughters and mothers become estranged in patriarchal culture and how they may be reconnected.

This chapter will explore how the nanny in these two psychological thrillers signify the patriarchal forces that estrange daughters from their mothers, and how mother-daughter reconnection is achieved through the daughter's eventual seeing and slaying of matrophobia, which is enacted by the nanny. Susan Maushart calls for the crucial act of "unmasking motherhood to reveal truths about maternity heretofore silenced or repressed" (7). I suggest that these two novels use the nanny trope to reveal the insidious and toxic forces that estrange daughters from their mothers and show how the mother-daughter connection may be repaired. In her article, "'The Synergy Between You': Mothers, Nannies, and Collaborative Caregiving in Contemporary Matroethnographies," Elizabeth Podnieks argues that writings on the mother-caregiver dyad "register and challenge prevailing maternal ideologies, shatter silences about what it means to be a mother and mother to accomplish their goals of unmasking truths about mothering and caregiving" (341). One of these truths, I suggest, is how ubiquitous mother-daughter estrangement is in patriarchal culture. These two novels, through their use of the nanny trope seek, in Podnieks's words "to create textual space to talk back to neglected cultural experiences of motherhood" (351), particularly those that cause mother-daughter estrangement, and to make possible empowering and empowered mother-daughter connections.

Reflecting on her novel *Little Disasters*, author Sarah Vaughan argues that "Nowhere is the willingness to be brutally honest clearer than in psychological suspense which often probes the darkest reaches of our psyches and delights in tackling taboo subjects." In my recent chapter "'They Both Begin with Blood, Pain, and Terror': Transgressing Normative Motherhood in and through the Contemporary Psychological Thriller: *The Perfect Mother* by Aimee Molloy, *Little Voices* by Vanessa Lillie, and *Little Disasters* by Sarah Vaughan," I explore how the three authors employ the tropes of the psychological thriller genre to transgress normative motherhood through evocations and excavations of troubling and troubled maternal feelings. In each novel, the authors employ the tropes of the psychological thriller genre to convey and confirm tabooed maternal sentiments, such as maternal regret and ambivalence, to validate and vindicate the mothers' experiences of them as well as to critique and challenge the normative institution of motherhood, which denies and disparages them in its idealization and naturalization of maternity. The psychological tropes used in each novel include psychological tension—in particular, maternal dread and anxiety as experienced by the mother protagonist—an element of shock and/or incomprehension, and a plot twist or surprise ending at the conclusion of the novel. Indeed, as Vaughan notes, these conventions "make for compelling suspense, as the reader is misdirected while being exposed to an honest exploration of the extreme difficulties of early motherhood." That it takes acute psychological tensions, shocking surprise elements, confusing plotlines, and twist endings, I argue in this chapter, shows how hidden the extreme difficulties of early motherhood have become in patriarchal motherhood and how necessary it is to expose and extricate them. I suggest that the two authors of the nanny psychological thrillers considered in this chapter similarly use the tropes of this genre to unmask another hidden dimension of patriarchal motherhood— namely, the disruption and distortion of empowered mother-daughter bonding theorized by Rich in her concept of matrophobia. In each novel, the nanny figure becomes an agent of patriarchy who seeks to divide and disempower mothers and daughters and who must be slayed to restore mother and daughter connection. More specifically, Hannah in *The Nanny* seeks to estrange the daughter from the mother to claim the husband/father role and the patriarchal power he represents, whereas Anneliese in *Nanny Dearest* seeks to estrange the daughter from the mother to become the perfect mother of idealized patriarchal motherhood. This chapter will explore how each novel through the tropes of the psychological thriller—psychological dread, shocks, and surprise endings—exposes, confronts, and eventually eradicates the matrophobia of patriarchal culture as enacted and symbolized by the nanny trope.

The Nanny

In her article discussed above, Fraser argues that the nanny is rarely positioned as inherently monstrous but rather is driven to evil through a tragedy or loss of her own and that the nanny is usually fiercely protective of the children. However, the nanny, Hannah, in MacMillan's novel is unambiguously malevolent and abuses Jocelyn, the daughter, as well as other children she cares for, although it takes the tropes of the psychological thriller for these truths to be revealed. The novel opens with a prologue wherein the daughter Jocelyn at the age of seven wakens to find that her beloved nanny Hannah has left under mysterious circumstances, leaving her feeling "as if the bottom has dropped out of her world" (6). Young Jocelyn reflects: "Hannah is her everything" and "Hannah is better than Mother" (6). Virginia, the mother, then tells her daughter Jocelyn that her nanny left because she "was a very bad girl ... and that Hannah couldn't stand to look after her anymore" (7). The mother's cruel words, and the daughter's love for the nanny over her mother, sets up the anticipated patriarchal script of matrophobia—wherein the mother is positioned as bad, and the daughter understandably hates her mother and identifies with an idealized mother, represented by the nanny figure. The idealization of the nanny figure, the scripting of the bad mother, and the resulting mother-daughter estrangement is fully established when Jocelyn returns to her mother's home with her own nine-year-old daughter some twenty years later following the sudden and tragic death of Jocelyn's husband, Chris. Without employment of her own, and with her late husband's business in financial ruin, Jocelyn has no choice but to return to her family home in England, where only her mother now lives following the recent death of her husband, Jocelyn's father. After walking away from Lake Hall, her family home, as a young woman, Jocelyn "distanced herself as much as she could. She changed her name from Jocelyn to Jo and refused to accept a penny from them. That is why it hurts so much to be here now, and dependent on her mother's charity" (43).

Upon her return to Lake Hall, Jo reflects upon her memories with her nanny with "sweet nostalgia" (16) and is resolved that her mother will not raise her daughter Ruby as she was raised— "crushing her spirit until she learns to repress every single raw and healthy emotion she ever feels" (23). However, much to Jo's surprise "a bond between granddaughter and grandmother is forming right in front of her eyes" (9), and she is "not even a tiny bit comfortable with it" (9). The opening chapter concludes with Jo and her daughter Ruby finding a fractured skull on the shore of the island lake. Jo is horrified by the skull and regards it as "tangible proof of a dark current running from the past to the present" (27). For Jo, this dark current signifies the intolerable relationship she is now forced to continue with her mother. As she later explains to her daughter, she calls Virginia "mother" rather than "mom," since the latter "would suggest an intimacy that never existed" (64). However, as the novel unfolds, we learn that the skull symbolizes the insidious patriarchal forces that estrange mothers and daughters as enacted and symbolized by Hannah, the nanny figure.

The following chapters are narrated in turn by Hannah, the nanny, Virginia, the mother, and Jo, the daughter. These are interspersed with chapters from the viewpoint of the detective, who is called in to investigate the murder of the woman whose skull is found. Jo increasingly believes that the skull is Hannah's, her nanny, who suddenly disappeared when she was a child, but Virginia is adamant that the skull cannot be Hannah's. Significantly, as the identity of the woman murdered is investigated and the psychological tension of the novel intensifies, the reader learns about Hannah's past and gains insight into the relationship of Jo and Virginia from the mother's perspective. In the mother's narrative, we learn that she did love her daughter and that she felt "an intense and unrelenting pain," as "the child she loved did not love her back, even when she was a very little girl, and not even when she was a baby" (36). As Virginia says, "I had so much love to give her, but she didn't want a single piece of it" (214) and then further ponders: "In that situation, it can only be the fault of the parent, but I have never worked out what I did wrong" (36). And later Virginia reflects: "When she was a child, our daughter belonged to another woman. This burden was heavier than a millstone around my neck. It broke me" (179). However, for Virginia, "there is a silver lining, and her name is Ruby [her granddaughter]" (36). As the grandmother and granddaughter's relationship develops, Virginia realizes: "*She is just like me*, and the thought brings her such a warm feeling" (49). And later Virginia reflects: "I know I'm not perfect, but I want to pass on all that is good about me [to Ruby] while I can" (89). I suggest that these narratives from the mother's perspective reveal Virginia to be a more loving and caring woman and mother than as perceived and presented by her daughter.

The mother's remembrances also suggest that the nanny Hannah is not the idealized caregiver as Jo remembers; instead, she created the "illusion that she was well-meaning and trustworthy" (90) and that "she used her eyes to seduce and control" (91). Indeed, as Hannah's past is shared in her narrative, the reader learns that Hannah is a woman named Linda, who applied for a job as a housekeeper only because she fell "a bit in love" with the man who she saw posting the ad. Once hired, Linda confesses to her friend that the sight of the father with his babies "thrilled her" and she felt "he was just right for her" (32). Linda later observes and begins mimicking the nanny of this family's household planning someday to become a nanny herself because "Linda was interested in power, and she recognized that in this family, Nanny Hughes had it in spades, because the man loved the children, and the children loved the nanny" (32). When one of the babies dies, resulting in the grieving husband becoming "not like he used to be" (36), Linda leaves her position and assumes the identity of Hannah, the husband's sister, who had died six months earlier. These glimpses into Linda, now Hannah's past, reveal that her desire to become a nanny was not about loving and caring for children as Jo idealized but rather to gain power particularly through identification and connection with the father/husband of the household. In this, Hannah enacts and symbolizes an allegiance to patriarchy, which in turn is used to sever the mother and daughter connection, which Virginia understands but Jo has yet to comprehend.

The first section concludes with the return of Hannah to Lake Hall, and the second section opens with Hannah's memory at arriving Lake Hall for the first time to care for baby Jocelyn, wherein she resolves that "she will look after this baby as if she were more precious than the crown jewels. Jocelyn is, after all, her key to a better future" (115). For Virginia, this woman simply cannot be Hannah because she knows that the skull of the woman found in the lake belongs to Hannah, indicating that Virginia was involved in the murder of Hannah and leaving Virginia to ask: "How can a dead woman come back to life?" (118). With the return of Hannah and Virginia's conviction that Hannah is dead, the novel sets up the compelling suspense and psychological tension of the thriller genre through which the matrophobia of patriarchal culture, as enacted and symbolized by the nanny, is exposed and eventually eradicated.

The second section of the novel continues with the multiple narratives through which the psychological tension builds through the competing truths of Hannah's identity—alive or dead, benevolent or malevolent—until it is resolved through the thriller trope of shock and/or incomprehension. As Jo and Hannah reunite, Jo recalls how she used "to fantasize about Hannah adopting her and how she wished Hannah could become her mother" (137). When Jo finally asks Hannah about why she left, believing it was, as her mother told her, because she behaved badly, Hannah exclaims: "No! That's not true. Your mother and I argued that night after she was terribly harsh with you when you spoiled your dress" (142). Jo is convinced that the dress she wore that night was blue, whereas Hannah corrects her saying it was green. Jo reflects, "I guess I'm wrong then"; to which Hannah responds, "Memory is a funny thing" (144). Although this exchange on the colour of the dress seems incidental at the time—Jo swearing the dress was blue but then thinking "what difference does it make" (144)—it reveals the nanny's rescripting of that night as a matrophobic narrative, in which the mother is blamed to estrange the daughter from her. Significantly, we later learn with the trope of shock that the dress worn was indeed blue, which repudiates the nanny's matrophobic narrative and repairs the mother-daughter estrangement.

The second section of the novel, until the moment of shock, continues the juxtaposition of these two opposing narratives: the nanny's matrophobic one, which seeks to estrange Jo from her mother, as well as those from Hannah's and Virginia's past, which seek to disrupt this patriarchal distancing of mother and daughter. In Hannah's narrative, we learn that she abused and drugged one of the children under her care, drugged the mother, and seduced the father (177, 205). Hannah explains to the child: "If you behave, I won't hurt you. Your mother does not want to care for your properly, and it is my authority that counts" (171). When Hannah leaves her nanny position, she is hopeful that the next family will be wealthy, as she would "love to have one of those rich men for herself" (296). Later, when Hannah first meets the Holts, she "feels a stab of jealousy" (308) when Virginia touches Alexander, her husband, but Hannah is resolved to become the nanny for Joycelyn, since "every muscle in her body already aches for him and every cell in her body tells her that she will never do better than him" (308). For Hannah, being a nanny is not about the care of children but about accessing patriarchal power through estranging children from their mothers to lay claim to the husband/father. Indeed, as Virginia reflects: "When Jocelyn was a child Hannah pulled the wool so far down over her eyes that all Jocelyn saw was a beloved nanny: fluffy, sweet, and safe" (185).

In the second section, we also learn the truth, albeit partially, about the night Hannah left: Hannah's assumed to be dead body is dumped into the lake by Virginia and her husband, but she survived and then extorted money from the husband until his death many years later. Upon Hannah's return and Virginia learning about the extortion, she agrees to pay an "eyewatering" sum and says, "she will do anything" to get Hannah to leave (209). But Hannah stays and moves into Lake Hall to be a nanny for Ruby, Jo's daughter. When Virginia hears this news, she feels as if "she had been punched in the stomach" (181) but decides to protect both her daughter and granddaughter from Hannah: "I've protected my daughter for so long I will not give up now" (181). As the suspense and tension mounts in the second section, Hannah's matrophobic manoeuvrings now include estranging Jo from her daughter Ruby. Hannah suggests to Jo that it was Ruby who left the hamster cage open causing the hamster's death and that "Ruby does lie sometimes" (272). When Ruby defies Hannah and tells her mother she does not like Hannah, (287), Jo only defends Hannah: "She is so much more than a practical solution to my childcare arrangements. She knows me, she knows us, and having someone whom I can trust is the most extraordinary feeling" (258). However, as Hannah once again contradicts Jo's memory, Jo begins to "feel uneasy" (244) and seeks to find more about Hannah on the internet only to discover that Hannah has no online presence: "She is invisible" (244). As the second section concludes, we learn that Hannah is abusing Ruby as she did with the previous children under her care. When Jo sees her daughter's bruises, she recalls another arm with bruises, and it is hers (315). Significantly, at this moment, Jo also remembers that the dress she wore that night was "definitely blue," although Hannah had assured her it was green. However, Jo remains "unsure what or whom to believe" (315). The section ends with an image of Hannah's face with "fake sympathy and concern" and Jo's "with contempt for her mother," which signifies that although the truths about Hannah's are being revealed, her narrative is still scripting matrophobia. However, Virginia is determined to disrupt this narrative: "*I love you* [Jo]. *I am not the threat*" (319); "Jo needs to see through the veils of falsity Hannah is shrouding us with.... It's our only hope" (320).

The second section ends with another thriller trope: shock and incomprehension. The fractured skull is found not to be Hannah's, as Jo initially believed; it belongs to a yet unidentified woman. The third section of the novel resolves the shock and explains the incomprehension by revealing the identity of this woman and disclosing what happened the night Hannah left Lake Hall. The fractured skull belongs to Jean, Hannah's friend when she was still Linda, and who threatens to reveal Hannah's true identity unless Hannah secures a job for her at Lake Hall. Hannah then kills Jean and disposes her body in the lake. The second disclosure, conveyed through a tape made by Jo's father and kept by Hannah as extortion, reveals that it was not Virginia who killed Hannah as implied thus far in the plot but young Jocelyn, who pushed Hannah down the stairs when she discovered her in bed with her father. Hannah's parents, believing Hannah to be dead, disposed of her body in the lake. Jo has no memory of this, and as Virginia tries to explain to her daughter that it was accident, Hannah responds: "You meant to kill.... You thought I wasn't good enough for your daddy, so you pushed me down those stairs" (384). Virginia tells Hannah that she "never wanted her to know" and gave her pills to obliterate the memory. After learning this truth about Hannah and all her mother did to protect her, Jo "allows in the thought that Mother made an effort to get close to me on so many occasions, over so many years, and I rejected her every single time. Because of Hannah. How much damage must that have done?" (395). Hannah tells Jo that her father used to drug her as a child so he could have sex with Hannah, that "he and her mother loathed her [and] that she was a disappointment, a plain and dull girl" (399). Enraged by Hannah's "poisonous" words and repulsed by Hannah's "doughy flesh and breakable bones" (399) as she puts on Virginia's dress, Jo now understands the following: "Hannah means to destroy me, my mother, and my daughter" (399). With this realization "something breaks inside of her with absolute finality" (399), and she suffocates Hannah with a dry-cleaning bag. As she does so, "every part of her is seized by a burning anger. Every part of her wants this to end" (399). And as Virginia tries to release Jo's hold on Hannah's murdered body, Jo wants "to keep the plastic tight forever" and wants "to punish her for everything she's done" (400). The mother and daughter then dump Hannah's body in the lake. This surprise ending of the psychological thriller marks the eradication of matrophobia—as enacted and symbolized by the daughter's killing of the nanny to make possible mother and daughter reconnection and reconciliation. As the novel concludes, Virginia attempts to hug her daughter, but Jo flinches, "and her mother steps away as if she had been burnt" (415). However, with the final sentence of the novel, Jo apologizes to her mother, moves forwards, and puts her arms around her, explaining that her reaction "was just a little souvenir from Hannah" (415).

In *The Nanny*, the tropes of the thriller genre—psychological tension, moments of incomprehension, and a surprise ending—work to unravel the threads that weave and sustain matrophobic scripts by exposing that what estrange mothers and daughters is the larger patriarchal culture, as enacted and symbolized by the nanny. Hannah seeks to disconnect and disempower Virginia and Jo to claim the husband/father and the patriarchal power he represents. However, through the tropes of the thriller genre, Jo comes to understand how the nanny, and the patriarchy she represents, sought to undermine her relationship with her mother. In killing Hannah, Jo rebukes and eradicates matrophobia and is then able to reconnect with her mother.

Nanny Dearest

Like *The Nanny*, *Nanny Dearest* begins with a prologue from the perspective of the daughter, four-year-old Suzy, entering her mother's bedroom trying to awaken her mama by "kissing her lips" because that "is how Sleeping Beauty in the story wakes up." But her mother does not respond because, as we learn later in the novel, she is dead, killed by the nanny Anneliese. Following the prologue, the novel opens with a woman approaching Suzy, now called Sue as a young woman, who introduces herself as Anneliese, explaining that she used to babysit her and then asks about Sue's father. At her question, Sue flinches and thinks "she knew my mother" (14); we learn later that Sue's mother became ill with cancer and died when Sue was a young child. Sue then tells Anneliese that her father died a year earlier in a car accident. As Sue is about to leave Anneliese, "Annelise stops her, one of her tiny hands on her wrist, almost tugging at her sleeve like a child" (15), saying she would love to see hear again and gives Sue gives her phone number. Like *The Nanny*, the following chapters in this novel are narrated by the nanny from the past, and in the present, and also from the perspective of Sue, the daughter.

An early narrative from the nanny's past recalls the close and loving relationship Anneliese had with her mother who protected her from her father's abuse and who told her daughter that "her imagination, that vivid, dynamic thing, would be her saving grace" (44). When Annie is twelve, her mother is hit and killed by a truck, but people speculated that "Maybe it wasn't an accident after all, that she'd gone to fatal measures to escape life with her husband, and all those children" (45). A year later, Annie's father is shot leaving him to channel "all his physical rage into verbal assaults, mostly toward Annie" (48). But we are told that Annie could take his abuse because she "had those friendly voices in her head to keep her company.... As she got older these friends, would on occasion, glide out of her head so she could see them, dazzling and effervescent. Cherishing her. Loving her" (45). The tragic death of Anneliese's mother, her father's abuse, and Anneliese's "vivid imagination with friendly voices" reveal Anneliese to be a troubled woman who, unlike Hannah in *The Nanny*, is positioned, at least initially, as a sympathetic character and who, as Fraser has argued, "is driven to evil through a tragedy or loss of her own." However, Anneliese's narratives from the past also introduce her matrophophic maneuverings. When Mr. Keller talks with Anneliese and "acknowledges her existence beyond Suzy," Annaliese "likes the attention" (66). Later when Georgia, Mrs. Keller's niece, visits, Annaliese is jealous of Suzy's love for her aunt, and when she sees the two of them hugging, she feels "the sudden urge to scream, to scalp this girl, to snatch Suzy and run to the lake" (89). Later when Suzy and her aunt spend the day outdoors, Anneliese deliberately forgets to put sunscreen on Suzy, hoping that Georgia will be blamed for her sunburn. (91). And when Suzy is inconsolable at Georgia's departure, Anneliese resolves that "Something needs to be done" (93). We learn that Anneliese steals a beloved bracelet and family heirloom from Mrs. Keller, knowing that Georgia will be blamed, which will forever estrange her from the Holt family.

As the novel unfolds in the present-day narrative, Annelise and Sue visit more and more, and with each visit, Annelise becomes entirely focussed on her (53). Like Hannah in *The Nanny*, Anneliese soon begins a matrophopic scripting of Sue's past. She tells her that when Sue cried in her room and was unable to leave the room because of the baby gate put in by her parents, Anneliese carried young Sue to her room to comfort her, never telling the parents. When she learns this, Sue responds: "I always thought my mom did that.... I guess I was giving the wrong woman credit" (52). Later when Sue asks Anneliese about her mother, Anneliese tells her that as a baby, Sue often cried for her mother because she was away so much that her mother did not have time for domestic matters and that the mother would take credit for special things that Anneliese did, such as baking her a birthday cake for Sue's preschool class. Sue instinctively feels that Anneliese is not telling her everything, but she attributes this to the trauma Anneliese experienced watching her mother die. We learn later through the thriller trope of incomprehension the real reasons for Anneliese's evasions.

As Annaliese shares stories and pictures of their time together and tells Sue that she was "such a fun child" and a "joy to look after," Sue realizes she is "ravenous for Anneliese's praise" (55). She wants her "identity proven all over again ... by this woman [she] hardly know[s]" (55). As their friendship grows, Sue begins to overcome the debilitating anxiety and depression experienced since the sudden death of her father, and as Sue explains to Anneliese: "The dreams have stopped. I think it has something to do with you, and I don't know why but I'm so grateful" (71). Sue then realizes the following: "I need her ... I'm fastened to her now" (71). She later presents Anneliese with the perfect birthday gift so that Anneliese will understand how much she cares about her. However, at Anneliese's birthday dinner, also attended by Sue's best friend, Beth, the suspense of this thriller, centred on the ambiguity of the nanny figure, is activated when Beth says to Sue "Anneliese seems really off. There's something not quite right about her" and when she wonders, "I just don't understand why she wants to spend so much time with you" (86). Later, Anneliese tells Sue that her friend Beth "only wants to keep Sue in a place where you need her; and that is not what true friendship is about" (100). Upon hearing these words, "Sue finds herself nodding along, encouraging her to say more" (100). Though not yet understood by Sue, but likely suspected by the reader, it is Anneliese and not Beth who is making Sue defenseless and dependent, and it is Anneliese who is deliberating seeking to estrange Sue from her friends and distort Sue's memory of her mother.

The gripping elusiveness about Annaliese continues to intensify as we learn more about Anneliese and her relationship with her sister as well as her sister's children, who Anneliese is caring for. Sue reflects: "The children are so obedient. They're so docile I'd be suspicious if Annie weren't so gentle, so sure in the way she handles them" (97). And later, the children's father, the ex-husband of Annaliese's sister, says to Sue as he is dropping the children off: "They have not seemed well that last few times I have come to get them" (131). Annaliese also becomes increasingly possessive of Sue. When Sue reconnects with her friend and former boyfriend Gavin and spends the day painting with him, she discovers she has missed several texts from Annaliese, each one more frantically asking where Sue is. When Annaliese learns Sue has spent the day painting, Annaliese offers a room in her sister's home for a studio, and when Sue declines the offer, Sue hears "a moroseness to Annaliese's tone," which Sue significantly likens to "a sour candy coated in sugar" (116). Hearing desperation in Anneliese's voice, Sue ends her painting before its completion to Gavin's surprise, visits Annelise, and they spend the night together drinking. Once again, Annelise seeks to estrange Sue from her friends, telling her that Gavin had been cruel to her after her father's death, and although Sue is "unsure if she agrees with Annaliese, it felt good to be validated" (119). Significantly, the first section of the novel ends with Annaliese and Sue dancing as "if they are one entity" and with Annaliese kissing Sue's forehead as "Sue falls under embryonic, into the dark comfort of sleep not unlike a womb" (121). The imagery of pregnancy conveyed in these words signify an idealized mother-daughter relationship that Annaliese seeks to create with Sue to estrange her from her own mother.

The narratives from Anneliese's past in the second section of the novel are replete with Anneliese's matrophobic manoeuvring with Sue as child. On Sue's first day of school, the teacher explains to her father that Sue was upset believing that she would be taken away (127). There is doubt it was Anneliese who suggested this, as Anneliese kidnaps Sue later when the mother dies. We also learn that on the first day of school, Sue cries for Annelise and not for her mother. Later and overheard by Annelise, the mother sobs to her husband: "Of course, Suzy likes her better" (139). When the family learns that the mother has been diagnosed with incurable cancer, Annelise feels "relief, this wash of feeling steadying her heart" (157). When young Sue says she is scared about her mommy (referring to the mother's illness), Annelise repositions Sue's words and replies: "I'm afraid of Mommy too.... But you'll always have me. You know that right? No matter what Mommy does, where she goes, I'll be right here with you" (166). Anneliese then begins to introduce herself as the mother of Sue with "the glow of supposed motherhood, thinking of those people who automatically imagined Suzy in her body... and wants to squeal with joy, with the absolute euphoric dream of it" (167). Annelise also begins to bruise her arms and tells the mothers and the nannies of Suzy's school friends that Mrs. Keller is abusing her and young Suzy, but she cannot leave because "she loves Suzy so much" and that she does not want "to leave her with that woman" (198). As Mrs. Keller's cancer progresses, Anneliese feels as if "her happiness would erupt and bubble out," since she realizes that Mr. Keller "will always need the help, after Mrs. Keller is gone, more than ever" (203). The final narrative from Anneliese's past in section two concludes with Anneliese killing Suzy's beloved cat because she has "to banish anything that comes between her and Suzy" (222).

Like *The Nanny*, the second section of this novel continues the opposing narratives through which the psychological tension builds through the competing truths of Anneliese's identity, benevolent or malevolent, until it is resolved through the thriller trope of shock and incomprehension. In the narratives of the present day, with Sue not yet aware of Anneliese's past matrophobic manoeuvrings, she becomes closer with Anneliese with every passing day. Sue reflects: "Something is happening, small shifts in my routine becoming regular, and thus becoming my new normal" (147). This new normal for Sue is spending every night at Annaliese's sister's home, and this "new family, for Sue, is what is important" (149). When she is away from them her chest "aches as if something's missing and she wonders if she should curb this sentimentality, this overflow of love [she is] feeling for them" (172). However, Sue then accidently finds in Anneliese's cupboard her mother's bracelet that Georgia was accused of stealing (174). When Sue confronts Annaliese with the bracelet, she hears in Anneliese's voice "an undercurrent of something else," and "her eyes narrow for the first time in all [her] months of knowing her" (191). However, Anneliese explains to Sue that she stole the bracelet out of financial need, planned to pawn it, but then felt too guilty to do so" (192). "Anneliese's soothing voice deflates Sue's tension," and Sue thinks her explanation makes sense, as she would have likely done the same thing in her situation. However, at the same time, Sue feels "a painful prick of uncertainty" (195) because her father earlier told her that the bracelet disappeared right around the time Georgia left their home. Significantly, when Sue later looks at a photo of her with her mother, "She can't help but let that fear, the uncertainty mount, and give [her] pause" (194). This pause marks a connection with her mother that will eventually enable Sue to see and slay the matrophobia symbolized and enacted by Anneliese.

Following the discovery of the bracelet, denoting the thriller trope of shock, the psychological tension intensifies. Gavin shares with Sue his discovery that Anneliese suffers from mental illness, and then after contacting the families that Anneliese had said she nannied for, Sue learns that she had never actually worked for them, which forces Sue to wonder, "What the hell has Annaliese *really* been doing these last two decades" (215). Sue begins to realize that she has lost herself becoming so close to Anneliese and has reverted to the toddler she was when Anneliese cared for her. She confronts Anneliese about her lying about her past nanny positions, but once again Annelise provides an explanation, accuses Sue of not trusting her, says she loves her unconditionally, and forgives Sue. Seeing Anneliese looking "so sincere, her face so placid and open," Sue decides "not to question any of it anymore" (229). However, at the conclusion of this section, the thriller trope of shock emerges when Sue discovers in the children's vitamin bottle, sleeping pills, which Sue now realizes Anneliese has been putting in the children's morning smoothies to make them obedient (240). This section concludes with Sue leaving Anneliese's home vowing never to return "with a ball of fire growing larger, igniting into an expanding cannonball of fury" (241).

The final and shorter third section includes several elements of shock and concludes with a surprise ending to finally unravel Anneliese's matrophophic scripting. From the narratives from Anneliese's past, we learn that as Mrs. Keller is dying from cancer, she asks Anneliese to kill her, and Anneliese does so by suffocating her with a pillow (251). We also learn that Anneliese became pregnant at sixteen but then miscarried. Three years later, when she sees Suzy on the street, "Anneliese's destiny fell into place," as she is convinced that Suzy is her daughter, and she longs "to run after her, her child. Fully formed and exactly the age she should be" (292). Anneliese then learns that the family is looking for a nanny, and Anneliese realizes that her "future was set" (292). After Mrs. Keller's death's, Anneliese kidnaps Suzy, believing that she now "has control of her life, her daughter" (295). However, young Suzy will not stop crying and hits Anneliese with a shoe while she is driving and throws to the floor the bracelet Anneliese gave her for her birthday. At this, Anneliese "has the urge to cover that little mouth, force the black smoke of her screams back into her lungs" (297). The final image in Annelies's narrative from the past is of the two of them "lying on the grass with Anneliese's arm tight around Suzy's waist, her ear to the earth, waiting for the howling to end" (298). These images confirm that what Anneliese seeks in claiming Suzy as her daughter is not a lived relationship with an actual child but an idealized one, in which Anneliese has complete control over a compliant daughter.

In the present-day narrative, Sue discovers the letter Anneliese left for her father when she kidnapped her as a young girl. Reading this letter Sue reflects: "The entitlement in that letter was shameless, pathological. It was downright insane. No wonder my dad had moved the two of us swiftly only a month later" (305). She then returns to the family home to discover Anneliese there. Once again, Anneliese attempts to rationalize all that she has done, but Sue now realizes that Anneliese is a "deeply troubled woman" (321) and tries to get Anneliese to leave. But Anneliese continues with her matrophophic narrative: "You were always supposed to be mine. I saw you before you were even born ... your mother neglected you and you cried for me" (321). At that moment, Suzy remembers her mother telling her that she is going away, but that she loves her and does not want to go away (322). Anneliese then tells Suzy that she killed her mother, explaining that she "did it all for her" (323). At these words, Suzy remembers going into her mother's bedroom as a young child and trying to wake her. Then like the ending of The Nanny, Suzy "screaming with all that tightly knotted anger ... and with every crevice boiling over with grief, and anger, and love and sadness, coiled together" (323) strangles Anneliese to death. And echoing Jo's words from The Nanny, Suzy feels relief: "My stomach uncoils. She's gone. She's gone forever. All this madness is over" (324). However, Suzy cannot immediately leave "because the greedy contours of this home forget nothing" (325). She cannot leave Anneliese, as these walls remind Sue of her. Thus, like the ending of The Nanny, when Jo initially flinches from her mother's embrace, this novel concludes with Sue holding the murdered Anneliese in her arms. With the killing of Anneliese, Sue, like Jo in *The Nanny*, finally does repudiate matrophobia, but Sue's holding of Anneliese, like Jo's flinch, suggests that although the nanny may be slain, the matrophobia of patriarchal culture she enacts and symbolizes may never be fully eradicated.

In contrast to *The Nanny*, wherein Hannah seeks to estrange the daughter from the mother to claim the husband/father and the patriarchal power he represents, in this novel, Anneliese seeks to estrange the daughter from the mother to become the perfect mother of idealized patriarchal motherhood. Anneliese covets Sue not because of an actual love for this child but because she is driven to fulfill her fantasy of perfect motherhood, which was first imagined when she became pregnant as a young woman. And to do this, Anneliese must rescript the actual mother as a bad one. For both Hannah and Anneliese, their nanny positions and their performance of idealized caregiving are not about loving children but about achieving power through patriarchal feminine identities: Hannah in being a devoted wife and Anneliese in being an idealized mother. And both women must estrange the daughters from their mothers to claim these patriarchal feminine roles and the power they convey. However, in both novels, the tropes of the thriller genre—psychological tension, moments of incomprehension, and a surprise ending—work to unravel the threads that weave and sustain matrophobic scripts by exposing that what estranges daughters from their mothers is the larger patriarchal culture and in particular the patriarchal identities of the devoted wife and idealized mother. However, through the tropes of the thriller genre, Jo and Suzy come to understand how the nanny, and the patriarchal culture she represents, sought to undermine their relationships with their mothers. In killing their nannies, Jo and Suzy eradicate the matrophobia of patriarchal culture to repair their relationship with their mothers.

Conclusion

Borrowing from the two novels, I titled this chapter "The Damage Done and May This Madness be Over" to signify how both novels expose the harm of matrophobia and seek to eradicate it using the nanny figure and the tropes of the psychological thriller. The lives of mothers and daughters are scripted by patriarchal narratives of matrophobia even as mothers and daughters live lives different from, and in resistance to, these assigned roles. A central aim of my research and teaching over the last three decades has been to unravel these matrophobic scripts by exposing them to be narrative constructions rather than reflections of the actual lived realities of mothers and daughters, hence neither natural nor inevitable. I have also considered how daughters and mothers may identify, challenge, and dismantle the patriarchal narratives of mother-daughter estrangement to achieve an empowered and empowering mother-daughter connection. In these explorations, I found quite unexpectedly a compelling exposé of, and resistance to, matrophobia in the least likely of places: the nanny psychological thriller. But perhaps it can only be through the terror of the thriller genre and the treachery of the nanny trope that the "damage and madness" of the matrophobia of patriarchal culture can be fully exposed and eradicated.

Works Cited

Collins, Flora. *Nanny Dearest.* Mira Publishers, 2021.

Fraser, Emma. "The Nanny as Protector and Tormentor in Horror." *SYFY WIRE*, 27 Oct. 2021, www.syfy.com/syfy-wire/the-nanny-as-protector-and-tormentor-in-horror-from-the-omen-to-bly-manor. Accessed 12 Oct. 2023.

MacMillian, Gilly. *The Nanny.* William Morrow. 2021.

Maushart, Susan. *The Mask of Motherhood: How Becoming a Mother Changes our Lives and Why We Never Talk About It.* Penguin Books. 1999.

O'Reilly, Andrea. "'They Both Begin with Blood, Pain, and Terror'" Transgressing Normative Motherhood in and through the Contemporary Psychological Thriller: *The Perfect Mother* by Aimee Molloy, *Little Voices* by Vanessa Lillie, and *Little Disasters* by Sarah Vaughan." *Mothering Outside the Lines: Tales of Boundary-Busting Mamas*, edited by BettyAnn Martin and Michelann Parr, Demeter Press, 2023, pp. 197-218.

Podnieks, Elizabeth. "'The Synergy Between You': Mothers, Nannies, and Collaborative Caregiving in Contemporary Matroethnographies." *Life Writing.* vol. 18, no.3, pp. 337-54.

Rich, Adrienne. *Of Woman Born: Motherhood as Experience and Institution.* W.W Norton & Company, 1986.

Vaughan, Sarah. "Why Motherhood is a Fertile Subject for Crime Fiction." *Crime Reads,* 21 Aug. 2021, crimereads.com/why-mother-hood-is-a-fertile-subject-for-crime-fiction/. Accessed 12 Oct. 2023.

Chapter 8

Family Exchange Norms and Mother-Nanny Relationships in Leila Slimani's *The Perfect Nanny* and Kiley Reid's *Such a Fun Age*

Jill Goad

Iconic literary-turned movie nannies Mary Poppins and Mrs. Doubtfire are known for their abilities to engage the children in their care while lending levity to the homes in which they work. Their selflessness and wisdom bring estranged parents and children together, rendering these nannies the missing piece for their employers' families. Well-known African American literary child caregivers, such as Mammy in Margaret Mitchell's *Gone with the Wind* and Aibileen in Kathryn Stockett's bestselling novel *The Help,* have more fraught legacies—with the first being an enslaved women forced into carework and the second having few options other than coerced carework. Like their white counterparts, these women are associated with nurturing and self-sacrifice.

Analyzing these fictionalized nannies is a worthwhile endeavour because their portrayals reveal cultural expectations of women in care-giving roles and the ways race and class affect these expectations. In the early twenty-first century, contemporary portrayals of nannies in popular fiction have taken a darker turn, involving overt conflicts that affect nanny-family relationships, even murder, and reveal deep-seated societal issues connected to the nanny's role as a "shadow mother" (Macdonald). Leila Slimani's *The Perfect Nanny* and Kiley Reid's *Such a Fun Age* are widely read examples of this shift and feature seemingly salacious conflicts that call into question why readers are drawn to nanny-centred narratives.

Close readings of the nannies as well as their interactions and connections with the mothers they work for in these two novels give insight into current middle- to upper-class cultural anxieties about mothering and the paid childcare system while exposing inequities in this system and addressing the lack of subjectivity often attributed to nannies by mothers who employ them as part of the family. My analysis of nannies Louise in *The Perfect Nanny* and Emira in *Such a Fun Age* applies concepts of family exchange norms and paranormal management to highlight racial preference in nanny hiring, the nanny's simultaneous role as essential helper and objectified employee, blurred nanny-employer boundaries due to the nature of in-home care work, and the conflict-fomenting economic disparity between nannies and the families for whom they work.

Background on Slimani's and Reid's Novels

Slimani's *The Perfect Nanny* won the Goncourt Prize when it was published in France in 2016 (Corrigan). The novel focusses, according to writer Belinda Luscombe, on the "dissection of the relationship between mothers and those who care for their children, of the soul-crushing tedium of looking after small humans, of the fury that radiates between the have-it-alls and the have-not-enoughs" ("Not Afraid"). Ultimately, it is this tedium and fury, along with a complicated mother-nanny dynamic, that builds to the novel's horrific act: Louise's murder of the two children in her charge, which is brutally depicted in the opening chapter before the novel goes back in time to Myriam, the mother-employer, hiring Louise. A 2012 murder of two children by their nanny in New York inspired Slimani's work (Corrigan). Kiley Reid's *Such a Fun Age*, longlisted for the 2020 Booker Prize, has been lauded for its balance between "a nuanced take on racial biases and class divides" and "a page-turning saga of betrayals, twists, and perfectly awkward relationships" (Canfield 108). In discussing her work's book-club readability alongside its treatment of serious themes, Reid notes, "I wanted a compulsive read ... but when it comes to the social issues, I would hate for anyone to think that my intention was to make systemic racism a light issue" (qtd. in Canfield 108). *Such a Fun Age* addresses how racial and economic differences are thrown into stark relief through the mother-caregiver relationship between wealthy writer, Instagram influencer, and mother-of-two Alix and twenty-five-year-old caregiver Emira. Exacerbating instances that heighten conflict between the two are Emira dating Alix's ex-boyfriend, Emira experiencing racial discrimination from a security guard while caring for Alix's child, and Alix leaking video footage of the incident to make Emira dependent on her and to compel Emira to leave her boyfriend.

Family Exchange Norms and Paranormal Management: A Theoretical Framework for Reading Slimani and Reid

Cameron Macdonald's theory of family exchange norms in carework, along with her more intricate assessment of mother-nanny relationships, provides a framework for examining *The Perfect Nanny* and *Such a Fun Age* to unpack the broader cultural significance of the nannies therein. In her study *Shadow Mothers,* Macdonald contends that professional childcare is undervalued socially and economically, rendering nannies and au pairs vulnerable workers who have fewer economic opportunities than their employers (45). In the nanny's perspective, she is "fictive kin" who must "balanc[e] [her] strong loyalties to the children in [her] care against [her] own needs and desires for regular hours, a clear job description, and decent pay" (Macdonald 45). Similarly, historian Sonya Michel argues that labelling nannies "one of the family" serves to "naturalize or normalize the presence of strangers in [a family's] midst," even though "family membership is tenuous and can be withdrawn as readily as it is granted" (40). Mothers who employ nannies, in contrast, must be concerned with their children receiving ideal care while ensuring the childcare worker's pay is not a budget strain. Class and culture may cause tension due to different perspectives on childrearing (45).

Macdonald refers to the norms applied to nannies' work as "family exchange norms" (59), a contrast to the market-based norms governing caregivers in nurseries and daycares. Within family exchange norms, "it is not unusual [for mother-employers] to expect flexibility, accommodation, and even sacrifice for the good of the group" from their nannies, including doing work outside of contracts and blurring lines between "on-duty" and "off-duty" time (Macdonald 59-60). Nannies are thus "family" and employee, working for both love and money. The informal norms tied to carework often lead to some employers feeling entitled to control the personal lives of nannies outside the home (Macdonald 62).

Examining *Shadow Mothers* more closely yields additional, subtler, yet significant components of the mother-nanny relationship. For example, Macdonald argues that race, ethnicity, and immigration status are important to mothers who see these categories as a means of instilling certain qualities in their children (70). However, mothers are "as likely to seek 'otherness' in their nannies as ... similarity" because mothers ascribe certain meanings to ethnicity (Macdonald 70). Class lies outside these considerations, though, because an economic status disparity will inevitably exist between the employer and nanny, which is important because "motherhood is classed, but social class is also actively transmitted through mothering practices" (Macdonald 204). Therefore, the mother can control only some aspects of the type of nanny she wants. If the mother has selected what she sees as the "right" type of nanny, Macdonald notes, she will later engage in a form of nanny management known as "paranormal management," where the mother sees the nanny as an extension of herself (95). Since, under this type of management, the nanny is supposed to intuit what the mother wants for her children, the mother assumes that decisions about the children's food, activities, and other aspects of caregiving can be safely left to the nanny's judgment. Paranormal management makes "shadow mothers" of nannies, whose carework is supposed to preserve the idea of the mother-employer as the primary parent (Macdonald 133). Thus, nannies often do not have the sense of autonomy or recognition they seek as skilled workers. To combat this, Macdonald contends, nannies engage in unspoken "competency contests," where they use their knowledge of their employers' sometimes imperfect parenting skills to internally gauge who the best caretaker is (151). This allows the nanny to see herself as a skilled worker and give herself the recognition denied her by her employer (Macdonald 152).

Race as a Hiring Determinant for Nannies

Both Slimani's and Reid's novels give insight into the ways a nanny's race and ethnicity have bearing on the hiring process. In *The Perfect Nanny,* which is set in Paris, Myriam and her husband Paul choose their nanny Louise largely based on immigration status, race, and ethnicity; she is French Moroccan. Myriam, thus, opts for "otherness" in the woman they hire. Although the couple never precisely say that they ascribe meanings to demographic categories, they reject an immigrant candidate for her lateness and inability to speak French or English fluently—an undocumented woman whose immigration status, they feel, makes her more suited for housecleaning than childcare. Myriam's refusal to hire a North African woman, even an experienced caregiver, lies in the fear that "a tacit complicity and familiarity would grow between her and the nanny," leading to "immigrant solidarity" and the nanny asking for favours "in the name of their shared language and religion" (18). With this refusal, Myriam rejects an element of her identity and ties it to undesirable qualities in an employee and caregiver. Louise is white and a French citizen. The purposeful selection of a nanny of a different race implies the mother-employer's desire to draw a clear boundary between herself and the nanny in terms of power and roles. At the same time, the racially based selection suggests that although the mother-employer wants a "shadow mother," she fears that a nanny too much like herself could be a replacement instead of a proxy.

Alix's hiring of Emira in *Such a Fun Age* is not explicitly attributed to race, but Alix clearly seeks "otherness" in her caregiver, too. After interviewing a series of "Carlys and Caitlins, camp counselors and resident assistants"—mainly white, middle-class young women who are fans of Alix's organization, LetHerSpeak—she knows they would "never work" (30). Alix subsequently requests an interview with Emira through a babysitter-hiring site because she is intrigued by Emira's lack of profile photo. Upon meeting the young, African American woman, Alix thinks, "*Huh,*" perhaps a reaction to their racial difference. A few minutes into the interview, Alix sees Emira as hirable because she has never heard of Alix or LetHerSpeak and speaks little, a contrast to the other candidates and to Alix herself. Emira's quietness also makes her the ideal audience for Alix's verbose daughter, Briar. Alix's employment of an "other," an opposite, has a slightly different purpose than Myriam's because "the Carlys and Caitlins," who too much like Alix in their upward career climb and vocal enthusiasm for her brand of feminism, would threaten to usurp her career, her top priority. Alix takes pride and pleasure in the accolades of her career, earned through her writing and photo ops, a contrast to the inconsistent demands of mothering. This hiring implies that the mother-employer wants the shadow mother to replace her in the aspects of motherhood she finds uninteresting and exhausting: listening to the toddler daughter's constant chatter and handling the boring minutiae of raising a small child, such as hosting birthday parties and attending dance classes. In effect, this othered nanny should make the mother-employer look like a good mother because the mother-employer's energy can be directed towards only the aspects of motherhood she finds fulfilling. The othered nanny's role in redirecting the mother-employer's energy also allows the mother to excel at work.

Class Disparity and Conflict in the Nanny-Employer Relationship

Although a nanny's economic status is not necessarily a hiring determinant for the mother-employers, it is an inherent part of the carework system, since class disparities are common between nannies and the families they work for. Unacknowledged class differences may aggravate the nanny's sense of otherness and lead to misunderstanding and friction between the nanny and mother-employer. In *The Perfect Nanny,* Paul and Myriam are initially ignorant, perhaps willfully, of Louise's dire financial status because her perfect grooming and calm demeanour reflect their class-based sense of decorum. Louise's "old-fashioned manners" and "taste for perfection" seem to ally her with the bourgeoisie (25). Early in the novel, however, readers see that Louise polishes the same battered pair of shoes every day, regularly mends her worn clothing, and wakes at dawn to meticulously work on her hair and makeup, all means of concealing her poverty.

Myriam later becomes more aware of the vast economic gap between her and Louise, which creates tension between mother and nanny and, as Macdonald notes of carework, exposes differences in what the two women see as ideal mothering and caretaking. As Louise becomes more enmeshed in her position, often staying the night in her employers' home and thus witnessing more of their lives, Myriam grows concerned that her shopping will make Louise feel jealous or wounded. Thus,

Myriam hides new clothing purchases and gives Louise her hand-me-downs, subsequently receiving praise from Paul on her tact and generosity. However, financial assistance that could positively alter Louise's life, including a raise commensurate with her workload, is never addressed as an option by Myriam or Paul, who worry only that they may be accused of exploitation due to Louise's long hours.

On a Greek vacation with their children and the nanny, Myriam and Paul are embarrassed into silence and angered by Louise's revelation that she cannot swim, a privilege never afforded to her, and they "blam[e] [her] for having brought her poverty, her frailties ... here ... poison[ing] the day with her martyr's face" (69). Instead of understanding that Louise may have many valid reasons for not learning to swim, the couple is angry that this gap in Louise's knowledge keeps her from taking care of the children in the water. Myriam and Paul's defensive reaction connects to the employer's inability to understand the nanny outside a disparate, class-based set of experiences. Louise's socioeconomic status contributes to increased family-employee tension, thus reminding readers that otherness in the carework system, which keeps the nanny from ever truly being "one of the family," can encompass class.

Additionally, Louise's economic status seeps into her work, influencing the way she cares for the children and manages the household in ways that anger Paul and make Myriam nervous. Approaches to caregiving may be heavily influenced by class, not solely the product of race and culture, as Myriam believes. Therefore, a paranormal, hands-off management style that does not account for class differences between nanny and employer is likely to lead to conflict. For example, Louise applies a full face of makeup to Mila, an act that enrages Paul because he feels that Louise, with her low-class vulgarity, has made his daughter look like a sex worker. This is the beginning of Paul finding everything about Louise sickening, from her appearance to her caretaking methods. He resents the nanny for "turn[ing] him into a boss," thus ruining his sense of the paranormal management style in place (118). Paul's visceral disgust is an indictment of a carework system that often requires the poor to fulfill the personal needs of the upper middle class and wealthy, who might otherwise not regularly interact with people outside their class.

No less judgmental than Paul, Myriam finds Louise's propensity for clipping coupons amusing and sees Louise's insistence on using every scrap of food disturbing instead of being a result of her economic status. When Myriam buys a replacement cardigan Mila lost that Louise had searched for incessantly, Louise responds with, "I can't believe I tried so desperately to find it. And what does that mean? You get robbed, you don't take care of your things, but it doesn't matter because Mama will buy Mila a new cardigan?" (170). Louise's focus on saving money, which has never been important to Myriam, peaks when Myriam comes home to find the expired roast chicken she has thrown out pulled from the garbage and stripped down to the bones. She discovers that Louise made the children eat all the meat as part of a "game," and Myriam concludes that Louise is punishing her for being "wasteful, frivolous, casual" and, terrified, resolves to fire the nanny (170). This final instance of frugality before the murders reads as angry and even abusive on Louise's part. It indicates that attempts to ignore or dismiss class differences in the nanny and employer relationship by the mother-employer could culminate in tension, alienation, and outright flouting of what the mother-employer considers parenting norms.

Such a Fun Age also addresses inherent class disparities in the employer-caregiver relationship as a contributor to mother-nanny disconnect. Despite Alix's attempts to deepen her relationship with Emira and to learn more about her, Alix is only marginally aware of the class differences between the two that make a true personal connection impossible. For example, Alix's paying an extra twelve hundred dollars to Emira out of guilt for an incident with a security guard while babysitting is an example of using money as a quick fix for problems that may require more considered approaches. While it appears Alix will not miss this money, Emira sees the extra pay as monumental and the chance to buy something nice for herself. Alix's laissez-faire attitude towards spending and her tendency to link money with appreciation are similarly evident when she gives Emira her leftover expensive wine and extra groceries in an attempt to bond. Emira is aware that Alix does not extend the same generosity to her wealthy friends and sees her employer's gifts as one of many boundaries preventing a friendship between them. She "had met several 'Mrs. Chamberlains' before ... all rich and overly nice and particularly lovely to the people who served them" but not to their friends (187). In effect, the way the mother-employer spends money on the nanny can, based on socioeconomic differences, highlight the gap between the two instead of bridging it because most financial gestures other than a living wage and regular raises do nothing to change the nanny's circumstances.

The economic gap between nannies and the mothers who employ them may lead to stereotyping on the mother's part and a desire to compensate on the nanny's part. In one instance, when Alix hears Emira use the word "connoisseur," she is momentarily confused that this is the same woman who listens to hip-hop songs with titles such as "Dope Bitch," assuming that a good vocabulary and acceptance of "coarser" language are mutually exclusive (79). These assumptions about Emira's intellect are both class-coded and racially coded. Significantly, Alix knows of Emira's musical tastes only because she sneaks looks at Emira's phone, which speaks to Alix's sense of entitlement to her othered employee's private information. Conversely, Emira is embarrassed at the prospect of Alix seeing the video of her confrontation with the security guard, in which Emira speaks colloquially and confrontationally, showing a different side than her employer sees. When Emira discovers Alix's betrayal in leaking the video, however, she no longer feels the need to code switch and confronts Alix with language the mother-employer sees as distasteful and aggressive. While in Emira's apartment, Alix deems the young woman's futon to be a "glorified bean ba[g]" and finds it endearing that Emira still rents DVDs from Netflix, not considering that either are a result of the frugality required of her due to low wages (254). The mother-employer's complete inability to understand her employee's circumstances is evident when Alix is shocked to hear Emira has held a second job while also caring for Briar. It does not occur to Alix that Emira is not paid enough in carework to have that be her sole job. Alix's obliviousness, not an isolated example in the carework industry, emblematizes the mother-employer's unfounded idea that love of the child and loyalty to employers are "compensation" sufficient to keep the nanny in her position. Within these assumptions, the nanny's second job reads as a betrayal to the mother-employer.

Nanny as an Essential Part of the Family, Nanny as an Employee Taken for Granted

Because in-home childcare operates under family exchange norms, which blends the personal and professional, the nanny's role as shadow mother can render her essential and beloved, yet one whose labour the mother-employer feels entitled to. Effectively, the mother feels she needs the nanny but may not see the nanny as someone needing acknowledgment and appreciation, time off, increased compensation, or even consideration as a subject. In *The Perfect Nanny,* Louise initially seems like a panacea for Myriam's postpartum anxiety and frustration. After giving birth to Mila and then Adam, former lawyer Myriam feels that daily life is both overwhelming and monotonous, with her most mundane tasks made more complicated by the presence of her children. Desperate for alone time and feeling that her children are "eating [her] alive," Myriam wants to "scream like a lunatic in the street" (8) but pretends to be fine for months. Ashamed to be a stay-at-home mother and to have nothing to talk about but her children, Myriam shuns time with friends. However, a chance encounter that results in a job gives Myriam a sense of purpose and a need for someone to take over the bulk of daily childcare. Myriam posts job ads for a nanny, waiting for the right person, the "Savior" (14), who will effortlessly understand Mila and Adam's needs as she does. Louise, with her "face ... like a peaceful sea" and who immediately engages the children with imaginative play, seems the ideal candidate (19).

French professor Julie Rodgers notes that the beginning of Louise's time as the nanny for Myriam and Paul is marked by "a positive, gratifying, even rapturous caregiving exchange between Louise and the children" (387) and arguably between Louise and her employers. In this early idyll, Myriam sees Louise as magic, "a rare pearl"—a miracle worker who "has pushed back the walls" of the family's cramped, hastily put together apartment and "let the sun in" (25-26). Louise is given free rein on disciplining, cleaning, clothing, and engaging with Mila and Adam, rendering her a paranormally managed employee from the outset. Myriam admires how animatedly Louise plays with the children, how Mila and Adam are well-groomed and calm after a day with their caregiver. Although Louise has been hired as a non-live-in nanny, her job, which operates under family exchange norms, does not "seem to come with any specific terms, conditions or even boundaries" (Rodgers 387), and outside of childcare, she washes, mends, and cooks, taking on the household tasks Paul and Myriam are unmotivated to do. For Myriam, the shadow mother, "Louise arouses and fulfills the fantasies of an idyllic family life that Myriam guiltily nurses" (26) by taking on "ridiculous [domestic] preoccupations" (39) that Myriam would rather not be bothered with, and in a few weeks, the nanny has made herself indispensable. Consistent with Rodgers's idea that nannies are rendered invisible by their employers, who cannot see them outside their role as caregiver, Louise reassures Myriam with every chore she completes, "You won't even see me" (53). To fulfill her role as shadow mother and preserve the idea that Myriam is the primary parent, Louise, "works in the wings, discreet and powerful ... control[ling] the transparent wires without which the magic cannot occur" (53), her role again couched in the language of invisibility. Because Louise is "part of the world of children or the world of employees" (71), her invisibility is so extensive that she is incorporeal to her employers, and Paul is startled to realize when he touches Louise during a swimming lesson that she has a body like any other person. Louise's vital role speaks to the balancing act the nanny must operate under within family exchange norms. To feel essential and secure in her employment, she may be compelled to work longer hours than agreed upon or complete tasks outside childcare, such as housekeeping and event planning. Although these often uncompensated efforts might lead to a stronger sense of being "part of the family," the boundary between indispensable and taken for granted is easy to cross.

Slimani's narrator says of Louise, "You look at her and you do not see her. Her presence is intimate but never familiar" (53), which indicates the potential for Louise to be undervalued. A key aspect to the nanny-employer relationship is respect of the caregiver's time, which, through the novel, becomes nonexistent. Myriam's late nights at work become more frequent, and after weeks pass, she no longer lets Louise know when she will be home, even if it is 4:00 a.m., nor does Myriam resist when Louise insists on cooking, cleaning, and putting the children to bed after the workday should have long been finished. This blurred line between on-duty and off-duty hours leads to Louise sleeping at her employers' home multiple nights per week, and Myriam is both "embarrassed and secretly thrilled" (54) that she has a nanny/housekeeper who sacrifices her time in service to the family. Because of this inconsistency in Louise's status as live-in nanny and non-live-in nanny, "this constant to-ing and fro-ing ... leads to feelings of liminality, non-belonging and dislocation" (Rodgers 390), where Louise progressively centres her schedule only on going back and forth to her place of employment and feels her own home is a stopover, a place to wait until she can return to carework. Not long before Louise murders the children, Myriam has progressed to such a point of devaluing her employee's time that she thinks, "Louise is sulking? Oh, who cares!" (160) when coming home late to a silent nanny who quickly rushes out. In fact, Myriam notes that "she doesn't owe her nanny anything" (124) in terms of making Louise aware of scheduling changes well in advance. As Louise's story shows, the nanny's movement from essential part of the household to invisible employee can be a quick one if the mother-employer does not consistently recognize the nanny's skilled contributions and instead burdens her with expectations of personal sacrifice.

As a contrast to Louise, Emira in *Such a Fun Age* is treated dismissively as soon as she is hired; her Monday, Wednesday, Friday presence is a given, and her subjectivity is of no concern to Alix. Emira's initial treatment in her carework role connects to Alix feeling entitled to the shadow mother position, thereby casting off a large portion of the domestic burden. On her workdays, Emira is greeted by Alix rushing out the door, pushing Briar at her with cursory comments about what the child has eaten. If Emira asks Alix questions about events or presents for Briar, Alix tunes her out. Although Alix's paranormal management style, where she gives Emira no direction and asks her little about time spent with Briar, implies a certain trust, it also implies the preference of keeping her nanny at arm's length. Additionally, Alix's refusal to hire Emira full time suggests that she takes her for granted; only after the security guard incident does Alix ponder the possibility that Emira might quit, and the idea makes her "physically ill" (44). This is not due to worry over Emira's wellbeing but panic that Emira's possible departure would make Alix responsible for all childcare at the expense of her career. In this moment, Alix's view of Emira as indispensable is more about Emira doing the work Alix does not want to do, representing the contradictions that can be manifest in the mother-nanny relationship: The mother needs the nanny but under the conditions of taking on mundane and messy work effortlessly and invisibly.

When Alix worries that she may lose Emira, the panic manifests itself in overly solicitous questions and conversation starters directed at Emira to make her feel like an essential part of the household. However, as Emira notes, all she needs to feel like family is the legitimizing label of nanny instead of babysitter along with "a contract and a 1095 form" (266), which Alix is unwilling to offer. Because Emira feels unseen as a skilled worker under these conditions, she engages in Macdonald's "competency contests," internally berating Alix for lying to Briar about the child's dead goldfish and for the times Alix is capable of being an outstanding mother but chooses not to be. While Emira feels that she encourages Briar's curiosity, verbosity, and extroversion, she sees Alix as unappreciative of her daughter's gifts, preferring the easy cuteness of her infant, Catherine. Emira's competency is on full display when at the Chamberlain family's Thanksgiving table, she is the only one who notices that Briar is ill and catches the little girl's vomit in a napkin before Alix, oblivious to Briar's increasing wanness, can even register her child's discomfort. This is one instance where taking care of "a small unstructured person...le[aves] Emira feeling smart and in control" (Reid 209). Emira's struggle to feel competent and mature when Alix's treatment of her and apathy towards childcare seems to delegitimize and downplay her work is indicative of the societal value of carework that is inconsistent with how this work is compensated and regarded, often by the mother-employer.

Blurred Boundaries in the Nanny-Employer Relationship

A final outcome of family exchange norms in carework is a blurring of lines between professional and personal, not just within job expectations and hours but also within the ways the mother-employer relates to the nanny. Alternating between being a boss and a friend, between ignoring the nanny or bringing her closely into the fold creates a sense of inconsistency and even conflict and frustration. In both *The Perfect Nanny* and *Such a Fun Age,* such vacillations operate in the extreme and precipitate drastic outcomes, representing in a more dramatic fashion what can happen when the mother-nanny relationship has no clear delineation. For example, in *The Perfect Nanny,* despite Myriam's emphasis on not being too close to Louise, she has no qualms about Louise seeing her nude emerging from the shower. Although Myriam does not hire a North African nanny for fear of mother-nanny shared intimacies, she complains about her mother-in-law to Louise, who "takes Myriam's side with excessive zeal," making Myriam feel "simultaneously supported and slightly uneasy" (124). The mother-nanny confidences, however, are markedly one sided, with Myriam caring so little about Louise's life outside of work that she is startled when she sees Louise walking around town. She realizes that is the first time she has had any curiosity about Louise as a person, not a nanny. Macdonald argues that family exchange norms involve the employer feeling entitled to know about aspects of the nanny's personal life that the employer deems important. In one instance, Myriam scolds Louise as though she is a child when she and Paul find out about Louise's extensive debts, which have no bearing on her carework. When Myriam continues to question Louise about her owed taxes, she takes the nanny's silence as "a way of maintaining the frontier between our two worlds" (174), a frontier Myriam feels authorized to breach when she sees fit.

Paul and Myriam attempt to bring Louise into the fold of their personal lives in social situations, but because they have nothing in common with their nanny outside the children, these interactions are often uncomfortable. When the couple invites Louise to sit down with them and their friends to enjoy the dinner the nanny has thoughtfully prepared with everyone's preferences and allergies in mind, Louise "is as nervous as a foreigner, an exile who doesn't understand the language being spoken around her" (59). As "fictive kin," Louise is welcome to prepare a lavish meal for a large group hosted by her employers every Friday night, but as a guest at the table she has elaborately decorated, Louise does not fit in and cannot contribute to talk of private schools, Paul and Myriam's career successes, and property values. When she withdraws to the kitchen, invisible, no one notices. On a vacation to Greece with Paul, Myriam, and the children, Louise goes to dinner with her employers while the children sleep, and she finally feels like part of the family: "She has the intimate conviction now, the burning and painful conviction that her happiness belongs to them. That she is theirs and they are hers" (78). In contrast, Paul and Myriam dread having dinner with her, knowing they have little to talk about besides the children, and they drink in excess to overcome potential awkwardness. After Paul and Myriam retire to their bedroom, the illusion of Louise as family is shattered when Adam cries, and she is the one expected to go to him. Her vacation is simply an extension of her employment, not an opportunity for leisure time as it is for her employers.

Through many examples of blurred lines between personal and professional, most perpetuated by Myriam and Paul and not Louise, Myriam expresses fear and concern that the relationship has progressed to the point that Louise "has embedded herself so deeply in their lives that it now seems impossible to remove her" (Slimani 175). Myriam compares Louise to a "wounded lover" (175) due to the professional boundary-breaching nature of their mother-nanny relationship while wishing that she could snap her fingers to make Louise disappear, taking with her the devotion Myriam once thought brought so much light into the home. Tragically, the blurred boundaries accompanying family exchange norms in Louise's carework and Myriam's paranormal management style allow information and hints about Louise's serious personal issues to fall through the cracks. The hands-off style of paranormal management and the mother-employer's selectivity of the nanny's personal details to focus on permit the most vital information—the nanny's childcare capabilities—to go unchecked.

Flashbacks to the past characterize Louise as prone to violent outbursts, in one case against her daughter. Before Louise's history of anger and sadism is revealed, hints of these inclinations emerge in her caretaking of Mila and Adam, some visible to her employers. During a game of hide and seek, for example, Louise hides for so long that the children "scream ... cry ... fall into despair" (44). Adam panics, sobbing, and Mila soon joins him, both thinking that their caretaker has abandoned them. When Louise emerges from her hiding place, knocking Mila down and causing her to hit her head, Louise is "triumphant ... staring down at [Mila] from the heights of ... victory" (Slimani 45-46). On an occasion where Mila wanders away from her, Louise hugs the child tightly and lavishes her with affectionate words while onlookers are present, but when the two are alone, "Louise holds Mila more and more strongly against her ... crush[ing] the little girl's torso against her until she begs: 'Stop, Louise, I can't breathe'" (92). After Louise threatens Mila by noting that a pedophile will snatch her the next time she wanders away, Mila has to bite the nanny to free herself from the iron grip, leaving a mark that Myriam later discovers. During the Greece vacation, Louise pushes Mila when the little girl insists the two swim together, an act

Paul and Myriam witness. Although the couple are not to blame for the horrific deaths of their children, their focus on the wrong details concerning Louise sets the stage for her unfathomable act.

Kiley Reid's *Such a Fun Age* ends in a less dark manner than *The Perfect Nanny*, but blurred lines between the personal and professional in the nanny-mother relationship perpetuated by the mother-employer make for an acrimonious ending. Professionally, Emira maintains a line between herself and Alix, referring to her employer as Mrs. Chamberlain, wearing a uniform each time she comes to work, and revealing little about her personal life other than a few friends' names. Alix, however, wants to treat Emira as both babysitter and friend, inviting her to share confidences about dates and social outings. Of this behaviour, Reid says: "I think that Alix is really lonely. But I also think there's complications in the fact that Alix hires Emira as a babysitter. And she asks her for a lot.... And suddenly it's, can you have a glass of wine with me, which is almost...will you be my friend? And unfortunately, for Emira, the power struggle is different. And so she's not really in a position to say no" (qtd. in Fadel). Reid offers insight into the power differential in the mother-nanny dynamic, which makes a true friendship impossible and renders a mother-employer's push for such a friendship as a way to ineffectively gloss over that gap.

Making Alix's approach even more ineffective is her focus on surface elements with Emira, who sees Alix's questions about her favourite cocktail and Friday night plans as superficial and unimportant. To Emira, Alix would not have felt shocked and betrayed at the discovery of her nanny's second job had she asked deeper questions. Similarly, Alix sees a friendship with Emira as an inevitable outcome of liking Alix's optics, the elements of her life that make her look like a good and well-rounded person, such as having a close Black friend and displaying serious literature in her home. Alix's goal, she thinks to herself, is to replicate the close relationships she views between her friends and their nannies; however, she does not understand that her friends asking their nannies to pick up emergency birth control or asking the nannies to pretend to be their employers to pushy salespeople does not constitute friendship. Furthermore, Alix's friendly gestures of inviting Emira to Thanksgiving dinner or to Briar's third birthday party mean little in creating a personal bond when Emira feels compelled to engage in care-work at these family events.

Alix's boundary-blurring behaviours with Emira do not end with invitations to drink wine, have dinner, or tell secrets. Spurred by Emira's reticence about personal matters, Alix intrusively looks at Emira's phone when Emira is caring for Briar. She reads her sitter's text messages, looks at her music playlist, analyzes her conversations, and researches the artists Emira listens to—an echo of Myriam and Paul reading Louise's mail and discovering her financial situation. While Emira may prefer to leave aspects of her personal life private in conversations with her employer, Alix feels entitled to this knowledge. Additionally, similar to Myriam's tirades regarding her mother-in-law to Louise, Alix uses Emira as a sounding board to vent her cruel observations of one of Peter's coworkers, a kind woman who wants to be Alix's friend. Instead of establishing intimacy, this behaviour makes Emira wary of Alix's rudeness. A month after the security guard incident, Alix "develop[s] feelings toward Emira that [aren't] completely unlike a crush," and one evening, when offering wine to Emira to get her to open up about her love life, Alix realizes "She [is] very much courting her babysitter" (76). Acting almost as a jealous lover and as an entitled employer in the family exchange system, Alix is upset when she sees on Emira's phone that the young woman has plans she had not divulged to Alix when asked. This sense of entitlement represents on a broader scale the unfettered access to the caregiver that is often expected by the mother-employer, who perhaps feels that the nanny's role as paid part of the family requires her to be an open book.

Alix's escalating intrusion into Emira's personal life and her desire to make a friend of her employee culminates disastrously in Alix's discovery that Emira has been dating her ex-boyfriend, Kelley, with whom she had a bitter breakup over issues tied to race and class. In response, Alix tries to cajole Emira into breaking up with him, and, when that does not work, she leaks the video of the security guard incident in a way that implicates Kelley and thrusts Emira in an unwanted spotlight. Ultimately, Emira suffers from the fallout of Alix's refusal to leave a professional relationship in the professional realm. Emira discovers Alix's deceit after breaking up with Kelley, she is subject to constant media scrutiny, and she quits her job when she realizes she has been lied to and used as a public relations tool for Alix's reputation. Through Alix's various manipulations and attempts to insinuate herself into Emira's life, one larger aspect of the nanny-mother relationship is clear: When the mother-employer blurs the line between professional and personal, it is not out of interest or affection but out of the desire for control.

Conclusion

Current popular literary portrayals of nannies appear inexplicably bleak and dramatic, with relationships between caregivers and families marked by tension that leads to arguments, terminated employment, even murder. A close reading of Leila Slimani's *The Perfect Nanny* and Kiley Reid's *Such a Fun Age* classifies the darkness and drama as symbolic of persistent problems in carework. Cameron Macdonald's *Shadow Mothers,* a sociological perspective on the relationships between nannies and the mothers who employ them, provides an apt vocabulary and framework for the phenomena in carework that breeds these problems. Applying her concepts of shadow mothers, family exchange norms, and paranormal management to the nannies and nanny-mother relationship in Slimani's and Reid's works reveals the complex roles race and class have within the carework system. Along with racial and economic issues, a close reading of bleaker nanny-centric literature reveals that the carework system is mired in boundary issues that require clearer expectations of and more respect for people paid to care for children.

Works Cited

Canfield, David. "A New Literary *Age*." *Entertainment Weekly,* Jan. 2020, pp. 108-109.

Corrigan, Maureen. "*The Perfect Nanny* is the Working Mother's Murderous Nightmare." *Fresh Air, NPR,* 22 Jan. 2018, https://www.npr.org/2018/01/22/579673595/the-perfect-nanny-is-the-working-mothers-murderous-nightmare. Accessed 18 Oct. 2023.

Fadel, Leila. "Kiley Reid on *Such a Fun Age*." *Weekend Edition Saturday. NPR,* 28 Dec. 2019, https://www.npr.org/2019/12/28/792022308/kiley-reid-on-such-a-fun-age. Accessed 18 Oct. 2023.

Luscombe, Belinda. "Leila Slimani is Not Afraid to Go There." *Time,* 4 Feb. 2019, p. 99.

Macdonald, Cameron Lynne. *Shadow Mothers: Nannies, Au Pairs, and the Micropolitics of Mothering.* University of California Press, 2010.

Michel, Sonya. "Beyond Mary Poppins: The Politics and Economics of Real-Life Nannies." *American Interest,* vol. 14, no. 6, 2019, pp. 40-43.

Reid, Kiley. *Such a Fun Age.* Putnam, 2019.

Rodgers, Julie. "Deviant Care: *Chanson Douce* and the Killer Nanny." *Australian Journal of French Studies,* vol. 57, no. 3, 2020, pp. 381-95.

Slimani, Leila. *The Perfect Nanny.* Penguin, 2016.

Chapter 9

Seeing Beyond Black and White in the Mother-Nanny Novel: Problematics, Purpose, and Possibilities of Empathy

Katie B. Garner

The mother-nanny relationship is an immensely complex matrix, in which issues of gender, economics, class, immigration law, parenting norms, feminism, cultural and religious beliefs, and more collide beneath the glossy veneer of "being one of the family" and altruistic carework.[1] While proxy mothering is expected of all nannies, Black and brown women can be charged with even more additional labour —that of assuaging or reinforcing an employer's subjectivity regarding being racist and engaging in race-based oppression. The United States (US) is far from postracial, but American women are living and mothering in a time when issues regarding class and race are more widely understood by the typical fiction reader than thirty years ago when Jamaica Kincaid's *Lucy* was first published.[2] Still, the nanny novels discussed herein, *Substitute Me* by Lori L. Tharps (2010) and *Such a Fun Age* by Kiley Reid (2019), challenge white readers to develop more astute empathy via their understanding of how power and race shape domestic carework in the US, despite Reid, and many Black theorists, remaining leery of the ways that white consumers of Black art may be extractive or may abdicate their responsibilities toward more active anti-racist work under the false belief that consuming Black art is enough. While the ways empathy functions in readers or is developed by authors is a key aspect of this work, the more pressing question concerns how Tharps' and Reid's novel can (unknowingly?) inspire progressive change in the mother-nanny relationship.

The stakes for deepening understanding and empathy in mother-employers are high.[3] Many nannies are women of colour, immigrants, and/or are financially struggling, with the average pay in the United States being $11.60/hour.[4] White women are complicit in perpetuating broken systems, according to economist Nina Banks, who argues that white women have a "material interest in maintaining White patriarchy as a system of control over racialized women's labor power" (355-56), since, by doing so, they themselves can more freely engage in waged work and pursue interests disconnected from domestic labour and carework. In "The Nanny Question in Feminism," political scientist Joan Tronto argues that childcare should be a public undertaking, not a private burden, and she also questions if white, Western feminists have assisted in the development and maintenance of current patriarchal and capitalist systems when they hire women with fewer social and economic privileges to complete reproductive labour. Many authors frame this latter issue in stark terms, including Grace Chang, Mignon Duffy, Mary Romero, Regina Jackson, Saira Rao, and many more. (Aya Kitamura addresses this in chapter eleven.)

Although trickle-down economics has been debunked as a sustainable financial system, a twinning occurs in trickle-down feminism, when white women erroneously believe they are helping someone less privileged by providing them employment. This is not to argue that all white women are engaging in these practices maliciously; they, too, are navigating very flawed systems of waged work and care responsibilities—a point that I will return to in the conclusion. White women have, however, been historically able to engage with issues concerning marginalized women as they wish rather than as a matter of necessity, and these novels by Black women can serve as powerful ways to engage white women. Although the voices of all women of colour are important, the figures and experiences of African American nannies are notable in the US due to the country's history of slavery, the ensuing ambivalence many African American and Black women feel about working in domestic service and carework, and, more recently, the intensity of white, liberal performativity.[5]

This chapter examines how two contemporary novels by Black, female authors that centre a relationship between a white, female mother-employer and a Black, female nanny can impact how white women frame their thinking about their role as a mother-employer. I argue that the novels herein are particularly important to white, female readers who employ childcare providers in part because, like testimonios, they "revers[e] the traditional direction of the anthropological gaze" and have the "potential to call into question [the] readers' very self-concept" (Nance 58). I contend if one accepts that novels can promote the development of empathy in readers, then it is reasonable to assert that reading novels about the mother-employer/nanny relationship may help mother -employers become more capable at navigating thorny labour relationships—a skill that would help all parties involved.

Encountering Empathy in the Hallways of Motherhood Literature

Novelists are often tasked with helping readers achieve a sense of empathy. The fly in the proverbial ointment, according to literary scholar Suzanne Keen, is that even if (and she retains strict allegiance to the "if") reading novels leads to increased empathy, this knowledge does not necessarily transfer into prosocial behaviour. Empathy is often described as a feeling that extends beyond sympathy and requires us to step into the shoes of another person. Empathy can be thorny, though, according to philosopher Mariana Ortega, who warns, "Ignorance goes hand in hand with the production of knowledge about the experience of women of color" (62). Arguably, the issue at hand here is not only ignorance but also what actions are undertaken based on ignorance, particularly when a person has more social power than those for whom they are speaking. Spanish literature scholar Kimberly A. Nance similarly cautions that "Obscuring power relations has tended to benefit the person already in power, either materially—or, in the case of people who would prefer not to be oppressors nor benefit from it, psychologically" (144).

Perhaps most problematically for this work, Reid hazards against focussing too strongly on race in her novel *Such a Fun Age*, explaining that she wants the novel to be enjoyed rather than tell readers "this is how you shouldn't be" (qtd. in Proudfoot). For Reid, reading novels as instructional is "missing the story ... on a very basic level," adding, "[to] layer black artists with other responsibilities like teaching you something new about race is just additional labour that a black artist shouldn't be faced with" (qtd. in Proudfoot). These are all valid criticisms; empathy is not a simple shortcut, identification can be distorted, power can be misused, and positioning art as instructional is problematic. My intent is not to disagree with Reid (or the others) but to consider an additive model in which we avoid thinking in terms of "either/or" and incorporate a "both/and" approach. Indeed, Reid notes that she enjoys reading novels empathically, and I posit that we can appreciate novels for the artistic works they are *and* allow the messages in these novels to challenge us as white readers to think critically about our connection to and within systems of racism, classism, and misogyny. Literary theorist Rita Felski argues that "only by internalizing the expectations of these others" that we acquire "interior depth" or question the "norms and values that formed us" (32). English literature scholar Kimberly Chabot Davis acknowledges in *Beyond the White Negro: Empathy and Anti-Racist Reading* that white readers may be extractive, mimics, and self-centered when consuming work by Black artists, but the empathy that art often evokes may also "lead white empathizers to a deeper understanding of racial injustice and the need for public action" (8). Relevant to this chapter, Davis also questions if public action should be defined beyond "elections, protest movements, and collective organizing," since "local, interpersonal encounters" can also be "effective social change" (109). In other words, it is unlikely that too many white mother-employers will join organizations that advocate for domestic workers (although this is a possibility) after reading a single novel, but it seems quite possible that reading the novels in this chapter (and others) can shift perspectives and actions in their own homes.

While Reid is correct in noting that Black authors should not be *charged* with shaping social norms of race or crafting didactic novels, it is impossible for readers, all readers, not to bring their own subjectivity to their reading and be shaped by what they read—recognizing both their strengths and flaws in the characters novelists create. Felski argues that "aesthetic value is inseparable from use" and that texts "lack the power to legislate their own effects" (8, 9). Instead, a reader remains in flux based on their subjectivity. It is this mutability that permits change.

This will be a key point of discussion throughout this chapter, not because reading *automatically* leads to empathy or to action but because it has the *potential* to do so. Nance posits that the critical role of testimonio authors, for example, is to ensure that readers understand that the "obligation to help does not more properly belong to others who are more responsible, more suited, and more likely to help in the reader's stead," and, importantly, the "reader must not be allowed to substitute other actions (like reading, for instance) for social action" (80). My intent is not to argue that Tharps and Reid should be positioned as activists in the way that testimonios writers are; rather, it is to assert the importance of accepting social issue writing's dual role in terms of shaping conversations, promoting empathy, challenging ideas, and even creating changes in behaviour.

Writing in Black and White: *Minding Ben, Substitute Me,* and *Such and Fun Age*

As we look at the connective tissue of these novels, it is useful to consider the similarities, which is one rationale for including these as companion texts. In *Substitute Me* and *Such a Fun Age* the nannies are both Black; Zora and Emira identify as African American.[6] Both the nannies are young, heterosexual, cisgender women under the age of thirty, and have had significant formal education. Neither woman has children of their own, is wealthier than their employer, nor is experiencing profound poverty. Both women encounter the types of race- and class-based oppression inherent in the biracial mother–nanny labour relationship and contemporary life more broadly in the US. Their mother-employers, Kate in *Substitute Me* and Alix in *Such a Fun Age*, are both white, cisgender, in a heterosexual marriage, employed, have had ample formal education, are financially comfortable, and live on the East Coast. Kate and Alix are aware, to differing extents, of the ways they are asked to navigate racism and classism, and it is this awareness, in part, that challenges readers to learn vicariously. Both *Substitute Me* and *Such a Fun Age* are engrossing social novels that could be deemed middle-brow in the sense that they are well-crafted yet remain quick-paced and entertaining in ways literature can eschew.[7] The following sections will provide a deeper analysis of the two novels.

Substitute Me

Unlike *Such a Fun Age*, *Substitute Me* shares the first-person narrative space between nanny and mother-employer. This technique lends itself to building readers' empathy as they may commiserate with a character and (learn to) understand how the character's actions or words are perceived by another character. The nanny in this novel is Zora Anderson, a thirty-year-old, African American, college-educated women. The mother-employer is Kate, a white marketing executive who is married to Brad. They have one child, Oliver. Brad is "outraged" that he and Kate have been "sucked into the New York City mind-set where hiring a Black nanny goes with the lifestyle" (177). Kate, conversely, holds what she deems is a pragmatic perspective, namely that it is reasonable to hire help when possible—an idea espoused by her mother. Kate's argument that "Not every person on this earth is destined to be a white-collar worker" (81-82) strips bare the neoliberal perspective of those who willfully ignore the overrepresentation of Black and brown women in carework, domestic labour, and other essential, under-remunerated positions.

Substitute Me opens with Zora heading to Kate's home in a Brooklyn neighbourhood that is "on the edge of respectability" (5). Zora, who was raised in an upper-middle-class family, remains ambivalent about the interview, claiming "working as a domestic for a White family" would mean a "thousand slave women were probably rolling in their graves as they watched her get ready to go back to the big house" while her parents will "completely disown her" (35, 1). This admission serves as a painful juxtaposition to Kate's economics-driven rationality. Zora admits she never felt "inadequate" but was not "oblivious to racism," since there was "no such thing as that much privilege" (35). Readers immediately see Zora become othered when Kate claims she cannot place Zora's accent. Zora is from Michigan. Because the narrative space is shared, readers learn that Kate feels "really White" for assuming Zora was from "an island somewhere" like so many of the other immigrant nannies in Brooklyn (9). Continuing the onslaught of race-based gaffes, Kate describes Brad as a "bleeding-heart" guy who craves "meaningful" work like traveling "to Africa to help save all the poor starving orphans" (39). Zora chafes at the comment but remains silent. Still, readers are privy to her telling herself that she "wasn't being paid to educate this woman on the vast economic diversity on the African continent" (39). In this response, white readers are privy to the ways Black people, including employees, take on additional labour by serving as teachers, a point Reid implicates in her argument that Black authors should not have to take on additional labour.

These are the awkward moments that likely cause white readers to pause and wonder if they have made similar blunders while also seeing how these blunders hurt racialized people. In reference to the mother-employer in her own novel, Reid cautions, "Many white readers ... work overtime to point out Alix's flaws, potentially in a way that separates her from themselves," adding that the "liberal élite" tend to highlight "overtly racist behaviour and say, 'I recognise this behaviour as bad, and therefore, it's not me, and there's no way that I could contribute to white supremacy'" (qtd. in Law). In *Substitute Me*, Kate reveals her allegiance to norms of whiteness and neoliberalism, while readers (hopefully) witness how benign racism infiltrates common interactions with Black (and brown) people while power differentials linked to employment can silence those with less power and add additional labour to already difficult work.

Kate hires Zora believing her decision is based on her comfort with a woman close in age; she fails to recognize that she is closer in class as well. When readers later hear from Zora, the authenticity of this easy connection becomes questionable. Zora explains that she knows what mother-employers desire; she must "play down her college education and her upper-middle-class suburban upbringing" [and] "play up her love for children, her homemaking skills, her ambition to do nothing in the world except care for somebody else's offspring" (36). Kate's comfort is based largely on Zora's (unrecognized) labour and ability to perform deference even while she recognizes and finds comfort in their common class placement.

Overall, Kate is magnanimous, although it is clear she does so in part to make her own life as an employer easier. Kate calls if she will be late, pays extra if Zora agrees to stay, and generally treats Zora with authentic respect. Like many mother-employers, Kate seems to genuinely struggle with how to define her relationship with Zora because she "didn't want to belittle Zora and introduce her as the nanny," but "she didn't feel justified calling her a friend" (107). Kate does not see herself as "friends" with Zora, but states, "It's not like we're not, either," adding, "I mean, we could be friends" (91). Regardless of the veracity of this statement, Kate remains pragmatic about her role as an employer, claiming she "knew if Zora was happy outside of work, she'd be happier at work," and ultimately, it is inferred, be a better employee (170). She recognizes that their relationship is commodified, and there are calculated (albeit perhaps mutually beneficial) ways to extract additional labour. Sondra, Zora's friend, astutely claims Kate "wants to feel like you're her friend so she doesn't have to feel guilty for asking you to work late every damn day of the week" (98). Muddying the matter even more, though, Zora pushes back, telling Sondra that she appreciates the extra money, and because Oliver is asleep, she can take advantage of the Carters' cable television subscription, which she cannot afford. She does not admit that she cannot afford cable because of Kate's low compensation wages. In this context, the novel does not suggest that there is a clear right answer and often there isn't one. White mother-employers are, however, encouraged to examine their own behaviour when it comes to blurring the lines between professional help and the unmonetized care often associated with kin and friends as well as whether the person they have hired desires the extra hours.

Like Reid, Tharps shows that white people are not the only ones who hold misconceptions regarding a person's racial-ethnic identification. In *Substitute Me*, Zora's friend Angel, who is also Black and is a nanny, believes women like Kate and her own (white) employer are "pretty stupid" because "they ask us to come into their homes, take care of their children, clean their houses, and feed their husbands, and then they expect their men not to fall in love or at least into bed with us" (296). Angel proudly claims, "We clean better, take care of their kids better, and fuck their husbands a whole lot better" (296). Zora, like Kate, pushes back, telling Angel: "What you just said is so racist and fucked up" (296). Mirroring this conversation, Kate's friend, Fiona, bluntly asserts that "Black women are naturally better caretakers than White women," which Kate expresses relief upon hearing as she agrees (288). While on the surface, this comment may seem like a compliment, the fact that she has associated specific skills with a specific racial-ethnic group is racist. Fiona continues, however, stating, "There's something else all Black women are good at," but here Kate tells her friend to stop because she feels "equal parts offended (for Zora's sake) and worried (for her own)" (289). By aligning these two statements in the novel, Tharps encourages readers to see how racism, regardless of whether it is complimentary is still racism, and yet, Zora remains a problematic character, a point I will return to shortly.

Fiona and Angel, both very minor characters, iterate what circulates culturally, but Tharps chooses not to have the novel's protagonists utter these racist comments. While both protagonists are not passively silent, only Zora is clear in naming the racist words for what they are. Tharps may want readers to feel empathy for both Kate and Zora, arguably with the hope that readers will continue to identify with them and learn from them. The recognition some white mother-employers might have with Kate encourages them to question if they would respond similarly to a friend like Fiona, but Kate's confession that she is selfishly concerned about Zora's impact on her marriage rather than being more forceful in her pushback against Fiona raises questions. Zora's response to Angel, while direct and arguably didactic, could be diluted in readers who point to the ways everyone is racist and do not recognize the differences between being prejudiced and having access to the power required to be racist.

As the novel progresses and Zora stays late more often, she and Brad begin eating dinner together. Like Kate, Brad benefits from Zora working additional hours as she prepares meals, provides amiable company, and helps with Oliver. Their shared time leads to Brad initiating a sexual relationship with Zora. While Zora offers enthusiastic consent, the power differentials between worker and employer make her acquiescence troubling. Published before the #Metoo movement, the novel presents the shift from platonic to sexual as relatively unproblematic. Kate's own racist thoughts become much more transparent after she discovers the affair. When Kate confronts Zora, Kate claims she wants to prevent the situation from escalating because "Zora might beat her senseless," and she tells Brad he is "free to run off" with his "little Black whore" (316, 311). The first comment reveals Kate's belief that Black people are inherently violent, and the second echoes the very language Kate objected to previously. The fact that these ugly statements are placed so late in the novel restricts readers from fully grappling with the (possible) shift in a central character, whom Tharps previously presented as benign (at least on the spectrum of bad employers) and relatively empathetic. It is difficult to discern the purpose of such a shift in Kate, and, while racism is still embedded in the fabric of our society, it seems unlikely that Kate would say this in a novel published after 2015 for reasons

I will explicate in the next section.

In the epilogue, which is set a year later, Fiona and Kate discuss the fact that Zora and Brad are still together. Fiona expresses surprise that the "quickie jungle-fever thing" was still in effect, to which Kate says, "Brad's always wanted to be different and countercultural" (341, 342). Kate calls into question whether all white Americans hide racist beliefs under the skim coat of social acceptability, which bubble to the surface when their position of privilege is challenged. It is difficult to determine if Tharps's presentation of Kate's strengths as a mother-employer and Brad and Zora's choice to pursue a relationship mask deep injustices in the mother-nanny labour relationship as it exists in a racist and patriarchal society. Readers could easily leave the novel believing Kate was the one who had been wronged, which ultimately releases her from the less problematic (at least in this novel) issue of neoliberal care circuits. Tharps also relies on the troubling trope of punishing a mother for working outside the home and abdicating her feminized role as the primary caregiver. This book was published at roughly the same time as a spat of neoliberal/choice feminist books valourizing working motherhood were published (e.g., Linda Hirshman, 2006; Sheryl Sandberg, 2013; and Anne-Marie Slaughter, 2015). Race, in other words, is arguably not a primary aspect of the plot, at least not the in the way that it is in *Such a Fun Age*. It is difficult to discern if this makes it easier for white mother-employers to engage, as they may feel less threatened, and yet, the conclusion of the novel troublingly suggests that Kate is the more sympathetic figure.

Such a Fun Age

Told in third-person omniscient, *Such a Fun Age* is set in Philadelphia in 2015, towards the end of former President Obama's tenure and before the political schisms of the ensuing president. For further context, significant media attention was being given to the murders of unarmed Black and brown men by police officers, including Michael Brown in August 2014 and George Floyd in May 2020, along with the ensuing political unrest, some of which was led by the Black Lives Matter movement. Although the previous novel challenges structural racism via an examination of individual characters, Reid's work, despite her seeming unwillingness in interviews to enter the political fray, is more direct in her engagement with current racial events. A critical early plot point occurs in a "rich people grocery store" (6), where Emira, an African American, young woman, is questioned for being with her charge, a young, white girl named Briar. Called in after-hours by her employer, Alix Chamberlain, due to an emergency, Emira is dressed for an evening out with friends. Readers are exposed to the surveillance of Black bodies; the sense of self-protection Emira experiences when challenged by the security guard; her eagerness to have him "hear the way she could talk" (10) so she would not be mistaken for someone with less education and social habitus; and the white woman (i.e., "Karen") who initiated Emira's interrogation.

This scene serves as a catalyst for Alix to re-examine her relationship with Emira. Like Kate in *Substitute Me*, Alix can be a thoughtful employer. She is considerate of Emira's time and happiness and looks for ways to show her appreciation, including buying an expensive mixer for Emira, who is considering a career as a chef. Although this act is problematic due to the motives that gird her choices, a point that will be discussed later, Alix models many aspects of being a good employer. As a social media influencer and head of her self-branded company #LetHer Speak, Alix is a modern, neoliberal feminist. Though not uber wealthy, she is stereotypically "white," which is marked by her CB2 purchases and owning twenty-dollar, trendy mascara. Having recently moved from trendy Brooklyn, Alix sneers at her white, suburban peers in Philadelphia, who carry dated Coach purses or wear t-shirts that drolly read "Plank Now, Wine Later." Alix is particularly concerned that Emira will view her as equally unhip. Interestingly, while Alix tries to keep her distance from her white, suburban peers, Emira disdains Alix's snubbing of these women, seeing them as kinder and more authentic than Alix.

Alix is loath to be viewed as the "textbook rich white person," believing she is not inherently that person, and she fears Emira views her the way Alix had viewed the "annoying Upper East Side moms" (139)—entitled, snobby, and out of touch. However, between cutting off tags from clothes she purchases so Emira will not see their cost, pretending she will eat leftovers but ordering sushi after Emira leaves, and hiding her Marie Kondo book, since Emira might think "how privileged are you that you need to buy a hardcover book that tells you how to get rid of all your other expensive shit" (139), Alix demonstrates a clear discomfort around class and race. She problematically "fantasize[s]" that Emira will see the "truest version of herself," (139) which is a woman who is close friends with a (wealthy) Black woman, Tamra; who has read everything from Toni Morrison; and whose favourite shoes are from Payless. As Nance alluded to earlier, readers witness a turning of the male/white gaze as Alix contorts herself to be appealing to Emira in ways that, importantly, are often missteps and do not ultimately upset the inherent power differentials connected to their roles as employer and employee let alone their placement in racist and classist structures more broadly.

In her quest to be accepted and reify her own liberal political leanings, Alix insentiently sees Emira as a means of showcasing her progressive outlook. In the modern politics of liberalism, Alix craves access to Emira's life as a young, Black woman. Reid insists in interviews that she holds compassion for Alix, and, as stated, readers likely empathize with her. Still, it is easy to read Alix as a self-centred social climber whose identity as a mother serves her public role as a woman who "has it all" and who hires a Black nanny as "proof" to herself and others of her progressive ideals. When considering her Thanksgiving invite list, for instance, Alix was "so pleased as she counted in her head how many African American guests would be present at her Thanksgiving table" (160). For Alix, acceptance by Black people both absolves her of the privileges she has gained from white supremacist institutions in America and gives her credibility as a nonracist, liberal white person. However, Alix does little else to promote racial equity, including paying Emira a living wage. Alix seems to want to both reap the benefits of her race and class privilege while not having to admit, even to Emira, the extent of her privilege. Unlike Kate in *Substitute Me*, Alix knows the right things to say, such as her comment after the grocery store: "I'm not going to even pretend to know what you're feeling right now or how you felt last night because I never truly will, but I just want to extend my support in whatever way you need it" (50). However, at the root, issues of racism still bear down, with Alix both participating in and benefitting from racist structures, most markedly low-wage childcare.

Despite some notable strengths as an employer, Alix displays troubling boundary crossing, which is rooted in complicated feelings for the young woman as well as her entitlement based on race and employment status. Alix frequently reads Emira's private text messages and attempts to find out more about her social life online. While their relationship remains completely platonic, Alix contemplates whether her "feelings toward Emira ... weren't completely unlike a crush," particularly when she is "excited to hear Emira's key in the door," feels "disappointed when it was time for her to leave," and basks in the sense she had "done something right" if "Emira laughed or spoke [to her] without being prompted" (76). Alix does consider whether Emira's laughter, which is "backed by a small token of toleration" (81), is coerced via the power structure of their relationship and is therefore polite rather than authentic. She wrongly concludes that this is not a crucial impediment to them forming an equitable friendship. The tension between Alix craving intimacy, even perhaps ownership, and Emira's calculated warmth provides an opportunity for white, mother-employers to investigate the ways they expect the nannies they hire to be emotionally available to them for comradery, entertainment, or personal validation.

Emira is a millennial everywoman who does not "love doing anything" but "does not terribly mind doing anything either" (37). Her two siblings are successful while Emira still flounders with a part-time babysitting position that she pairs with a part-time secretarial position. Combined, the two jobs barely cover her bills. Emira blames herself for the altercation at the grocery store, thinking, "This wouldn't have happened if you had a real fucking job.... You wouldn't leave a party to babysit. You'd have your own health insurance. You wouldn't be paid in cash. You'd be a real fucking person" (39-40). Reid indicates throughout the novel that despite the way babysitting is socially belittled, childcare is worthy work, and Emira does express pride in her ability to connect with and support Briar. Emira's self-abasement for not fulfilling her role as a neoliberal subject is challenging to read, and she elicits considerable empathy from readers. Reid takes pains to show that the problem with childcare is not that the work is unimportant, but that it offers scant remuneration. Mother-employers are thus encouraged to question their own role in maintaining flawed systems even though some mother-employers may accurately cite financial limitations due to their own under-remunerated work and their unwilling position in an under-supported care infrastructure.

Emira is relatively indifferent to Alix, whom she views as similar to the many other "white women [who] were often overly accommodating to her when she found herself in specific white spaces" (88). Emira recognizes Alix's push for friendship as race- (and possibly class-) based: "Mrs. Chamberlain would never display the same efforts of kindness with her friends as she did with Emira" such as "accidentally" ordering extra food and practicing the type of maternalism sociologist Judith Rollins warns against. Emira is pragmatic, claiming that if she weren't working for Alix, she would be working for another white woman just like her. Overall, Alix is a minor figure in Emira's life, though. Emira's attention is spread between her female friends, her boyfriend Kelley, figuring out her life, caring for Briar, and reconciling her ambivalence about childcare. This decentring of Alix encourages white, mother-employer readers to consider not only the personal lives of the women they hire but interrogate their possible belief that they are central figures in the lives of the childcare providers they hire.

Alix and Emira's relationship shifts after Alix asks Emira to purchase a replacement fish for the one that died before Briar realizes what has happened. Unbeknownst to Alix, Emira chafes at Alix's unwillingness to tell Briar about the fish's death, believing the young girl has a right to know and can handle the information. Following this, Emira distances herself, and Alix is hurt that Emira has "lapsed back into formal toleration" (118) of her for reasons she cannot name. Of course, the fish is not the real issue. Readers learn from Emira that as her affection for Briar grows, she becomes increasingly resentful of Alix for not appreciating her daughter. Emira explains that Alix could be an "outstanding mother," but simply was not "by choice rather than default" (127), which she deems more cringeworthy. Readers, thus, are reminded of the norms of motherhood and the judgement that is incurred should they choose not to conform.

As the novel progresses, it is revealed that Alix and Kelley had been high school sweethearts, with Kelley labeling Alix a racist after she called the police when his fellow (Black) teammates would not leave her home. Both Alix and Kelley put themselves, not Emira, at the centre of their decades-long feud. When Emira checks her email on Alix's computer and does not log out, Alix realizes she can access the video from the grocery store that Kelley, who had recorded the altercation, had emailed to Emira. Alix secretly posts it to social media against Emira's wishes, and it immediately goes viral. Presuming Kelley is the one who betrayed her wishes, Emira and Kelley fight with Kelley deriding Emira's work as a babysitter and condemning her choice to work for an entitled, white woman like Alix. Meanwhile, Alix decides to hire Emira full-time, thrilled with the idea that she can mentor her—mentorship Emira did not request. While Alix attempts to craft a closer bond over wine and chitchat, Emira sagely thinks to herself that "receiving a contract and 1095 tax form" (266) said volumes more about her importance to Alix than empty platitudes and friendly conversation. The novel closes with Emira learning that Alix was the one who posted the video, and she annuls their contract during a live television interview that she and Alix appear in, embarrassing Alix publicly and tarnishing her position as a feminist icon.

Like Kate in *Substitute Me*, Alix is a white, neoliberal subject who maximizes her privilege in part by outsourcing labour that has historically been provided by women with less social and financial privilege. While Reid provides readers with avenues to empathize with Alix, she ultimately paints her as contemptible, and readers likely relish her comeuppance. Alix's efforts to impress Emira are notable in a relationship typically depicted as offering few sites of empowerment for the nanny. As Emira realizes, kindness does not pay the bills; a living wage and health insurance are necessary. Emira is somewhat exceptional in terms of childcare workers because, even though she is still subject to racism, she comes from a supportive, middle-class family; obtained formal higher education; is young, attractive, and able-bodied; and, while still navigating her path forward, has the wherewithal to succeed by traditional metrics in ways that are often significantly reduced for those who are poor, have immigrated, do not speak English, have disabilities, and/or have tenuous work status. Although these markers do not necessarily undercut a mother-employer's trust, level of dependence, and interest in crafting a closer relationship, it is likely that increased social difference may limit the ability to connect personally (see O'Donnell and Wood and in chapter two). Like many nannies, Emira does not have real agency in her position as a childcare provider or in her relationship with Alix even though she does ultimately upend the power differentials. Moreover, her ability to do this is not an option that many nannies can access.

Reid may not want her novel to be viewed as polemical, but it is impossible not to empathize with Emira and see the ways her work is devalued and underappreciated. Unfortunately, Reid's relatively hopeful ending (Emira gets hired full time at her other job with health benefits) is not a common reality for many of the women doing carework in the US. Moreover, many mother-employers do not have the option of paying more, as they, too, are bound by a broken system that does not support care and in which feminized labour is under-remunerated. Despite these limitations, it is critical to note that Alix does showcase a level of vulnerability that is less obvious in Kate.

Novel Approaches to Mother/Nanny Novels

When we view *Substitute Me* and *Such a Fun Age* together, a few key motifs emerge, namely the exploitative nature of the mother-nanny relationship, white women's ignorance about racism as it exists in themselves and their communities, the ways neoliberal feminism has impacted allyship between white women and women of colour, the deeply negative impacts of our refusal to address care as required infrastructure in the US, and the ongoing refusal to implicate men as part of the carework problem. These are all points I will address briefly below before returning to the primary purpose of this work, which is to argue that while empathy may not be a balm that addresses all of these concerns, novels about mothers and nannies can evoke a powerful sense of emotive understanding that can lead to deeper awareness, critical self-reflection, and even pro-social action.

The relationships in *Substitute Me* and *Such a Fun Age* illustrate the complexity of hiring a worker to fulfill an employment need in one's home. Both Kate and Alix use the race of the nanny they hired strategically, and in both cases, while it is not indicated directly, benefit from the centuries of suppressed wages and limited options for employment that Black women have experienced in America. In *Substitute Me*, Kate is willfully ignorant of the more nuanced aspects of how racism functions (particularly considering her husband's pushback) under the guise of pragmatism. She practices "aversive racism," which is the "type of racism well-intentioned, educated, progressive people are more likely to enact" and which "exists under the surface of consciousness because it conflicts with consciously held beliefs of equality and justice among racial groups" (DiAngelo 132). In *Such a Fun Age*, Emira's race validates Alix's progressive persona as well as providing personal access to a culture outside of her own. Readers are asked to examine the ways in which mother-employers benefit from racist structures, particularly in a world where "the racial messages we receive (and broadcast ourselves) are subtle and are often invisible, especially to white" people (131). The Black nannies in these novels are paid, but they are paid to care for the employers' children, not to grant access to their personhood, their culture, their ability to heal white guilt, or to serve as a token that proves a white person's progressiveness.

Black activists often contend that it is impossible for any white American not to be racist in the US, or truly any person, with Charlene A. Carruthers writing: "None of us are immune to the effect of white supremacy, capitalism, anti-Blackness, and patriarchal systems" (51). We eat, breathe, and learn racism from the time we are born, even if it has been enacted differently across the decades and geographies. Historically, white women have exerted their racial privilege by knowing only as much as they cared to know about the women who worked in their homes every day, while domestic servants often witnessed the intimacies of their employers' lives whether they wanted to or not.[8] Today, progressive whites are at times rewarded (typically by other whites) for their ability to perform allyship and for successful relationships with people of colour (e.g., "I can't be racist; my best friend is Black," or to a lesser extent, "I can't be racist because I hired a Black woman to have an active role in raising my white children"). A progressive white mother may believe hiring a Black nanny will offer ongoing "teachable moments" to their own white children via the nanny's time, labour, and identity—not recognizing the flaws in extracting this labour without compensation or the ways a nanny's own children are disadvantaged as a result (see Cummins Muñoz, chapter 1).

The mother-employer/nanny relationships in *Substitute Me* and *Such a Fun Age* bring into stark relief the problems inherent in neoliberal feminism, which can also be called choice feminism and white feminism (although there are arguably differences between these three). Journalist Koa Beck describes white feminism as a "type of feminism that takes up the politics of power without questioning them—by replicating patterns of white supremacy, capitalistic greed, corporate ascension, inhumane labor practices, and exploitation, and deeming it empowering for women to practice these tenets as men always have" (xvii). According to gender and women's studies scholar Kyla Schuller, "White feminist politics promotes the theory that women should fight for the full political and economic advantages that wealthy white men enjoy within capitalist empires," while encouraging the use of "Black and Indigenous people, other people of color, and the poor as raw resources that can fuel women's rise in status" (4). At the macro and micro level, this practice has been at best ignored and at worst endorsed by men and women whose allegiance to capitalism outweighs their allegiance to parity. Feminist writer Rafia Zakaria aptly warns: "The we-can-all-agree-on-this brand of choice feminism has not only proven impotent, it has eluded accountability" (205). Indeed, it is important to question the ways profound restriction of viable choices leads nearly all mothers to craft imperfect solutions in a neoliberal landscape that has failed them.

Kate and Alix are both neoliberal subjects, committed to capitalism and "having it all," even if it means outsourcing the work (i.e., childcare) that would otherwise prevent them from achieving their goals to women who are more marginalized socially, racially, and/or economically. Their quest for free time, self-satisfaction, and career recognition are referenced as reasons they outsource childcare, which is notably different than if they were lower-income, single mothers. It is this aspect of choosing to outsource childcare that seems to lead problematically to both Tharps and Reid punishing the mother-employers in profound ways. Kate loses a husband she loves and Alix is publicly humiliated in a way that deeply tarnishes her brand. Kate and Alix, even when sympathetic, are guilty of many of the most powerful insults one can label a white mother: self-centred, work obsessed, emotionally aloof, and/or racially insensitive. This complicates our sense of empathy even while providing learning opportunities. It also challenges what journalists Rachel Abramowitz and Kim Masters deem rampant public scorning of white mothers. They write, "In a world in which it's considered politically incorrect to mock almost any group, there is one exception: the middle- to upper-class mother [...] who dares to hire child care." Whereas Tharps and Reid craft Kate and Alix as likeable characters, many readers are quick to castigate them, myself included.

Meanwhile, the husbands in both novels are presented as benign bit characters, even while Brad initiates an affair with Zora and Peter takes no active role in parenting his children or overseeing Emira. As with most novels concerning nannies, the mother is the one who is the second protagonist or foil. Men, when present, seem to engage with nannies only for the purpose of initiating a sexual relationship.[9] Many contemporary novels do address women's dissatisfaction with gendered roles in the home, inequitable division of reproductive labour, and men's inattention to issues concerning childcare, but these tend to focus primarily on the heterosexual marriage itself rather than the ways men benefit from current systems of outsourced carework.

While it is important to reference (white) men's culpability in continuing broken systems of carework, more salient to the work in this chapter is the ways that this impacts empathy. Kate, who is a character developed during a time in which many mainstream, white feminists were espousing a "have it all" mode of empowered womanhood, is ultimately seen as pitiable in light of losing her husband to Zora. In some ways, her very racist comments are cloaked under this more dramatic plot line. Tharps still shines a light on the ways that white women tolerate racial difference only to the extent that they benefit from it. Reid's novel is much clearer in its depiction of racism even while Alix is arguably less overtly racist.

It is worth noting that Tharps and Reid seem to endorse empathy over division, particularly in author interviews. Tharps confesses that she left waged work because she was so "overwhelmed with the process" of hiring a nanny, adding "Kate Carter is far braver than I" (qtd. in Shalema). She suggests that any woman who engages with the process should not be criticized for her missteps. Reid states in an interview that she has sympathy for Alix and describes her novel as a "comedy of good intentions" (Hays). This makes sense from Reid, as she claims she wants to avoid her novel being read as a political treatise. Reid notes that when on tour for her novel many white women were deeply critical of Alix, while Black women simply saw her as one of the many white women they work with. Reid recalls in one interview, "I thought it was really interesting that Black women had this empathy for Alix and could see her as more of a symptom of bigger issue. Alix is a victim of a system that connects your health care to your employer, a system that doesn't offer subsidized childcare" (qtd. in Akhtar). Still, Alix does have health insurance and childcare and has chosen not to extend the same protections to Emira. While Kate and Alix often want to do right by people, their execution falls short—sometimes quite significantly and in racist ways—and they are both ultimately punished.

The question this chapter addresses is how effective novels can be in the process of consciousness raising, particularly for white mother-employers who read novels that depict their own fraught care decisions.

As posited earlier by Reid, to put additional responsibility for race education on Black authors would be to behave no differently than the mother-employers discussed herein. Still, white mother-employer readers can benefit from the opportunity to use what bell hooks calls the "oppositional gaze" and should challenge themselves to interrogate their privilege. Philosopher Alison Bailey contends: "By learning about lives on the margins, members of dominant groups come to discover the nature of oppression, the extent of their privileges, and the relations between them. Making visible the nature of privilege, enables members of dominant groups to generate liberatory knowledge" (286). It is of utmost importance that we, as white women, read stories about Black protagonists from Black authors, but I simultaneously argue that we must interrogate our desire to position Black female authors as our guides via their art or literature. Novels, by their nature, can be instructional in ways that encourage self-reflection, invite readers to deepen their empathy, and provide lessons through storytelling, but they do not replace active resistance.

As Davis notes earlier, though, change that happens in the home can have profound consequences for the people involved and for change more broadly. She further posits that "local and personal examples of taking a moral stand do work to undermine racism and are probably necessary stepping stones for individuals to move towards more public-oriented anti-racist acts that require greater risk" (109). Ultimately, these novels ask readers to engage emotionally with the lives of people who may be quite different from them and come out wiser and better positioned to act in ways that are equitable.

Are books the gateway to improving this broken system? Pulitzer Prize-winning literary critic Margo Jefferson said it best in an interview when she was asked if she could "separate a book from its social context." She replied, "Yes. Isn't the challenge when, why, and how? To separate isn't to deny or obliterate. We can read a book for its aesthetics; reread it for the social/political/cultural context. We can do this sequentially or simultaneously. We're not single-cell creatures. Books make complicated demands on us" ("By the Book"). While literature is not a salve for all social wrongs, the potential remains that white women can become stronger allies and more aware employers by building empathic understanding and engage in more critical self-examination. The power in the mother/nanny relationship still resides with the employer for all the reasons asserted in this anthology; no single novel or even collection of novels will change that. However, changing social norms creates strong undercurrents for potential reform—reform that is crucial to all women.

Ultimately, while these novels are useful in building empathy, particularly in white mother-employers who may not be aware of the unethical aspect of outsourcing care to a woman of colour, this is not enough. The inherent power differentials present in our classist and racist society remain intact in the mother/nanny relationship as do our neoliberal-based economic and employment structures. White mother-employers continue to self-analyze as they choose and can often be nearly as extractive and exploitative as they wish due to the plethora of Black, brown, and/or immigrant women who have few options to support themselves and their families in a failed political/legal system that does not provide basic employment protections to vulnerable groups.

Broken system or not, white women can do better. Hand in Hand is one organization that offers advice on how to be a better employer when hiring domestic workers, including nannies, and they offer sample contracts that outline work responsibilities, paid leave, taxes, and more. *Care.com* (and others) offers easy-to-understand advice on how to file tax forms related to waged carework. Alia Benefits allows for multiple families to contribute to health insurance or other benefits when they are in a nanny share arrangement. These tools are tangible ways that we can be part of solutions that impact injustices, but employers (due to the lack of government policy) need to feel invested in ethical practices. Reading, even empathically, is not enough; however, like the consciousness-raising novels from the 1960s and 1970s, these novels provide a "starting point ... from which to begin doing more public, activist organizing, rather than end in an investigative model" (Hogeland 25). Cultural change can be rooted in individuals and can, in turn, shift policy.

Endnotes

1. I have argued previously, a nanny is often charged with being a proxy mother and platonic spouse to the mother-employer, yet she is seldom compensated for this additional emotional labour (Garner, "Love"; Garner, "Mirroring").

2. Historically, American novelists seldom centre Black housekeepers, childcare providers, and mammies. *The Sound and the Fury* by William Faulkner (1929), *Gone with the Wind* by Margaret Mitchell (1936), *The Member of the Wedding* by Carson McCullers (1946), *The Street* by Ann Petry (1946), *To Kill a Mockingbird* by Harper Lee (1960), *The Good Nanny* by Benjamin Cheever (2004), *The Secret Life of Bees* by Sue Monk Kidd (2008), *The Help* by Kathryn Stockett (2009), and *The Dry Grass of August* by Anna Jean Mayhew (2011) all depict Black childcare providers; however, the amount of narrative space provided each woman and the deftness of the author's depiction of complex issues regarding race vary substantially. Notably, Ann Petry is the only Black author in this list. A handful of nanny novels feature non-Black women of colour with the primary conflict addressing cultural clashes and immigration, including *The Love Wife* by Gish Jen (2004), *My Hollywood* by Mona Simpson (2010). and *Re Jane* by Patricia Park (2015).

3. Rather than using only "mother" and "employer," I am using the term "mother-employer" from Cameron Macdonald's *Shadow Mothers*, in which she draws attention to the fact that many nannies are also mothers. In this chapter, I will only refer to the nannies as nannies because both protagonists are child-free.

4. Many scholars believe this number is inflated with those paying the least also not reporting the wages they pay.

5. The late 2010s and early 2020s were notable for a corpus of books published by Black or brown writers aimed wholly or in part at white people, sometimes specifically white women. Some aim to present a different, more intersectional point of view to mainstream (i.e., white) feminism (e.g., *White Feminism* by Koa Beck and *Unapologetic: A Black, Queer, and Feminist Mandate for Radical Movements* by Charlene A. Carruthers); some offer corrections to the whitewashed feminist history that is often provided in formal schooling and remains entrenched in our culture (e.g., *Hood Feminism: Notes from the Women That a Movement Forgot* by Mikki Kendall and *Against White Feminism: Notes on Disruption* by Rafia Zakaria); and some are straightforward instructional texts (e.g., *White Women: Everything You Already Know about Your Own Racism and How to Do Better* by Regina Jackson and Saira Rao and *So You Want to Talk about Race?* by Ijeoma Oluo).

6. Popular nanny novels based in the US often foreground young, white, securely middle-class employees (e.g., *The Nanny Diaries* and others) who are biding their time until they find "real" employment and thus sidestep the nuanced and challenging issues intrinsic in employing domestic help, particularly childcare providers. Novels that focus on white, working- to middle-class women may highlight the economic power imbalances in the mother-nanny labour relationship, but these novels seldom address systemic racism in a meaningful way. In novels where both employer and employee are white, conflicts tend to be based on adultery, conflicts around mothering, and/or interpersonal struggles. Romance novels tend to spotlight father/nanny romantic relationships, although typically the mother is not present due to death or divorce, and the relationships are typically consensual.

7. Though outside the scope of this work, it is interesting to consider the ways that a novel's literariness could impact reader identification, development of empathy, and its ability to serve as a conscious-raising novel.

8. See *The Maid Narratives: Black Domestics and White Families in the Jim Crow South* by Katherine Van Wormer for more information.

9. I have currently begun researching an article that addresses father-employers' relationships with nannies and have found a void of scholarly writing on the topic.

Works Cited

Akhtar, Jabeen. "How Such a Fun Age Came to Be: An Interview with Kiley Reid." *Los Angeles Review of Books*, 2 Jan 2021, https://lareviewofbooks.org/article/how-such-a-fun-age-came-to-be-an-interview-with-kiley-reid/. Accessed 17 Oct. 2023.

diAngelo, Robin. "What Does It Mean to Be White? Developing White Racial Literacy: RevEd" *Counterpoints*, vol. 497, 2016, pp. 125-55.

Bailey, Alison. "Locating Traitorous Identities: Toward a View of Privilege-Cognizant White Character." *Decentering the Center: Philosophy for a Multicultural, Postcolonial, and Feminist World*, edited by Uma Narayan and Sandra Harding, Indiana University Press, 2000, pp. 283-89.

Banks, Nina. "Black Women in the United States and Unpaid Collective

Work: Theorizing the Community as a Site of Production." *The Review of Black Political Economy*, vol. 47, no. 4, 2020, pp. 343-62.

Beck, Koa. *White Feminism: From the Suffragettes to Influencers and Who They Leave Behind*. Atria Books, 2021.

"Caribbean Feminisms on the Page." *Bernikow* https://barnard.edu/magazine/fall-2015/caribbean-feminisms-page. Accessed 17 Oct. 2023.

Brown, Victoria. "Reading Jamaica in New York." *Apogee*, https://apogeejournal.org/2015/08/05/nonfiction-reading-jamaica-in-new-york-by-victoria-brown/. Accessed 17 Oct. 2023.

Brown, Victoria. *Minding Ben*. Voice, 2011.

"By the Book." *New York Times*. Interview with Margo Jefferson, 7 Apr. 2022, https://www.nytimes.com/2022/04/07/books/review/margo-jefferson-by-the-book-interview.html. Accessed 17 Oct. 2023.

Carruthers, Charlene A. *Unapologetic: A Black, Queer, and Feminist Mandate for Radical Movements*. Boston, Beacon, 2018.

Chang, Grace. *Disposable Domestics: Immigrant Women Workers in the Global Economy*. South End, 2000.

Cheever, Benjamin. *The Good Nanny*. Bloomsbury, 2004.

Collins, Patricia Hill. *Black Feminist Thought*. Routledge, 2000.

Duffy, Mignon. "Reproducing Labor Inequalities: Challenges for Feminists Conceptualizing Care at the Intersections of Gender, Race, and Class." *Gender and Society*, vol. 19, no. 1, Feb. 2005, pp. 66-82.

Faulkner, William. *The Sound and the Fury*. Norton, 1994.

Felski, Rita. *Uses of Literature*. Blackwell, 2008.

Flanagan, Caitlin. "How Serfdom Saved the Women's Movement: Dispatches from the Nanny Wars." *The Atlantic*, https://www.theatlantic.com/magazine/archive/2004/03/how-serfdom-saved-the-women-s-movement/302892/. Accessed 17 Oct. 2023.

Garner, Katie B. "Mirroring a Mother's Love: A Chodorowian Analysis of the Complicated Relationship between Mothers and Nannies in *My Hollywood*, *The Perfect Nanny*, and *Women's Work: A Reckoning with Work and Home*." *Nancy Chodorow and the Reproduction of Mothering: Forty Years On*, edited by Petra Bueskens, Palgrave, 2020, pp. 301-28.

Garner, Katie B. "Love Bi the Book: A Chodorodian Examination of Heterosexual Mothers' Love for Nannies in Contemporary Fiction." *Motherhood, Sex, and Sexuality: An Anthology*, edited by Holly Zwalf, Demeter Press, 2020, pp. 167-89.

Gordon, Mary. *Men and Angels*. Random House, 1985.

Hays, Stephanie. "*Such a Fun Age* Satirizes the White Pursuit of Wokeness." *The Atlantic*. 8 Jan 2020, https://www.theatlantic.com/entertainment/archive/2020/01/review-such-fun-age-kiley-reid/604552/. Accessed 17 Oct. 2023.

Hogeland, Lisa Marie. *Feminism and Its Fictions: The Consciousness-Raising Novel and the Women's Liberation Movement*. Pennsylvania University Press, 1998.

Hondagneu-Sotelo, Pierrette. *Doméstica: Immigrant Workers Cleaning and Caring in the Shadows of Affluence*. Berkeley: California University Press, 2001.

hooks, bell. "The Oppositional Gaze: Black Female Spectators." *Black Looks: Race and Representation*. South End Press, 1992.

Jackson, Regina, and Saira Rao. *White Women: Everything You Already Know about Your Own Racism and How to Do Better*. Penguin, 2022.

Jen, Gish. *The Love Wife*. Vintage, 2004.

Keen, Suzanne. *Empathy and the Novel*. Oxford University Press, 2007.

Kendall, Mikki. *Hood Feminism: Notes from the Women that A Movement Forgot*. Viking, 2020.

Kidd, Sue Monk. *The Secret Life of Bees*. Penguin, 2002.

Kincaid, Jamaica. *Lucy*. Farrar, Straus and Giroux, 1990.

Law, Katie. "Interview." *Evening Standard*, 31 Dec. 2020, https://www.standard.co.uk/culture/books/kiley-reid-such-a-fun-age-racism-interview-b323163.html. Accessed 17 Oct. 2023.

Lee, Felicia. "Nannies Still Draw a Keen Audience." 13 July 2010, https://www.nytimes.com/2010/07/14/books/14nanny.html. Accessed 17 Oct. 2023.

Lee, Harper. *To Kill a Mockingbird*. HarperCollins, 1960.

Lepucki, Edan. *Woman 17*. Hogarth, 2017.

Macdonald, Cameron Lynne. *Shadow Mothers: Nannies, Au Pairs, and the Micropolitics of Mothering*. California University Press, 2010.

Mayhew, Anna Jean. *The Dry Grass of August*. Kensington, 2011.

McCuller, Carson. "Member of the Wedding." *Collected Stories of Carson McCullers*.

McLaughlin, Emma, and Nicola Kraus. *The Nanny Diaries*. St. Martin's Griffin, 2002.

Mitchell, Margaret. *Gone with the Wind*. Macmillan, 1936.

Moore, Lorrie. *A Gate at the Stairs*. Vintage, 2009.

Morland, Denise. "Review." *Powells*, https://www.powells.com/book/-9781401341510/1-4. Accessed 17 Oct. 2023.

Nance, Kimberly A. *Can Literature Promote Justice? Trauma Narrative and Social Action in Latin American Testimonio*. Vanderbilt University Press, 2006.

Oluo, Ijeoma. *So You Want to Talk about Race?* Seal, 2018.

Ortega, Mariana. "Being Lovingly, Knowingly Ignorant: White Feminism and Women of Color." *Hypatia*, vol. 21, no. 3, Summer 2006, pp. 56-74.

Park, Patricia. *Re Jane*. Penguin, 2016.

Parreñas, Rhacel Salazar. *Servants of Globalization: Women, Migration, and Domestic Work*. Stanford University Press, 2001.

Pastan, Rachell. *Lady of the Snakes*. Harcourt, 2008.

Petry, Ann. *The Street*. Houghton Mifflin, 1946.

Proudfoot, Jenny. Interview. *Marie Claire*. 27 Jan 2021. https://www.marieclaire.co.uk/entertainment/books/kiley-reid-724642

Reid, Kiley. *Such a Fun Age*. Putnam, 2019.

Rollins, Judith. *Between Women: Domestics and Their Employers*. Temple, 1985.

Romero, Mary. *Maid in the U.S.A.* Routledge, 2002.

Schuller, Kyla. *The Trouble with White Women*. Bold Type Books, 2021.

Shalema. "Substitute Me." *Authors in Color*. http://authorsincolor.blogspot.com/2010/08/substitute-me-by-lori-l-tharps.html. Accessed 17 Oct. 2023.

Simpson, Mona. *My Hollywood*. Knopf, 2010.

Slimani, Leïla. *The Perfect Nanny*. Penguin, 2016.

Stockett, Kathryn. *The Help*. Amy Einhorn Books, 2009.

Strum, Verity. "Writer Kiley Reid on Why We Cringe in Her Debut *Such a Fun Age*." *The Michigan Daily*, 7 Jan 2020, https://www.michigandaily.com/arts/writer-kiley-reid-on-why-we-cringe-in-her-debut-such-a-fun-age/. Accessed 17 Oct. 2023.

Styron, Alexandra. *All the Finest Girls*. Little, Brown, and Co., 2001.

Sullivan, Courtney J. *Friends and Strangers*. Knopf, 2020.

Tharps, Lori L. *Substitute Me*. Atria, 2010.

Tronto, Joan. "The 'Nanny' Question in Feminism." *Hypatia* 17, no. 2, 2002, pp. 34-51.

Zakaria, Rafia. *Against White Feminism: Notes on Disruption*. Norton, 2021.

Chapter 10

"I'm Quitting Your Service; I've Had Quite Enough": Representations of Caregivers' Subjectivity in Tamara Mose Brown's *Raising Brooklyn* and Victoria Brown's *Minding Ben*

Elizabeth Podnieks

D uring her interview for a caregiving position in Manhattan with the Bruckner family, protagonist Grace Caton, a migrant from Trinidad, is asked to read to her prospective charge, the eponymous child in *Minding Ben*. Taking Ben's favourite picture book, Nancy Willard's *Pish, Posh, Said Hieronymus Bosch*, Grace begins:

> "Once upon a time there was an artist named Hieronymus Bosch who loved odd creatures. Not a day passed that the good woman who looked after his house didn't find a new creature lurking in a corner or sleeping in a cupboard. To her fell the job of feeding them"—Ben recited along with me—"weeding them, walking them, stalking them, calming them, combing them, scrubbing and tucking in all of them—until one day—" (34).

The passage breaks off here, but in a later episode, Grace completes the verse for us; she describes hearing Ben and his parents, Miriam and Sol, reading the same section, and bursting out in unison, "Until one day ... I'm quitting your service, I've had quite enough ..." (102). If Miriam and Sol seem oblivious to the implications of these lines, Grace surely appreciates their meaning. As the "good woman" looking after the Bruckners' child and home, Grace embodies the plight of caregivers—who are overwhelmingly racialized and often (undocumented) immigrants—to children of privileged, typically white families in the Global North. Although they are often overworked and undervalued, for these women, quitting is usually not an option. *Minding Ben* provides the space where caregivers like Grace and her cohort articulate their pent-up feelings of enduring "quite enough" oppression on the job and how they are led to the brink physically, psychologically, and emotionally.

An oeuvre of fiction centred on caregivers—what Elizabeth Hale dubs "nanny lit"—was brought to the cultural fore by Emma McLaughlin and Nicola Kraus's *The Nanny Diaries* (2002). In addition to Victoria Brown's *Minding Ben* (2011), it has been expanded by stories like Nandi Keyi's *The True Nanny Diaries* (2009), Lorrie Moore's *A Gate at the Stairs* (2010), Mona Simpson's *My Hollywood* (2010), and Leila Slimani's *Chanson Douce* (2016) (translated and published in 2018 as *Lullaby* [UK] and *The Perfect Nanny* [US]). The genre can be traced to Anne Brontë's *Agnes Grey* (1847), although it did not proliferate until recently (Hale 104). Comparing *The Nanny Diaries* and *Agnes Grey*, both featuring caregiving heroines (respectively Nan and Agnes), Hale finds shared revelations about the exploitative working conditions for nannies and the complicated dynamics between the mother and nanny figures (104). The texts "convey their narrators' (and authors') sense of real disappointment in their workplaces and working lives, as well as offering them an outlet for their anger and even a measure of vengeance" (105). That said, books like *The Nanny Diaries* and *Agnes Grey* portray white and entitled caregivers. Agnes is a "gently bred" governess (Hale 104), and Nan, a college student at NYU, is the granddaughter of an elite society matron. In contrast, in *Not Your Mother's Mammy*, Tracey L. Walters examines *The Nanny Diaries* beside *The True Nanny Diaries* and *Minding Ben*, both of which depict migrant protagonists from Trinidad. These latter novels spotlight the racialized and immigrant identities of the domestic workers and are more authentic in that they cover "harsher realities," such as fears of deportation and homelessness (48-49).[1]

I had such a group of nanny-focal novels in mind when previously, in my chapter "Matrifocal Voices in Literature" (2019), I recommended that a vital future direction for motherhood studies would be to extend an examination of mother-centred narratives to include those from the first-person perspectives of caregivers. Moreover, taking myself at my word, I wrote "'The Synergy Between You': Mothers, Nannies, and Collaborative Caregiving in Contemporary Matroethnographies" (2021). In the article, I catalogued nonfiction books that document relationships between mothers and their waged caregivers (who often have children of their own). Examples include, among others, Jessika Auerbach's *And Nanny Makes Three: Mothers and Nannies Tell the Truth about Work, Love, Money, and Each Other* (2007); Lucy Kaylin's *The Perfect Stranger: The Truth about Mothers and Nannies* (2007); Analyn D. Aryo's *Nanny Tales: Voices from the Diary of an Overseas Filipina Worker* (2009); Cameron Lynne Macdonald's *Shadow Mothers: Nannies, Au Pairs, and the Micropolitics of Mothering* (2010); and Tamara Mose Brown's *Raising Brooklyn: Nannies, Childcare, and Caribbeans Creating Community* (2011).

In the article (and with specific attention to Kaylin's and Aryo's work), I coined the term "matroethnography" to classify texts like these as a new genre of matrifocal writing. Affixing "matro" (Latin root for mater) to ethnography, the term gestures to autoethnography, itself a hybrid form emanating from the fields of autobiography, sociology, and anthropology. Autoethnography is defined by Tony E. Adams, Stacy Holman Jones, and Carolyn Ellis as a qualitative research method that blends "the *self* (auto), *culture* (ethno), and *writing* (graphy)" (46). Autoethnography seeks to "name and interrogate the intersections between self and society, the particular and the general, the personal and the political" (2). Autoethnographers "look *inward*—into our identities, thoughts, feelings and experiences—and *outward*—into our relationships, communities, and cultures' (47). With an agenda to "Disrupt Taboos, Break Silences, and Reclaim Lost and Disregarded Voices," practitioners "create a textual space for talking back to neglected cultural experiences and, simultaneously, offer accounts that allow others to 'bear witness' to these experiences" (40-41). A related methodology and genre is collaborative autoethnography, defined by Heewon Chang, Faith Wambura Ngunjiri, and Kathy-Ann C. Hernandez as being "simultaneously collaborative, autobiographical, and ethnographic" (17). With autobiographical narratives, "each participant contributes to the collective work in his or her distinct and independent voice" while generating a "harmony that autoethnographers cannot attain in isolation" (24). Within these contexts—and concentrating on the intersecting narratives of employers and their hired caregivers—I argued that matroethnography is autoethnography from pointedly matrifocal perspectives, fusing individual and personal maternal identities and experiences with those that are collective and communal.

Here, in my chapter for *Care(ful) Relationships*, I draw on these genres to show how we can read both fiction and nonfiction works as iterations of matroethnography. Specifically, I use Brown's *Minding Ben* as it overlaps with Mose Brown's *Raising Brooklyn* as evidence of how, by bringing creative storytelling into dialogue with ethnographic research, we broaden our understanding of "stories of/about the self told through the lens of culture" (Adams, Jones, and Ellis 1). Such stories serve as "artistic and analytic demonstrations of how we come to know, name, and interpret personal and cultural experience" (Adams, Jones, and Ellis 1)—in this case, the personal and cultural experiences of racialized caregivers. Brown and Mose Brown are a rich source for "artistic and analytic" pairing. They are both of West Indian descent; lived and studied in New York; are academics, wives, and mothers who themselves rely on paid caregivers; and predicate their narratives on their own immersion as participant-observers within communities of migrant Trinidadian caregivers in Manhattan and Brooklyn. *Minding Ben* and *Raising Brooklyn* testify to their comparable authorial goals of translating their insider knowledge of these communities into narratives that give voice and dignity to its individual and collective members. In reading them together, I posit that their matroethnographic accounts exemplify new literatures that not only name but also give voice and agency to immigrant caregivers as complex beings.[2] As I argue below, their texts claim our attention to caregivers as underappreciated maternal figures performing undervalued mother-work. The texts press for our urgent recognition of—and the need for social justice intervention into—how contemporary mothering unfolds within the geopolitical contexts of globalization at the inescapable nexus of ethnicity, race, and class and the dynamics of power, labour, and love.

Modelling Matroethnography

I view *Minding Ben* and *Raising Brooklyn* as constitutive of an intertextual conversation or collaboration between Brown and Mose Brown and the caregivers profiled in their respective books. *Minding Ben* is narrated by Grace, a young immigrant from Trinidad. The story revolves around the period from February to August 1991, when she is employed by Miriam and Sol Bruckner to look after their nearly four-year-old son, Ben. Grace lives with the Bruckners in their upper-middle-class flat in Manhattan during the week and returns to a derelict apartment in Brooklyn on the weekends. In relaying her story, Grace not only renders imbalances of power she experiences with Ben's parents but also gives voice to her caregiving colleagues. Brown wrote from her 'insider's' position acknowledging that her novel is "mixed with a little biography, and autobiography" (qtd. in Sidman). Indeed, Brown's middle name is Gracie; and like protagonist Grace, Brown emigrated from Trinidad to New York alone at age sixteen, becoming a babysitter (Sidman). In the spirit of the collaborative autoethnographer, Brown affirms that she "wanted to tell a larger story" and thus, "The main character is Grace, but I've incorporated a lot of nannies' stories into her own" (qtd. in Sidman).

Reflecting on her role as a child minder, Brown admits, "I was one of those anonymous women pushing a child on the Upper East Side"; "I'd be in the building's lobby with the little boy, and the neighbors would say hello to the little boy but not to me. There was a degree of invisibility. It may sound corny, but I wanted to give these women some inner life" (qtd. in Lee). Additionally, Brown is an academic. After several years working as a caregiver, Brown took courses at LaGuardia Community College, made her way to Vassar College (where she earned a BA in English), and then attended graduate school at the University of Warwick, where she wrote *Minding Ben*. She is now an associate professor of English at Rollins College in Florida as well as a wife and mother of two (Lee; Sidman). Interviewing Brown in 2010, Felicia R. Lee comments, "She now has a baby sitter (whom she pointedly does not call a nanny)."

Published in the same year as *Minding Ben*, *Raising Brooklyn* showcases the very real women fictionalized by Victoria Brown. *Raising Brooklyn* is the product of Mose Brown's research at the Graduate Center at City University of New York in the early 2000s—she is now a full professor of sociology at CUNY's Brooklyn College. She frames the project as an ethnographic study of West Indian caregivers at various parks around Brooklyn: "While not a paid childcare provider, I am a mother of two toddlers and have spent many hours of many days in public spaces while caring for children" (vii). She continues: "I was intrigued by the familiar West Indian accents I heard from the many black women caregivers using public parks. I recognized those accents, for I had grown up in a Trinidadian immigrant household in Canada with a father of African, Indian, English, and Irish ancestry and a mother of African, Indian, Carib, Spanish, and French ancestry" (vii). Mose Brown appreciates her role as an ethnographic participant: "As a member of the same racial and ethnic group these women belonged to, I found myself treated as a cultural 'insider'" (11). From this vantage point, she "began to see that the use of public places by West Indian childcare providers was related to matters of race, ethnicity, immigration, political economy, and transnational motherhood" (viii).

Mose Brown outlines her agenda to "illustrate how a group of women who are traditionally viewed as one-dimensional in their work have multidimensional experiences influenced by cultural traditions" (4-5) and to show "how childcare providers, through their use of public spaces, can create a collective space and collective definitions of what they are doing during the day" (3). In this, we can see connections to the practices of collaborative autoethnography. Focusing on the gentrifying neighborhoods in Brooklyn, her book is based primarily on her interviews with approximately twenty-five (pseudonymous) sitters who migrated from Grenada, Trinidad, Guyana, St. Lucia, Jamaica, St. Vincent, and Barbados (10, 161). The diverse cast of caregivers in *Minding Ben* could well be taken for being among the list of Mose Brown's interviewees. Mose Brown details, "This ethnography is one of the first contributions in the twenty-first century to give prominent voice to this group of workers and to their complicated networks that result in a collective life" (159). Mose Brown also interviewed a handful of employers but indicates that she placed their commentary "in the background, focusing more attention on the childcare providers' accounts of their own daily experiences" (164). Consequently, the childcare providers were eager to participate in her study: "It was their lives that were being documented, and I became their number one resource for 'telling the truth about the work'" (169). Mose Brown thus explicitly echoes Brown, who "wanted to tell a larger story" and who "wanted to give these women some inner life" (qtd. in Lee).

Taken together, Brown and Mose Brown use their insider status to construct individual portraits of themselves and the caregivers in their communities while merging those narratives into collaborative matro-ethnographies. These matrifocal perspectives illuminate caregivers as performers of mother-work. In defining mother-work, I begin with Sara Ruddick, who proposes the "idea of mothering as a practice or work" (xi), which includes "preservative love, nurturance, and training" (17). More expansively, "mothers are not identified by fixed biological or legal relationships to children but by the work they set out to do" (xi). To this end, "Some may work so closely with others that it is impossible to identify one 'mother,' others share their work with many mothering persons," while "Mothering in households is joined in many ways with mothering in day-care centers, schools, clinics, and other public institutions" (xii). Caregivers are easily situated within this fluid definition. In her study *Shadow Mothers*, Cameron Lynne Macdonald explicitly connects the term "mother-work" with caregiving, being "those daily tasks involved in the care and protection of small children" (9). I am led by Macdonald's insistence that, "mother-work represents a significant component of what it means to be a mother. Therefore, the practice of delegating mother-work to a paid caregiver could be expected to challenge fundamental understandings of motherhood" (10). Matroethnographies like *Minding Ben* and *Raising Brooklyn* inscribe these challenges.

Dreams for Hire

I turn now to a comparative reading of Brown's and Mose Brown's stories, guided by Mary Romero's description of immigrant women's labour in the United States: "Globalization of childcare is based on income inequality between women from poor countries providing low-wage care work for families in wealthier nations" (832). Foregrounding this reality, Mose Brown outlines the history of specifically West Indian migration to New York, thus contextualizing the settings of both *Raising Brooklyn* and *Minding Ben*. She traces, for instance, geographical movement in the late nineteenth and early twentieth centuries generated by the "unemployment 'push' factors from the Caribbean and opportunity 'pull' factors from the United States" (24). The American domestic sector had been dominated by African American women, but with the onset of World War II, they had "left domestic employment to obtain work in factories, shipyards, and other war-related industries, where they could earn relatively decent wages" (25). Even though many were expected to return to their previous roles postwar, they preferred to work in manufacturing and office jobs. This upward mobility of African Americans, from 1945 on, led to West Indian migrants accepting vacated low-wage positions (25). These positions continued to proliferate throughout the 1970s and beyond so that, "By 2001, West Indians ages twenty-five to fifty-four made up 58 percent of New York's black population" (25).

Mose Brown accounts for the reasons West Indian caregivers are preferred hires by white upper-middle-class employers: "For most, their native language is English, they have more education on average than their Latino immigrant counterparts, and they will accept lower wages than some other groups of childcare providers" (26). Overall, in leaving their homes and families, migrant women have "made substantial sacrifices" in their pursuit of the "American Dream" (25). Mose Brown qualifies, "That dream, however, has been limited for first-generation West Indian women, who have for the most part experienced downward mobility, housing segregation, and limited economic opportunities leading to their employment in the domestic services sector" (25). This failed or tarnished dream is evidenced throughout *Raising Brooklyn* and informs the plot of *Minding Ben*.

The novel opens in late 1989 on the day Grace, sixteen, leaves her native Trinidad for New York. Grace's estranged Aunt Velma had a daughter and grandson living in Brooklyn, and Velma had supposedly arranged for Grace to live with her cousin. Grace would attend school in the day and look after the young boy in the evenings. However, arriving in New York, Grace learns that her cousin had never consented to her mother's scheme and that Grace cannot stay with her. Aided by friends—migrants from home—Grace finds work as a caregiver with Mora, who has four children. The novel's central plot unfolds after this year-long position has ended; Grace has been unemployed for two months, and is living in a filthy, dilapidated apartment in Brooklyn with Sylvia, a fellow Trinidadian with three children: Micky, Derek, and Damien. Situating Grace within these caregiving contexts, the novel establishes its matrifocal perspectives.

We are immediately introduced to the plight of women like Grace, seeking employment, as she responds to an ad placed by the Bruckners.

Discussing the job over the phone, Miriam Bruckner lists their excessive requirements: "We need someone to live in and take care of [Ben] full-time, Monday to Friday. Give him his meals, his baths, take him to the park and his activities and playdates. You have to come in on Sunday nights because my husband and I both work. You get off at seven on Fridays. One Friday a month you'll have to work late." Miriam continues: "And there's housework. I need someone to do laundry and keep the apartment clean. You'll have to mop the floors and keep on top of the dust and do the bathrooms. And we need someone to cook and to clean up after we finish eating." Additionally, "There's ironing" (21). Miriam's demands can be critiqued via Romero's reflections: "The most burdensome mothering activities (such as cleaning, laundry, feeding babies and children, and chauffeuring children to their various scheduled activities) are shifted to the worker" (835), highlighting uneven divisions of mother-work in the caregiver-employer dyad.

For all of these duties, Miriam offers the non-negotiable salary of two hundred dollars a week, although Grace knows that between four hundred and fifty and five hundred dollars have been commanded by other sitters in Manhattan. When Miriam asks, "Does this sound like something you're interested in?" Grace thinks, "No," but replies, "Yes" (21). Financially desperate and eager to leave Sylvia's place, Grace is a vulnerable undocumented labourer. Many of Mose Brown's interviewees entered into similar situations. Mose Brown observes: "The women's work that the providers do not only goes unnoticed but is ill paid. The low wages and lack of appreciation for childcare providers in general lead to the conclusion that having private childcare involves both racial and class oppression" (39). Concomitantly, "Middle- and upper-middle class families benefit from this social inequality and find themselves with ample opportunities to hire poorer women of color who are frequently first-generation immigrants" (39).

Addressing class imbalances, Romero asserts,

The solution of hiring a live-in domestic, used by a relatively privileged group, is a component of reproductive labor in the United States, and serves to intensify inequalities between women: first, by reinforcing childcare as a private rather than public responsibility; and second, by reaping the benefits gained by the impact of globalization and restructuring on third-world women. (838-39)

Miriam, a teacher, joined this "privileged group" when she married Sol, a well-paid lawyer from a wealthy family. Mose Brown, for her part, emphasizes of her own class status, "I was earning less than what the sitters were making" as an adjunct instructor, yet "I still felt that they associated me with the bourgeois residents they encountered on a daily basis while in the neighborhood since I had the 'option' of staying home with my children and not having to worry about making an income" (11). Mose Brown's position as a racialized insider within her caregiving community is thus complicated by her class-inflected identity as a graduate student with a college-educated husband and a part-time caregiver for her children.

Following her in-person interview—during which Grace "impresses" the Bruckners with her literacy skills[3]—Grace is invited back for a trial weekend. Here, she learns that even though she is to be a live-in caregiver, she will not have an actual bedroom, "just a small space partitioned from the kitchen by a jalousied sliding door set on tracks" (50) with a single bed. As Miriam rationalizes: "This will be your space. It's not big, but you'll spend most of your time in Ben's room or doing stuff around the apartment. You'll only be in here to sleep" (50). Miriam denies Grace a private life (and a room) of her own. To be sure, Miriam will later lash out to Grace, "You don't live here, you work here" (311). As a live-in caregiver exposed to Miriam's oppressive attitudes, Grace experiences how "the social reproduction of inequalities begins in the employer's home" (Romero 846). The explicitly racialized context of this situation is underlined in *Raising Brooklyn* by Jennie, a child minder from Grenada, who affirms, "When you're at home [the employer's home], you know you're just working, you're not among your own people" (30), evidencing how immigrant caregivers are forced to endure environments hostile to their self-worth and identities.

Grace is hired by Miriam, and from the beginning, she learns that her "hours were a sham" (92) and that she "was on twenty-four-hour call" (163-64). Her situation resembles that of Arlene, a sitter from Guyana, who tells Mose Brown that her employers are "using me like a donkey" (50). In foregrounding oppressive labour conditions, both *Raising Brooklyn* and *Minding Ben* invoke slavery. Mose Brown records the following of Jennie: "One of the poignant remarks she made during our interview showed me that she viewed her work as a childcare provider in a broad historical context." Jennie relays, critiquing her situation,

"After you know that we were once enslaved, and knowing how we were treated by white people and how our forefathers were treated by white people, how could you not treat us better after you know what it's like. I mean what it still is.... I think we have slavery now, it just happens differently" (23). Mose Brown assesses Jennie's comment: "[She] was expressing a politicized understanding of black childcare providers' shared history of subordination and exploitation" (23).

To be sure, when Grace went for her interview with the Bruckners, she had encountered a lobby full of candidates from Jamaica, Trinidad, and Haiti, illuminating the shared plight of immigrant domestics at the mercy of abusive employers like Miriam. As one potential hire reported back to the group following her interview, "She want no babysitter, sah. Me din leave Jamaica fih be nobody slave in New York" (30). Elsewhere, when Grace accompanies Miriam and Ben to a farm, Grace describes that on the wagon ride, Miriam starts singing, "*Gonna pick a bale of cotton, Oh lordy, Gonna pick a bale a day*" (260). Miriam notes that her father sang these lyrics during her childhood summers in the country- side. Miriam is either appallingly racist (as was her father, clearly) or improbably naïve here, but in either case, she subjects Grace to unten- able degradation. Grace's humiliation is driven home by the Black farm hand—a summer intern from Cornell University, son of a Washington DC lawyer—who, learning that Grace is Ben's caregiver, chides, "So you're the mammy?" and follows with, "You island people keep setting us back, man. What you doing minding white people's kids?" (262).

In *Black Feminist Thought*, Patricia Hill Collins argues that "con- trolling images," such as "mammies, jezebels, and breeder women of slavery" dating back to the slave era, continue to be applied today, tes- tifying "to the ideological dimension of U.S. Black women's oppression" (7). Drawing on Collins, Walters emphasizes of the mammy that "Her supposed loyalty to the family she worked for helped create the idea of the domestic being like a family member and, subsequently in the eyes of the black community, a race traitor" (5). We witness this sense of contempt in the response of the successful Cornell student, who accuses Grace of "setting us back." Significantly, he follows with this injunction: "You need to be reading some books, girl" (262), insisting that it is through education as the conduit to advancement that such stereo- types—and real economic disparities—can be countered. Grace's only response is to get away from the young man "as quickly as I could" (262), suggesting he has tapped in to her own uncomfortable recognition of her subjugation.

Patriarchy, Surveillance, and Survival

Explaining the attraction of the US as a migratory destination, Mose Brown introduces us to the Guyanese sitter Catharine, who already had some family members living in Brooklyn (28). Indeed, "West Indians found it easier to settle in Brooklyn (also in Queens and the Bronx) because these boroughs feature a distinct Caribbean ethnic enclave" (Mose Brown 28). Mose Brown also reports of Jennie leaving Grenada: "When I asked her why she had come to New York, she said she had cousins, an uncle, and her sister living here and wanted a fresh start in life" (23). Similarly, as mentioned earlier, Grace chose Brooklyn because her cousin is there, while Victoria Brown notes of herself, "My mother knew there was nothing for me in our village, and I credit her for letting me go" (qtd. in Sidman). Grace's desire to migrate is inspired by the American dream. Talking with Kath, her Trinidadian school friend who had recently emigrated, Grace recounts: "I've been planning to leave home since I was ten. My neighbor spent six months in New York" (43). Her description of the city proved irresistible to Grace. Grace notes that Kath's family "was well known and rich," owning a supermarket chain, and Kath was raised "to be a princess" (43). The fact that Kath rejected a path of privilege established by her parents underscores the diverse reasons women chose to migrate, carving out their own destinies.

Kath, like Grace, is a live-in domestic in Manhattan, looking after a baby. As Grace and Kath reflect on their situation—including Kath's romantic (and dead-end) involvement with a married man—Kath wonders, "God, Grace, what are we doing here? This is what we come New York for?" (42). To which Grace justifies, "Is only for a time, Kath. Once we get our papers, it won't be like this forever, right? A little bit of catch-ass and then we can work it out" (42). Grace and Kath represent the countless caregivers like Catharine in *Raising Brooklyn*, who neither planned for a career in caregiving nor regarded it as their future. Catharine rationalizes their situation: "This is just for now until I make enough money. ... I want to go to school for nursing eventually, but haven't found the time to research how to go about doing it. ... Many of the sitters feel the same way" (28).

Hired by the Bruckners, with Kath by her side, Grace is inducted into the local caregiving community. Grace is initially met with hostility from a group of child minders at the park, to which Kath explains, "You need to learn playground politics. I bet you half of them had somebody for your job" (89). Moreover, the women, who are friends of Carmen, Ben's former caregiver, resist Grace. Caregiver Ule contextualizes the situation between Carmen and Miriam: "Is a nasty somefing that boy mother do Carmen" (98). Ule expands: "That woman is a snake. She used to spy on Carmen" (98). She warns Grace that "You best watch yourself, you hear me" (99). Sitter Evie cautions: "All me can tell you, child, is to watch out for your new boss lady. That woman is pure snake, and I wouldn't trust she if me was you" (55). The dynamic accentuates the complexity of loyalty: On one hand, they want to stand up for Carmen, but on the other, they rally to support Grace as a new community member. Indeed, Evie later clarifies to Grace: "I don't want you to think I don't like you, child. This thing that this woman do have everybody so upset" (103-4). Ule informs Grace about Miriam, "She fire Carmen on Tuesday night and Grace was with Benjamin on Wednesday morning" (174). Former caregiver Bridget then weighs in: "What a dirty, low-down thing to do to a hardworking woman" (174). The caregivers are united against Miriam. It is important to qualify that Carmen broke the Bruckners' rules when she took Ben on the subway and perhaps deserved to be let go. Her cohort highlights, however, that Carmen had been consistently mistreated herself. Furthermore, they articulate their awareness that caregivers—no matter how hard they work (and no matter how much they are loved by their charges—Ben wails at losing Carmen, "I want my ya-ya" [84])—are in the precarious situation of being fired at a moment's notice and that their ability to survive economically is constantly jeopardized.

Just as Ule reveals Miriam to be a "spy," so Grace later calls one woman by the sandbox "a stay-at-home, spy-on-us mother" (171). Grace learns that caregivers sense they are being watched and are thus constantly on guard. She observes that when the employers visit the playground, "The sitters were usually restrained, speaking good English and giving one-word answers and nods whenever one of the mothers came by and tried to pal around. They simply didn't trust these women" (173), evidencing the toll of surveillance on caregiver-employer relationships. Mose Brown relatedly details how child minders are scrutinized by diverse groups of people like other park users, and organizers of children's activities at libraries and dance classes, for instance (79), who report their negative observations to parents. She concludes that surveillance "emphasized an 'us-versus-them' dialogue (between employers and nannies, between other parents and nannies, and between parents themselves), thus stirring up conflicts and divisions between the parties engaged in the work of childcare and mothering that took place on everyone's behalf" (117).

Mose Brown finds that sitters developed empowering strategies to offset criticisms levelled against them. In particular, "they found ways of justifying their frustrations" by promoting themselves as more capable maternal figures than their employers and by "their inversion of outsiders' assumptions as to who was 'fit' and or 'unfit' to take care of children" (79). In this way, they were able to articulate and affirm their own maternal ideologies and practices. To be sure, Grace's mother-work is often positioned in relation to Miriam as a disengaged mother. Grace observes, "Mrs. Bruckner held Ben awkwardly" (58). When Miriam, pregnant with her second child, takes Ben to pick strawberries, Grace assumes that Miriam will participate. Instead, Miriam "sat down on the bench and took out a fat Danielle Steel novel"; Grace "just stared" in disbelief (260). Miriam claims her pregnancy precludes physical activity, but Grace, referring to another group at the farm, thinks, "How I wanted to tell her that the pregnant Orthodox women seemed to be able to bend over and pick strawberries just fine" (261).

As we heard earlier, Miriam hires Grace to be a full-time child minder who must "give [Ben] his meals, his baths, take him to the park and his activities and playdates" (21). In *Raising Brooklyn*, we meet the sitter Deondra, who castigates her own employer for similar requirements. Deondra explains to Mose Brown: "Motherhood means that you feed your children, you bathe your children, and you spend time with your children. ... These mothers go to work and don't do anything for their children and then want the sitters or nannies to do everything, that's not motherhood" (95). Even though Mose Brown works, Deondra praises her: "See, you want to be with your children, feed them, give them a bath to be with them, that is a good mother" (95). Mose Brown suggests that Deondra is failing to account for her class privileges— having a financially supporting husband and flexible graduate school hours—that enable her "good" mothering. However, Mose Brown also recognizes the political impetus behind Deondra's assertions: "By making such broad claims, Deondra was expressing the inequality she felt as a domestic worker and demonstrating to me how power could be asserted through superior performance in the 'job' of 'mothering'" (95). Deondra's reflections on Mose Brown's own mother-work signal, too, how Mose Brown is a matroethnographer, who as both participant and documentarian is positioned both inside and outside of the child-minding community.

Relatedly, when Grace observes to Ule, "It's late to have a small baby outside," Ule agrees: "Is the same thing me try and tell the mother, but she don't want listen. I tell her dew falling already and America dew is colder than in the West Indies. A likkle child so should be inside. But nobody listen. She want me to bring the child outside for air, so me bring him outside for air. As long as when you see he catch pneumonia and drap dead them nah say is my fault" (98). Ule illuminates how the mother-work of racialized labourers is often performed in opposition to or even in fear of their employers' own mothering practices while implying that she is the better or more "fit" mother for her concern over pneumonia.

Duty and Discipline

Both texts further address differences or divisions in maternal attitudes towards discipline. Grace's mother-work is pitted against that of Miriam when Miriam surprises Grace and Ben at the park one day. Grace informs her that she has been trying to teach Ben how to share; to which Miriam counters, "Grace, Ben doesn't have to share his toys with anyone if he doesn't want to. It's totally up to him" (144), thus undermining Grace's efforts and authority. Another time, when Miriam wants to make it clear to Grace that her weeknights belong to Miriam—"You're full time live-in, and I need to have access to you at night"—Miriam presses, "Do you understand?" (293). Grace then narrates: "And Ben, who had been listening to his mother, said, 'You understand, Grace?' Miriam turned to him and laughed. She put her hand under her big belly and cradled it as she laughed. 'Oh, baby,' she said. Ben, happy that he could amuse his mother so, said it again, and Miriam laughed even harder" (293). This passage showcases how the employer, by enforcing her parenting style at the expense of the caregiver, humiliates the caregiver, while the employer's own mother-work (encouraging disrespectful behaviour in her child) is called into question or problematized. As one West Indian caregiver disparages with Grace, "These white children talk to you like them is the man, and the parents don't tell them no better" (29). Mose Brown supplies numerous comparable examples. In one, Victoria (the only white caregiver in her study) is spat on by her four-year-old charge in front of his mother. Victoria reports, "I was waiting for her to say something and she didn't say anything" (57).

Analyzing the impact of mother-work on the children in the sitters' care, Romero states, "The primary mission of reproductive labor in contemporary mothering is to assure their children's place in society" (836). Consequently, as Romero continues:

> If mothering is directed toward assuring their child's social and economic status in society—a society that is racist, capitalist, and patriarchal—then her goals are strengthened by employing a low wage, full-time or live-in immigrant woman. Conditions under which immigrant women of color are employed in private homes is structured by systems of privilege and, consequently, employers' children are socialized into these norms and values. (837)

Mose Brown would concur, for she contends, "The relationship between female employer and employee in the private household is fundamentally a patriarchal one in which the mother of the children being cared for takes on the role of traditional father figure" (38).[4] The responses—respectively enjoyment and indifference—by Miriam and Victoria's employer to their children's unacceptable behaviour reveal this patriarchal socialization in action. It is important to note that while Grace stood by and accepted her humiliation by Ben and Miriam, Victoria not only spoke back to her charge—"I actually said to him, 'Please never do that to me again. That is very mean'"—but also left work early, threating to quit if she is "ever put in that position again" (57). Mose Brown suggests that unlike the majority of racialized sitters who remain silent, Victoria may have felt empowered as a white woman to stand up to her employer.

While revealing how caregivers are mistreated, *Minding Ben* and *Raising Brooklyn* conversely tackle the serious issue of caregivers mistreating their charges. For instance, in *Minding Ben*, as a playdate winds down in a Manhattan apartment, Bruce, the boy in the care of Petal, announces, "Nanny, I want to go home." Petal lashes out: "Petal, who seemed to be the calmest woman in the park, turned on Bruce in a rage. 'You hear, don't call me nanny. A nanny is a she-goat, Bruce. My name is Petal. P.E.T.A.L. Say it.' She squeezed his arm tight. 'Say it'" (184). Certainly, Petal's corporal response to Bruce is inexcusable. Her unexpected outbreak might signal, however, the pent up rage of many caregivers, indicating the impact of her being pervasively disrespected and rendered invisible—just as Grace was mocked, and Victoria was spat on. Petal feels that she has been negated as a person, unrecognized and unnamed as a unique individual. Her loss of control with Bruce can be considered as having less to do with the child (who obviously cannot be held responsible for Petal's abuse) and more to do with the dire consequences of racist, capitalist globalization on migrant women's self-worth.

Such consequences are further tied to economic fears. From Mose Brown's reportage, we learn that "Providers disagreed about the acceptability of various ways of disciplining children, but many agreed that a provider shouldn't hit a child because that would most certainly get you fired, especially if done in a public place" (59). (Petal, we later learn, is indeed fired.) Reflecting on the episode with Bruce, Ule instructs Grace: "Don't mind what you see today. Petal is a good woman, and she love that little boy like she own son" (185). When Grace criticizes Petal's actions, Ule is defensive: "But what we going to do? Take bread out we own mouth?" (185). Ule attempts, however problematically, to redeem Petal as a loving child minder, concomitant with articulating the self-preservative needs of their financially constrained and systemically unsupported cohort.

Whose Boat Are You In?

The fallout from the scene above—with Grace and Ule in disagreement—testifies to how both *Raising Brooklyn* and *Minding Ben* portray collaborative mother-work as well as conflict among community members. This thematic is registered when the caregivers gather for the playdate at the Zoller residence, where Evie looks after twins Sammy and Caleb and where the Petal incident unfolded. Grace opens with a collegial montage: "The babysitter lime had moved to the fifteenth floor of Tower One. Petal had come by, so had Marva, Meena, and Ule. The

Bloomberg baby was asleep in his carriage, and, perhaps subdued by the weather, all the children were seated around Caleb and Sammy's work-table coloring, amazingly, quietly," while the caregivers play cards (181). Evie articulates the exigency of their shared situations and needs, telling Grace: "If you ever want to go and do your business, just bring Ben for me to watch. Is not a problem at all. All of we in the same leaky-ass boat" (183). Thus allied, the caregivers support each other in their moth-er-work and beyond. So, too, in *Raising Brooklyn*, as Mose Brown reveals: "I often saw West Indian sitters asking other West Indian sitters to watch their charges while they got something from the local bakery or ran back to the employer's house for something that they had forgotten" (53). Significantly, as a matroethnographer, Mose Brown was a partic-ipant within this collaborative system:

> Many West Indian childcare providers seemed to claim our rela-tionship as a reciprocal one. As they became more comfortable with me in the field, they would call on me for small favors, such as watching the child in their care at the park while they grabbed some lunch down the street, or calling me at home to use my bathroom during the day because a local park lacked a public restroom. On colder or rainy days we would cook together, often while listening and dancing to reggae and calypso music. (168)

Consequently, "These types of favors, along with the fact that I could often be seen with my two young children, led to a seemingly positive and receptive relationship between the women and me" (168).

At the same time, there could be dissonance within and between the communities. Mose Brown observed some tensions "between babysitters who came from different islands in the Caribbean" (33), just as Brown highlights the "playground politics" (89) of the sitters in her novel. In one instance, Ule cautions Grace about Evie, who has been trying to generate conflict between Grace and Ule: "Child, all I could tell you is watch your self with Evie. That woman know everything that going on in these four towers. Sometimes is best to just sit down and listen and don't say a word" (185). In this light, Ule negates Evie's earlier assertion of sisterhood: "You not in no same boat with nobody" (185).

Notions of union and disunion are further complicated by Grace's relationship with Sylvia. Grace attends the Brooklyn West Indian Day parade: "Trinidadians, Jamaicans, Bajans, Haitians, Guyanese, we were all there" (14), the "we" signaling a collective diasporic sensibility. Here Grace meets Sylvia, the Trinidadian who invites her to stay with her after Grace's first caregiving contract ends. Sylvia, however, takes advantage of Grace, expecting her to assume all childcare and housekeeping responsibilities while she, Sylvia, goes out to her own job at a domestic service agency. Once Grace begins working for the Bruckners, Sylvia forces Grace to pay fifty dollars a week for room and board over the weekends as well as to continue child-minding and cleaning duties for her. Even within the diasporic community, members can exploit other members. Confronting this fact, *Minding Ben* resists reducing caregivers to a monolithic entity, instead portraying them as complex individuals with complicated personalities and relationships. Moreover, we must empathize that as a racialized, domestic-working mother herself, Sylvia requires childcare as much as Miriam's legion of professionals. The systemic problems are assessed by Mose Brown: "Working mothers, whether they are immigrant childcare providers or the providers' employers, all find themselves repeatedly facing childcare crises. [...] We need a structural change in how people are connected economically" (148-49). I will return to this issue in my conclusion.

Seeking Social Justice

In *Raising Brooklyn*, Rachel, from St. Lucia, comments on the matrifocal support she receives from Molly, from Guyana: "Molly is older than me and she's like my mom in a sense. She gives me advice and talks to me and says you can't do this forever, you are young, you need to go to college and get yourself a degree" (33). Ule similarly warms to Grace, "You like me own daughter," and encourages Grace to seek a better life. Indeed, throughout the novel Grace—like all the caregivers—has been seeking her own version of the American dream. Surveying the Bruckners' apartment, she fantasizes living in "someplace like this," and "Not just to be the help" (57).

For most of the novel, Grace has pinned her hopes for advancement on securing sponsorship to become a landed immigrant. Her earlier invocation to Kath, "Once we get our papers" (43), illuminates one of the novel's key themes: the plight of the undocumented caregiver. Grace had been especially eager to work for the Bruckners after Miriam informed her, "We're looking for someone to be part of the family, someone we can sponsor maybe" (22). Not only do the Bruckners never treat Grace like "family," but as Mose Brown emphasizes of child minders, "These are employees, not 'family' as some might like to think" (151). This statement resonates with Mose Brown's acknowledgment of the pressures of caregiving: "I myself was often surprised at the amount of physical labor involved in this 'labor of love'" (70). The Trinidadian Irene speaks to Mose Brown about being poorly paid for this labour, criticizing her employers, "But if you're mean ... it makes us feel uncomfortable because, remember, we're with your kids most of the time, and you know, we'll end up loving those kids just like they're our own" (51). Relatedly, on one hand, Grace wants to be valued for her contributions to the Bruckner family, contributions that are not only physical but also personal and intimate, and constitutive of kinship. On the other hand, Grace needs to be paid (and to secure her papers) to survive. The intersecting issues of family, love, labour, and remuneration highlight the complex negotiations involved in nurturing for hire.

When Grace tells Kath about the promise of sponsorship, she wisely warns, "Be careful with these people, once they have that to hold over your head, they'll make you see hell before they sign anything" (44). Thus trapped, Grace is enraged by her situation while berating herself for being unable to express herself. In response to Miriam's often untenable demands, Grace longs to respond, "'I'm off,' or 'I'm done for the evening,' or 'This is my time.' But I could not" (100); and she tells us, "How I wanted to say no. [...] But I didn't. I couldn't" (261). Hope for a green card underlies Grace's willingness to be exploited and how, unlike the "good woman" in *Pish, Posh*, she cannot simply quit the Bruckners' service.

Mose Brown draws attention to issues of immigration status and workers' rights in her chapter on the Domestic Workers United (DWU), a non-profit organization founded in 2000. In an interview with Mose Brown, the DWU director, Ai-jen Poo, outlines the reality of caregiving: "The work is made invisible, it's not protected, the wages are low"; in response, there must be "education around respect for the work itself, not just as a form of wage labor, but as a form of work that traditionally women have done in the home for generations and continue to do, that isn't compensated" (135). Even though West Indian caregivers were "one of the targeted groups for this organization" (132), and many were working illegally (136), Mose Brown discovers that the women in general were not interested in activism, and their rationales resonate with the theme of sponsorship in *Minding Ben*. Irene affirms that "Fear of getting sent back to the islands was a common reason for sitters' nonparticipation in organizing efforts" (144). Furthermore, Molly notes that "Even people who did have a green card were afraid to report [abuse by employers]: they were 'still taking the abuse from bosses' and they endured such circumstances because they needed the money" (145). Mose Brown summarizes, "Just the prospect of getting fired, even if one didn't have to fear deportation, was catastrophic enough to scare many women away from DWU" (145) and thus from help to improve their socio-economic condition.

The urgent need for such an organization is implicitly driven home in *Minding Ben*, as many of the characters fail to realize their American dreams. For instance, throughout the novel, Sylvia is depicted not only as an exploitative figure towards Grace but also as a victim of the system. She inhabits a low-income flat covered in toxic lead paint that is literally impairing the development of her toddler, Damien, who has been ingesting paint chips. At the end of the book, Damien falls out of their apartment window to his death, traumatizing Sylvia as well as Grace, his caregiver.[5] Moreover, as mentioned earlier, Petal was fired, after which she becomes a homeless religious zealot, ranting on the streets that "This America is a wicked, nasty place" (332). Watching her, Grace reflects, "Something about Petal scared me. She had worked in the towers and limed with us in the playground and in the Zollers' apartment, and now here she was resurrected as mad as mad can be taking her crazy message to the highways and byways" (332). Kath winds up pregnant by the married man she loves, but as he refuses to leave his wife, she feels she has no choice but to have an abortion. Devastated, she returns to Trinidad; she will become the manager of her parents' new store, but she leaves the US depleted. As maternal figures and immigrant caregivers, these West Indian women experience not the American dream but diverse matrifocal nightmares.

Damien's death precipitates the end of Grace's employment. Grace is alone with Ben on the evening she gets a phone call from the hysterical Micky, begging Grace to come to Brooklyn the night of her brother's fall. In rushing to comfort the terrified child, Grace is forced to take Ben with her on the subway. When Grace returns to the Bruckners hours later, they fire her on the spot—just as they had done with Carmen. In disregarding the rules, Grace sealed her fate. However, her treatment is problematized by the fact that Grace learns the family had been lying to her all along—they had no intention of filing sponsorship papers—and that they were going to let her go anyway, as they had sold their Manhattan apartment and were preparing for their imminent move to the countryside. Grace, it seems, never stood a chance with these employers.

Conclusion

If *Minding Ben* ended here, with Grace turfed into the streets, it would unquestionably exemplify the type of narrative described by Walters as a "more authentic rendition" of the caregiving experience than offered in texts like *The Nanny Diaries* (50). However, this authenticity is compromised in the novel's Afterword. Having been befriended earlier in the story by Dave, a wealthy gay man living in the penthouse of the Bruckners's building, Grace is, *en fin*, rescued by him. He decides to move to Florida and offers her the job of taking care of his apartment's solarium greenhouse, including free accommodation in his massive Manhattan suite. Grace thrillingly accepts his invitation and further prepares to return to school, no longer needing to work as a caregiver. She revels, "I couldn't believe my luck"; "Minding plants instead of ... you know. Oh my God, yes!" (334). Walters notes the significant fact that the publishers of *Minding Ben* marketed the text "similarly to *The Nanny Diaries* and *Mary Poppins*—the book jacket features a nanny holding the infamous umbrella" (51), suggesting its association with these more whitewashed and, in the case of *Mary Poppins*, fantastical portraits of caregivers.

As Walters posits, "As a memoir combined with the stories of other domestics, *Minding Ben* is a cautionary tale about the American dream and the insecurity of undocumented domestic workers whose status makes them vulnerable and exploited" (51). However, Walters does not comment on *Minding Ben*'s fairy-tale ending, which recapitulates to a happily-ever-after imaginary. Romero uncovers "little if any social mobility" among immigrant workers: "For these women, domestic service is best described as a ghetto occupation rather than a bridging occupation" (816). While Grace escapes, her cohort remains at the playground. Mose Brown attests, "Domestic workers find it difficult to better their education or improve their chances for economic mobility because of their non-negotiable dependency on childcare work" (154). Mose Brown cites Jennie, who believes, "Things aren't going to get better unless sitters get out of this position. ... Well, I mean it will never get better even if they get out because another generation is going to do it" (142). In writing about the ending of books like *Agnes Grey* and *The Nanny Diaries*, Hale queries, "I wondered why the best reward for enduring a terrible workplace was not to reform it but to leave it" (104) and confirms, "The implication is that the workplace can never be changed" (115). Could it be that the plight of caregivers is so dire, so pessimistic, that the only way to imagine their advancement is through an act of magic—say, an improbable plot turn that lifts child minders like Grace, Mary-Poppins style, up and away to the penthouse?[6]

If *Minding Ben* does not seek to reform the domestic workspace, Grace's delight in being able to swap minding Ben for minding plants testifies to the novel's overwhelming impetus to expose imbalances of power between employers and their domestic labourers. Before Miriam, Grace worked for Mora, a mutually beneficial exchange: Grace affirms, "I liked working for Mora"; and Mora gives Grace a "very good reference" for Miriam (35). Yet scant mention is made of her. Brown tells interviewer Amanda Sidman that she herself worked for three families and that while Miriam is based on one real employer, "the last of her employers, Nancy Ney, was 'the family every nanny would want to work for'" (qtd. in Sidman). Why, then, did Brown not focus her story on the figure of Ney and on the positive experiences she had as a caregiver? The answer might come from Grace, who acknowledges that her relationship with Mora "was very different from how most of the women in the towers got on with their help" (173). That is, Brown shares a matroethnographic account of the majority, encompassing broader truths and realities experienced by her particular caregiving collective.[7]

Raising Brooklyn is likewise an assemblage of honest confessions and admonitions from West Indian sitters. The study documents the very real and oppressive conditions under which racialized caregivers perform their mother-work, and more so than *Minding Ben*, it gestures to realizing radical restructuring of domestic labour. Mose Brown references volunteer organizations like DWU created in 2000 and its push for a Domestic Workers Bill of Rights, which at the time of her writing had been put before the New York State Legislature (133-40). The Bill went into effect on November 29, 2010, guaranteeing "rights for privately employed nannies, housekeepers and elder caregivers," including "defining an eight-hour day as a legal day's work" and "workers compensation insurance for full-time and part-time domestic workers," among other benefits ("Domestic Workers Bill of Rights Campaign"). In 2007, the DWU became part of the broader National Domestic Workers Alliance (NDWA). Today, with Ai-jen Poo as its president,[8] it continues to press for results. As of 2023, Domestic Workers Bills of Rights have been passed in ten states, two cities, and Washington, DC.[9] However, as urged on the website for the NDWA, "We continue to push for bills of rights in more states and cities as well as federal recognition and protection for domestic workers" ("Domestic Workers Bills of Rights").[10]

One caregiver speaks for the many to Mose Brown: "We just want to be appreciated for the work we do. Pay us so that we can live a decent life. Help us to get our documents, or help us when our children need us to tend to them. ... Don't punish us because we have a life outside of working for you. We all want this not just me, but all of us ... as a community of sitters" (151). Mose Brown believes, "This is the message West Indian childcare providers want the public to hear" (151). *Minding Ben* and *Raising Brooklyn*, published in the same year and appearing at the same zeitgeist of reform, are predicated on giving voice to neglected caregivers, who exhort each other and their audiences to listen to their warnings, their truths, and their needs. In this, they fulfill the objectives of authoethnography, providing "accounts that allow others to 'bear witness' to these experiences" and to "Break Silences, and Reclaim Lost and Disregarded Voices," including "talking back to neglected cultural experiences" (Adams, Jones, and Ellis 40-41)—like those of the West Indian caregivers featured herein. *Raising Brooklyn* and *Minding Ben* contribute to what Mose Brown sees as the way forwards to social justice: "We need not only an ongoing dialogue about how New York and the United States in general integrate childcare providers into the larger social and economic structure, but also efforts to alter the structures in ways that respect these workers' *collective autonomy*" (149). Tamara Mose Brown and Victoria Brown are matroethnographers inscribing their own individual as well as collective and collaborative matrifocal narratives. In so doing, they provide forums for representing, respecting, and heeding the "collective autonomy" of real and fictionalized caregivers like Jennie, Molly, Rachel, Evelyn, Deondra, Grace, Kath, Ule, Evie, and Petal.

Endnotes

1. Walters expands: "Keyi and Brown belong to a tradition of Caribbean authors who have written about challenges for Caribbean domestics in North America, such as Paule Marshall's *Brown Girl, Brownstones* (1959), Dionne Brand's *Sans Souci* (1989), and Jamaica Kincaid's *Lucy* (1990)" (50).

2. Regarding terminology, I note that Mose Brown states, "I use *childcare provider* when speaking of my participants in general, but where the providers themselves used a specific title, I adhere to that specific term" (17)—these include "*babysitter, sitter, nanny,* and *childcare provider*" (14). For my part, I use caregiver as a broad term while taking my cue from Mose Brown's study as well as the characters in *Minding Ben,* who identify as child minder, nanny, babysitter, and sitter.

3. It is here that Grace is asked to read *Pish, Posh,* to Ben as a "test"; Miriam offers a compliment laced with racism: "You read and speak so well for someone … from the islands" (35).

4. Here Mose Brown draws on the work of Judith Rollins.

5. Although Sylvia was home at the time, she was unaware that a visiting friend of her brother, Bo (who lived with Sylvia and the children), had opened a window.

6. Note that in a happily-ever-after turn, the "good woman" housekeeper returns to the family at the end of *Pish, Posh, Said Hieronymus Bosch.*

7. Consider, for instance, that in her own study, Cameron Lynne Macdonald concludes: "The great majority of the mother-nanny relationships I observed did not evolve into" mutually rewarding experiences (167). For her, it was rare to uncover partnerships between caregivers and their employers that were overwhelmingly positive (168).

8. For more on Ai-jen Poo, see "Ai-jen Poo."

9. Bills have been passed in California, Connecticut, Hawaii, Illinois, Massachusetts, Nevada, New Mexico, New York, Oregon, and Virginia; Philadelphia and Seattle; and Washington DC ("Passed Legislation").

10. According to the NDWA, "Federal recognition and comprehensive

protection for this workforce is long overdue. That's why we are working with Senators Kristen Gillibrand and Ben Ray Luján and Representative Pramila Jayapal to introduce the National Domestic Workers Bill of Rights, which will establish rights for millions of home care workers, nannies and house cleaners in the U.S." ("Domestic Workers Bills of Rights").

Works Cited

Adams, Tony E., Stacy Holman Jones, and Carolyn Ellis. 2015. *Autoethnography: Understanding Qualitative Research*. Oxford University Press, 2015.

"Ai-jen Poo." Domestic Workers, domesticworkers.org/press/spokes-persons/ai-jen-poo/. Accessed 13 Oct. 2023.

Aryo, Analyn. *Nanny Tales: Voices from the Diary of an Overseas Filipina Worker*. ResearchMate, 2009.

Auerbach, Jessika. *And Nanny Makes Three: Mothers and Nannies Tell the Truth about Work, Love, Money, and Each Other*. St. Martin's Press, 2007.

Brontë, Anne. *Agnes Grey*. Thomas Cautley Newby, 1847.

Brown, Tamara Mose. *Raising Brooklyn: Nannies, Childcare, and Caribbeans Creating Community*. New York University Press, 2011.

Brown, Victoria. *Minding Ben*. NY Books, 2011.

Chang, Heewon, Faith Wambura Ngunjiri, and Kathy-Ann C. Hernandez. *Collaborative Autoethnography*. Left Coast Press, 2013.

"Domestic Workers Bill of Rights." *National Domestic Workers Alliance*, https://www.domesticworkers.org/programs-and-campaigns/developing-policy-solutions/domestic-workers-bill-of-rights/#:~:text=The%20Domestic%20Workers%20Bill%20of%20Rights%20typically%20includes%20provisions%20that,discrimination%2C%20harassment%2C%20and%20retaliation. Accessed 13 Oct. 2023.

"Domestic Workers Bill of Rights Campaign." knowyourrightsny.org, Accessed 13 Oct. 2023.

Hale, Elizabeth. "Long-Suffering Professional Females: The Case of Nanny Lit." *Chick Lit: The New Woman's Fiction*, edited by Suzanne Ferriss and Mallory Young, Routledge, 2006, pp. 103-18.

Lee, Felicia R. "Nannies Still Draw a Keen Audience." *The New York Times*, 13 July 2010, https://www.nytimes.com/2010/07/14/books/14nanny.html. Accessed 13 Oct. 2023.

Kaylin, Lucy. *The Perfect Stranger: The Truth about Mothers and Nannies.* Bloomsbury, 2007.

Keyi, Nandi. *The True Nanny Diaries.* Bread for Brick Publishing, 2009.

Macdonald, Cameron Lynne. *Shadow Mothers: Nannies, Au Pairs, and the Micropolitics of Mothering.* University of California Press, 2011.

McLaughlin, Emma, and Nicola Kraus. *The Nanny Diaries.* St. Martin's Griffin, 2002.

Mose Brown, Tamara. "About Me." tamaramose.com/bio. Accessed 13 Oct. 2023.

"Passed Legislation." National Domestic Workers Alliance, https://www.domesticworkers.org/programs-and-campaigns/developing-policy-solutions/domestic-workers-bill-of-rights/. Accessed 13 Oct. 2023.

Podnieks, Elizabeth. "Matrifocal Voices in Literature." *Routledge Companion to Motherhood*, edited by Lynn Hallstein-O'Brien et al. Routledge, 2019, pp. 176-90.

Podnieks, Elizabeth. "'The Synergy Between You': Mothers, Nannies, and Collaborative Caregiving in Contemporary Matroethnographies." *Life Writing*, vol. 18, no. 3, 2021, pp. 337-54.

Rollins, Judith. *Between Women: Domestics and Their Employers.* Temple University Press, 1985.

Romero, Mary. "Nanny Diaries and Other Stories: Imagining Immigrant Women's Labor in the Social Reproduction of American Families." *DePaul Law Review*, vol. 52, no. 3, Spring 2003, pp. 809-48.

Ruddick, Sara. *Maternal Thinking: Toward a Politics of Peace.* Beacon Press, 2002.

Sidman, Amanda P. "'Minding Ben' author Victoria Brown drew from New York Nanny Experiences for New Novel." *Daily News*, 18 Apr. 2011, https://www.nydailynews.com/2011/04/18/minding-ben-author-victoria-brown-drew-from-new-york-nanny-experiences-for-new-novel/. Accessed 20 Oct. 2023.

Slimani, Leila. *Chanson Douce*. Gallimard, 2016.

Slimani, Leila. *Lullaby*. Faber & Faber, 2018.

Slimani, Leila. *The Perfect Nanny*. Penguin, 2018.

Simpson, Mona. *My Hollywood*. Vintage, 2010.

Walters, Tracey L. *Not Your Mother's Mammy: The Black Domestic Worker in Transatlantic Women's Media*. Rutgers University Press, 2021.

Section III

Care(ful) Relationships around the Globe: Sociological and Anthropological Analyses

Section III

Care(full) Relationships around the Globe: Sociological and Anthropological Analyses

Chapter 11

Between Cosmopolitan Mothering and the Global Care Chain: Japanese Mothers, Intra-Asian Migration, and Everyday Struggles of "the Nanny Question"

Aya Kitamura

Introduction: Maids and Madams in Global Cities

This chapter explores the inherently unequal relationship between women of privilege and the other(ed) women they employ in their private households—"the nanny question" (Tronto)—in the context of intra-Asian migration. It focusses on Japanese women who relocate to Singapore and attend to the conflicting roles that they perform in the Asian global city. While these women are likely to enjoy a variety of privileges associated with their nationality, ethnicity, and class, their gendered status—as a wife of a global elite and a mother of cosmopolitan children—may confine them within particular traditional gender role expectations. Moreover, when they employ a Southeast Asian domestic worker at home, they newly assume the "madam" role that is common in Singapore but is rarely present in Japan. Through original interview data, this chapter explores such mothers' struggles, including intra-Asian migration, to inquire into the connectivity between the women's personal experiences and sociopolitical hierarchies and disparities in the Asian global city.

As early as the 1990s, Saskia Sassen argued that global elites enjoy class privilege in their foreign destinations while accelerating the precariousness of the livelihoods of poorer populations, including those of migrant workers (324-5). Such global inequality often goes hand in hand with gender inequalities. The intimate work of migrant and other underprivileged women who cook, clean, and provide sexual services are also part of the daily reality of flourishing global cities (Ochiai and Aoyama). Even as they provide such highly sought after carework, those women are socially stigmatized and acutely vulnerable (Boris and Parreñas; Brooks and Devasahayam; Ehrenreich and Hochschild; Githens).

Particularly in Asia, racial, ethnic, class, and gender oppression often intersect with one another in the neoliberal regimes of global cities (Ochiai and Aoyama; A. Ong). In many Asian global cities—including but not limited to Singapore, Hong Kong, and Kuala Lumpur—the ways in which migrant domestic workers can be hired by local and expat families are institutionalized through hierarchical and targeted visa and work-permit categories as well as through a transnational industry of commercial agencies specializing in connecting upper-income households with low-skilled maids from nearby countries. The governments of these global cities support upper-middle-class, double-income, heterosexual households through providing institutional access to domestic workers from poorer regions of Southeast Asia. While the state programs benefit privileged families (i.e., ideal neoliberal citizens who can self-care and self-manage), the schemes also inscribe class disparity along with national, racial, and ethnic divisions of labour in private homes. Carework is regarded not as a public but as a private matter that individual families can and should take care of.

Consider, for example, how privilege is institutionalized through the work permits for different classifications of foreigners in Singapore. Expat "professionals" and their families are defined by their income and exclusive educational background; typically, those working for global multinational firms will typically be there on an employment pass visa, which requires them to earn a minimum of five thousand Singaporean dollars per month as well as to have qualifications from an accredited overseas college or university that is recognized by the government of

Singapore (Singapore Ministry of Manpower, *Eligibility*). Family members accompanying these expat professionals will likely be there on a dependent's pass.[1] The basic requirements for obtaining a migrant domestic worker (MDW) work permit in Singapore stand in stark contrast. An applicant must be: (1) a woman; (2) between the ages of twenty-three and fifty at the time of applying; (3) from a state-approved source country or region; and (4) have at least eight years of formal education (Singapore Ministry of Manpower, *Migrant Domestic Worker Eligibility*).[2] That is, foreign domestic workers are defined by their gender and age, their countries of origin, and their lack of higher education. Even this brief look at the basic categories of work permits for foreigners in Singapore reveals how inequality and dependence are prescribed as the basis of relationships between foreign domestic workers and their employers.

In such institutional contexts, many ethnographic studies have revealed the inhumane realities of the "global care chain" (Hochschild). Migrant women primarily from the Philippines, Indonesia, Myanmar, Thailand, Sri Lanka, and a number of other Asian countries often have little choice but to go through commercial agencies at both their places of origin and their destinations and can thus become highly vulnerable financially, legally, and socially. Inside their employers' houses, they are often exposed to surveillance, discipline, discrimination, and other worse forms of physical and mental abuse (Constable; Lan; Piper and Yamanaka). The global cities regard them merely as "a single product: a hardworking, submissive, and obedient domestic helper" (Constable 69) and treat them as "subhuman" (A. Ong 208). Although migrant women often organize collectively, utilizing their social and linguistic capital, the social security provided to these workers by the state in the host countries is usually far from sufficient (Lindio-McGovern). As such, the idealistic picture of global elites managing their global households in prospering global cities in fact masks multiple layers of socioeconomic inequalities, and women, both maids and madams, especially experience the resulting disparities within the most private sphere—the home.

Japanese Mothers as Madams in Singapore

A Japanese mother in Singapore, shopping at high-end Japanese and international grocery stores, hiring a Southeast Asian domestic worker, and raising cosmopolitan children is one example of global-elite cluster that is increasing in Asia. A rapid and massive inter-flow of business between Japan and Singapore has developed especially in the early 2010s, before the COVID-19 pandemic hit, and thus, more and more cosmopolitan Japanese elites and their families move transiently or permanently to the Southeast Asian hub. According to the Japanese Ministry of Foreign Affairs, as of October 2022, Singapore hosts the eleventh largest population (32,743) of Japanese outside Japan.

This expat population includes women who accompany their husbands on international job assignments or entrepreneurships as a full-time homemaker as well as others who negotiate their own career by, sometimes, transferring to her company's Singapore division or switching to a freelance job that requires only online correspondence. Yet others live permanently in Singapore as immigrant families from Japan, or as wives of a Singaporean or other national. This group of Japanese women enjoys a variety of privileges associated with their nationality and ethnicity as well as with their social class. In this intra-Asian context, they are largely exempt from the type of racial stereotypes that they might come across in North America or Europe, for instance.

Notably, as discussed above, the privileged lifestyles of such Japanese women in Singapore are predicated on and help to reify unequal power relations characteristic of the global city-state. Behind their well-off lifestyles is the labour of local and migrant workers that the global cities heavily depend on, albeit in a highly invisible way. Japanese mothers are integrated into Singapore's inherent contradiction between its state-sanctioned multiculturalism and "everyday racism" (Velayutham) and "everyday un-cosmopolitanism" (F. Ong and Yeoh). The clear hierarchy among the haves and the have-nots is irrefutable.

Meanwhile, this particular madam-maid context could be a significant source of frustration for Japanese mothers in Singapore. While global-elite husbands/fathers may have no problem devoting themselves to their work, the wives/mothers, working or not, are often expected to create a "bubble of Japanese-ness in the middle of foreign-ness" for her family (Kurotani 12). They are often expected to prepare Japanese meals, clothes, and baths, to keep up a Japanese standard of cleanliness in the home, and to maintain the children's Japanese language proficiency. They are, above all, the guardians of Japanese-ness in their home away from home. They must navigate this perplexing situation while assuming a new role of household employer. They experience difficulties as international relations scholar Catherine Goetze discusses about cosmopolitan mothering:

> Much of this process of navigating, translating and mitigating strangeness is the responsibility of mothers, a task adding to already existing dilemmas and difficulties women experience when they need to position themselves as spouses, mothers, daughters, and former, future or current working women in multinational and multicultural contexts. (220)

Similarly, playing the role of global-elite mother in a highly stratified Asian global city is rarely a smooth process.

Below, I will draw upon my original interview research from 2017 and onwards, conducted with sixteen Japanese women who were living or had lived in Singapore for one to thirteen years. At the time of the first interviews, they were aged between thirty-three and fifty-one. Six were full-time homemakers, four were full-time corporate employees, one was an entrepreneur, and the remaining five had part-time jobs. Most of them were college educated with some having earned graduate degrees. Seven of them were married to Japanese husbands, while nine had a Singaporean, American, or British partner. All of them had one to three children and had hired a domestic worker from the Philippines, Indonesia, and/or Myanmar. I employed a snowball sampling method; I first met a few of the research participants through a mutual acquaintance, and as the research proceeded, I met the others through another research participant who introduced us.

Each interview was carried out in Japanese and in a semi-structured method, starting with a common opening question, "How do you like your life in Singapore?" After that, the research participant led the conversation, narrating their experiences inside and outside their home in Singapore. As I disclosed my identity as a mother-researcher also from a bilingual/bicultural background, we confided and empathized with each other about our familial struggles. This mutually open feminist method (Harding; Oakley) allowed for the interviews to last for two to four hours. With some participants, I conducted second and third interviews while exchanging follow-up emails with others. Research participants are referred to by a pseudonym in the following.

The analysis below will explore the following questions: What privilege and confinement do the Japanese mothers in Singapore experience, and what are some consequences of their choices and actions? How care-full or care-less can the relationships in their global households be? I will argue, first, that the research participants tended to narrate their decisions to hire a migrant domestic worker as a "rational choice," employing a neoliberal discourse prevalent in both Japan and Singapore. Second, many women also emphasized the difficulties of assuming the household-employer role, drawing on their constant anxiety and insecurity—of which, curiously, the husbands and children seemed to be devoid. Third, such personal struggles at times drove Japanese mothers to act collectively by using informal networks and social media. Japanese expat communities, once firmly confined with corporate relations (Kurotani), are now found to be relatively uprooted from traditional ties and to be more diverse, voluntary, and specifically needs based (Nagatomo). The Japanese women's online and offline network provides an exigent example. As such, the mothers from Japan are indeed "oppressed and agentive" as well as "curtailed and mobilizing," as migrant women tend to be (Erel 32). Simultaneously, the analysis uncovers how the Japanese women, unquestioningly subscribing to the racial/ethnic/class hierarchies, could also be oppressive and curtailing in their relationship with migrant domestic workers. Through illuminating such multidirectional nature of oppression, this chapter aims to analyze the dilemmas and difficulties of cosmopolitan mothering in an under-studied context of intra-Asian migration.

"It's Cheaper and Easier that Way": Rationalizing Their Choice in the Global City

For the research participants, life in Singapore is by and large enjoyable yet burdensome. They spoke highly of how clean and accessible the city-state tends to be and praised the government's efficient use of information technology, as well as the general vibrancy of the multiethnic, multicultural, and multilingual society. Many also referred to their Singaporean female friends and acquaintances whose careers were not hindered by their gender, unlike those of their counterparts in Japan. However, in a more day-to-day context, managing a household in a foreign culture/language often turned out to be exhausting, especially for those who had young children, for those whose husbands were frequently away for international business trips, as well as for those who managed their own career while taking care of their household. Furthermore, many mothers lamented the harsh competitiveness of Singapore's educational system that physically and mentally burdened children and parents both. Working mothers had to keep up with the equally severe business world too, and most considered the double shift as beyond their capacity. Clearly, the Japanese mothers were not entirely liberated from domestic chores, concerns, and responsibilities in Singapore.

Therefore, it is only "natural" and "rational"—as many research participants described—for those overburdened women to start outsourcing carework. In Singapore, not only a local but also an expatriate family is eligible to apply for a work permit for a domestic worker of foreign origin. Owing to the state's advanced information technology services, the government offers comprehensive online support for prospective employers. In addition, there are many private agencies—some bilingual/multilingual—that undertake the whole process on behalf of the employer. The minimum wages, stipulated not by Singaporean government but by the domestic worker's country of origin, range between 450 and 570 Singaporean dollars, which, from an employer's viewpoint, is "totally manageable," according to one research participant, Ms. Suzuki:

> Obviously, it's a great system. It's cheap. Cost performance is all there is to it. You have a lot to do around the house and so you hire a live-in maid from the Philippines; it's just cheaper and easier that way. Let's say you [the wife] earn three thousand Singaporean dollars a month. You pay eight hundred to a Filipina maid. It's totally manageable. And what do I buy for that money? Time and energy for my children. I don't have to do dishes; I can read to them in bed instead. With that extra ease of mind, I can be nice. I can be a good mom.

She further explains:

> Here in Singapore, the assumption is that you have a maid. The whole society is built on it. Without hiring one, you are screwed. Look at our house. It's small but has three bathrooms and multiple balconies. All the children do all different types of activities, and adults are supposed to be there, too. For example, when my son wants to join a soccer team, and my daughter wants to learn ballet, I can't take them both by myself. I need help, right?

As such, a general agreement seems to be that not just among Japanese expat families but also in Singaporean society in general, one is to hire a migrant domestic worker if she is a proper parent raising a proper child in the global city. She can buy time, energy, and mental ease for a reasonable price. Why shouldn't she?

This rhetoric, undeniably rooted in a neoliberal logic that is predicated on socioeconomic disparities, reverberated throughout my interview research. Although the research participants spoke of their choice of hiring a domestic worker just like any other commercial transaction—a "rational" and "cost-effective" choice—the fact that this relationship between worker and employer occurs in a shared living space, and not as a one-off exchange but continuously through all hours of the day, should give us pause regarding such a characterization. Political scientist Joan Tronto argues that carework, which often occurs in an enclosed space and in an immediate and intimate relationship, is different from other marketized actions, yet it is put under the capitalist logic, to be rationally outsourced if one—a mother, for example—wants to succeed at it. Tronto writes:

> Fueled by a fear of the increasing competition for scarce future seats in competitive colleges, jobs, and so forth, the needs of children become greater and more expansive, without limit or public discussion. Thus, the injustice of hiring domestic servants is obscured by the ideological construction of intensive and competitive mothering. (44)

Under the rhetoric of "in the best interests of the children," such mothers justify their unjust acts of exploiting other women, who are often from working-class and other underprivileged backgrounds.

Ms. Suzuki above emphasized that she outsourced cleaning for the sake of her children, to read to them in bed, to "be a good mom." The domestic worker she hires is instrumental for this purpose; that is, the "live-in maid" in her narrative exists only as an instrument, a means to an end, and not as another woman who might equally need "extra ease of mind" or have a child of her own left behind in the Philippines. In her telling, the worker is first and foremost a convenient (and financially "totally manageable") commodity whose services she purchases to meet the demands of housework and childcare.

Anthropologist Aihwa Ong is critical of the manner in which migrant domestic workers are alienated in Asian global cities:

> Having a maid at home is a social right, like access to good schools, housing, shopping malls, and leisure, all entitlements of the middle-class bent on buying their way to the good life. But even as the host country finds itself more intimately entangled with poor neighbors who participate in the reproduction of family life, disciplinary mechanisms and ethical exclusions invest the foreign maid with a *bio political otherness* in the public and domestic realms. (my emphasis, 202)

Ms. Suzuki and other privileged mothers from Japan certainly do not seem to regard themselves as someone who "disciplines" or "excludes" migrant women. They hire a domestic worker only because they "need help." However, they are the ones who decide when, where, and how the worker spends her time, night and day, if they so choose. They are the ones, as required of employers, who send the migrant women to an annual checkup for pregnancy and HIV, which is a violation of the migrant women's reproductive rights. As such, the Japanese mothers too are a part of the "bio political otherness" inflicted upon migrant domestic workers in Singapore. However, any critical self-awareness of their role in the exploitation of the migrant women is conspicuously absent among the research participants, masked by the neoliberalist discourse of "rational choice." All the while, the global care chain with its inherent inequalities remains intact.

"A Lot of Trouble": Othering Migrant Domestic Workers

Notably, such "rational" and "cost-effective" living like Ms. Suzuki's does not necessarily come true at once. The women from Japan in my interview research had little to no experience with being a "madam" before. It is rather rare in Japan to hire outside help in a private household; moreover, the Japanese government had long prohibited labour immigration until a new visa category for "foreigners conducting housekeeping services" was introduced in 2017. This scheme is intended specifically for migrant domestic workers from Southeast Asia who perform housework in Japanese homes, under the supervision of specially appointed personnel companies in only four designated prefectures over a strictly limited duration of five years. There are approximately two thousand such workers nation-wide as of 2021 (Cabinet Office of Japan), and because of this scarce availability, none of the women I interviewed, many of whom had left Japan before the scheme, had ever used the service in Japan.

Thus, the Japanese mothers often had to train themselves to assume their new role as a household manager/supervisor. Each needed to learn to assess her employee's skills, distribute household chores between the worker and herself, and supervise the everyday running of the household. The process has been painstaking for many of these first-timer madams, who had to negotiate with a professional domestic worker from a different linguistic, cultural, and socioeconomic background. Ms. Hirata provides an illuminating example. When I first met her and told her that I was interested in her life in Singapore, she started without pause. "There's a lot of trouble. A lot. Hiring a maid doesn't mean life gets any easier," she explained, as if to keep me from holding the naïve assumption that she and other Japanese mothers enjoyed their class privilege and had an easy life in Singapore.

Ms. Hirata was a working mother of two children and had hired more than a dozen domestic workers in her twelve years in Singapore. (She said she had lost track of exactly how many.) Like Ms. Suzuki, she claimed her decision to pursue her career while outsourcing carework was financially rational; however, in the first half of our two-and-a-half-hour interview, she recalled various distressing incidents that she had experienced with domestic workers from the Philippines. Some came under-skilled, so much so that Ms. Hirata had to do the laundry and ironing herself. She had to give precise and minute instructions as to what to buy, how to store each food item, and how to cook it "so as to avoid food poisoning in my home." Many of them "lied" and "cut corners," she explained, and Ms. Hirata once fired a worker who was found to have gone out to have fun, all dressed up, after she and her family left home in the morning. Some other employees called her at work, saying, "Ma'am, I forgot to pick up your daughter," and "What time was the doctor's appointment again?"—phone calls that "almost stopped my heart." For a while she had shuttled between her work, her children's schools, and her home by herself, "literally running around, couldn't even breathe" because the nanny at the time was too unreliable. She said she had so many such stories that she could write a whole book.

Ms. Hirata, as well as some other research participants, probably felt she had to showcase these incidents in a rather exaggerated manner in front of a researcher who might otherwise misunderstand her as a carefree lady of the leisure class in Singapore. As if to preempt such a characterization, she drew on the widespread notion that it is acceptable to publicly complain and criticize the maids from her urban, upper-middle-class, Japanese viewpoint. In her narrative, domestic workers from the Philippines are together labelled as being inept and untrustworthy, a source of "trouble." The unpredictable and difficult nature of carework was never mentioned, and the possibility of the Japanese mothers themselves falling short of their responsibilities was rarely considered. It was solely the maids—migrant women from poorer regions—who were to blame.

In Aihwa Ong's words, it is the "ethnoracial hierarchy" in Asia that underlies such mistrust toward migrant domestic workers. She observes that while public expressions of racism are now prohibited in Asian global cities, "these rules do not apply when it comes to the treatment of foreign migrants who perform a variety of 'low-skill' or 'unskilled' jobs avoided by local citizens" (203). The stigmatizing stereotypes, as in Ms. Hirata's narrative, are left unquestioned and even justified in ethno-racist terms. The workers' autonomy is thereby scarcely respected, and their dignity is made light of. Japanese mothers in Singapore, despairing at their intensive mothering duties, simultaneously intensify the biopolitical otherness of other migrant women.

"I Have to Be the Yeller": Gendered Division of Labour Maintained

The domestic dependence of husbands and children was another common concern that surfaced during my interview research. Ms. Suzuki, who was positive about her rational choice above, said hiring a domestic worker also improved her relationship with her husband:

And it [hiring a maid] has reduced arguments between my husband and me a lot. I don't have to ask him to pick up children or to look after them when I can't. We both have this space to ourselves, and he enjoys it even more than I do.

Yet she acknowledges that her husband as well as her children took it for granted that someone other than themselves would take care of housework. As Ms. Suzuki relates:

> Sometimes I think about letting go our maid now that the children are older, but my husband says, "No, no, no, don't do that. I will pay for it. Keep her." He knows that he can focus on his work like he does now because we have a maid.... One thing we mothers here [in Singapore] discuss often is how children get spoiled because we have a maid. My children don't pick up after themselves. They think our maid will do it for them. Embarrassingly, I myself realize that only when we go back to Japan and see other children there. It's a problem.

Ms. Hirata, the mother above who found maids to be a source of stress, echoes the anxiety:

> My husband does so little at home. All husbands are like that when there is a maid at home. That's another problem. Children would see that and copy that. I don't want my son to think that a father has nothing to do with housework. So, I keep yelling at them: "Put away your own dishes," "You can't just assume there's always someone to take care of you." I have to be the yeller of the family all the time. Sometimes I ask the maid not to help the older one, but they are both too used to the old habit by now. We all are.

Both Ms. Suzuki and Ms. Hirata might no longer worry about cleaning, cooking, and washing, but they were still the ones who oversaw family relations, assuming the role of "the yeller" and trying to change household dynamics in vain. The husbands were exempted from all that, outsourcing his share of housework and childcare. Sociologist Evelyn Nakano Glenn argues, "Mothering is constructed through men's and women's actions within specific historical circumstances" (3). Highlighting how mothering is racialized as well as gendered, Glenn argues: "Middle-class men can keep the illusion (or reality?) of the home as a private haven, while enjoying the services of their wives or their wives' substitutes in maintaining that haven. Thus, the notion of mothering as women's responsibility is left unchallenged" (7).

As such, the question of whether the Japanese mothers in Singapore have it easy is complicated, as Ms. Hirata had indicated. Many women shared with me that all work related to hiring and managing maids was considered their responsibility, from researching local hiring rules, visiting agencies, arranging and conducting interviews with prospective employees to training and supervising employees—the additional "third shift" labour (Hondagneu-Sotelo). Apparently, they are the ones who worry over the consequences, too. After all, the gendered division of labour in their home remains, and their "rational" choice is a double -edged sword that may solve everyday predicaments but ultimately confines the mothers to a domestic role along with the domestic worker they hire.

"How Are You Doing with Your Maid?": Networking, Empowerment, and Disempowerment

Another equally troubled mother, Ms. Nakajima, took a different, more collectively engaged, approach to tackling her mothering difficulties. She first told me about her "typical Japanese husband," who reluctantly agreed to hire a domestic worker from Indonesia but kept complaining about how the maid cooked and cleaned. He only ate Japanese food and expected a high standard of cleanliness at home. In the end, he always criticized Ms. Nakajima, who also worked full-time in a local trading company, for not doing enough as a wife and mother. Apparently, getting housework done to a Japanese standard was all on her shoulders.

Ms. Nakajima then told me that she and other working mothers from Japan started a social media group where they "joke about all those frustrating things in Singapore." When she first joined the group and read what the other Japanese working mothers had to say about their home management circumstances, she felt that she was not the only one feeling lost and stressed. She soon opened up to the other working mothers and shared the struggles she was experiencing with her domestic worker as well as with her husband. Others responded with empathetic comments. The spontaneous group gradually expanded to a larger network among Japanese mothers in Singapore. They have organized face-to-face gatherings and now have an official website with articles contributed by members.

Ms. Nakajima was especially proud of her own initiative in the group: organizing an off-line gathering to share each other's experiences of hiring a migrant domestic worker:

Hiring a maid is so common here that whenever we mothers get together, we start talking, "How are you doing with your maid?" "Where did you find the new one?" There also are new people who want to give it a try but don't know how to. They ask me questions all the time, and I thought, "Why don't we all get together and share our thoughts and tips?"

According to Ms. Nakajima, the event featured several mothers from Japan who all hired migrant domestic workers, including Ms. Nakajima herself, and involved candid questions and answers with the audience. "I was just sharing what I do and feel every day, and the other women really appreciated it. I was thrilled," Ms. Nakajima recounted. She herself also learned tips from other madams; one panelist created a separate bank account for her maid to withdraw money from to buy household necessities, so that the madam would not have to deal with cash everyday but could still keep track of expenses. Another mother had her maid watch YouTube videos that explained the basics of nutrition and oral hygiene for children, so that she would not need to explain everything in English. In Ms. Nakajima's words, the goal was "to create a venue where we can think together, not to find one best way to do everything."

One could argue that the group that Ms. Nakajima and other mothers organized functioned as a space to express their worries and share troubles, a support system, in a sense. Laura Major, observing an online group of working mothers in Israel, describes how the women give and receive encouragement and support, both to empower and be empowered, through interacting in a virtual safe space: "Here, motherhood is at the centre of the discourse—as lived experience, as complicated identity, as institution, and as agency" (188). The Japanese women around Ms. Nakajima created a common space—online and offline—to utilize their "bonding capital" in Singapore (Keles).

Nevertheless, it is crucial to emphasize that this particular network for Japanese mothers exists at the expense of the migrant domestic workers they hire. When the privileged mothers engage in virtual conversations at night or gather in a hotel lounge on weekends, it is the migrant women who stay home with their children and husbands, cooking and cleaning. More disturbingly, when the madams bond together over the predicaments of their employer status, their conversations may circulate and reinforce the already stigmatizing stereotypes of domestic workers from Southeast Asia—that, for example, madams have to keep track of maids' monetary transactions because they might steal, or that the madams have to educate the "ignorant" maids. When discussing how to be a better, more efficient household supervisor, the women sometimes end up urging each other to watch out for the "lazy," "cunning," and "inept" maids, even when they personally might not have had such negative experiences interacting with their own workers.

As discussed earlier, such circulative narratives are what lie underneath the repetitive exploitation and abuse of migrant domestic workers in Singapore and other parts of Asia (A. Ong; Lan), and the Japanese women as employers are securely invested in this global injustice. That is to say, the Japanese mothers' empowerment of each other certainly does not empower the underprivileged women they hire—another significant irony of cosmopolitan mothering.

Conclusion: Self-Managing Mothers and "the Nanny Question"

The analysis above has demonstrated how individual Japanese mothers' personal experiences derive from, and in return reify, the sociopolitical structure of Asian global cities. The migrant mothers from Japan obviously strive to be a good mother in Singapore as well as to be, no doubt, a good madam. Class-privileged but simultaneously gender-confined, they may hire a domestic worker hoping to lighten their daily workload at home. Through this "rational" choice, she manages to juggle career, housework, and childcare while maintaining a personal space for herself. Encountering difficulties, she may find or even create a communal space with other women in which she can express despair about her newly assigned madam role, exchanging tips to make her life even more rational and efficient.

Well-functioning as she may seem, the Japanese mother is not free from the dilemmas of cosmopolitan mothering. First, in addition to the expectations of motherhood, she encounters a new set of physical and psychological burdens as a madam. It is her job to supervise the smooth running of the household through learning how to effectively interact with a migrant domestic worker and to avoid conflicts and problems at home. The third-shift labour is all hers. Second, as some of the women's narratives above suggest, the overwhelming job of managing a worker in one's home could easily lead to increased anxiety and mistrust towards migrant domestic workers. The collective discourses that circulate among research participants are highly problematic in that they unquestioningly draw on and reinforce the stigmatizing stereotypes of migrant domestic workers that prevail in Asian global cities in particular (Lan; A. Ong; Piper and Yamanaka). In this sense, the migrant mother in this intra-Asian context can be curtailed and curtailing, both the oppressed and the oppressor, all at once.

As such, the Japanese mothers in Singapore in my research are in the exact pitfall of "the Nanny Question" (Tronto), aided especially by the intense neoliberal regime of the global city-state. Those women are privileged global citizens as well as self-managing and self-caring individuals. They are rational mothers capable of utilizing what is available to them, never disrupting or challenging the social relationships they are embedded in. What these images obscure, however, is that their successful household management and collective discourse amplify the global inequality in which, ultimately, women are chained to carework globally. And all the while, their children are exposed to an ethno-racial hierarchy in the Asian global city, embedded in the context of racism, global inequality, and a gendered division of labour. The nanny question remains amid the everyday realities of an Asian global household, between two migrant women of utterly different socioeconomic positions.

Endnotes

1. These expat families gain the right and financial means to hire an MDW once they have attended the mandatory three-hour employment orientation program and fulfilled some other basic requirements, such as the ability to provide reasonable accommodations for a domestic worker to live in their home.

2. Once hired, an MDW is required to reside with their employer family for whom they must work full time and is prohibited from taking on any other work part time. Basic rights to be provided by their employers include reasonable living quarters, three nutritious meals a day, one non-working day a week, and medical insurance, in addition to their wages.

Works Cited

Boris, Eileen, and Rhacel Salazar Parreñas, eds. *Intimate Labors: Culture, Technologies, and the Politics of Care.* Stanford University Press, 2010. Print.

Brooks, Ann, and Theresa Devasahayam. *Gender, Emotions, and Labour Markets.* Routledge, 2011.

Cabinet Office of Japan. *Kokka senryaku toku betsu kuiki no hyoka ni tsuite.* [Evaluations of National Strategic Special Zones], Cabinet Office of Japan, 7 Jun. 2021, https://www.chisou.go.jp/tiiki/kokusentoc/pdf/2021_hyoka_2.pdf. Accessed 26 Sept. 2023.

Constable, Nicole. "The Commodification of Intimacy: Marriage, Sex, and Reproductive Labor." *Annual Review of Anthropology,* vol. 38, 2009, pp. 49-64.

Ehrenreich, Barbara, and Arlie Russell Hochschild, eds. *Global Woman: Nannies, Maids and Sex Workers in the New Economy.* Henry Holt, 2002.

Erel, Umut. "Thinking Migrant Capitals Intersectionally." *Migrant Capital: Networks, Identities and Strategies,* edited by Louise Ryan, Umut Erel, and Alessio D'Angelo, Palgrave Macmillan, 2015, pp. 18-32.

Githens, Marianne. *Contested Voices: Women Immigrants in Today's World,* New York: Palgrave Macmillan, 2013. Print.

Glenn, Evelyn Nakano. "Social Constructions of Mothering: A Thematic Overview." *Mothering; Ideology ,Experience, and Agency,* edited by Evelyn Nakano Glenn, Grace Chang, and Linda Rennie Forcey, Routledge, 1994, pp. 1-29.

Goetze, Catherine. "Raising Children in Strangeness: Cosmopolitan Mothering and Domestic Helpers in Expatriate Families." *Troubling Motherhood: Maternality in Global Politics,* edited by Lucy B. Hall, Anna L. Weissman, and Laura J. Shepherd, Oxford University Press, 2020, pp. 214-32.

Harding, Sandra. *The Science Question in Feminism.* Cornell University Press, 1986.

Hochschild, Arlie Russell. "Global Care Chains and Emotional Surplus Value." *On the Edge: Globalization and the New Millennium,* edited by Will Hutton and Anthony Giddens, Sage, 2000, pp. 130-46.

Hondagneu-Sotelo, Pierrette. *Doméstica: Immigrant Workers Cleaning and Caring in the Shadows of Affluence.* University of California Press, 2007.

Keles, Janroj. "Diaspora, the Internet and Social Capital." *Migrant Capital: Networks, Identities and Strategies*, edited by Louise Ryan, Umut Erel, and Alessio D'Angelo. Palgrave Macmillan, 2015, pp. 102-16.

Kurotani, Sawa. *Home Away from Home: Japanese Corporate Wives in the United States.* Duke University Press, 2005.

Lan, Pei-Chia. *Global Cinderellas: Migrant Domestics and Newly Rich Employers in Taiwan.* Duke University Press, 2006.

Lindio-McGovern, Ligaya. *Globalization, Labor Export and Resistance: A Study of Filipino Migrant Workers in Global Cities.* Routledge, 2013.

Major, Laura. "Advance Forward Moms! A Paradigm for an Online Community of Working Mothers That Actually Works." *Journal of the Motherhood Initiative*, vol. 8, no. 1-2, 2017, pp. 177-90.

Ministry of Foreign Affairs of Japan. *Kaigai zairyu houjinsu chousa toukei* [*Statistics of Japanese Nationals Abroad*]. Ministry of Foreign Affairs of Japan, 20 Dec. 2022, https://www.mofa.go.jp/mofaj/toko/tokei/hojin/index.html. Accessed 26 Sept. 2023.

Nagatomo, Jun. "Changes of Social Cohesion within Ethnic Communities: A Case Study of the Japanese Community in Sydney, Australia." *International Journal of Arts & Sciences*, vol. 9, no. 4, 2017, pp. 45-60.

Oakley, Ann. "Interviewing Women: A Contradiction in Terms?" *Doing Feminist Research*, edited by Helen Roberts, Routledge and Kegan Paul, 1981, pp. 30-61.

Ochiai, Emiko, and Kaoru Aoyama, editors. *Asian Women and Intimate Work.* Brill, 2014.

Ong, Aihwa. *Neoliberalism as Exception.* Duke University Press, 2006.

Ong, Fred C.M., and Brenda S.A. Yeoh. "The Place of Migrant Workers in Singapore: Between State Multiculturalism and Everyday (Un)Cosmopolitanism." *Migration and Diversity in Asian Contexts*, edited by Lai Ah Eng, Francis Leo Collins, and Brenda S. A. Yeoh, Institute of Southeast Asian Studies, 2013, pp. 83-106.

Piper, Nicola, and Keiko Yamanaka. "Feminized Migration in East and Southeast Asia and the Securing of Livelihood." *New Perspectives on*

Gender and Migration: Livelihood, Rights and Entitlements, edited by Nicola Piper, Routledge, 2008, pp. 159-88.

Sassen, Saskia. *The Global City: New York, London, Tokyo.* Princeton University Press, 2001.

Singapore Ministry of Manpower. *Eligibility for Employment Pass,* https://www.mom.gov.sg/passes-and-permits/employment-pass/eligibility. Accessed 26 Sept. 2023.

Singapore Ministry of Manpower. *Migrant Domestic Worker Eligibility.* Ministry of Manpower. https://www.mom.gov.sg/passes-and-permits/work-permit-for-foreign-domestic-worker/eligibility-and-requirements/fdw-eligibility. Accessed 26 Sept. 2023.

Tronto, Joan C. "The 'Nanny' Question in Feminism." *Hypatia,* vol. 17, no. 2, 2002, pp. 34-51.

Velayutham, Selvaraj. "Everyday Racism in Singapore." *Everyday Multiculturalism,* edited by Amanda Wise and Selvaraj Velayutham, Palgrave Macmillan, 2009, pp. 255-73.

Chapter 12

Paradoxes of Power in Carework

Laura Bunyan and Barret Katuna

Introduction

The entry of mothers into the paid labour force has led to the hiring of women for childcare. Research shows the hiring of childcare providers is typically the task of women (Macdonald; Bunyan), as women are viewed as experts on family life (Bean et al.) and are hiring replacement care. The personal and work relationships of childcare providers and employers are the most complicated aspects of childcare work (Macdonald; Nelson; Uttal, "Custodial Care"; Wrigley). These relationships have been described as "tenuous" based on the absence of clear boundaries between tasks reserved for mothers and those delegated to paid child caregivers (Uttal and Tuominen).

We ask under what conditions can paid caregiving work be an empowering space for the careworker? Research on carework and childcare often focusses on the challenging working relationships between mothers and caregivers of dissimilar social statuses, where the caregiver is of a much lower socioeconomic status in comparison to the mother, and clear boundaries are drawn between the two groups (Greenfield et al.; Hochschild; Macdonald; Romero). Research also focusses on the transfer of caregiver labour from the Global South to the Global North (Busch; Macdonald).

Immigrants and women of colour have divergent working conditions and experiences compared to white nannies born in the United States

(US). This is rooted in the historically underlying and conflictual racial -ethnic employment hierarchy (Wu). Taking this into account, our research asks: What happens when women of privileged racial, socio-economic, and educational statuses perform carework? Are they empowered in these relationships? How does this elevated status affect the employer-employee relationship? We address these questions through qualitative interview data from twenty-five women who work as nannies and nineteen mothers who employ a nanny. Interviews were not conducted with direct employers and employees to allow both groups to speak freely about their experiences without being matched on their responses.

In an employer-employee relationship, the employer generally retains the bulk of the power and influence given that the employer is the overseeing party. On the contrary, our study finds that educated nannies have power in many areas over those who are not educated. Examples of the power nannies hold in the nanny and employer relationship include employer willingness to work around the ever-changing school schedule of the nanny, payment of higher wages for educated nannies, employer dependence on the nanny for care, and identifying the nanny as an insider as opposed to an outsider based on the presumed social status of the nanny. Insider status may lead to acknowledging her place in the family and treating her as a family member. This is in contrast with those who hire nannies who differ on sociodemographic variables. Hiring strategies are intentional, and those who purposefully maximize social distance find it easier to delegate tasks to someone dissimilar to them (Busch; Macdonald; Uttal; Wrigley). Educated nannies identified additional ways they held power including the ability to speak freely and offer opinions without repercussions. Beyond these areas, nannies and childcare workers as a whole are not viewed as having much power, and that is tangibly evident in their low wages. Prior research shows the power differentials between nannies and employers based on the private employment location, in the employer's home (Romero), hidden from public purview (Bakan and Stasiulis), without opportunities for supportive employee networks to form (Bunyan). The evidence provided in this chapter demonstrates relative power in the occupation for white, cis, college-educated nannies as compared to those without higher educational credentials, yet even nannies with degrees were still constrained within their positions. This chapter documents the following themes. First, we examine the power that educated nannies gain in wages and schedule flexibility and the privileged treatment they received based on race and educational attainment. We then address whether or not nannies gain power in their interactions with employers. Finally, we examine the role of nannies as a friend or family member, social status, and nannies' perceptions of an increase in workload. We conclude with a discussion of whether nannies feel they are taken advantage of by their employers.

Methods

The first author recruited participants by posting calls on social networking sites, such as Craigslist and in public spaces where parents and nannies spend time with children (e.g., libraries, grocery stores, and children's classes). Snowball sampling was also a helpful recruitment mechanism. The analysis presented in this chapter will focus on interviews with nineteen mothers who employ a nanny and twenty-five women who work as nannies.

Interviews were audiorecorded, transcribed, and analyzed using a constant comparative method (Glaser and Strauss) and were semistructured, allowing participants free range of responses. Interviews lasted an average of one hour, and they took place at a location of the participants' choice. Employer participants included those who worked for pay in or outside of the home, and those who did not work for pay. Nannies identified their nanny employment wages as their primary source of income. Nannies ranged from nineteen to thirty years of age. In contrast to the demographics of all those who work in nanny work in the US, this sample was overwhelmingly white. Twenty-three of the nannies identified as white and two as nonwhite. Sixteen of the mother employers identified as white, one as Asian, one as white and Hispanic, and one as white, Native American, and African American. This racial composition of the sample is largely due to the recruitment strategy that excluded non-US born women and the stratification by educational attainment in the sampling strategy. Employers were not asked questions about the race of their nanny. Only one white employer noted her nanny was Indian. Part of the reason this sample was not at all racially diverse is due to the characteristics of nannies that white employers sought out, which also led to a highly educated sample of white nannies. Over half of the employers hired a nanny who had a bachelor's degree or higher, and over half of the nanny participants had a bachelor's or higher (12) or were enrolled in college (4). Nannies and employers resided in Connecticut, Eastern New York State, and New York City. All the nannies interviewed were US-born citizens, and the employers interviewed employed a nanny who was a US-born citizen. A token of appreciation of twenty dollars was given to interviewees participating in this study. Most employers declined compensation. Names of participants were changed for privacy reasons.

Findings

Power in Wages and Schedules

Although nannies are not expected to be college educated or hold advanced degrees, employers in this sample greatly valued a college-educated nanny over a non-college-educated nanny, and this is evident in the pay structure. Formally educated nannies had a clear wage advantage over those without a degree. Both groups, nannies, and employers alike, reported college-educated nannies received a higher hourly wage. Educated nannies earned a median hourly wage of fifteen dollars per hour, whereas those without degrees disclosed a rate of thirteen dollars and twenty-five cents per hour. The median salary that employers reported paying educated nannies was twelve dollars per hour and ten dollars per hour for those without degrees.

Hiring an educated nanny came with several benefits for employers. Employers sought nannies that could serve as role models for their children. However, role model status led to scheduling conflicts based on the multiple roles that nannies fulfilled as engaged college students and employees. Despite the variability in college class schedules from semester to semester and the movement of students between home and school for college breaks, employers were flexible with college student nannies and worked to meet the demands of schedule changes. Cathy, a white employer, hired several college students for care each semester. Cathy downgraded her position at work to be able to work remotely so that she could still be present with her children for periods of time throughout the day, noting "That is kind of why I chose to do what I am doing. To be a part of my child's life, to teach the other person how to care for my child and how I want them to be cared for." Lynet Uttal notes, mothers who are employed outside the home are unable to "follow the traditional ideal of the mother who is constantly available in her young children's daily lives" (*Making Care Work*, 118). Although Cathy reported that following the college schedule was "difficult," as was employing multiple nannies, hiring college student nannies allowed Cathy to feel she was making a positive and responsible choice about care while still remaining present in her children's lives due to her work from home status.

Nannies who were enrolled in college had a lot to juggle between academics and work and were seen as high achievers, who were sought after for hire for this reason. Margaret, a white college student, told the story of her conversation with her employer over her course schedule for the next semester. She noted that her employer, a doctor, said the following: "She really likes the fact that I'm in school that I'm headed somewhere.... She said that she'd much rather have someone like me, younger and ... headed towards getting a degree... than an older woman who isn't really doing much.... She said she'd be flexible because she likes the fact that I'm in school, so she's more willing to be flexible." Margaret's employer appreciated the fact that she was in college and seeking a career outside of childcare. Thus, she was willing to accommodate the changes in Margaret's schedule from semester to semester.

Employer Silvia, a white lawyer recently hired a teacher to care for her children over the summer. She paid this nanny four dollars and fifty cents more per hour than her prior nanny, a woman who was highly experienced but lacked higher educational credentials. When the interviewer commented on the wage increase, she replied, "She's a teacher." In hiring this nanny, Silvia was willing to both pay a premium for her and search for replacement care at the end of the summer when the nanny returned to work as a teacher. Silvia recognized the status of her nanny as an asset and was willing to take on the extra work of hiring replacement care and the financial burden of paying more. This stands in contrast to what is typically assumed about feminized care.

Mariana, who described herself as a Hispanic college student nanny, noted her frustration with her employer and her schedule. "School's my priority. She knew that even hiring me, especially with a college student." At times, her employer would get home very late, leaving her little time to get from work to school, demonstrating that not all employers were respectful of the balance nannies needed between school and work. Mariana's schedule was more flexible in the prior semester, and she said she never paid attention when her employer was late previously. With the new semester and schedule change, Mariana noted, "Now that I have a strict schedule, it's like tensions are rising between us." Mariana was one of the few nannies of colour interviewed for this research. Because of the low number of nannies of colour in this study, it is hard to claim it is race related, but this does highlight differential treatment and sheds light on the mistreatment that nannies often face. Her experience stands in contrast to that of the other white nannies interviewed.

Privileged Treatment as Compared to Others

Nannies who worked for families that hired more than one household employee could directly compare their treatment with that of the other employees. Stephanie, a white college-educated nanny, discussed her employer's adverse treatment of those who were not white. She noted the housekeeper "didn't speak English very well" and her employer "did not treat her very well." Elaborating, "Anything would go wrong, things would go missing, blame it on [the housekeeper]. She'd talk to her really disrespectfully."

Claire, a white college student, grew up in the same town the family she worked for resided in. She discussed her experience in opposition to the family's other household employees, nannies, and housecleaners. She described her social class similarity as appealing to her employers stating: "You can reach eye to eye; it may sound bad but it's true." In contrast, a Black nanny of lower socioeconomic status, the family hired, did not work out. Claire explained, "she sang all this gospel stuff, and they don't want that rubbing off on their kids." Claire also drew distinctions between her status and nannies of other racial and class statuses. "I was invited to their bat mitzvah, and even their old nanny was invited, but her husband wasn't invited. My boyfriend was invited, and her husband wasn't. It just goes to show..." Claire's voice trailed off, but she was discussing the status distinctions that arise between herself and other household workers based on her race, socioeconomic, and educational status. She reiterated the importance of social class: "Being of the same social class, you can relate to the kids on, you know, just even from things that you wear, or stores that you shop at, or things that you can afford."

Although Claire's employer was far wealthier than her own family, Claire felt growing up in the same town her employer resided in allowed her to connect with her employer. Claire noted the "extreme" wealth in the Westchester suburb of New York City she grew up in and explained, "they have more money than my family does, but I was very privileged in the fact that I travelled every single summer." Noting, "I've been to Europe four times." Claire felt these shared demographics and experiences allowed her to better fit in with her employer's family than the other nannies and the housekeeper they hired, typically women of colour. She continuously discussed differences between herself and the other employees of the family: "Their housekeeper, who's from the Philippines, she's a housekeeper. That's her role, that's her identity.... I'm perceived as someone who's in college who's doing this to help out the family while at the same time who is getting paid." The other employees, Claire felt, could not "reach eye to eye" like she could. The housekeeper would return to her apartment in the Bronx at the end of her shift while Claire would return down the road to her parents' home in the same affluent suburb. The theme of "helping out" persisted in interviews with educated nannies. Most families they worked for treated them in a way where educated women felt like friends or family, not as an employee. This stood in contrast with employees who were cultural outsiders.

Kristin, a white graduate student, commented on the differences between herself, and the nannies her employer's friends hired: "They don't treat them as nicely." She elaborated, "the ones that are not treated as nicely are not college graduates, are not in their twenties, and are not Caucasian." Further separating her status from nannies of other social statuses is the close relationship Kristin formed with the family she worked for. For example, she indicated her brother who attended a local college came over regularly for dinner with the family. Nannies from college-educated backgrounds are expected to be so much more than a childcare worker. While they care for and entertain the children, there is an underlying understanding they will also be companions for the family.

Power in Interactions?

Nina, a white college graduate, found employment through an agency that works only with educated nannies. She explained that Margie, her employer, "was looking for someone that she could relate well to, that she would be comfortable having around, someone that could hold a conversation." Many of their chats centred around Nina's recent move-in with her boyfriend as well as college attendance and her graduate school aspirations. As a stay-at-home mother, Nina said, "I think she values that, having someone to talk to." Nina expounded upon the importance of mother-employers getting along with their nannies and disclosed she thought Margie enjoyed being able to relate to her. Margie told her, "We like the fact that you're college educated. We like the fact that you're intelligent." Nina indicated her educational status allowed for Margie to better navigate their relationship. Nina too was able to successfully adapt to social situations in the New York City neighbourhood her employer lived in based on her race, educational attainment, and perceived socioeconomic status.

Educated nannies felt they were given credit for knowledge in specific areas based on college attendance alone. Lynn, a white college graduate, remarked her employer saying, "I know you know this because obviously you went to college." Stephanie, another college graduate, noted her boss expected her to know how to perform specific tasks because she went to college: "You're a college graduate. You can figure that out." Although her employer said it in a condescending way, the message was clear: College graduates were expected to possess critical thinking and problem-solving skills. Given the skill requirements for these jobs, which are quite low by society's standards, we argue it is problematic to assume that based on college attendance, a nanny would have more practical knowledge of household tasks and childcare than a nanny who was not formally college educated. For example, it could be potentially harmful to a child's safety if it's assumed that a college-educated nanny would know what to do in an emergency just because of her college degree, which may or may not be related to the nature of the emergency.

Employers expected nannies with degrees to possess markers of similarity, including intelligence, and a level of familiarity with their social world. When hiring an educated nanny, employers felt they were hiring someone with a degree of cultural competence who could navigate social situations as Claire discussed previously. Employer Melyssa hired a nanny with a bachelor's in education. Melyssa described her nanny as "knowledgeable" and "intelligent." Referencing her nanny's degree, she stated: "I'm glad that she has that knowledge behind her because then she can gauge what's going on and kind of understand it a little better." Melyssa continued: "If I say, 'Oh, watch out because Elizabeth is having fits lately...' She'll say, 'That's just how kids are at that age; it's okay.'" Melyssa said, "It's nice to have that feedback" as a form of validation for her parenting. Melyssa viewed her nanny as an equal in parenting. Elevated educational status eased interactions and allowed nannies to feel more accepted and gain better treatment. It also allowed employers to accept nannies on more equal terms. Ironically, employers who followed the advice and opinions of their nannies were a minority, according to nanny respondents.

When differences between educated nannies and employers emerged, employers expressed surprise. In regard to her college educated nanny, Theresa, a white employer, explained: "She's not that sophisticated, and it sort of surprises me given her background, you know, with these educated parents. That there are just certain things she doesn't always know or places she hasn't been or things like that. So that I see a discrepancy that I notice because it surprises me." Class peers carry some authority, but studies show that employers must tolerate their assertiveness (Pratt; Tuominen; Wrigley). Educated nannies were also often asked their personal views on a range of topics commonly extending beyond childcare—such as fashion, restaurant recommendations, nutrition, and fitness—because they are perceived as class peers. Mothers also appreciated the ability to seek their nanny's perspective on the child's behaviour. This occurred most often when the nanny was in graduate school in a field of study related to education.

Despite feeling included, nannies also identified moments when clear boundaries were drawn. Nina said, "Sometimes Margie, the woman I work for, she'll ask my opinion on things. Like, 'what do you think we should do?" And I had to learn that I can give it [advice], but very rarely is she actually going to take it." Nicole, a graduate student, said, "I think that they trust my opinions about certain things with childcare." Nicole quickly learned that her opinion had limitations in terms of how much it was acknowledged. As a graduate student in education, Nicole felt strongly about how learning should occur. When her employers purchased a phonics kit and workbooks to do with their four-year-old,

Nicole expressed her thoughts. This was a battle she lost: "I don't think that you should sit there with a workbook with a four-year-old and teach them that way. I think phonics should be taught naturally. And I've tried to explain that, and they don't think that it's true."

While employers did not always side with educated nannies' opinions, they were generally acknowledged and not outrightly dismissed, which contrasts with what nannies of colour experienced. Mariana, a self-described Hispanic nanny, recalled being reprimanded for the food she fed the children. Mariana noted that her employer insisted on a balance of protein and carbohydrates and scolded her for providing jelly on bread without peanut butter as a snack. Abigail, a white nanny working on her associate degree, was one of the few nannies who was hesitant to speak directly to her employers about her thoughts and opinions on childrearing. She noted, "There were a lot of things that I was afraid to bring up because I was just a stupid little kid, who didn't know their kids and didn't know what I was talking about." When asked what happened when she addressed an issue, she described how the father employer would toss the baby in the air to play with him. "And one time I said to him, 'He laughs, but his brain is being shaken right now.' And he was like, 'No, it's not.'" She further explained, "When I tried to bring it up, it was just, 'Oh, you don't know what you are talking about. He likes it.'" Abigail was disturbed by the situation and felt powerless to change it. She explained when the father was present, she would have to leave the room because she felt physically ill from the harm that she perceived he was doing to the baby in these instances. In these situations, nannies felt their opinions and feelings were dismissed, and their lack of power in certain instances was evident.

The Role of the Nanny: Nanny as a Friend or Family Member

This power dynamic appears often in the nanny and employer relationship. Research shows parents are commonly confused over the nanny's place within the family (Macdonald; Uttal, "Custodial Care"). Employers struggle with how to treat someone who is intimately involved in their daily lives and loves and cares for their child but is also a paid employee. Is this person a friend? Or are they an employee? Hiring strategies shape relationships formed between nannies and employers. Key differences emerge between our sample and other studies. Employers in this sample who hired status peers were more apt to view them as part of their family or as having a friendship as compared to prior research (Macdonald; Uttal, "Custodial Care"). Perhaps reducing this employer-employee boundary made them feel better about delegating to someone that was not entirely dissimilar from their racial, cultural, and class status. Thirteen of the nineteen employers interviewed stated their nanny was either a close friend or a family member. One explanation may be because the employers sampled often minimized the social differences between themselves and their care providers, whereas employers in other samples sought to emphasize these dissimilarities in terms of race, educational attainment, and socioeconomic status (Uttal, "Custodial Care"; Uttal and Tuominen; Wrigley), potentially making it easier to maintain an employer-employee relationship. Over 75 per cent of the employers who categorized their nanny as a friend or family member classified her as being socially similar to them. These employers sought to reduce the number of social differences between themselves and their nanny both directly and indirectly by hiring educated nannies. Minimizing these differences allowed them to forge personal relationships. For employers, shared social locations had a significant impact on their relationships with their nannies. The choice to define their relationships as family or friendships versus employer-employee centred on their level of comfort in these relationships, which stemmed from their interpretations of social similarities and differences.

A degree of social class differences between both parties is a feature of many employer-employee relationships (Wrigley). Employers in the sample pointed out that this space was lacking. Only three of the employers who reported not possessing shared socioeconomic characteristics to their nanny defined their relationship with her as a friendship. This is important to note as friends often come from similar social class backgrounds and possess other markers of social similarity, such as educational attainment and shared hobbies.

For employer Cynthia, the bond her nanny shared with her children linked them together as a family: "The relationship with my children is very strong and when someone is very close to your children you look at them differently, and you're more open to them. So, you know in that way, I view her as a part of the family because she's very important in my kid's lives." Cynthia's nanny, Hannah, was currently enrolled in college and the first in her family to attend college. When she first started working with them, Hannah was a live-in nanny, who "had no interest in college." Cynthia liked that her children and Hannah did their schoolwork together: "They understand that she did not go to college right after high school like most of the people that they know.... This is something that she's decided to do as a grownup."

The ability to have encounters and personal discussions, which transcended childcare and the children, also shaped some employers' views of their relationship as a friendship. Melyssa's nanny was invited to family gatherings. She and her nanny are both involved in each other's extended families. Lindsay described the closeness she felt with her nanny, "I think of her as a younger sister," and she was more trusting of her nanny than her own family. She described examples of this: "She stayed here, and slept here, and took care of our dogs while we were away for a week. And again, that is something that my own actual younger sister, I wouldn't have felt as comfortable with her." Lindsay elaborated: "I truly feel like we would be in her life for a long time even when she is not sitting with the kids. And I would like to think that." Similarly, Melyssa said, "I expect with her that even when she stops working with us that she would continue to have a relationship with my children."

Previous research found employers spoke about their caregivers in familial or friendship terms but did not engage in family-like friendship behaviours with them. Moreover, they reserved some aspects of care only for family members (Uttal, "Custodial Care"), such as overnight care and doctor's appointments. Again, our research differs because of the whiteness and high educational attainment of our sample. Contrary to prior findings, Lindsay and Melyssa's statements illustrate the idea that their nannies are both valued and treated as close family members. The areas of family life they wanted and allowed their nannies to partake in were more intimate than those they allowed family members.

Despite this hope for future connection, prior research has found only a minority of employers actually stayed in touch with their caregivers after the conclusion of the work relationship (Macdonald). While it is impossible to determine whether mothers in this sample will maintain ties to their nannies beyond their childcare relationship, fifteen out of the nineteen mothers stated that they hoped to do so. Six noted that they were currently in contact with their former nannies because their relationships transcend the employer-employee relationship based on their social statuses. Susan explained that one of her former nannies, "visits us every year just as one of her vacations because she just finds it really nice to.... She likes spending time with us." This nanny visited Susan's family, but Susan did not describe her own family as making efforts to visit their former nanny. These mothers expected and welcomed that their nanny would move on to formal employment but hoped that she would stay with them for the years to come in a familial or close friend capacity. This desire may be related to the role model status many nannies took on based on their educational credentials and their ability to move on to formal employment. These employers wanted relationships with people they saw as peers, and they did not want to feel as if they were "taking care" of their nanny. Regarding a prior nanny, Susan elaborated: "There were times when we had to take care of her. It seemed like her life went from crisis to crisis." To avoid this, Susan no longer hired career nannies. She noted that those who utilized nanny work as a temporary status had "more resilience," and they would take care of her children instead of Susan caring for them.

Most nannies, fifteen out of the twenty-five, saw themselves as a part of the family. They also expressed that their employer shared this feeling. Regardless of the view of the type of relationship held, relationships worked best for nannies when they and their employer agreed on the type of the relationship they shared, whether that meant strong or weak ties.

Sage, a graduate student, described her relationship with her employer as "loving" and "caring": "They treat you like family, you know, and that's how we look at each other." Much like the employers in this sample, the nannies who were happy in their arrangements were very likely to state that they would remain in contact with their employer and the children they cared for long after their work arrangement came to an end. Sage said, "I really feel that they will be in my life forever, not necessarily, I mean I'm not going to be babysitting them when the youngest is twenty years old. But more as, like an additional family member." The way they spoke to her made her feel "included." They asked her to do things; they did not tell her. She described: "It's always a choice... 'Do you want to do this?'" Sage preferred this because it made her feel valued. Being spoken to in this way made Sage feel included and more than an employee.

Social Status and Nannies' Perceptions of an Increase in Workload

Nannies frequently noted their employers' practice of adding additional chores to their list of tasks. Research shows this is a feature of in-home labour (Romero). The increase in duties evolved in two ways. Either the employer asked the nanny to do a chore directly, and then it became expected, or the nanny offered to perform a task, which later became required of them. Chores related to cleaning, for example, commonly increased over time or were sprung on nannies without notice. It also was not uncommon for employers to ask nannies to perform tasks not related to childcare, such as house or pet sitting, when the employers and children were away or caring for new pets in addition to childcare.

For some nannies, the fluidity of their job requirements posed a challenge to them, and they were bothered by the addition of non-child-care-related tasks. Surprisingly, most nannies were not upset by their employers' requests of them to provide extra services. This finding is related to the solid personal relationships formed between employers and employees in this sample, including healthy employer-employee communication. In contrast, Cameron Macdonald's work discussed the difficulty nannies had in drawing a line on their mounting job requirements. From a work and occupations standpoint, we felt employees would be upset by an increased workload that was not met with a raise. Nannies' views of these additions were intertwined with the feelings they held for their employers.

This was a key area where we perceive nannies' demonstrated powerlessness and acceptance, yet they did not typically see it as such. Employers were quick to add on extra jobs to their nanny's workload. When nannies felt valued by their employers on a personal level, they did not feel burdened by these additional requests. Instead, some were simply not aware that it was wrong, while others even felt honoured, as they were treated as a loved one.

One of the most egregious examples of the overstepping of boundaries occurred in Sara's story, a white nanny who had taken some college courses but was not currently enrolled. Her employers added two puppies to their family and expected Sara to train and care for the puppies while caring for their young children. One day while rollerblading with the children, one puppy ran away. Sara chased after the dog and fell and broke her elbow. This issue was compounded because Sara did not have health insurance. Her employers never offered to pay her medical bills. When asked how she felt about this, Sara replied: "It didn't really phase me…. I didn't realize how unacceptable I guess it was." Lack of employer consideration for the health and wellbeing of nannies was not uncommon. Nannies also failed to address these essential instances that reflected their lack of power, especially in situations where they were considered family. This view of the nanny as part of the family was often detrimental to the nanny and to the employer when critical, personnel-related issues had to be addressed that would likely not have surfaced in a familial relationship.

College student Claire was not bothered that her employer did not automatically increase her pay over the years when she watched over the dog while they were away. She attributed her employer's failure to initiate a raise to their close relationship. When nannies felt valued by their employers, they did not feel burdened by these additional requests. Instead, they felt honoured that they were included as a trusted loved one.

Most nannies in this sample reported viewing their employers as "family" or "friends" and noted their employers shared this outlook. Aside from those who sought time away from their employer, nannies who readily accepted additional tasks did so because of this status. In these instances, they did not view these extras as burdens but saw them as something they were more than willing to do to help their loved ones. Their agreement on status helped them feel as if they were doing a favour as opposed to providing a paid service. Nannies and employers in this sample rarely drew employer-employee boundaries. This was far more detrimental to nannies than employers.

Being Taken Advantage Of?

College student Claire was one of the very few nannies to ask for a raise. When asked how she felt that her employer did not automatically think to give her a raise, Claire stated: "I became part of their family, so I don't really feel funny that she wouldn't think of it." Employer Susan described a situation that occurred with a prior nanny where the nanny felt taken advantage of because Susan never gave her a raise. Her nanny stated: "I'm really upset with you because we didn't discuss a raise." Susan explained: "It just didn't occur to me. I'm not like, you know, we're a family…. It's not something that's in our rubric to be thinking that we've met the one-year mark." The instances that demonstrated these oversights were not always intentional but were incredibly problematic in employer-employee relationships and led to issues for nannies and employers alike. Nannies experienced wage loss, and employers had dissatisfied nannies.

Issues that arose were not always oversights. Some nannies described being used by their employers. Samantha, who held a graduate degree, discussed a time when her employer asked her to house sit for a week and sleep at their house. Samantha described the disparities between her living situation and her employer's. She felt her employer "just thought her house was so great" and "looked down at us as these basement dwellers" given that she and her husband resided in a basement apartment: "She made it seem like, 'Lucky you... You get to stay at my house!'" She recalled expecting to be compensated for this week, but upon her employer's return from vacation, she was instead given chocolates as a token of appreciation and in lieu of payment. The interviewer asked if the employer left food for them to eat while they were away. Samantha remarked, "no" adding her husband said, "She totally took advantage of us." Samantha never addressed the issue. Similarly, college-educated Suzanne described being asked to stay at the house of her employer for the maintenance person when her employer left with the baby she watched. Suzanne felt very uncomfortable: "You're here to not even take care of the baby; you're here to do us a favour and stay with the maintenance guy." In recalling the event, Suzanne relayed her discomfort having to remain in a home that was not her own with a person she did not know. It is important to note that nannies who felt used by their employers were a minority. Yet those who did not express these sentiments experienced similar treatment; they just did not perceive it as an issue based on their familial status. College student Kelly's employers went away and asked her to dog sit. She was compensated for the week but at a much lower rate. Rather than being paid her typical salary of six hundred dollars, they paid her 160 dollars. Kelly did not express even the slightest amount of dissatisfaction with the situation. Furthermore, when she watched the children overnight, she did not charge extra money: "I feel like I'm more family with them now so I kind of feel like I was cutting them a deal." Kelly also did not expect paid vacation time, or any other treatment associated with paid employment in the formal economy.

These relationships were ones where the employers typically gained, and the nannies lost. From a labour standpoint, nannies were being used by their employers. From a family perspective, most nannies were fine with this. The fact that these jobs were not their forever jobs or their careers also opened them up to abuse because they were less inclined to speak up for themselves in hopes of preserving their relationships long term. Speaking up or pointing out unjust treatment would challenge this notion of family and disrupt the relationship. The consensus was that employers preferred nannies to remain with them as employees for as long as possible and defer their career aspirations. College graduate Nina described this as a "contradiction with them because they'll say one thing and do another." Her employer attended graduate school and would indicate a level of understanding of Nina's desire to leave nanny work and attend graduate school. Nina explained the hypocrisy of the situation: "On the same hand, she wants me there forever, all of the time, taking care of their seventeen [exaggeration] children forever." As evidence of this, Nina's employer asked her to defer graduate school. "Margie has said to me, 'is there any way that you would put off grad school for like another year?'" Hindering the motivation for an employee to pursue further education oversteps the bounds of this dynamic and limits the potential job prospects for the future. Yet employers who benefited immensely from these relationships wanted to prolong them for as long as possible. Often, they dangled the promise of a raise over their nanny as Nina's employer did to maintain their lifestyle, an act which was not very familial at all.

Conclusion

Our chapter uncovers the relationships formed between women who work as nannies and mothers who employ nannies. We address the ways in which nannies gain power, albeit very limited power, in relationships given their privileged statuses that are linked to race, class, and educational attainment. One of the limitations of this research is the lack of racial diversity in the sample. Only two of the twenty-five nannies identified as nonwhite. After reviewing the pool of candidates, employers more commonly hired white, educated nannies over nannies of colour and nannies without higher education credentials. Our access to more white women than women of colour is also largely attributed to our sampling focus on nannies born within the US as well as the location of the research, in the Northeast. Because of these demographics, employers in this sample clearly gravitated towards white, educated nannies. We provide insight into these complex relationships that informs our understanding of how power operates in the informal carework sector.

Many of the nannies we interviewed were empowered in comparison to other nannies (nannies of colour, immigrant nannies, and nannies without degrees) based on their race, citizenship status, social class, and educational attainment, leading to their heightened validation and appreciation. We identify this empowerment as relative as they lacked critical power in key areas. As employees in a household performing childcare, who were often considered "family," nannies felt constrained around negotiations and had difficulty addressing issues as they arose. Part of this is in line with feminine gender norms where women are not expected to have solid negotiation skills. Gendered interactions impact understandings of entitlement in different ways for women and men (Ridgeway).

The household as the site of labour complicates negotiations, but the issues are ultimately shaped by several factors. Gendered assumptions surrounding expectations of women's workplace behaviour impacts their ability to successfully advocate for themselves without the threat of repercussions both real and imagined (Bunyan; Besen-Cassino). The household is the site of this labour further obscuring the view that this labour is in fact work. Carework is presumed to be low skill and labour that women perform based on their presumed natural propensity. Thus, nannies feel they are unable to ask for higher wages, and employers are ultimately surprised when they do. This lack of acceptability of negotiations on behalf of nannies and lack of forethought on the part of employers exposes women nannies to abuse and exploitation of power on behalf of employers.

Some nannies felt they gained power, status, and decision-making authority and overall better treatment based on their privileged statuses as educated white nannies. However, most recognized their work was bound up in a system of oppression and inequality. Childcare by default is low status, low prestige, and low pay. It has been labelled "women's work," as it is left up to women to perform and replace the care that mothers are expected to supply. Due to the social construction of these "innate" domestic childcare skills as women's domain, the job itself is seen as both low skill and low prestige. These white and educated women nannies were privy to these job opportunities because of their racial, educational, and presumed socioeconomic statuses. Their experiences, documented here, show that they were quite often, highly valued, and respected employees even if they were not always paid fairly or fully treated as equals. This research sheds light on the relative advantage white, educated nannies have as compared to prior research examining the hiring and employment of immigrant women of colour for carework. It raises the question: what happens to uneducated nannies and nannies of colour who form the majority of labourers in this industry when educated women are available for care? Future research should consider the experiences of college educated and affluent women of colour working as nannies. How might race then influence how these nannies are treated in these carework settings with affluent white employers and affluent employers of colour? Will they be empowered in these settings, or will they confront disempowering treatment?

Works Cited

Bakan, Abigail, and Diva Stasiulis. *Not One of the Family: Foreign Domestic Workers in Canada*. University of Toronto Press, 1997.

Bean, Heather, et al. "Can We Talk about Stay-at-Home Moms? Empirical Findings and Implications for Counseling." *Family Journal*, vol. 24, no. 1, 2016, pp. 23-30.

Besen-Cassino, Yasemin. *The Cost of Being a Girl: Working Teens and the Origins of the Gender Wage Gap*. Temple University Press, 2018.

Bunyan, Laura. *Modern Day Mary Poppins: The Unintended Consequences of Nanny Work*. Lexington Books, 2020.

Busch, Nicky. "The Employment of Migrant Nannies in the UK: Negotiating Social Class in an Open Market for Commoditised In-Home Care." *Social & Cultural Geography*, vol. 14, no. 5, 2013, pp. 541-57.

Cox, Rosie. "Competitive Mothering and Delegated Care: Class Relationships in Nanny and Au Pair Employment." *Studies in the Maternal*, vol. 3, no. 2, 2011, pp. 1-13.

Glaser, Barney and Anslem Strauss. *The Discovery of Grounded Theory: Strategies for Qualitative Research*. Routledge, 2006.

Greenfield, Patricia, Flores, Ana, Davis, Helen and Salimkhan, Goldie. "What Happens When Parents and Nannies Come from Different Cultures?" Comparing the Caregiving Belief System of Nannies and Their Employers." *Journal of Applied Developmental Psychology*, vol. 29 no. 4, 2008, pp. 326-36.

Hochschild, Arlie. Russell. "Love and Gold." *Global Woman: Nannies, Maids, and Sex Workers in the New Economy*, edited by Barbara Ehrenreich and Arlie Russell Hochschild, Metropolitan Books, 2003, pp. 15-30.

Macdonald, Cameron. "Manufacturing Motherhood: The Shadow Work of Nannies and Au Pairs." *Qualitative Sociology*, vol. 21 no. 1, 1998, pp. 25-53.

Macdonald, Cameron. "Shadow Mothers: Nannies, *Au Pairs*, and Invisible Work." *Working in the Service Society*, edited by Cameron Macdonald and Carmen Sirianni, Temple University Press, 1996, pp. 244-63.

Macdonald, Cameron. *Shadow Mothers: Nannies, Au Pairs, and the Micropolitics of Mothering*. University of California Press, 2011.

Macdonald, Cameron. "Ethnic Logics: Race and Ethnicity in Nanny Employment." *Caring on the Clock: The Complexities and Contradictions of Paid Care Work*, edited by Mignon Duffy, Amy Armenia, and Clare Stacey, Rutgers University Press, 2015, pp. 153-164.

Nelson, Margaret. "Negotiating Care: Relationships between Family Daycare Providers and Mothers." *Feminist Studies*, vol. 15, no. 1, 1989, pp. 7-33.

Pratt, Geraldine. "From Registered Nurse to Registered Nanny: Discursive Geographies of Filipina Domestic Workers in Vancouver, B.C." *Economic Geography*, vol 75, no 3, 1999, pp. 215-36.

Ridgeway, Cecilia. *Framed by Gender: How Gender Inequality Persists in the Modern World*. Oxford University Press, 2011.

Romero, Mary. "Unraveling Privilege: Workers' Children and the Hidden Cost of Paid Childcare." *Chicago-Kent Law Review*, vol. 76, no 3, 2001, pp. 1651-72.

Romero, Mary. "Nanny Diaries and Other Stories: Immigrant Women's Labor in the Social Reproduction of American Families." *Revista de Estudios Sociales*, vol. 45, 2013, pp. 186-97.

Uttal, Lynet. "Custodial Care, Surrogate Care, and Coordinated Care: Employed Mothers and the Meaning of Childcare." *Gender & Society*, vol. 10, no. 3, 1996, pp. 291-311.

Uttal, Lynet. *Making Care Work: Employed Mothers in the New Childcare Market*. Rutgers University Press, 2002.

Uttal, Lynet, and Mary Tuominen. "Tenuous Relationships: Exploitation, Emotion, and Racial Ethnic Significance in Paid Child Care Work." *Gender & Society*, vol. 13, no. 6, 1999, pp. 758-80.

Wrigley, Julia. *Other People's Children*. Basic, 1995.

Wu, Tina. "More Than a Paycheck: Nannies, Work, and Identity." *Citizenship Studies*, vol. 20, no. 3-4, 2016, pp. 295-310.

Chapter 13

Kin Care Versus Hired Caregiving: How Black College Women Navigate Dual Roles and Work to Earn a Degree

Yolanda Wiggins

For financially disadvantaged families, caregiving duties cannot be outsourced (Burton). As such, many young adult children are called upon by their families to engage in such tasks. With over forty-three million family caregivers living in the United States (US), families are the largest providers of informal care in the country. Throughout the US, family caregivers provide critical support to younger siblings, elderly family members, and to kin with chronic, disabling, or otherwise serious conditions. Each year, about forty million adults in the US provide support with basic functional (e.g., help with eating, bathing), household (e.g., meal preparation, assist with shopping), and medical/nursing tasks to help family members remain in their homes and communities for as long as possible (Bureau of Labor Statistics). Of these forty million family caregivers, about one in four is a member of the millennial generation (NCES).

For the past four decades, researchers have focussed on demographic characteristics of caregivers (gender, age, illness types, relationship aspects, etc.). Evidence suggests that most caregivers are women and a spouse or child of the family member(s) (Karlin; Scott and Roberto).

More than half of young adult caregivers are of colour (NCES). Black and Latinx young adults are more likely to live in multigenerational households, sharing their home with parents, siblings, grandparents, and great-grandparents (Bureau of Labor Statistics; NCES). As such, they are essential workers in their households, providing care in the form of domestic household chores, intimate care (e.g., helping to dress or bathe their loved ones), and medicine administration. In households with non-native English speakers, caregiving can include language translation in which children speak or write on behalf of a family member (Cabrera). Even before the COVID-19 pandemic, youth of colour who assumed the role of caregivers looked after siblings by helping with homework, cooking family meals, engaging in play, and providing companionship (Burton; Stack). Research has found that Black and Latinx youth are performing greater amounts of caregiving tasks in the home in comparison to other demographic groups (Cabrera; Winkle-Wagner).

Although a great deal of research has been conducted at colleges and universities, very little data have been collected examining their experiences as paid and unpaid caregivers. Of importance is the fact that enrollment in degree-granting institutions has increased dramatically (US Department of Education). It is expected that college enrollment will continue to increase for those between the ages of eighteen and twenty-four and for those over the age of twenty-five. Those students who are committed to enrolling in a degree-granting institution while also working as caregivers—both within the home and outside—may have distinct experiences that average students may not have. This chapter seeks to explore the experiences of Black undergraduate women who take on a caregiving role while taking classes at an institution of higher education. It aims to begin a discussion on the unique characteristics of these caregivers.

Caregiver Workload

Paid caregiving, especially in the form of babysitting and eldercare, is a common early work experience in the US, particularly for college students (Besen-Cassino; Morrow). Though paid caregiving can be thought of as temporary, many college women engage in this type of work. This study highlights the central role that undergraduate women play as caregivers. Given prevalent gender typing of household duties, some studies reveal that college women may place more importance upon assisting their families than college men do (Klein). Yen Espiritu and Diane Wolf found that daughters feel restricted by assisting family, whereas sons feel less restricted by their parents and are therefore not expected to provide practical assistance to the same degree as daughters, if at all. Latinx and Asian American young women are more likely than young men to be called upon to assist with household chores, translate for their parents, and care for younger siblings (Dayton et al.; Maramba; Kane). Susan Sy and Aerika Brittain explore the impact of family obligations on Latina, white, and Asian American young women and found that women of colour engage in duties, such as paying bills, disciplining younger siblings, and caring for sick or physically disabled relatives. Rachelle Winkle-Wagner finds that Black daughters who are expected to continue to contribute to their families while in college experience this tension of having to fulfill multiple and often competing obligations at the same time. Similarly, Sara Goldrick-Rab finds that financially disadvantaged women in particular often feel the pull of home and family, which Dodson argues often discourages them from concentrating on education. No single piece of literature examines the ways in which Black undergraduate women who act as paid and unpaid caregivers must oscillate between these dual roles and how these responsibilities affect their college experiences. This paper fills these gaps.

Informal or unpaid caregivers not only juggle normal day-to-day routines but also incorporate a secondary workload into their daily lives. According to the Family Caregiver Alliance, more than one in six Americans who work full- or part-time report that they assist with the care of an elder or disabled family member, relative, or friend. Furthermore, the report states that 50 per cent of all caregivers eighteen-years-old and older who care for an individual aged fifty years or older are also employed full-time.

Balancing full-time employment, aspects of an individual's personal life, and the challenges associated with being a caregiver result in an increased workload. This workload varies among individuals and encompasses parameters of time, difficulty, tasks, demands, and ability in the conceptualization of the task (Juratovac et al.). On average, caregivers spend twenty hours per week providing care (Juratovac et al.). Those who live with their care recipient are estimated to spend thirty-nine hours or more per week caring for that person (Family Caregiver Alliance). This level of time commitment as a caregiver student may create extreme demands on young adults who are full-time college students, thereby creating overwhelming burdens.

The ability to commit this amount of time and energy into caring for a family member's needs varies among caregivers. Many factors contribute to the extent to which these responsibilities are taken on, including age, gender, support levels, and willingness to sacrifice aspects of one's personal life. Among caregivers that work outside the home while caring for a family member or friend, 69 per cent report having to rearrange their work schedule, decrease their hours of paid employment, or take an unpaid leave to meet family caregiving responsibilities (Family Caregiver Alliance).

Positive Aspects of Providing Care

The impact of being a caregiver affects each individual care provider differently. A pattern in current research tends to focus on negative aspects of being a caregiver of a loved one or client, although a cursory look at the positive aspects has been addressed. For example, Barbara Habermann and Linda Lindsey Davis suggest that positive aspects of caregiving, such as finding meaning in caregiving, may mitigate psychological harm. Most caregivers (75 per cent) report that the act of providing personal care contributed significantly to their self-identification as a caregiver and made a positive difference in their lives and in the lives of their family member (Habermann and Davis). Research on caregivers of patients with Alzheimer's disease found that despite suffering loss, sadness, pain, stress, and frustration, most caregivers (78 per cent) report positive aspects of and meaning in the caregiving process (Butcher). Meaning making for participants in this study was found through their commitment to the care recipient, by identifying the benefits of caring for another person, and by creating moments of joyfulness together. While the positive experiences reported by some care providers may pose differences in individual care provider's lives, this may not always be the case.

Gender

Many studies report that the gender of the caregiver plays a role in the overall experience (Nidhi et al.; Swinkels et al.; Stefanova et al.). Typically, women assume a greater burden for aging parents than men (Finley). Over time, it has been found that this level of responsibility is due mostly to the division of family labour. However, this division is not enough to explain gender caregiving differences particularly with young adults who view roles differently than previous generations.

This chapter is a starting point to better understand primary caregivers who are also students. There has been little to no published research addressing caregivers who are also college students. Gaining insight into their level of burden and their ability to balance academics, family, and employment (or not) on an average day may provide information concerning the needs and experiences of young adult caregivers.

Building on a tradition of scholarship on family interdependence and kin care within and outside of the Black family, this paper explores the experiences of millennial women who assume the simultaneous roles of both unpaid family caregivers and paid caregivers to individuals outside of the family. Therefore, I ask: What support do Black undergraduate women provide to their family? How do Black undergraduate women understand their roles as paid caregivers? In what ways do these similar and distinct roles parallel and conflict with one another and reproduce inequality?

This work is based on in-depth, semi-structured interviews with Black college women from financially disadvantaged backgrounds who are employed as paid and unpaid caregivers and will explore the ways in which they alternate between college, work, and family. This study argues that caregiving is a nuanced role and points to the academic and economic toll placed on students as they juggle occupational and familial responsibilities. I will show that in addition to attending college, Black young women secure employment as paid caregivers, assume the role of unpaid caregivers to various family members, and send money that they feel obligated to share with their families to ensure their survival.

Methods

As part of research including two hundred interviews with Black, Latinx, Asian American, and white undergraduates attending a large, predominantly white institution in the northeastern region of the US (hereafter Flagship University), I conducted in-depth, semi-structured interviews with fifty-two Black students, including twenty-six undergraduate women and twenty-six undergraduate men.[1] Black students comprise three per cent of the undergraduate population at Flagship. It is a good place to study the impact of the family in college students' lives, as the majority of college-aged young people attend public universities like this one (NCES). The student body here is also more economically diverse than students attending more elite, private colleges and universities that other research examines (Aries; Jack; Mullen; Stevens; Stuber).

Purposeful sampling was used to recruit students; a research team of four graduate students and a faculty advisor obtained a list of all enrolled students from Flagship's Undergraduate Registrar Office. The list included each student's name, race/ethnicity, age, email address, home address, and grade point average (GPA). In addition, we obtained a university list of all students receiving the Federal Pell Grant.

Based on the data we obtained, we divided the students into two class categories: financially advantaged and financially disadvantaged. We operationalized these as a combination of parental educational attainment (i.e., whether one or more parents had graduated college) and Pell Grant eligibility, as these seemed to provide the most accurate reflection of students' economic class. I use the language of "financially advantaged" and "financially disadvantaged" throughout the chapter, as it is a difficult but useful descriptor that does not evoke all the baggage of so many designations of class, such as upper and lower class, working and middle class, as well as white and blue collar. Qualitative research can illuminate the cultural narratives, meanings, and resources people use to make sense of the world they encounter and help shape (Geertz). In-depth interviewing is especially useful as a method to illuminate people's narratives, conceptions, reasoning, and the potential contradictions within them (Lamont; Pugh).

In-depth interviews with participants ranged from one to three hours, with most interviews lasting approximately ninety minutes. Interviews included questions and probes about interactions with family and kinds of support (including money, guidance, connections, as well as practical and emotional support) given by and to family members (including parents, siblings, aunts, uncles, cousins, grandparents, and other extended kin), perceived obligations and contributions from students to family during college, assessment of the impact of family involvement on the college experience, and perceptions of college success. These questions allowed me to analyze not only the range of financial, social, and cultural support families provide but also track the support students receive from kin and the support students provide to kin. During my interviews with financially disadvantaged Black women, I learned that 85 per cent of them not only provided kin care but also worked as hired caregivers in the New England town where they were enrolled as college students. These young women were employed as nannies, babysitters, and eldercare providers. When I asked these women why they provided carework to earn money rather than work in other service-sector positions (retail, grocery stores, movie theaters, etc.), they said their supervisors were more accommodating of their class schedules as students and often these roles compensated them under the table. Few statistics exist on nannies' salaries, for example, primarily because most of these workers, very much like the college women in this study, are part of the informal economy.

Findings

The experiences highlighted in this chapter are drawn from the larger study's findings. In comparison to the other racial groups, most financially disadvantaged women mentioned working over twenty-five hours a week in low-wage, service-sector jobs as babysitters, nursing assistants, and part-time in-house nannies. My findings complicate the normative view that separates home, work, and college life. I address educational inequalities by showing there is no "postfamily" stage in the life course; undergraduate women remain tied to their families even as they work as paid caregivers. The type and amount of caregiving they provide to their families and at their place of employment varies significantly for different women.

My findings show that Black college women from financially disadvantaged backgrounds alternate between college, work, and family. Financially disadvantaged students' narratives suggest they do not immerse themselves in college life. Instead, they emphasize their involvement within their families as caregivers and their part-time jobs as hired caregivers pulls them away from campus life. Students discussed their commitment to family broadly, highlighting that they not only provide caregiving support to their nuclear family members but also other kin—including grandmothers, grandfathers, aunts, uncles, and cousins. Students talked about working as hired caregivers outside of their families and how this role often detracts from the amount of time and care they can realistically give to their family.

Financially disadvantaged students report having to fulfill significant domestic responsibilities. They sometimes find themselves torn between their role as family members, students, and hired caregivers, and express a desire to give even as they simultaneously worry about what that means for their college trajectory and employment. A case in point is a financially disadvantaged student, Cecilia. She talks about the strain she feels as a result of the domestic duties she is responsible for at her part-time job and when she visits home regularly:

> I have to help out when I go home because my mother works late. At the same time, I feel bad when I can't go home because I have to work late at the nursing. I feel torn because I'm helping out someone else's family member when I should be helping my own relatives, but I need the money. These extra responsibilities interfere with me really focussing on my classes and getting work done…. Sometimes I think, "am I ever going to graduate because all of this work and family stuff?"

Some of the young women interviewed felt indebted to family due to the sense of guilt they felt from cultural expectations. As such, the excerpt above suggests a sense of repayment that more financially advantaged students may not consider, since giving back to family during college is not as important.

In addition to paid care, these women also provide assistance to their families. They spoke not only of caregiving for younger siblings but also for their mothers and grandparents. Sometimes assuming these dual roles meant students had to formally take time off from school. Rhonda is a first-generation college student who took a semester off to work in an assisted living facility for pay while providing domestic support to her family. Now re-enrolled, Rhonda shares how she continues to shoulder household and employment obligations: "I took a semester off from school because going so far away was really hard on my mother. I have three brothers but all the weight of getting stuff done around the house—the cooking, cleaning falls on me."

Though Rhonda, like other women I spoke with, talked about the cognitive and emotional labour aspects of this by saying things like, "It's taxing" and "It really weighs on me mentally." They also understood providing paid and unpaid practical assistance in gendered and racialized terms:

> I'm no stranger to changing the diapers of the elderly people I work with at the facility and even doing the same thing for my eighty-year-old grandmother. It's something that strong women, strong Black women, have been doing for a long time. Putting on so many hats, juggling work, school, and family all at once is hard, but we know how to make it work to keep things going on so many fronts. They need me at work and I'm there. They need me at home, and I'll be there. So many pockets of society rely on Black women to hold things down.

In some respects, young women saw their caregiving roles as empowering rather than disempowering. Not only do many financially disadvantaged women talk about their work and family caregiving responsibilities as a means to ensure the functioning of a facility or their family, but they also emphasize that they often combine these duties with spending desired time with their families, clients, and the patients they regularly assist. Each young woman I interviewed framed their experiences in these ways. As one undergraduate woman named Sarah put it, she feels responsible, as a caregiver, for "holding my family and my clients, whom I consider family, up." Whereas most feminist writing on carework often discourages employers from referring to care workers as being part of the family, participants shared that they found referring to clients as family members helped to build friendships and establish rapport. Sarah, like many others, refers to both her biological relatives and individuals that she shares no biological ties to her as family. She moves beyond the nuclear family relations to include those she has made connections with as a result of her employment. As paid and unpaid caregivers, these young women make the exchange of support possible.

Young women reported working long hours and late shifts to cover basic material needs for themselves, and, importantly, to send money home to their families. They say that sending money home to family can also be thought of as a form of caregiving; it is essential for their families to thrive and, in some cases, survive while they are away at college and working as hired caregivers.

In contrast, young men's understanding of their roles in relation to giving money differed from women's. No undergraduate man interviewed indicated that they worked as a caregiver or went home regularly to provide unpaid care to kin. They perceived their financial contributions to the family as their duty as a man. Typically raised by single mothers, some say they see themselves as their families' primary breadwinner. As the oldest of eight, a financially disadvantaged student named Martrez, who calls himself the man of the house, states how his mother and younger siblings rely on his financial support for basic necessities:

> My mom has a disability, so she can't work...but she and my little sisters still need to eat. Some might think, "he's still in school, he shouldn't be doing this," but I have to do this. I wouldn't be able to sleep. I'm still the man of the house even though I'm at school. I work at least twenty hours a week, sometimes more, just so I can send money home so my mom can pay bills. They're counting on me.

Another financially disadvantaged man, Khalil, talks about how giving money to his family comes before his academics: "If I had to choose, my family comes first. If I need to work longer hours to make more money and if working more hours means that I have to miss a final or write a paper because they need me at home, I'll do it. They're expecting me to hold my weight."

Undergraduate women describe the importance of monetary support as a way to pool resources and care for family and, in doing so be, as many put it, be a "good daughter." Brittany, an undergraduate woman, states: "I've been in a live-in nanny ever since I've been in college. I do it because I am able to send money home every pay period. It's what a good daughter does. I make sacrifices for my family by caring for another family's children. It's an even exchange in my book. Both families are taken care of."

Furthermore, students like Brittany report giving money as a result of self-imposed expectations and feelings that they "left the family" by working as hired caregivers. Another student, Tanesha, expresses a sense of guilt for going to college and taking a job in a hospital as a medical assistant rather than staying close to home. She talks about assisting her family financially and her attempts to remain a "good daughter" even from a distance:

> Leaving and going away to college was hard enough. Taking a job and caring for patients and not my own sick relatives felt like I was a bad daughter. I felt like, okay, I'm going to live this other life and do this other thing in this other place. I didn't want my family to think I was turning my back on them by caring for other people. I get a refund check every semester and I always give my family half. I feel guilty giving money and not being able to be there to really help out.

Note that both financially disadvantaged women and men talk about giving money, but they engage in gendered assessments. Martrez emphasizes that he is the "man of the house," reporting the continuation of an "adultified" position (Burton) and sustaining a sense of duty even if it comes at great costs (missing a final, turning in incomplete assignments, not dedicating enough time to study for upcoming midterms, final exams, etc.). Financially disadvantaged men talk of themselves as "heads of household"—a hierarchical formulation—while young women talk of themselves as being "good daughters" in familial or relational terms that still situates them within—rather than at the top of—their families.

Here we see how young women place a value on maintaining family relationships. Referencing the support they provide to a range of kin, these undergraduate women talk about how they fit into the helping tradition of their families and how they also contribute to the paid caregiving industry. This chapter shows that although the provision of support to family may sustain family (which these students so clearly value), providing paid and unpaid care also reproduces inequality. Financially disadvantaged women work as paid caregivers, often with extensive hours, so they can give money to family members. In this sense, they share the cultural assumptions of employed Black workers whom sociologist Michelle Lamont describes as displaying a moral sense of self that is centred on sharing with others in need. Lamont calls this the "caring self," which she (and the Black workers) contrast with more individualistic white workers.

Colleges and universities have been called upon to develop organizational policies and practices that support an increasingly diverse student body. To develop these pathways, it is crucial to understand the ways that Black undergraduate women who assume the role of paid and unpaid caregivers experience college. I show that ongoing caregiving exchanges and familial relationships are central to many financially disadvantaged women's experiences.

Conclusion

This study contributes to the literature on caregiving by beginning a discussion that addresses the experiences of students who do not fit traditional demographics. Regarding future research, more intensive analysis is needed to explain the resilient nature of this group of caregivers. Degree seeking may provide a buffer from the traditional burden and depression often experienced by other caregivers who are not attending college. Although my participants indicated experiencing levels of struggle and strain, they also viewed caregiving as empowering. More research is needed to understand the immediate and long-term impact of providing care as a full-time, degree-seeking adult. Due to the lack of male caregivers, this chapter could not examine potential gender differences in the experiences of Black undergraduates.

The millennial generation is changing how we explore the question, "How do the roles of family caregiver and hired caregiver align and differ?" A focus on Black, millennial women who assume these dual roles provides an opportunity to foresee the challenges that lie ahead in family caregiving and hired caregiving. It is important to monitor the trends over the coming years, as they likely have broad implications for millennials of colour, who will continue to increase as a proportion of the overall caregiving population.

Caregiving is a nuanced role. The academic and economic toll for students with such responsibilities is clear. Many of my study's participants reported that their work and family duties affected their ability to focus entirely on and effectively manage their academic commitments. Many of my participants chose to keep the stress they were experiencing hidden from university officials and staff who may be well positioned to lend help, including financial assistance or more flexible assignment deadlines. Early identification of student caregivers is key. Student caregivers should be encouraged to inform their college or university, but academic institutions must create a caregiver-friendly environment that fosters this communication.

Data suggests that caregiving does have a significant impact on matriculation. According to a study from American Association of Retired Persons (AARP), five million students in colleges, universities, or vocational schools are taking care of adults who may be elderly or suffering from an illness (AARP). The association reported that these students are forced to balance their studies with the demanding work of caregiving. Of the four hundred people the study surveyed, seven in ten said caregiving has affected their coursework to at least some extent, and six in ten said their family responsibilities have hurt their ability to pay tuition or other costs of education.

Few colleges and universities have dedicated services to support caregivers enrolled on their campuses. In many cases, the students fit into existing programs that provide academic help, financial aid, and mental health counselling. However, they also encounter some distinct challenges and have unique sets of experiences that require campuses to think differently about the services they offer.

Further complicating efforts to support student caregivers is the fact that they may not always identify with the role, often claiming they are just doing what they are supposed to do for a loved one or to maintain employment. Others fear that school officials will not understand. A majority of the participants in this study (over 90 per cent) said they had not informed an instructor or staff member at their institution that they were a caregiver because they felt as though "they wouldn't understand" or would "think I'm making excuses for missing class or turning in assignments late." The COVID-19 pandemic has shed light on young adults who also serve as caregivers. As such, colleges and universities are slowly realizing that the number of students who are struggling with the emotional and physical strains of caregiving is growing and that those students are at greater risk of delaying coursework or dropping out.

Looking ahead, in order to better find and support student caregivers, postsecondary institutions will need to better think through how to reach this student population. Emphasizing dignity, communicating concern, embedding student advocates on campus, and practicing trauma-informed care include initial sets of strategies that institutions can employ. Creating a more robust or targeted assistance for caregivers on campus will not happen overnight. Budgets are tight, and the issues are complex, as this chapter shows. But there are steps, large and small, that colleges can take to make sure that students who serve as caregivers do not slip through the cracks. By developing policies, promoting available resources, and normalizing the number of students who are employed outside of an institution and enrolled as students, academic institutions can build an environment that fosters success and reduces unnecessary stress as students juggle family, work, and college demands.

Endnotes

1. I use the term "Black" rather than "African American" throughout the paper to reflect the preferences of the participants in the study.

Works Cited

AARP. *5 Million Student Caregivers Need More Resources and Flexibility From Schools.* AARP, 2020.

Besen-Cassino, Y. *The Cost of Being a Girl: Working Teens and the Origins of the Gender Wage Gap.* Temple University Press, 2018.

Bureau of Labor Statistics. 2021. *The Economics Daily, Nearly One-Quarter of Eldercare Providers Provided Daily Care from May 2020 to May 2021.*

Espiritu, Yen, and Diane Wolf. "The Paradox of Assimilation: Children of Filipino Immigrants in San Diego," Ethnicities: Children of immigrants in America. Edited by R. G. Rumbaut and A. Portes. University of California Press, 2011, pp. 115-32.

Family Caregiver Alliance. *Factsheet. Selected Caregiver Statistics.* 2012.

Finley, N. J. "Theories of Family Labor as Applied to Gender Differences in Caregiving for Elderly Parent." *Journal of Marriage and Family,* vol. 51, no. 1, 2008, pp. 79-86.

Gladieux, Lawrence and Laura Perna. Borrowers Who Drop Out. National Center for Public Policy and Higher Education Report. 2005.

Goldrick-Rab, Sara. *Paying the Price: College Costs, Financial Aid, and the Betrayal of the American Dream.* University of Chicago Press, 2017.

Habermann, B. and Davis, L. L. "Caring for family with Alzheimer's disease and Parkinson's disease. *Journal of Gerontological Nursing,* vol. 31, no. 6, 2005, pp. 49-54.

Juratovac, E., et al. "Effort, Workload, and Depressive Symptoms in Family Caregivers of Older Adults: Conceptualizing and Testing a Work-Health Relationship." *Research and Theory for Nursing Practice,* vol. 26, no. 2, 2012, pp. 74-94.

Kane, Connie M. "Differences in Family of Origin Perceptions among African American, Asian American, and Hispanic American College Students." *Journal of Black Studies,* vol. 29, no. 1, 1998, pp. 93-105.

Karlin, N. J., et al. "Comparisons between Hispanic and Non-Hispanic White Informal Caregivers." *Sage Open,* vol. 2, no.4, 2012, pp. 1-10.

Klein, Wendy, et al. "Children and Chores: A Mixed-Methods Study of Children's Household Work in Los Angeles Families." *Anthropology of Work Review,* vol. 30, no. 3, 2009, pp. 98-109.

Lamont, Michelle. The Dignity of Working Men: Morality and the Boundaries of Race, Class and Immigration. *Harvard University Press,* 2000.

Maramba, Dina C. "Immigrant Families and the College Experience: Perspectives of Filipina Americans." *Journal of College Student Development,* vol. 49, no. 4, 2008, pp. 336-50.

Morrow, V. "Policy Implications: The Worth of Women's work," edited by A. Statham et al., State University of New York Press, 2008.

Nidhi, Sharma, et al. "Gender differences in caregiving among family – caregiving of people with mental illnesses." *World Journal of Psychiatry,* vol. 6, no. 1, 2016, pp. 7-17.

Stefanova, V., et al. "Gender and the pandemic: Associaions between caregiving, working from home, personal and career outcomes for women and men." *Current Psychology,* vol. 42, no. 6, 2023, pp. 395-411.

Swinkels, Joukje, et al. "Explaining the Gender Gap in the Caregiving Burden of Partner Caregivers." *The Journals of Gerontology,* vol. 74, no. 2, 2019, pp. 309-17.

Sy, Susan, and Aerika Brittian. "The impact of family obligations on young women's decisions during the transition to college: a comparison of Latina, European American, and Asian American students" *Sex Roles, 58,* 2008, pp. 729-737.

US Department of Education, National Center for Education Statistics. *Digest of Education Statistics.* US Department of Education, 2019.

Winkle-Wagner, Rachelle. "The Perpetual Homelessness of College Experiences: Tensions Between Home and Campus for African American Women." *The Review of Higher Education,* vol. 33, 2009, pp. 1-36.

Chapter 14

Friending with the Caregivers: An Autoethnographic Study of a Bengali Household

Medhashri Mahanty

"Keeping"[1] servants is a common practice in India that rests on a "feudal imaginary" of the faithful retainer who enters the family by inhabiting faux-familial ties but always stays away from an amorphous inner sanctum of the house by invisible and unbridgeable touch barriers (Ray and Qayum 7). The nature of this relationship between employers and their help has evolved over the last few decades, taking the specific feudal trait of domination and servility and moulding it into various affective indices ranging from love or friendship to an ambivalent zone that is beset with an arbitrary mix of carelessness and familiarity. I identify ambivalence as a complex emotional register to justify the non-committal yet deeply intimate space shared by employers and caregivers as they navigate through the domestic space.

Ambivalence, in this relationship, is a tool that employers use to reproduce the class boundaries while maintaining a patronizing, loving, and often safe space between each other. What sets this zone as ambivalent is the arbitrary limit that applies to demarcate, stop, and sometimes disregard the emotional investments in the relationship. This development in the caregiver-employer relationship is relatively new as the economic liberalization hit the two parties very differently, increasing income inequality and class gap beyond comprehension. The servitude culture of India rests on a scaffold of various identity markers which are interchangeable with touch barriers (for example, caste determines the range of an employee's entry to the house, a Dalit usually cleans the house whereas a Brahmin is almost always hired for kitchen work) within the heteropatriarchal family. While the relationship with one's domestic help has updated itself from a feudal, infantilizing, and abusive relationship to a more patronizing and less abusive one, post liberalization, with better infrastructures, especially in the communication sector, finding domestic labour became easier. As families started to become smaller mobile units and move away, retainers were replaced with helps who worked on a contractual basis. Relationships with the help started on the pretext of a familial bond but became more personal, slick, and complex. With retainers, love and obedience were predominant, but with the emerging helps, love shifted to a less serious, casual, flexible, and intimate relationship. The rhetoric of love remained at the base of this, providing support to manage various touch barriers.

The employer-caregiver relationship in the everyday domestic space is a product of an ambiguous, liveable but non-navigable class barrier that falls short of the love rhetoric in its promise of familial inclusivity, while never aspiring to resemble friendship. To understand such a non-consistent, albeit personal transaction of synergies occurring in the domestic space, I use my situatedness to determine the "filters" through which my perception of the familial and its exigencies occur to critique and infer how they contribute to the larger realm of the social and political (Behar, 20). As a broader rubric to understand the complications of employer-caregiver relationships in India, I have used "friending" as a term to denote the seemingly friendly, familial, and safe nature of the relationship that employers and caregivers mutually feel towards their relationship. Friending is an irregular state that balances itself on the various touch barriers that affect the relationship and amplifies the impossibility of friendship precisely on the lines of those barriers. Friending, insomuch as it mimics friendship is vastly different from it in its goal. Friendship as such has no goal, in that it is a goal in itself, but friending begins with the purpose of "making up" for work that cannot be compensated with material remuneration. This knowledge about the impossibility of friendship reflects itself in a quick hack, that can be unstructured, limited, and deeply conditional. The touch barriers in this case (i.e., class, caste, and gender) act as fasteners in the relationship, such that these relationships can always change their nature, depending on the situation. Friending is also a tactical measure against the love rhetoric that employers use to infantilize and abuse their employees while creating familial obligations using guilt. Friending gives opportunity to the employees to voice their opinions and choices because of the personal nature of the relationship. In friending, a more direct and personal relationship with the employer lets the employee put herself before the employer, i.e., the employee uses discomfort, hesitation, or negligence in her work as a way of "devalorization" of labour, by taking away her labour power as well as putting "labour on a distinct footing from other means or inputs of production" (Gidwani 179, 180). I do not suggest that the rhetoric of love is outdated, rather, friending is an emerging structure that complements the love rhetoric while taking various strands from it.

With increased mobility, migrant labourers often come with their families to the cities with the hope of earning more money from multiple sources. Usually, the women from these migrant families work as part-time domestic workers while also being employed in other unorganized sectors of the economy in various capacities. The "aggressive" nature of the accumulation of commodities in post-liberalization India is commensurate with increasing caste and gender prejudices and economic inequality—a structure that reinstates violence as a given, in earning profit (Mishra xvi). While the labourer is motivated by capital to sell her labour whenever she chooses, it is capital that determines where she can sell it. Recruiting agencies such as bookmybai.com use identity markers to customize the search for maids which always work against the minorities and marginalized communities, especially the Dalits and the Muslims. Since labour power is a "variable capital," its movement is determined by the exigencies of capital which means that workers have to abide by the rules of these agencies, which in turn have a customer base that is middle and upper-middle class (Harvey 381). If capital encashes its "indifference" to convey that labour always produces money, then it also imposes on the worker that she does not restrict her choices and accepts all "variations" in her work; this means that employers' preferences ("basic grooming" and "background check") always overrule the choices of the employees (Harvey 380-82; "Hiring Housemaids in India"). The rhetoric of love undergoes a significant change when freelancers are hired by agencies or directly. With agencies and especially with young employers, the personal element of "keeping" a maid fades away to a more specific need that works on an ambiguous emotional plane. Often many employers prefer freelancers but also extend the rhetoric to bind them into a long-lasting relationship that continues beyond one's service has ended. Such relationships often imitate the tendencies in friendship but betray the structure of friendship at odd moments of expectations that arise from potent awareness about one's class and caste.

In this chapter, I study moments from my life to demonstrate the intricate nature of the relationship between mothers and their domestic help. I recount a few incidents of stealing and discuss what it means to steal from the home of one's employer. In the first part of the essay, I remain with the literal act of stealing and contemplate a common Bengali proverb associated with domestic helps and stealing. In the latter part, I work with other meanings of stealing that define the limits of the relationship between the domestic help and her employer, while studying the domestic space as a shared unit between the mother and the help she hires. In reading the space as a mutually inclusive space of balance between two women, I add a queer meaning to the otherwise heteropatriarchal family.

My chapter reflects primarily on the interactions between my mother and the house help she has hired and specifically focuses on the nature of ambivalence in their relationship as a metonymic reference, to trace the evolving culture of servitude in neoliberal India. Autoethnography as a research tool helps me read the unquantifiable excesses in social life to perturb the complacent nature of a givenness usually associated with personal idiosyncrasies in dealing with housekeepers. My reliance on memory to recount the stories comes riddled with various linguistic terms whose connotations vary widely in Bengali, the language spoken by the caregivers, their employer(s) that I write about, and myself.

Autoethnography as a method is reassuring because it not only makes power relations more visible with the "I" as the entry point thus making me, the writer more accountable to those about whom I am writing but also takes into account that I, since the I is both a writer and the person whose stories are being written about, can hold up many narratives at once, to keep up with the wholeness of social life (Erdmans et al). It is interesting that while autoethnography has been established as an academic (read reliable) method of study, it still creates anxiety among scholars to take personal experiences as valid content to expand on and critique cultural systems, claiming that such a lens is both limited and dangerously homogenous in making inferences. I think that autoethnography makes an incision in the ethnographic "gaze" by reflecting and aligning the self with others (Dauphinee 806). This is a clinical process of (de)attachment where the self as another comes to be seen and critiqued by the writer, against the broader cultural fabric. Autoethnography questions the passive voice of the scholar using the third-person narrative as an effective source of absolute knowledge.

I want to mention an incident about this. I used autoethnography (mostly because I was writing during the pandemic without any access to the archives, but also because I wanted to understand the relationship with waste personally) as one of the methods in writing my MPhil dissertation. It was on waste and the intimate relationship it has with the people, especially the city and its architecture. During my viva voce, my external examiner told me that while my writing is filled with "journalistic brilliance,"[2] autoethnography does not count for much of an academic tool. It struck me that the personal, even though political, is being discarded as nonacademic because it cannot convince the examiner as an authentic tool of inquiry. The personal with its active reflexivity shows the formation of the narrative through various actors, including the researcher and always gazes back. This can be disconcerting since it calls for ethical accountability from the researcher/writer/colonizer; in other words, the power relations out there and the body of the researcher now an undeniable presence make it personal (Erdmans). The auto of autoethnography hints at the researcher's body being palimpsestic and evidential. This means that the body of the researcher builds upon the preexisting knowledge in the community and refers to the codes and patterns that manifest themselves in nonacademic terrains. When the researcher uses autoethnography as a tool to tell her story, she critically refers to these codes to tell the story for an audience that is not related to her because of any shared identity but because these codes, when broken down, construct a more unbiased, political, and perhaps, an inclusive story. Autoethnography mashes up the subject/object divide and always makes the researcher uncomfortable by creating personal accountability.

When my examiner felt that autoethnography as an academic tool was not viable, I realized that I was failing to communicate an affective reality of my writing, which is its informality. Informality in academic writing accommodates political accountability that uses the personal as a critical vantage point. Informality takes the shape of messy prose, often wobbling with emotional histories that disregard the possibility of finitude in third-person objective writing. In this chapter, I use autoethnography more as a prerequisite than a research tool to understand the relationship between mothers and caregivers because the affective quality of this relationship is hardly a consistent workplace relationship. It seeps into the deeper layers of familial strata and develops into an informal, vulnerable, and unequal relationship. That the relationship begins with class and caste inequality is slightly less disconcerting than the discomfort that manifests itself through the faux-familial bond and creates sudden and lopsided desires in the employer and the caregiver. The casual acceptance of touch barriers surviving class and caste divides rests peacefully unless triggered by emotional histories in an otherwise difficult relationship that devolves into deep familiarity, because of the materiality of the workspace. The personal accounts that Raka Ray and Seemin Qayum document in their book bring out many vulnerable moments in the domestic space, that reflect the unspoken but deeply biased and set rules that keep the class and caste divide intact by using touch barriers. These barriers present themselves physically, such as sitting arrangements, places designated unofficially for domestic helps to take off their shoes before entering the house, what suffix they might add after the names of employers, especially young members of the house, etc., while these barriers extend to the bodies of the employees and employers through affects such as hesitation, shame, or despair that often remain unaccounted for because of the ingrained inequality that cements this relationship.

In the 2018 Hindi film *Is Love Enough? Sir,* when Ashwin falls in love with his domestic help Ratna and confesses his feelings to her, Ratna rejects him due to the unsurmountable class gap that separates them. In the end, when she receives a call from Ashwin and calls him by his first name after calling him sir throughout the film, she has already left work at Ashwin's and is an assistant to a fashion designer. Ratna's class was not just only immutable vis-à-vis her work as domestic help, but mostly because as long as she worked at Ashwin's, Ratna constantly remained, by an act of "transfer", in a class that is deemed low because it serves the classes above it (Ray and Qayum 9). This transfer of reproductive work is feudal, and it comes from the deep-seated prejudice that already classifies the help as worthy to do what the employer would not want to do. By deeming the work unworthy and impersonal such that it can be done by someone else, the class boundaries are constantly recreated inside the house as a byproduct of keeping domestic help. When my mother insisted that I hire a housekeeper to help me prepare my meals every day, she stressed how unimportant chopping vegetables is and that I have better things to work on. The arbitrariness in the importance of the kind of work (re)sets the class distinction so that a romantic relationship between the employer and caregiver is always fraught by the unsurmountable lack of identification. The impossibility of the romance between Ratna and Ashwin was not only because of their class barrier but also because loving Ashwin while being employed by him would require Ratna to value the loved object (Ashwin) by identifying her position in a desired state of being. To identify her position is undesirable for her because she would not only identify herself as the beloved but also as the help, who does everything for "Sir," to love here would be a romantic extrapolation of the classic "rhetoric of love" (Ray and Qayum 92). This rhetoric is a function that works for both the employers and the employees as they navigate through and justify their unequal relationship using the garb of affection and familial care.

In my experiences with caregivers and domestic help, I have seen this trope working as an emotional offshoot of the feudal imaginary that coddles the expectations of the help by letting them expand their being inside the family and giving them a space of their own. The help feels this love in the familial space that coopts their labour so it feels like doing everyday things for one's own family and also because of the friendships that develop between the women employers (in this case, my mother) and themselves. Chandana, one of my mother's past house help, said that she has never found a friend as close as my mother. The desire for such friendships comes from the need to identify with someone that faces discrimination by the heteropatriarchal family. This relationship becomes an alternative to the heterofamilial structure while sharing space within the family. It becomes necessary to ally to live through the violence of the patriarchal family as the relationship between two women traverses the boundaries of an employer-caregiver relationship into a rhetoric, very different from the patronizing albeit abusive rhetoric of love. The mother-domestic help relationship hits a new level of common purpose as they start sharing affairs, recipes, and struggles.

But this friendship is not between people who hold "all things in common"; in fact, it is an incidental friendship that exists as an ambiguous unequal alliance, chiefly a byproduct of a job opportunity (MacPhail 616; Aristotle 147). The relationship mimics and fails to be a friendship insofar it exhibits a moral superiority on the part of the employer always providing advice, help, and assistance to the childish, innocent caregiver. My mother often thinks that Chandana is like a desperate child, so she needs to be controlled. But children are also selfish, they often do not care after they have got what they want. Chandana, for my mother, is not exactly like this, but she fears her eccentric side and believes she is capable of this if my mother spoils her too much, and draws arbitrary limits to shut her away. Chandana, for her part, is not unaware of this, and strategically maneuvers their space but always maintains an intimate distance.

In the Nicomachean Ethics, in Book IX, Chapter 7, while talking of friendships, Aristotle says that the love between a benefactor and his beneficiaries is unequal as the benefactor will always love the beneficiary more than the beneficiary will love the benefactor. Comparing the benefactor with the mother or the poet who loves her child/poem more than the latter ever will (in the case of the poem, if it comes alive), Aristotle makes a case for labour by equating the amount of effort gone in producing (giving birth) the object of love with the object itself. In a way then, this is an economic exercise where the evaluation of love for the loved object begins with valuing the labour that has gone into producing the object (Singer). Since such love is self-reflexive, it is also narcissistic and "returns" to the subject, in this case, the mother (The Cultural Politics of Emotion 127).

After Chandana quit working at our house because her salary was more than my mother could afford, my mother said (in a tone that suggested she always knew it) that Chandana always puts her income and comfort before anything. She felt more anger than betrayal given the nature of the relationship, which stretches beyond Chandana's work years, but my mother regretted her inability to control her, referring to the feudal nostalgia when servants, domestic helps and housekeepers never thought of refusing to work for less pay, as that would be 'betrayal' against the family. My mother's crises in regards to Chandana was akin to the benefactor whose emotional labour was not valued by her beneficiary and was in fact, expendable. My father said that their class (meaning domestic help, housekeepers, and caregivers) is unfaithful no matter what one does. My mother was offended by this statement and said that Chandana was never unfaithful to her. At this moment, it was more complex than the employer-employee relationship of gratitude and faithfulness usually attributed to the servitude culture. It was love. Who loved more, my mother or Chandana? For my mother, the childlike dependence that she had expected from Chandana in exchange for her maternal advice left her disappointed as she learned how to continue the relationship with Chandana post her heartbreak.

I suggest friending as a way that supports these unequal relationships, which may resemble friendship. Friending allows the employers and caregivers to continue their relationship on a personal level but with a layer of conditional affection, constraining the limit of the relationships when the expectations of a party, especially that of the employer, go unmet. Friending is a fluid state of relationship making that involves a frequent, fissured, and continuous tussle in asserting random and personal claims. It is also a sustainable way for both parties to maintain a symbiotic, noncommittal, and ambiguous intimacy even after the professional relationship ends. But friending is also a political means for caregivers insofar as it becomes an attitude in dealing with employers. Moments of insolence, which in the employer's parlance becomes acts of betrayal, are essential to the concept of friending where employees do not bring the relationship to an abrupt end but only irritate the employer into shifting the register from expected servility to a felt agency. Since friending is a process of networking, it works as an infrastructure for a tactical gesture that allows one to be selfish about their emotion but also maintains the connection for future benefits. Friending provides a "political terrain" that complicates, using intimacy, the relationship between the mothers and the housekeepers they hire (Chattopadhyay 171).

A Little About Stealing

"Bhaat choraley kaaker obhaabh hobena."
"If you spread rice all over, there will be no absence of crows."
—My father about housemaids

I.

My parents are both working so my mother hired Minu for regular housework which included making tea, cleaning the house and utensils, and washing the clothes. On holidays and weekends, she would accompany my mother to her terrace garden, they would bond over tea and help mother in gardening and cleaning. I learned from an early age to call all the housekeepers by adding a suffix of didi (elder sister) or mashi (maternal aunt). Not only were these names a way of forging a familial relationship with the help but also these relationships were very maternal. The feminine quality that these relationships normatively bear, such as the elder sister or the maternal aunt taking care of the house while the mother is away—is, after all, a synecdochic idea of the woman taking care of the man. The husband's house is considered the wife's sansar, colloquial for the Sanskrit term samsara meaning world. The wife is already a maternal equivalent who nurtures the husband and his home, the home being a material extension of the husband's being. To forge a maternal connection, such as didi or mashi is not just to hire a maid who will keep the household clean but also to use the figure of the maid as a familial relation to replace the space of the maternal figure temporarily when the wife/mother is away.

Even when there is no child to look after (although, with the presence of the child, the relationship becomes more complex and difficult) there already is at work a fragile balance between the wife, the housekeeper, and the house. This triad becomes sacred when the wife and the help find in each other, a sustenance to live by. The house becomes their common space of belonging. A popular example of this comes from the Indian epic Ramayana, where Manthara, the family servant of Kaikayi (the second queen of Dasaratha) convinces her to ask the king to send Rama to the forest and put her son, Bharat as the crown prince. A little context—Rama's mother Kaushalya (the first queen of Dasaratha) was mistreated by Kaikayi and Manthara played on this fear by telling her that Rama's kingship might ruin Kaikayi's stay at the palace. But more than this, Manthara was securing the future of Kaikayi's descendants, making her the Queen Mother. Manthara was not simply looking out for Kaikayi like a guardian, she was advising her on how to take charge of a home. Further, she was also securing her place in the palace because Kaikayi's queenship meant Mathara's permanent place in the house. This is not sudden because Manthara has been a maternal companion to Kaikayi since her childhood when her mother was banished, so Manthara had already shared a home with Kaikayi in her father's palace, followed her to her husband's palace, and now she only wanted to have a share in a house of their own.

The palace (or kingdom, in this case) becomes the third element with their relationship status changing from queen-chambermaid to mother and caregiver, as Manthara gives her a plan to secure her son's life, somewhat like a nanny. As Tripti Lahiri notes, such relationships can be "very unhappy" when the nanny undermines the position of the mother, but the mother agrees, threatened by her helplessness in the face of the child's life (179). It is important to note how a servant becomes a crucial ingredient in changing the future of Rama and the whole epic. Manthara has been called a traitor in most versions of Ramayana and is accused of ruining Kaikayi's character, but this is an oversimplification. Manthara's filial love for Kaikayi has been treated in Ramayana as an evil, even a cautionary tale, but the poet Valmiki describes her as hunch-backed, which I read as a personification of all that love she could not give to Kaikayi, except in a very twisted manner. The hunchback, which has been used as a trope for the evil disabled in various translations, was made fun of by Rama who hit her because of that, precisely pointing out that the patriarchal family will always do everything in its power to end such friendships because it cannot bend these structures of love to the general will of the family. Manthara, remains a significant character in the lived every day of India, as families compare their employees to Manthara whenever they feel irritated, suspicious, or betrayed—feelings that are often created by shifts and nicks in the touch barriers between the employers and their caregivers.

In the modern day, the sacred unity in these relationships is threat-ened by the permeable nature of the class boundaries in the family, which leads to a leakage of information through the help (Dickey). Housekeepers and domestic helpers are often labelled as gossip mongers, liars, and thieves which directly reaffirms the idea that the patriarchal family structure imposes arbitrary limits at its will to maintain the purity of the class. Sara Dickey traces the anxiety families feel with the servants in her study of households in Madurai, as she mentions a strat-egy of playing with limits that employers often use with their help. The right kind of proximity i.e., neither too close nor too far is always main-tained with the employees, such that the servants constantly monitor their behaviour lest they surpass the touch barrier.

Minu and my mother became friends to the point where each knew what the other liked. When it was discovered that Minu had been stealing money, clothes, and groceries, my mother regretted their friendship, blaming herself for the transgression that encouraged Minu to steal. It was, as if, a metaphorical leakage had already happened through their friendship before the stealing. Minu never confessed and she left the job immediately.

Another incident: My mother hired Kunti to help her prepare meals, since her work got hectic. Kunti was affectionate, helped my mother, and took care of my grandfather at times. Within a few days, my mother discovered that a lot of items from the kitchen including spices and cutleries were missing. Kunti left the job soon after confessing.

When my mother worried about finding another help, my father said that if one is willing to spread some rice, there won't be any absence of crows. This is a common proverb in Bengali and it means that once you have the money, you will find many people willing to work for you.

What my father suggested further was that house helps are like the proverbial crow because of the following reasons:

i) Crows steal. Crows steal eggs from other birds, they also steal shiny objects like spoons. Servants steal all the time, he said. No matter how much you try to help them, their jaat is such, that they will cheat and steal. Jaat means caste in Bengali, but here he did not try to evoke the literal meaning of caste as an identity marker but rather jaat as in the kind of material they were built of. For example, in Bengali, we often say, "loha onyo jaater dhatu" meaning that iron is a different kind of metal, thus jaat is used to mean class as an arbitrary but unique marker that sets an object apart from other things. In the case of iron, that statement could mean iron is a different kind of metal because it is strong or it cannot be used to make fancy items like a dish. Similarly, domestic help, my father inferred, was made of a unique material that made them who they were.

ii) Crows are omnivores. Crows are not loyal to others, but they have a strong sense of community. Omnivores indicate that domestic help will feed on anything as long as it is food, that is to say, it is a given that they will only be loyal to the one who has food and will not have any preference for the kind of food. But it also, perhaps ironically suggests, that they will feed on insults, abuse and rebukes, if need be, for the food.

They are omnivores who eat anything, as long as it can be eaten. Moreover, like crows who have a strong sense of community, domestic helpers often have a strong solidarity network to deal with the trauma and injustice they go through which comes in handy when they have to lodge complaints against the employer. In a patriarchal family, this goes against the very rhetoric of love that coddles the servant into a familial structure and is often considered betrayal.

In the case of stealing material goods such as tangible items, stealing is often forgiven as a petty issue to keep the love rhetoric intact. Stealing, in the case of long-time retainers, is almost an open secret as has been poeticized in a popular Bengali poem by Rabindranath Tagore, "Puraton Bhritto" or "The Old Retainer." The narrator affectionately reminisces how his wife always considers Keshta, their old servant, to be a thief whenever she loses anything. For the retainer, at least in the poem, theft was never on his mind, and he died serving his master. But on a deeper level, it can also be suggested that stealing from employers and the employers' accusations of theft is a kind of desire that provides both parties with the possibility to navigate the anxiety of knowledge of an unbridgeable class gap that comes with such proximity (Engebrigsten).

Stealing becomes more than an act, a way to challenge the "egalitarian version of the rhetoric of love" that employers such as my mother use to keep their relationships with the helps stable (Ray and Qayum 185). Even though my mother misses Minu, she was hardly a friend to her, given that she always chose to give certain clothes or advice to Minu, thinking for Minu and assuming she would need them. I am not trying to extract an ethical meaning out of stealing here, but I think Minu stole to wear clothes that were not given to her out of charitable pity. In friendship, gift-giving is a rigorous chore that demands an intimate knowledge of what the other desires, but in friending, the illusion of that knowledge with the constant awareness of "being friends" thrives the relationship. Friending also moves cautiously along the touch barriers, always disconcerted by the identity markers; while Minu had been stealing clothes, she was also confiding in my mother, knowing that my mother discussed her life with the others in the family (a metaphorical theft committed by my mother, if you will). She confided out of an obligation to give her employer material to build a base for friending. Stealing, for Minu, was a quiet act of disobedience.

II.

The fear of symbolic theft through gossip within the network of care-givers or chatting too much with one's employees reproduces class boundaries subtly. Identifying the caregiver as a close outsider through affective registers such as hesitation or unhappiness works in favour of keeping the structure of the family safe. The family is always identified as a safe space, a place that is essentially good and will provide happiness. Happiness registers here as an assurance of following the norms in a way that unhappiness registers itself as our inability to follow that ideal. Sara Ahmed explains this using the variable of queer amid family. The family is a set representing heteronormativity such that when a queer variable comes into play, it easily identifies the queer as an unhappy figure, someone who will not be happy and someone for whom the family will be sad. This happens when the family becomes the ideal whose norm the queer does not follow.

I suggest that the relationship between the mother and her caregiver begins with the normative codes but often devolves into arbitrary and secret codes of its own, whose norms fall far beyond that of the family. In such situations, things turn unhappy. The mother is blamed for her closeness with the caregiver to which she sometimes agrees after realizing how she overstepped the norm. Sometimes, the caregiver, in cognizance of her status as an unhappy object in the family, reiterates the patriarchal values to get back at the impossibility of the seeming friendship between the employer and herself, as if to call out the act.

Afraid of losing material from the family, mothers often try to compensate for the loss with an inflow of materials from the caregiver's life. This exercise has great value in friending because both parties feel indispensable to the other during the exchange without risking any individual loss, even though employers often feel they are risking a lot since maids often disclose secrets of one employer to another, a strategic move in friending with every employer.

After quitting her job, Chandana often visits my mother and talks about her life, the struggles she has to face, and so on. My mother helps her out when she can but if we consider these narratives from Chandana's life to be "figurations" to learn from, then mothers often use this in a very abstract way, almost to safeguard their children, from the true significance of the narratives of employees in particular, and the under-represented and marginalized in general (Haraway 47). Calling them figurations and treating them metaphorically like mothers do also hints at the colonizing discourse of Haraway herself who uses terms such as Trickster or Coyote to crack open various knowledge boundaries, instead of considering these terms on an essentialist plane (Todd 245-46). An example of this comes from my life: When I was a child and went to the park with Chandana, I introduced Chandana to an acquaintance as our kajer lok. Kaaj means work and lok is a person, so it should mean a person who works, but in India, kajer lok or kaamwali (kaam means work, waali is the suffix for a female worker) typically refers to a maid. Work becomes synonymous with reproductive labour as one does not need to define the kaj or kaam. I felt guilty and Chandana was hurt, my mother scolded me but she had no definitive answer except asking me to introduce her as my didi. I think my mother should have taught me better to accept her position instead of hiding it in a faux-familial tie. But would Chandana be okay with that? She was aware of the class difference and knew that maids in India are not respected because reproductive work is not respected. The labour goes unnoticed and is looked down upon.

Chandana loves gossip so much that my mother calls her the fluttering bird. Chandana is the name of a bird found in Bengal, and my mother relates her whimsical choices with the restless nature of the bird. In friending, nobody is servile, so Chandana throws a jibe at my mother, mocking her for her idiosyncrasies, and that puts my mother's family in a state of discomfit. Friending is significantly political and is very personal such that she has this relationship with my mother and not with my mother's family. When the family witnesses their relationship with the uncompromisingly indifferent nature, especially of the former employee, it unnerves them because Chandana is an "unhappy object" (Ahmed). She lacks servility and is independent in her choices in life. She dresses in clothes that do not mark her as lower class, and she is on Facebook—all these things render her visibly undifferentiated from the employer's class, and the family cannot deal with this. Class exists only when it can exhibit itself in difference. The family gets anxious to protect its class when the boundaries become permeable often blaming the mothers/employers for encouraging employees to simulate the former's behaviour. The anxiety of theft hence stems from the desire for the border. The desire to feel safe is a primal desire that tallies with following the norm of the family. Since friending is a customized variant of the rhetoric of love, it posits the help as an independent entity without familial ties to the employer, the family hesitates in the presence of such a relationship because it is already exempted from the relationship. Friending is a very personal relationship with the employer, that modifies the rhetoric of love from a familial emotion to a more independent, personal, and tactful space for registering intimacy.

Friending is also a protective measure when it comes to employees. Gossip counts for a political stance that aids the caregivers against abusive employers and families. Caregivers in India, almost always, suffer from a subordinate power position which makes them easy victims of domestic violence and sexual abuse (Alfano and Robinson). While NGOs and activists help domestic workers and there are associations for caregivers, it becomes very difficult to take legal steps especially when the employers are from the upper middle or upper classes. Gossiping provides the possibility to spread the narrative of the oppressed informally without the pressure to provide proof (which in most cases is difficult to provide) or abide by dominant institutions such as the court that always betray the marginalized communities in support of the norm (i.e., power). Gossip is a method of resistance and a "burdened virtue" in these circumstances as employees' narratives often garner support and bring out similar narratives from other victims while ostracizing the abuser (Tessman). One of the primary reasons that gossip is seen as a method of stealing is that employers fear their stories of abuse will get out. Since friending calls out the fake friendship between employers and caregivers, telling stories of past abuse to present employers often alerts the present employers by letting them know that employees will leak out the narrative again, should the abuse reiterate.

Friending is a speech act, that recognizes the rhetoric of love as an abusive and feudal tendency in employers and manages to undo it in various ways. Friending uses the ambivalent space between family and the help to harp on the class distance to achieve various goals. It is not a preventative tool against class distinction but it certainly reaches a more rich, personal, and complex emotional strata with the mother and the caregiver. Friending provides an alternative structure to the family by offering an independent and nuanced structure of dependence between the mother and the caregiver. It is not selfless or nonviolent, but it also does not promise the happiness that comes from the assurance of familial love. In that sense, friending offers a queer alternative to the

rhetoric of love as it destabilizes the dream of unconditional and recip-
rocated love between the family and the caregiver.

Afterthought

I began this essay as a personal piece, reflecting on a rather unequal but
deeply personal relationship my mother has had with her housekeepers
and maids over the past years. As a method, autoethnography has been
challenging as it forced me to be honest while critiquing my position in
the world. As a lens, it foils the distant and colonizing discourse in the
voice of an observer, but it also makes personal relationships with the
people involved, difficult. My relationship with my mother changed
significantly during the course of writing this essay, as I also lost a dog
that I adopted. I realized that my mother and I have also essentially been
friending for a long time, even though we call each other friends.
Friending allows us to remain intimately unavailable while doing everything with the other. It is not deceit; rather, it is a way of buttressing
a relationship of difference using mutual areas of interest. To be intimately unavailable means to resist an entrance to the fundamental
workings of one's being while also using a permeable space to filter in
things of each other's lives.

A fantastic example of this is in the recent film, *The Mirror* (2023) by
Konkona Sen Sharma. Played by actors Tilottama Shome (Ishita, an
upper-middle-class working woman, living alone in an apartment in
Mumbai) and Amruta Shubhash (Seema didi, Ishita's housekeeper), the
film uses the empty apartment to play with the relationship between
employers and their caregivers in neoliberal India. Ishita comes home
early one day from work to find her help making love to a man on her
bed. Ishita does not call her out on this; in fact, she gets turned on by the
voyeuristic pleasure she derives from watching them in a mirror, while
Seema who is also aware of her employer's quiet presence in the house,
gets turned on by the exhibitionism. Both women continue this until
Ishita disrupts their lovemaking by screaming at a house lizard and
confronts Seema and the man. When Ishita tries to blame Seema for
taking advantage of her, Seema says that she has not done anything
wrong, like stealing which is a common problem in such employee-employer relationships, neither is she answerable to Ishita who "can't do
any housework on her own, not even bring a man, and has to get pleasure

by looking at them." Seema says that at least she is sleeping with her husband. The film delves deeper into their relationship and whereabouts and even after this, Seema gets back the key and keeps working at Ishita's place.

What is interesting is that Seema and Ishita have two very important things in common: they keep on referring to each other by didi, and both have access to the house. The sansar is theirs and there is hardly any use of the love rhetoric except once where Ishita says she trusted Seema with the key, only to be answered back that she did not misuse it by stealing. Their relationship exists in an erotic economy where friending takes the form of a mutual understanding of desire so that they are relieved to have their employee-employer relationship back again. The rhetoric of love would never allow for such blasphemy because here, the barrier is not just broken but effaced. After all, the rhetoric exists for reproducing such barriers using elements like trust, guilt, and love. When Seema says she has not stolen anything, she refers to what Michel de Certeau calls "la perruque," where the worker uses the excuse of the employer's work to do her work. Seema had access to the house for cleaning and cooking, during which she also used it to make love to her husband (26). She took great care of the house (as she repetitively says) but she also made love on the same bed, using the employer's resources. This is also identified as symbolic theft by employers, such as my mother, who thinks that employees steal the sanctity of the employer's house—the right of the employer to have sexual relationships inside her home. My mother fired Tuni because she would bring her boyfriend when nobody would be at home. My mother felt cheated and evoked the love rhetoric by calling her ungrateful, but she was also afraid of a very literal theft (i.e., my safety), since I would come back early from school sometimes.

In the film, however, the two women separated by class, rest on an ambiguous plane as they get back to their home, separately, and manage it differently. It is also important to note that Ishita, for most of the film, becomes an outsider to her own house, entering quietly, hiding from her maid and her husband, touching herself in silence, and leaving just before the other is about to orgasm. Friending here expresses itself in a relationship of silence and builds on knowledge and respect for desire. The two women engage in slandering each other as neither truly understands why they did what they did, but they agree that they need each other. It is this acknowledgement of a symbiotic existence that I have tried to identify in the essay. When Seema says she has not done anything wrong because she slept with her husband and that it is Ishita who should be ashamed, Seema mimics and speaks on behalf of the patriarchal family for whom a home is a place for the heterosexual couple and not a single woman. The film, however, breaks this idea, as they make up and decide to come back to the apartment (Seema says: "I worked here thinking this is my home too") and offers a queer reading as the two women (both called didis or sisters) return to their home.

The film takes the concept of friending to an ideal as it neither resolves the problems of Ishita and Seema nor tries to simplify the abusive strains in Seema and perhaps, rightly so. Friending is after all a tactic of survival; it cannot resolve issues it cannot invest in because that would be impossible in such unequal relationships. Friending is different from other models of friendship because it is a constant negotiation in an ambivalent zone between two people. My mother's relationship with Chandana rests on an ambivalence given her desire to not interfere in Chandana's life by giving her advice as Chandana remains lackadaisical to my mother, like making fun of her idiosyncrasies. It is not insulting, but there is a limit that cordons them off from an uninterrupted friendship to a constant tussle of balancing, as they continue to need each other in various ways. Unlike in the film, the ambivalent zone protects my mother from Chandana's interference in her sansar, a space she strictly reserves for her family. Friending with Chandana helps my mother to maintain the relationship with her while keeping her separate away from the home. Friending in that sense is personal since Chandana now has a relationship with my mother and not our family, even though both would be uncomfortable to accept it as the love rhetoric is a foundational unit for such relationships. Insofar as the relationship between mothers and their caregivers goes, I think friending provides a sense of belonging to both parties in a noncommittal way by providing a mutable safeguard against the classist utopia of friendship in such situations. If according to Aristotle, true friendship is "disinterested" then it rules out that mothers and their employees can have friendships because such relationships are always goal oriented, a constant assurance of the future ("I'll come again from tomorrow," Seema says, or "Please call me if you don't come tomorrow," my mother says) besides being unequal (MacPhail 616).

Worrying about the future (who's going to take care of everything?) is a primary question that infests both the mother-caregiver relationship and their ghar-sansar.[3] It is difficult to imagine an Indian household that does not run on the efficiency of the mother and her domestic help. I do not mean that the mother owns the domestic help but rather a symbiotic space of work and belonging that is deeply personal between them. For the moment, the caregiver acts as if she is only close to nobody but her didi or boudi (sister-in-law). An example of this comes from my friend who said that she was very happy when their caregiver and their cook said that they only "listen" to their boudi. My friend felt it gave her mother a "sense of validation" for all the work her mother has done for the family. By using familial ties (like boudi) to refer to her employer, an employee does not forget the faux nature of the familial tie but uses it as a lubricant to navigate the touch barriers easily in the domestic space. In this chapter, I studied some relationships between my mother and her caregivers to look into an emerging pattern in the servitude culture of India. While friending runs parallelly to the love rhetoric both as a tactic and a less abusive alternative to the feudal relationship, the basic sentiments (obedience and dedication of the 'servant') that rest on the scaffold of servitude remain the same. Take for example a story shared by one of the websites for hiring domestic help. The website is called "Broomees," a direct reference to the popular middle-class imagination where the broom accompanies the domestic help for most of the day. The story reads: "Meet Shashi, a dedicated helper who truly embodies the spirit of hard work and determination. Despite experiencing a devastating loss when her mother passed away, Shashi did not let her grief hold her back. She started working the very next day, showing her unwavering commitment to serving others."

Even in 2023, such stories echo the feudal sentiments of Puraton Bhritto, albeit in a contorted manner. Shashi's desperation to turn up for the job the next day has been silenced and is portrayed as her willingness to serve like Keshta, who never speaks and dies serving his master even though he is called a thief for most of his life at his employer's. The rhetoric of love becomes starkly visible at such moments. My friend M (name withheld) said that her employee Pratima came to work at her apartment the day her brother died. Pratima did not tell this to her at first, but she looked sick and only said this after M asked her about her health. M was "shocked" and asked her to take the day off. The need felt by Pratima or Shashi to come to work despite personal crises reflects the contradictory nature of faux-familial ties. While the incomprehensible class gap threatens the employee (she fears that taking a day off without notice might cost her the job), she ignores her personal crises not only at the cost of her income (in friending, as I have mentioned earlier, there are many acts of disobedience) but also to betray the idea of the familial. By turning up, she challenges the love rhetoric that considers her as family, thereby using her presence as an anomaly in such a situation (i.e., in a real family), one mourns for the dead. M could not fathom why Pratima did not tell her about her brother's death before coming to work. It is at this moment of the employee's repression that I feel the "abuse-ready" nature of the servitude culture. That she could have "disappointed" M[4] was Pratima's first thought; to read them as acts of "commitment" is dangerous as it reinstates among other inequalities, class violence ("Humans of Broomes").

Disclosure of Conflict

Due permission was obtained from my subjects whenever their real name was used in this essay. To the best of my knowledge, I have no conflict of interest to disclose.

Endnotes

1. In Bengali, it is usually said, "Ami akta kaajer lok rekhechi" ("I have kept a housekeeper"). It is hardly ever said that one has employed a help or hired help. To keep something or someone in this case reflects the casual nature of violence embedded in the structure of the relationship. The help becomes an object, something that the employer simply keeps, without the liability that comes with employing.

2. My external examiner told this to me over Zoom during my Mphil viva voce in 2022. The dissertation was submitted successfully to Jadavpur University, Kolkata.

3. In several Indian languages, such as Hindi and Bengali, "ghar-sansar" is used interchangeably or together to refer to one's home which is the equivalent of one's world. Usually, this term is specifically used in the context of married women and their households.

4. I spoke to Pratima who said that M is one of the best people she knows. M said she could not believe Pratima did not tell her about such a personal loss and was "scarred."

Works Cited

Ahmed, Sara. "Happy Objects." The Affect Theory Reader, edited by Melissa Gregg and Gregory J. Seigworth, Duke University Press, 2010, pp. 29-51.

Ahmed Sara. The Cultural Politics of Emotion. Edinburgh: Edinburgh University Press, 2004.

Alfano, Mark, and Brian Robinson. "Gossip as a Burdened Virtue." Ethical Theory and Moral Practice, vol. 20, no. 3, 2017, pp. 473-87.

Aristotle. Nicomachean Ethics, edited by Roger Crisp, Cambridge University Press, 2004.

Behar, Ruth. The Vulnerable Observer: Anthropology That Breaks Your Heart. Beacon Press, 1996.

Broomes. https://broomees.com/. Accessed on 5 Nov. 2023.

Chattopadhyay, Swati. Unlearning the City: Infrastructure in a New Optical Field. University of Minnesota Press, 2012.

Dauphinee, Elizabeth. "The Ethics of Autoethnography." Review of International Studies, vol. 36, no. 3, 2010, pp. 799-818.

de Certeau, Michel. The Practice of Everyday Life. University of Berkeley Press, 1984.

Dickey, Sara. "Permeable Homes: Domestic Service, Household Space, and the Vulnerability of Class Boundaries in Urban India." American Ethnologist, vol. 27, no. 2, 2000, pp. 462-89.

Erdmans, Mary Patrice. "The Personal Is Political, but Is It Academic?" Journal of American Ethnic History, vol. 26, no. 4, 2007, pp. 7-23.

Gidwani, Vinay. Capital Interrupted: Agrarian Development and the Politics of Work in India. University of Minnesota Press, 2008.

Haraway, Donna. "Ecce Homo, Ain't (Ar'n't) I a Woman, and Inappropriate/cl Others: The Human in a Post-Humanist Landscape." The Haraway Reader, Routledge, 2004, pp. 47-62.

Harvey, David. The Limits to Capital. Verso, 2006.

"Hiring Housemaids in India: 11 Things You Should Know About." Servicesutra, 24. Nov. 2015, https://www.servicesutra.com/blog/hiring-housemaids-in-india-tips/. Accessed 10 Nov. 2023.

"Is Love Enough? – Sir." Directed by Rohena Gera, performances by Tillotama Shome and Vivek Gomber, Platoon One Films, 2020.

Lahiri, Tripti. *Maid in India: Stories of Inequality and Opportunity Inside Our Homes*. Aleph Book Company, 2017.

MacPhail, Eric. "Montaigne on Friendship." *The Oxford Handbook of Montaigne*, edited by Philippe Desan, Oxford University Press, 2016, pp. 615-28.

Ray, Raka, and Seemin Qayum. *Cultures of Servitude: Modernity, Domesticity and Class in India*. Stanford University Press, 2009.

Singer, Irvin. The Nature of Love: 1. Plato to Luther. University of Chicago Press, 1984.

Todd, Zoe. "Indigenizing the Anthropocene." Art in the Anthropocene, edited by Heather Davis and Etienne Turpin, Open Humanities Press, 2015, pp. 241-54.

Tami Spry. "Bodies of/as Evidence in Autoethnography." *International Review of Qualitative Research*, vol. 1, no. 4, 2009, pp. 603-10.

Tessman, Lisa. *Burdened Virtues: Virtue Ethics for Liberatory Struggles*. Oxford University Press, 2005.

"The Mirror". Lust Stories 2. Directed by Konkona Sen Sharma, performances by Amruta Subash and Tillotama Shome, RSVP Movies, and Flying Unicorn Entertainment, 2023.

Chapter 15

Temporary Sisterhoods: Thinking Ethics through Postnatal Care among South-Asian Muslims

Safwan Amir

Introduction

South Asian regional and diasporic communities approach maternity as a collective affair. Muslims, who make up a considerable population in South Asia, have their own grammars of birthing, mothering, and rearing children. This chapter demonstrates that maternity in South Asia is not only about the new mother and the baby but also involves various other actors, including the postnatal carer, the grandmother, neighbours, relatives and friends who partake in the larger processes in and around maternity. It specifically argues that in a largely caste-driven and patriarchal society, Muslim women of Malabar come together during and after childbirth to form informal networks of companionship and enter into practices of healing and caring that have a deep impact on their ethical outlook and wellbeing. While they are limited to particular time periods and occasions, such "temporary sisterhoods" allow for bonds between women that are open to possibilities other than those that modern liberal organizations and political associations aim for.[1] In these temporary sisterhoods, then, lie valuable lessons for both Islamic tradition and liberalism. The concept of sisterhoods—tried and tested in feminist circles and sparsely engaged with in mainstream Muslim set-tings— comprises most of the discussion in this ethnographic study. This chapter will first give an overview of the field and locate the concerns that it deals with. It will then move on to introduce the idea of temporary sisterhoods with the help of ethnographic vignettes and provide a brief comparison with other ideas of sisterhood, primarily those of liberal feminism. The chapter then locates the nonlinear shift from the midwife to the postnatal carer in modernity and reads "care" as not merely limited to a feeling of concern. The final section delves into possibilities that women participate in to further our perspective on Muslim feminine subjectivities and socialities in which the midwife/postnatal carer has played a significant role. The attempt made here is to initiate discussions on friendship and ethical possibilities that marginal spaces are capable of in minority traditions.

The discursive traditions around childbirth and postnatal care among Muslims of South Asia are always contextual and caught in interactions with other traditions, especially predominant South Asian ones of caste and modernity (which are themselves often overlapping as this chapter will suggest).[2] In male-dominated secular and religious spheres, it might be surprising to a few to imagine that Muslim women can offer insight into both Islamic and liberal traditions. This ethnographic study specif-ically focusses on the practices and relations between midwives/post-natal carers, birthing/new mothers, and various other actors who are involved in the socioreligious practices and everyday processes around maternity. These usually revolve around day-to-day activities that take place during birthing and the following forty days, or until the end of postpartum bleeding.

The Field

In this introductory section, I will briefly elaborate upon the regional context in which this study takes place as well as introduce one of the primary interlocutors: the midwife and postnatal carer. Malabar, a region located along the southwestern coast of the Indian subcontinent, is the site for this research and is home to some of the first Muslim settlements in South Asia. Caste orders this society in the contemporary, and people in the lower strata are stigmatized by their family occupa-tions. Barber families in South India usually include both midwives and hairdressers. Women perform barbering and midwifery roles. Men perform barbering and circumcision roles. The barber role is always attached to them regardless of the multiple roles they may come to perform or occupations they may take up. Muslim female midwife-barbers and male barber-circumcisers, Ossathi and Ossan respectively, have provided services to the Muslim communities of Malabar for centuries. This can be found to be the case in other Muslim regional settings as well (Sajdi; Giladi). Midwives have their regional locations and families that they tend to. In the past, these could be seen to replicate feudal patron-client relations and payment was in kind, often being rice grains or clothes. Oral origin narratives trace barber family lineages to the very first Muslim settlements in Malabar and status claims are made accordingly (Saidalavi; Amir). Such claims are also caught within discourses of caste and hierarchy, and occupation plays a central role in defining their contemporary social standing. Barber families among Muslims of Malabar occupy the lowest rungs in terms of caste (Saidalavi) and face contempt of varying degrees today (Amir). Many midwives and barber-circumcisers have moved away from their earlier occupational practices, yet stigma is attached to them especially in the case of marital preferences. Many midwives have taken up the role of postnatal carers over the past century with the larger privileging of modern medicinal practices. This has meant a steady decline in earlier practices of midwifery. Whereas midwives and postnatal carers are considered to be healthcare practitioners in most parts of the developed world, the case is different in South Asia. They still carry the baggage of their ascribed status, and South Asian barbers and midwives are seen through registers of caste as unclean, impure, and living at the peripheries of society. Currently, postnatal carers—eettukari or eettumma in the local dialect—include women from the lowest sections of the social order and are not only restricted to barber families (Marva).

Changes in an agrarian economy, in the previous century, also brought about some kind of geographical mobility, though not social mobility, among midwives and postnatal carers. They travel to places and stay at houses where services are required for periods ranging between seven and forty days. During this time, they stay away from their family in almost all present-day cases. They also take up work in the Middle East where more than 8.5 million Indian expatriates reside. Some midwives stay back illegally and hop from one birthing house to the next while others come in via temporary visas pretending to be family. Salaries range from INR 40,000 (USD 530 approximately) inside India to INR 100,000 (USD 1,330 approximately) outside the country, depending on prior agreements between the carer and those who hire her. These salaries are fixed for a period of forty days rather than a month. While there are no formal contracts, recruitment agencies also play a considerable role in the present on the basis of commissions. Travel expenses, visa fees, and accommodation are taken care of by the family that requires assistance. There are also maternity clinics in Malabar that range from luxurious speciality centres to small postnatal care services provided in buildings. While the former cater to affluent classes and functions for a week after a delivery, the latter are preferred for over a month by the lower-middle classes especially if they find arrangements at home difficult. These difficulties might arise from the unavailability of space in houses with extended joint families residing in them. In another instance, one respondent put it as a way to evade the stress of having to continuously serve guests who come to visit the child and new mother.

Academic discourses of caste in Islam have usually followed the models and methods of studies on caste in general (D'Souza; Ahmad; Nazir; Mondal). These have their origins in Hindu social and religious orders that are structuralist, functionalist, and ahistorical in their readings. The concepts of purity and pollution, occupational descent, and neat hierarchies continue to be central to sociological and historical readings of caste in Islam. Neither discipline (sociology or history) makes it a point to explore how such relations of contempt came about and takes it for granted that a singular narrative of caste-based hierarchy has existed throughout the history of Islam in South Asia. This is directly reflective of the kind of larger assimilation and diffusionist theories that are rife around Islam, within and outside India, that reproduce binaries around textual/lived and pristine/syncretic Islam (Geertz; Gellner; Ahmad; Robinson; cf. Das). Such an anthropology of Islam has further taken a divide. On the one hand are proponents of pious ethical cultivation (Mahmood; Hirschkind; Agrama), and on the other are exponents of an ordinary turn that focusses on ambiguities and transgressions in Islam (Marsden; Soares; Deeb; Schielke). Rather than follow one of these trends or find common ground, this research explores informal networks and unofficial practices. These are not highly visible instructive practices like religious education, audio-visual aids to cultivation of ethics or institutions like fatwa (legal ruling) councils or family courts. While these networks are some of the most ordinary settings, they are not spaces of transgression but an affirmation of the love, friendship, and sisterhood that oscillate between the material and the spiritual. However, to colour a singular picture is not the intent of this study. Although possibilities exist, we will see in subsequent sections that caste and modernity have drastically diminished such maternal worlds.

Temporary Sisterhoods

This section introduces "temporary sisterhoods" as an idea worth engaging. It uses ethnographic vignettes to enter into a discussion on the same.

Afreen, twenty-seven, is to deliver her first child in another month. Her mother has already made arrangements for a postnatal carer through mutual contacts. Fathima, the postnatal carer or eettukari, has been highly recommended by Afreen's relatives who had availed her services earlier. The role of the baby's grandmother is in a way designated as the one who establishes contact with the midwife or postnatal carer. She searches and researches for the best candidate. This is also not an outsourcing of work, since the general assumption can be that the grandmother is supposed to take care of every maternity-related need of the birthing daughter. Rather, the grandmother can be seen as a central authority who is ever-present in the background to almost all the practices and processes in the maternal world. If anything, she can be considered the figurehead for all decisions pertaining to these worlds and sisterhoods.

Anticipating the due date, the family goes to meet the gynaecologist a few days prior to the delivery. Fathima is in continuous contact with Afreen's mother and arrives at the hospital the very day the child is delivered. She immediately establishes her skill, knowledge, and authority by explaining and engaging in various processes that happen at the hospital. These include the child being observed for a few days due to swallowing of meconium during labour, introducing instant formula milk due to delayed milk production, and taking charge of holding and transporting the baby from the ward to the various doctors and medical check-up rooms. The family, especially Afreen's mother, is terrified by all the new terms and technicalities that the hospital presents and finds instant comfort in Fathima's enormous support. Relatives and friends pour into the hospital to meet the new mother and child. Coincidentally, Fathima's next client, a second cousin to Afreen, also visits, and they exchange pleasantries. While this might be an exceptional instance, most birthing mothers only meet their postnatal carer during or after delivery. Afreen, unlike her mother, is uncomfortable around Fathima during the first few days at the hospital, especially when it comes to using the restroom. Fathima, in contrast, understands people's privacy and gently prods her into ease and confidence.

Over the next forty days, the mother and the postnatal carer enter into various intimate associations. The new mother learns from the caregiver who shares some of the innermost secrets of womanhood. These happen during the night when the baby is up and crying. The new mother and the midwife/carer share the same room, and they discuss a variety of topics ranging from men, sex, and the features of the body. The carer instructs, coaxes, scolds, and cajoles the mother into doing her bidding, especially since these are times when the mother is most vulnerable and utmost care is necessary. The new mother's own mother is often unable to perform most of these tasks due to excessive empathy. This is best seen in cases that require the mother to consume local medicines that often leave a bad taste in the mouth. The grandmother, out of pity, will not press her daughter to consume them, but the postnatal carer will use all techniques at her disposal to ensure that the mother has taken all her medication. Helping the mother regain her health in the face of postpartum stress, swabbing, feeding, massaging, bathing, dressing, binding the belly, and grooming are all taken care of by the eettukari. Usually referred to as ittha, or sister, the carer is called on every now and then by the new mother for the rest of the forty days.

Time periods do vary according to client requirements and relationships between mother and carer. For instance, Noora, a thirty-two-year-old Beary-speaking woman from Mangalore, discontinued her carer's services because she could not put up with her "continuous prattle." In another case, Nadiya, twenty-six, from North Malabar was forced to drop her carer due to the fear of COVID-19 and since the latter was not willing to stay overnight. These changes have begun to affect the manner in which the postnatal carer leaves the house. Generally, on the fortieth day, the new mother receives her final bath, and this is followed by a gathering known as nalpathkuli or napoli with close relatives and friends attending. This time period has now shortened to twenty-eight days or even as brief as a week. The eettukari is laden with gifts, and in almost all instances, she leaves never to be seen again.[3]

Sisterhoods is an apt description only when all actors involved in the maternity world are taken into consideration. Relatives, neighbours, and friends are essential components to the concept of sisterhood. They participate in all important events before, during, and after birthing. This starts right from the time of "good news" or after three months, since conception when it is acceptable in these regions to publicize that a woman is pregnant. The seventh month of pregnancy is also a crucial time, and the expecting woman's health is monitored by her relatives, in-laws, friends, and neighbours constantly. They make their presence felt in various ways. These can be around arranging the midwife/carer, to key information regarding hospitals, gynaecologist preferences, to helping with household chores. Food, additionally, serves as an important ingredient in these networks and the sisters predecide responsibilities as to who brings in what and when. All of this is to support the pregnant woman and her mother during these hectic and vulnerable times. Giving is not always based on usual ideas of gift reciprocity where there are prior expectations or anticipated case scenarios, where the one giving thinks of a future where she might need similar help. Rather, these are also networks of giving that build on the notion of "Giving to God," which is about material detachment from this world, gaining closeness to God, finding rewards in an afterlife, but basing it on the here and now (Mittermaier).

Ittha does not merely point to simplistic fictive kinships but can be found to resonate with larger ideas around sisterhood that feminists have long engaged with. While recognizing issues of patriarchy and male dominance, critiques have maintained that the concept of sisterhood includes racial and regional biases (Hooks) and involves tensions between collective interests and individualistic strategies of members even when a strong language of sisterhood is employed (Handler), which have forced feminists to think of alternatives in concepts, such as companion or friend (Lugones). This is best summarized in the following statement:

When sisterhood is analysed as a product of the larger socio-economic structure, then its use for class-specific purposes that divide women against each other is no surprise... No two women are likely to be "sisters," then, if their material needs, lineage connections, and economic resources diverge significantly. Cross-class sisterhood is almost a contradiction. (Hewitt 25).

Class is not the only analytical lens through which sisterhoods go through such rigorous scrutiny and dismal rejection. More particularly, female activists and scholars of Islam, as well as Muslim women who identify as Muslim feminists, have been at loggerheads with Western feminists for decades and have come to some partial semblance of respectful difference only in the recent past (Shannon). Women across platforms and traditions not only find it difficult to come to common grounds but even those within similar settings find such paths constrained. In the South Asian context, a parallel can be found in anticaste movements, where people espousing similar political ideologies are unable to come, or even imagine, any kind of solidarities—be they feminine or masculine. Rather than taking disunity as the norm, perhaps we need to ponder the very essence of modernity and modern political organizations that disallow any kind of long-term solidarity. However, that is beyond the scope of this chapter, and we can only touch upon it cursorily.

Such conversations, engagements, conflicts, approvals, and disapprovals do not mean that spaces for solidarity themselves are completely absent. They do point to the temporal nature of such attempts, and "temporary sisterhoods" encompass this relationship as symbolized in the ethnographic narratives of the new mother and the midwife/postnatal carer. Here, the premise is built on the intimately personal and not limiting the focus to an abstract political. The two are interconnected, as bell hooks suggests, and it is imperative to begin with immediate spaces where people belong in their own "longing and dreams" (Hooks 825). Rather than locating maternal worlds out of the realm of power, such a parallel with ongoing divisions among feminists directly brings to the forefront realities with which women grapple without negating it under the guise of privacy. These predicaments also speak of larger modernizing projects that are underway, the nuances they present, and the intricate reach they have into almost every aspect of life. If so, does one completely do away with sisterhood, and in this course give up on forms of care, love, and affection? What kinds of methodologies, ontologies, and epistemologies are available which might give direction to, if not permanent, temporary possibilities? Temporary sisterhoods is an acknowledgement that Muslim women, who enter into informal networks over the course of maternity, also adopt neoliberal logics, and hence these sisterhoods are also temporary like the rest. However, there are other possibilities—minor that they may seem—in Islam. Practices of care that the women in this research enter into are deeply embedded in an Islamic tradition, which allows for a transformation of the self that modernity is incapable of. *Temporary sisterhoods,* through the Muslim women of Malabar, is then an affirmation of the possible solidarities that exist and help illuminate a realm of ethics that often goes amiss in liberal and mainstream Islamic traditions. Before entering into such possibilities, it is important to locate how midwives, our key interlocutors, have fared through modernity.

Midwives and Modernities

The assumption is that midwives transformed into postnatal caregivers overnight with the coming of modernity. However, the shift from an ossathi to an eettukari is not always linear. Although ruptures do take place, preferences for home-based birthing, as opposed to hospitals, have not completely declined in either the East or the West. This shows that modernity cannot be addressed as a singular unit, and its complexities always need to be considered. Modernity does not represent a binary between two geopolitical regions, and the multiple responses to it are more complicated than can be fathomed. In the context of Malabar, there are instances where women have had terrible experiences at hospitals in their initial deliveries and then went on to opt for birthing services at home. Ruptures from an earlier era, nevertheless, can best be noticed in seemingly trivial affairs like dietary patterns. Farah, an upper-middle-class Malayali expatriate of twenty-six living in Doha, is in her fifteenth week and is freshly learning about matters related to pregnancy and care. Her close friends who have recently gone through similar experiences are her primary sources while the internet provides detailed information. One of them tells her that roles related to diet that postnatal carers perform—planning, cooking, feeding—can be avoided. The rationale given to supplement her argument was that the food prepared by the carer will be filled with carbohydrates and does not make for healthy food options. Health, in such instances, is often caught up in images related to beauty and appearance, on the one hand, and to specific nutritious diets, on the other. Thus, while the eettukari tries to ensure that the mother regains her health immediately, in the carer's way, and that proper nutrients are transferred to the child, various other concerns influence the mother. The mother with her advanced access to information and the market has a wide range of delicious options in front of her and expects the best for her child and herself. While post-natal carers also work on the body of the mother, the process of reducing weight is gradual and takes secondary status. Hence, they end up rush-ing with an influx of carbohydrates and non-daily food—varying from starch water to specially prepared herbal medicine—which is considered unhealthy and unpalatable in contemporary situations. Farah's instance should not be read as a textbook example but as one that provides an opening into divergent knowledge practices regarding care and the socialities that emerge from them.

To understand care in the postnatal caregiver, it is pertinent to ex-pand this enquiry to midwives because they are the sources from which many of the eettukari's practices emerge or are on the wane. Further-more, it is necessary to consider all three—midwife, mother, and birthing practice—into analysis rather than limiting to either one of them as most studies around maternities have often prescribed. Throughout fieldwork for this research, people spoke of natural child-birth or sughaprasavam (literally "comfortable birth") as the preferred kind of parturition. Midwives and barbers, additionally, connected reciting Qur'an, blowing du'a (supplication), chanting dhikr (repeated chanting in remembrance of God), repeating salawat (praises on the Prophet Muhammad), and singing the Nafeesath mala (panegyric praising Syeda Nafisa, an important descendant of the Prophet Muham-mad) as aiding in this process. Such genres as the mala are not mere literary texts but practices—performed, as opposed to privately con-sumed—that help cultivate ethical selves in the context of Malabar (Muneer). Additionally, pinjanamezhutu (writing in ceramic) and ezhuteel kudikkal (drinking the written) are administered to the preg-nant woman (Arafath). Pregnancies overseen by midwives are different to hospitals, where the family stays anxiously apart. Female relatives and neighbours of the birthing mother are part of the larger midwife's entourage. Few, like the mother and sister, have direct access to the birthing mother, but they all remain around the room where the birth-ing takes place. The midwife leads, quite similar to an usthad (religious instructor), the chanting and singing. It is perhaps for this very reason that the anthropologist Dennis McGilvray observes that the Sri Lankan Muslim barber, Osta, derives their name from usthad and kinship terms are added to the barber-midwife, Oytta Mami, out of affection (McGilvray).

The atmosphere is tense around the room where the birthing is about to happen. The midwife carefully assesses the woman's body in labour to discern the fetus's position. She uses her fingers to check the cervix for dilation. She begins with some of her regular Qur'anic verses and supplications. These are said aloud and are audible to the women around and outside the room. She sings the Nafeesath mala, and this is picked up by all. The tempo rises gradually with the chanting and singing following a rhythmic pattern. The focus is less on the actual words of the Nafeesath mala and more on the bodily movements, swaying, gestures, and intonations. Some deliveries take a lot of time and these rhythms have a therapeutic effect on the mother as well. Gregor Dobler, in his analysis of women's work, shows how rhythmization "frees those parts of our attention" from those that "are not needed" while reacting to complex and tiring work situations; and "the better the tools are adapted to the specific material on which they act, the freer we are usually to choose our own rhythm" (Dobler pp. 16-18). Getting things in a rhythm helps one forget the pain and allows the women—birthing and tending—to focus on other aspects apart from the pain. Nafeesath mala is much better understood as a tool in this situation: a tool that is not in aid of the midwife alone. The midwife interacts with the birthing mother as well as with multiple carers (now an idea that is not limited to physical care) outside the room. Healing and caring are not singular procedures that involve the birthing mother and midwife alone, but revolves around the entire assemblage of women gathered around. Here, "care" as a moral idea is "not merely in the sense of concern but in the sense of actual connection and sharing" (Roberts 246).

In an important study on midwives in South India, Kalpana Ram shows how the midwife is often romanticised in anthropological literature as a source of Indigenous knowledge or in opposition to western knowledge. She examines such binaries and says that the midwife presents a unique predicament given that even so-called Indigenous traditions (Indic in this instance) end up further devaluing such knowledge practices while others limit it to the realm of common sense (112-

14). She goes on to ask:

> When an ethnographer finds that the midwife in South Asia has
> been devalued by the values of purity, she concludes that
> knowledge and care of the birthing woman is limited. How might
> it alter the picture of birth in South Asia if we view knowledge,
> not as the province of specialised texts or of specialist midwife
> practitioners, but as widely *diffused embodied practices*, sustained
> by *shared assumptions* that have not entirely been placed into
> *language*? (my emphasis, 119).

Without falling into the traps of idealizing or restricting the midwife to
the common-sensical, the midwife-initiated birthing instance above
demonstrates how Muslim women participate in sisterly socialities
where "diffused embodied practices" are "sustained by shared assumptions" even when they "have not entirely been placed into language."
Medicine administered through the use of writing in water (ezhuteel
kudikkal) literally represents this activity. While a few have an inkling
to what has been written by the midwife, language itself as writing
dissolves into the water only to be consumed by the pregnant mother.
It is precisely in these practices and interrelated socialities that one can
recognise the depth of such informal networks and shared knowledge.
Practices around sughaprasavam and Nafeesath mala are ethically sustained by shared ideas of care that Muslim women—related/ unrelated
and stranger/intimate—enter into. These are yet to be read through
grammars of Islamic tradition that are caught in masculine brotherhood
archetypes, neotraditional idealism, and reformist epistemic preclusions.
To enter into ways of knowing among women and maternal worlds, Ram
asks for new methodologies that do not fall into conventional methods
of social sciences that are filled with assumptions of what constitutes
knowledge (114, 117-120).

It is not coincidental that ethnographies of the midwife, and worlds
around her, have almost always had to tackle the question of modernity
(see for instance Ram and Jolly; Van Hollen; Ghoshal). These discourses
around the midwife come up in a plethora of ways: the midwife as representing her tradition as opposed to Indigenous or Western modernity;
her practice as fast ending and allowing rare glimpses into earlier lifeworlds; and the knowledgeable midwife's decline in an era of progress.
The attempt is not to critique these important anthropological and

sociological studies, but to find in them a common denominator. These works are based on their present and often fumble about with the past. The "are" and "were" are so closely caught up that it is difficult even for the authors to untangle them, often interchanging one for the other or placing them adjacent to each other. The "past" then needs not be seen as distant and can rather be considered as co-existing with the present in the case of Muslim maternal worlds and sisterhoods. These pasts do not mean going back to a "regressive" bygone era and rather looks out for those epistemologies and ontologies that can help attain a better ethical self. What would be the possibility of a methodology that embraces the past with such an attitude? Viewing this as a methodology is not to negate the effects of modernity or to suggest that these are spaces where modernity has no influence, but to rather accept that modernity has had its run, and it is now time to heal.

"Forty" Possibilities

The final section of this chapter deals with the kind of possibilities that Muslim women delve into through temporary sisterhoods. An average period for lochia or postpartum bleeding is between twenty-four and thirty-six days. Quick connections to the specific number of forty, as the day for parting between the midwife and new mother, can be associated with this. Nifas kuli, cleansing and bathing post bleeding, is a practice prescribed for new mothers in the Islamic tradition. The midwife bathes and assists the mother, a final time, and adorns her with scented perfume (attar). However, to read these forty days or the fortieth parting day as a simple stagnant ritual is to restrict the kind of sociality and sisterhood seen in earlier sections. First and foremost, the fortieth day (Napoli/nalpath kuli) is also a celebration with friends and family. The midwife's entourage in the initial days of birthing are priority invitees. In a way, the fortieth is then a celebration of the coming together of these women as sisters at a period when the mother and child are no longer vulnerable. During these forty days, they inquire about the health of the mother and child with the matriarch of the house through phone calls, WhatsApp voice notes, and brief visits. They will also discuss the midwife and her eccentricities in muffled voices. The midwife/postnatal carer might also receive her next assignment and client during these days. These sisterhoods are then dependent on the midwife/postnatal carer because even while concerns are around the new mother and child, they are mediated or referred to via queries around the midwife. To ask of the midwife is then to enquire about the wellbeing of the baby and mother. These sisterhoods are, nonetheless, temporarily given that they come to an end on the fortieth day.

Yet the number forty itself goes on to play a huge temporal role in the lives of Muslims in this temporary world.[4]

The ordinal and cardinal numbers, fortieth and forty respectively, are of great importance in the Islamic tradition. This numbers appear in various life narratives of prophets and saints as well as in multiple pre-scriptions and bodily activities. Right from the first prophet, Adam, to the last, forty years or forty days can be seen to recur as a time for penance or a period for cleansing. On the fortieth (year or day), the prophet or saint transforms, which can be seen in the stories of Adam, Noah, Jonah, Moses, and Muhammad in a conspicuous manner—be it spending forty years repenting after the original sin, forty days of the flood, forty days inside the belly of a fish, forty days of fasting before meeting God, and the fortieth year in which divine revelation was re-ceived, respectively. The prevalence of this number can also be seen in the retreat practice of chilla (from the Persian word chehel, or forty) that is practiced by Tablighi Jamat and Sufis, where forty days are spent in meditation and supererogatory prayers and practices. Here, too, the process is understood as going through a cleansing phase and then transforming oneself. But these can all be classified as extraordinary situations and examples. To come back to the ordinary, everyday (or every-forty-days) practices that Muslims take up also include cutting nails and shaving pubic hair before every other fortieth day. This con-tinuous activity, done over a period of forty days throughout their adult lives, is then instructive for this study.

Marcel Mauss, in his influential study on body techniques, notes that habitus are those aspects of the tradition that are effective, learned, and acquired by the body through transmission, which are essentially oral, imitative, and repetitive actions (Mauss). These serve in the process of cultivating the self and bringing about certain dispositions that help adherents of traditions orient themselves in particular ways. The act of cleansing oneself (tatheer) is mostly connected with repentance (tawba).[5] Yet the very act of converting it into everyday practices, like cutting nails and shaving pubic hair, tells us much more. To continuously discipline the body (and here disciplining is directly on the very form and shape it takes) through simple habitual steps allows for maintaining balance as well as transformation. Rather than changing the course of oneself, balance itself becomes a necessary stage that needs to be attained. The forty-day cycle then allows for the body (through hair and nails) to grow only then to be cut and groomed before every fortieth day. Grooming helps in consistency, and acts such as these are read as part of being Muslim. They are not secular activities, and here the Muslim actively, and habitually, orients their life by following the practices and habits of saints and prophets. We will see that the midwife then facilitates such emulation of revered and ordinary practices through temporary sisterhoods.

Emulation is an important concept that works here. Muslims do not learn most of these practices from madrasas (religious institutions) or usthads (religious instructors). Rather, they hear, imitate, see, and are visibly part of a larger order of things that do not necessarily need formal instructions all the time. Suhba, or companionship, plays a major role in this. For habitus to work in these settings, companionships of various kinds operate throughout. Siblings, cousins, neighbours, friends, and other members of the peer group help in navigating and learning these practices from a small age. But how do these companionships take place? What kind of habitus, bodily cultivation, and soulful techniques help in the making of affiliations themselves? Focus in the anthropology of Islam has been on the cultivation of ethical selves, to date, and these have fixated around the individual alone. What about relationships and the very fact that practices themselves are seldom individualistic? The socialities that such practices bring about are hardly recognized as playing their part in these situations. Emulating the Prophet Muhammad is seen as the best way to go about one's life as a Muslim. These behaviours were then emulated by his companions and the various notable saints that followed. Embodying such practices of emulation are enacted in pir-mureed (teacher-student), parent-child, and friend-friend relationships. They are also followed in congregations and are not only limited to a two-person activity. It is pertinent to further divide the concept of habitus for analytical purposes. A habitus of emulation, then, is one where the Muslim engages in networks of other Muslims, learning from them through imitation and instruction, fostering relations of care that are not limited to concern, actively participating in each other's daily lives, inspiring and chiding as the situation demands, and ensuring practices are followed by setting examples rather than injunctions. A habitus of emulation is also a habitus of cultivating relationships that move beyond the singular self and the base self.[6]

The central characteristic of the midwife, which has declined and been downplayed over the century, needs to be read along the lines of such complex relationships that the Islamic tradition fosters. If so, the kinship terms for the midwife that McGilvray connects with instruction and religious instructor (usthad), as mentioned earlier, revolves around instructing through various mediums that we might not recognize immediately as didactic. She helps in the transformation of the sister's self (mother and others involved), quite similar to Foucault's "technologies of the self." Here "*the help of others*" (emphasis added) is availed to orient one's "own bodies and souls, thoughts, conduct, and way of being" to attain particular states of living (Foucault 18). The postnatal carer carries remnants of these embodying traditions now and then. In leading the du'a (prayers) and dhikr (chanting), she brings the sisters together, and birthing is then only an occasion to make such coming together possible. The male usthad (religious instructor) can never teach Islamic practices related to birthing or maternity, and in all possibilities does not have any knowledge regarding the same. It is in the postnatal carer's practices and temporary sisterhoods that Muslim women form, that one can recognise and better appreciate the diverse ways in which the tradition is translated into the everyday.

The maternal world being studied in this chapter has hardly ever been analysed via the Islamic tradition. For various reasons, including neglect and ignorance of women's practices, such relations of sisterhoods and their intricacies do not fit into the grand narratives of formal, organization-based contemporary Islamic settings. The Napoli celebration needs to be read as a celebration of sisterhood, relations of care, friendships, and an affirmation to stand for each other when the time comes—in another pregnancy or birthing instance among these very women or in any of the umpteen crises and joyful situations that can come up anytime. The midwife and the matriarch also form a strong bond, and they learn to respect each other's viewpoints and differences. This relationship stays stronger than the one fostered with the new mother because it is the matriarch who later recommends the midwife/postnatal carer. The cleansing of the nifas and the forty days, when read through multiple meanings of cleanliness, points to interpretations of such female practices as directly intertwined in the Islamic tradition. It is a way of cultivating ethical selves for all involved—the midwife, new mother, matriarch of the house, and the women who assemble. There are two habitus working simultaneously in such settings: those that focus on the body and those that work on relationships. These relationships and continuous working on the self-help navigate new terrains as they come up, and the shift of the midwife to postnatal carer can be interpreted in this way. Here, women are not only adapting to the pace of modernity but restructuring their networks. The temporariness allows them to restructure these according to the context. However, acts of caring and practices of healing are continued, and in this, Muslim women put forward an idea of support that does not necessarily come under the purview of radical politics, which is about drastic change. While temporary sisterhoods among Muslims might seem to end then and there, the potential for having long-term consequences continue. It is picked up again through the schedule of the midwife/ carer every now and then, and we find with every new birth and birthing mother, temporary sisterhoods arise across geographies over time. Women networks are maintained, created, and expanded through such informal settings in multiple ways, and at the core of it, an Islamic ethics of care helps nurture sisterhoods. And through this, they also forward different ideas of support that are welcoming of life and being.

While caste dynamics and politics in South Asia have been about a growing right-wing force, such enduring networks that are intrinsically embodied point to other forms of associations and ways of being. They hold the potential to challenge preconceived notions of caste and hope for a better future. While relationships are skewed and power flows unevenly, such a coming together of sisterhoods stands in contrast to the kinds of relationships that caste otherwise pervasively ensures. While untouchability has never been an issue among Muslims, the temporary sisterhoods that we have seen also create promises of companionships. Even when these sisterhoods are temporary, the kinds of transformations that they allow within its members help them to rethink and remake their relationships with one another. The midwife/carer is not a client or servant, and the mother's patronage is complicated throughout. As a friend, instructor, sister, and carer, the midwife gains authority in temporary sisterhoods. While this cannot be considered a reversal of power equations, it is, nevertheless, demonstrative of an embodied ethics that the Islamic tradition, though faint, allows for.

Conclusion

During my last phase of fieldwork, I was fortunate to interact with my neighbour and learn a great deal from her. In her late sixties, she would hardly move outside her home. Yet women kept meeting her every other day. She shared a couple of photocopies with me, and they were filled with specific du'a and dhikr, some of which I had never come across in any of my interactions with male religious scholars. On further inquiring the source of such material and literature, she gradually told me how a female scholar, almost four towns apart, helped her with it. They had never met, but several women acting as messengers between them would help pass requests, blessings, and other kinds of information. None of these women had any association with Muslim organizations or sects in Malabar. They did not even have a name for their collective, nor did they necessarily recognise themselves as one. They participated in one another's life events, knew of their hardships, helped each other ease them through financial, emotional, and spiritual support and learned from one another under the aegis of the female scholar. Such networks of women help in the larger collective and individual betterment of its members. Informality helps sustain these networks expand and restrict them in various ways. There is very little that we know of these networks except for their existence. The midwife and maternal worlds that this chapter has focussed on are networks that are often ignored in studies that take up either liberal or Islamic traditions as their point of analysis. Temporary Muslim sisterhoods in the maternal world and similar networks while different from the ones that liberal feminists espouse and/ or decry can yet be useful examples to think of epistemic breaks that are necessary for the given era.

Throughout this study, midwife and maternal worlds have been entered into to think through epistemological and methodological ways of dealing with gender, Islam, caste, and modernity. This cannot be seen as a conclusive project but one that attempts to open questions and suggest directions. The past is not an end in itself. It stands as an embodiment beyond mere symbolic representations. Here, the Muslim actively engages with the past not in stagnant or romantic ways but through contextualizing and adapting to the situation. Bodies and on-tologies are not merely the recluse of the individual self but have to be read as actively formed through interactions with others. Such interactions are networks of care that are ontological bonds themselves. In a way, through the core principles of emulation, multiple meanings of cleansing and networks of care, such ontologies are themselves the very epistemologies through which women partake in the Islamic tradition. The possibilities that these ethical networks, and interconnected practices, allow for in the transformation of the self, time and again, in a world that is continuously changing has been the mainstay in this chapter. This requires assessing ethical landscapes that might not be immediately present. It is through such vestiges that caste and modernity can be challenged if such endeavours were to strike at their innermost core.

Endnotes

1. Rather than take up tradition in opposition to modernity, the attempt is to look at how ordinary members of a tradition navigate modernity. This does not mean that people can be categorised into boxes with either labels. In the contemporary moment, women are often at the margins of both modernity and tradition. While modernity is all encompassing, and tradition struggles, alternatives can be found in the margins.

2. Following Alasdair MacIntyre's idea of a tradition, it is not caught in the past or a binary opposite of modernity. Rather, multiple traditions exist in varying power relations. These can include liberalism, Marxism, religious traditions like Christianity or Islam, etc. Tradition in this fashion implies "a historically extended, socially embodied argument" that identifies a past as influencing the present and future (MacIntyre 222).

3. The carer reappears in subsequent births or when she needs money. The focus here is to suggest how a thriving sisterhood comes to an abrupt end.

4. In the Islamic tradition, life in this world is temporary, and it is in the afterlife that there is permanence. However, this does not deter them from living their lives in this world to its full, since it is based on their actions here that the after is contingent on.

5. This can be seen through the multiple uses of imageries, in the Qur'an and Hadith, of sinning where the heart is seen to accumulate blemishes or read as a diseased body. Repentance is then always accompanied by cleanliness (tahir) and cleansing (tatheer). These also represent inward (batin) and outward (zahir) states that needs to be seen together. Further, repentance in Islam is different from the Christian (obsessing around repentance) and Hindu (inheriting sins from ancestors) sense of the term. Focus is on bettering the self so as to transform and attain a degree of not returning to deplorable actions and habits.

6. The self in Islamic psychology is divided into three: nafs al ammarah (base self, inclined to wrongdoing), nafs al lawwama (doubting self), and nafs al mutmainnah (tranquil self) (Rothman and Coyle).

Works Cited

Agrama, Hussein Ali. *Questioning Secularism: Islam, Sovereignty, and the Rule of Law in Modern Egypt.* University of Chicago Press, 2012.

Ahmad, Imtiaz, editor. *Caste and Social Stratification among Muslims in India.* Aakar Books, 1978.

Ahmad, Imtiaz. "The Islamic Tradition in India." *Islam and the Modern Age*, vol. 12, no. 1, 1981, pp. 44-62.

Amir, Safwan. "Contempt and Labour: An Exploration through Muslim Barbers of South Asia." *Dalits and Religion: Ambiguity, Tension, Diversity and Vitality*, special issue of *Religions*, vol. 10, no. 11, 2019, p. 616.

Amir, Safwan. *The Muslim Barbers of Malabar: Histories of Contempt and Ethics of Possibility.* 2021, University of Madras, PhD dissertation.

Arafath, Yasser. "Saints, Serpents, and Terrifying Goddesses: Fertility Culture on the Malabar Coast (c. 1500–1800)." *Histories of Medicine in the Indian Ocean World*, edited by Anna Elizebeth Winterbottom and Facil Tesfaye, Palgrave, 2015, pp. 99-124.

D'Souza, Victor S. "Social Organization and Marriage Customs of the Moplahs on the South-West Coast of India." *Anthropos*, vol. 54, no. 3/4, 1959, pp. 487-516.

Das, Veena. "For a Folk-Theology and Theological Anthropology of Islam." *Contributions to Indian Sociology*, vol. 18, no. 2, Nov. 1984, pp. 293-300.

Deeb, Lara. *An Enchanted Modern: Gender and Public Piety in Shi'i Lebanon.* Princeton University Press, 2006.

Foucault, Michel. "Technologies of the Self." *Technologies of the Self: A Seminar with Michel Foucault,* by Huck Gutman et al., University of Massachusetts Press, 1988, pp. 16-49.

Geertz, Clifford. *The Interpretation of Cultures.* Basic Books, 1973.

Gellner, Ernest. *Muslim Society.* Cambridge University Press, 1981.

Ghoshal, Rakhi. "Death of a Dai: Development-Modernity's 'Success' Story." *Economic and Political Weekly,* vol. 49, no. 42, 2014, pp. 27-29.

Giladi, Avner. *Muslim Midwives: The Craft of Birthing in the Premodern Middle East.* Cambridge University Press, 2015.

Hirschkind, Charles. *The Ethical Soundscape: Cassette Sermons and Islamic Counterpublics.* Columbia University Press, 2006.

Van Hollen, Cecilia Coale. *Birth on the Threshold: Childbirth and Modernity in South India.* Cambridge University Press, 2003.

MacIntyre, Alasdair. *After Virtue: A Study in Moral Theory.* University of Notre Dame Press, 1984.

Mahmood, Saba. *Politics of Piety: The Islamic Revival and the Feminist Subject.* Princeton University Press, 2005.

Marsden, Magnus. *Living Islam: Muslim Religious Experience in Pakistan's North-west Frontier.* Cambridge University Press, 2005.

Marva, M. "Traditional Maternity Carers of Malabar: Caste, Religion and Knowledge." *Ala 4,* 2018, http://ala.keralascholars.org/issues/4/maternity-carers-of-malabar

Mauss, Marcel. "Techniques of the body." *Economy and Society,* vol. 2, no. 1, 2006, pp. 70-88.

McGilvray, Dennis B. *Crucible of Conflict: Tamil and Muslim Society on the East Coast of Sri Lanka.* Duke University Press, 2008.

Mittermaier, Amira. *Giving to God: Islamic Charity in Revolutionary Times.* University of California Press, 2019.

Mondal, Seik Rahim. "Social Structure, OBCs and Muslims." *Economic and Political Weekly,* vol. 38, no. 46, 2003, pp. 15-21.

Muneer, Aram Kuzhiyan. "Poetics of Piety: Genre, Self-Fashioning, and the Mappila Lifescape." *Journal of the Royal Asiatic Society,* vol.

26, no. 3, 2016, pp. 423-41.

Nazir, Pervaiz. "Social Structure, Ideology and Language: Caste among Muslims." *Economic and Political Weekly*, vol. 28, no. 52, 1993, pp. 2897-2900.

Ram, Kalpana. "Rural Midwives in South India: The Politics of Bodily Knowledge." *Childbirth Across Cultures: Ideas and Practices of Pregnancy, Childbirth and the Postpartum*, edited by Helaine Selen and Pamela Stone. Springer, 2009, pp. 107-22.

Ram, Kalpana, and Margaret Jolly, editors. *Maternities and Modernities: Colonial and Postcolonial Experiences in Asia and the Pacific*. Cambridge University Press, 1998.

Robinson, Francis. "Islam and Muslim Society." *Contributions to Indian Sociology*, vol. 17, no. 2, 1983, pp. 185-203.

Rothman, Abdallah, and Adrian Coyle. "Toward a Framework for Islamic Psychology and Psychotherapy: An Islamic Model of the Soul." *Journal of Religion and Health*, vol. 57, 2018, pp. 1731-44.

Saidalavi., P.C. "Muslim Social Organisation and Cultural Islamisation in Malabar." *South Asia Research*, vol. 37, no. 1, 2017, pp. 19-36.

Saidalavi, P.C. "Status Claims among Muslims in Malabar, South India." *Anthropological Notebooks*, vol. 23, no. 2, 2017, pp. 103-05.

Sajdi, Dana. *The Barber of Damascus: Nouveau Literacy in the Eighteenth-Century Ottoman Levant*. Stanford University Press, 2013.

Schielke, Samuli. *The Perils of Joy: Contesting Mulid Festivals in Contemporary Egypt*. Syracuse University Press, 2012.

Soares, Benjamin F. *Islam and the Prayer Economy: History and Authority in a Malian Town*. Edinburgh University Press, 2005.

Notes on Contributors

Editors

Andrea O'Reilly, PhD, is a full professor in the School of Gender, Sexuality and Women's Studies at York University, founder/editor-in-chief of the *Journal of the Motherhood Initiative* and publisher of Demeter Press. She is coeditor/editor of thirty plus books including *Feminist Parenting: Perspectives from Africa and Beyond* (2020), *Mothers, Mothering, and COVID-19: Dispatches from a Pandemic* (2021), *Maternal Theory, The 2nd Edition* (2021), *Monstrous Mothers; Troubling Tropes* (2021), *Maternal Regret: Resistances, Renunciations, and Reflections* (2022), *Normative Motherhood: Representations, Regulations, and Reclamations* (2023) and *Coming into Being: Mothers on Finding and Realizing Feminism* (2023). She is the editor of the *Encyclopedia on Motherhood* (2010) and coeditor of the Routledge *Companion to Motherhood* (2019). She is the author of *Toni Morrison and Motherhood: A Politics of the Heart* (2004); *Rocking the Cradle: Thoughts on Motherhood, Feminism, and the Possibility of Empowered Mothering* (2006); and *Matricentric Feminism: Theory, Activism, and Practice, The 2nd Edition* (2021). She is twice the recipient of York University's Professor of the Year Award for teaching excellence and is the 2019 recipient of the Status of Women and Equity Award of Distinction from OCUFA (Ontario Confederation of University Faculty Associations). She has received more than 1.5 million dollars in grant funding for her research projects, including two current ones: Older Young Mothers in Canada and Mothers and Returning to 'Normal': The Impact of the Pandemic on Mothering and Families.

Katie Bodendorfer Garner, PhD, focuses on motherhood, childcare, and labour equality via her PhD in English and is the executive director of IAMAS. Katie is currently writing *The Illusion of Choice*, which incorporates interviews with 100 U.S. mothers, and recently coedited *Creating Supportive Spaces for Pregnant and Parenting College Students* (Routledge). In addition to publishing articles with myriad academic outlets, Katie has been consulted for or appeared in releases by the Center for Public Integrity, *Chicago Tribune*, Fast Company, *Nature*, NPR, and numerous podcasts. She is the mother of three human children and two furry ones.

Contributors

Safwan Amir is a social anthropologist with a keen interest in the histories of the present. He specializes in the anthropology of religion and the sociology of caste with a focus on Muslim lifeworlds. Amir is an assistant professor at the School of Arts and Sciences, Ahmedabad University. He was a Fulbright Visiting Doctoral Fellow at the Department of Anthropology, Columbia University. He is currently working on a manuscript which is a revision of his PhD dissertation.

Laura Bunyan is an assistant professor in residence at the University of Connecticut, Stamford. Laura's areas of research and teaching include gender, work, family and ways to support first-generation college students. Laura is the author of *Modern Day Mary Poppins: The Unintended Consequences of Nanny Work* (2020), published by Lexington Books.

Lynn Deboeck (MA, PhD) is an associate professor of theatre and gender studies at the University of Utah. Her research interests include gender performance, the representation of maternity and motherhood in Western theatrical traditions, advances in pedagogy, and feminist directing of live performance. Her scholarship has been published in *Theatre Journal*, *antae: A Journal on the Interspaces of English Studies*, *PARtake: The Journal of Performance as Research* and *Frontiers: A Journal of Women's Studies*. Most recently, her book chapters "The Momboy: Maternal Tomboys on Stage" in *Reclaiming the Tomboy: The Body, Representation and Identity* by Lexington Books and "Negotiating the Fifth Wall" in *Theatre in a Post-Truth World* by Bloomsbury Methuen Drama were both published in 2022. She also coedited and published an anthology: *(M)Other Perspectives: Staging Motherhood in 21st Century*

North American Theatre & Performance which came out in 2023.

Jill Goad is an associate professor of English at Shorter University in Rome, Georgia. She has recently published articles on the new American baroque in Indigenous literature, water symbolism in Natasha Trethewey's poetry, the upended pastoral in Eudora Welty's short stories, and representations of women's labour in Trethewey's work. Her dissertation focused on re-envisioning the Freudian mother in Southern American literature according to a feminist psychoanalytic framework.

Jane Griffith is an assistant professor in the School of Professional Communication at Toronto Metropolitan University. Her first book, *Words Have a Past: The English Language, Colonialism, and the Newspapers of Indian Boarding School* was published by the University of Toronto Press. Her current work focuses on critical public relations and hydroelectricity. She is the book review editor (English language) for the journal *Historical Studies in Education/Revue d'histoire de l'éducation.*

Barret Katuna, PhD, is the executive officer for Sociologists for Women in Society, a nonprofit professional feminist organization dedicated to actively supporting feminist scholars and promoting social justice research. Barret's research focuses on gender, leadership, higher education, and human rights. Barret received her Ph.D. from the University of Connecticut in 2014. She is the author of *Degendering Leadership in Higher Education* (2019), published by Emerald Publishing.

Aya Kitamura is an associate professor at Tsuda University, Tokyo. She specializes in sociology, gender studies, and ethnography, and her current research explores global mothering in Asia. Her publications include "Hesitant Madams in a Global City: Japanese Expat Wives and their Global Householding in Hong Kong," *International Journal of Japanese Sociology* 25(1), 2016, and "Who Cooks What, How, and for Whom? Gender, Racial, Ethnic, and Class Politics of Food in Asian Global Household," *Journal of the Motherhood Initiative* Fall/Winter 2022.

Gertrude Lyons has dedicated her professional life to exploring the transformative capacity of all people, with a focus on mothers. Dr. Lyons received her EdD in 2017 and has lectured, appeared on television, radio, and podcasts, publishes widely, and produces her podcast, *Rewrite the Mother Code.* Her podcast empowers people who identify as women to love themselves by rewriting their mother codes. She has presented to audiences at various companies, including Google and Acuity.

Medhashri Mahanty is currently pursuing a PhD in cultural studies at the Centre for Studies in Social Sciences, Calcutta. Her research interests include queer theory, political theology, ruins, and postcolonial literature among other things.

Chrissie Andrea Maroulli is a PhD candidate in English Literature and Comparative Cultural Studies at the University of Cyprus. Her research is on women in early modern balladry. She has a BA in musical theatre and an MA in Shakespeare studies. Maroulli currently teaches at the European University. She is a musical theatre professional, and as a performer, she has worked with the leading theatre companies in Cyprus, including the National (THOC). She has created four original musicals that received wide critical acclaim.

Elizabeth Cummins Muñoz is a writer, researcher, and lecturer at Rice University. Her fiction and essays have appeared in several journals and anthologies. Her book, *Mothercoin: The Stories of Immigrant Nannies* (Beacon Press 2022), recounts the experiences of Central American and Mexican women working as cleaners and caregivers in the private homes of Houston, Texas, while telling a larger story about global immigration, working motherhood, and the private experience of our public world.

Rachel O'Donnell is an associate professor in the Writing, Speaking, and Argument Program at the University of Rochester. She has written about the political economy of bioprospecting in the Americas and revolutionary forces during the Guatemalan civil war. She has previously published with Demeter Press in *Coming into Being, Interrogating Reproductive Loss, and Mothers Under Fire: Mothering in Conflict Areas.*

Elizabeth Podnieks is an English professor at Toronto Metropolitan University. Her work on mothering, fathering, and caregiving has appeared in, among others, the *Encyclopedia of Motherhood* and the *Routledge Companion to Motherhood.* She is the editor of *Mediating Moms: Mothers in Popular Culture,* and *Pops in Pop Culture: Fatherhood, Masculinity, and the New Man;* and coeditor of *Textual Mothers/Maternal Texts: Motherhood in Contemporary Women's Literatures.* Her most recent monograph is *Maternal Modernism: Narrating New Mothers.* She is at present coediting *The Palgrave Handbook on Parenthood in Popular Culture.*

Tracy Royce is a feminist poet and writer living in Los Angeles. Her work has appeared in *Affilia: Feminist Inquiry in Social Work*, *The Fat Pedagogy Reader*, *The Fat Studies Reader*, *Modern Haiku*, Demeter Press's *Mother of Invention: How Our Mothers Influenced Us as Feminist Academics and Activists*, and elsewhere. Her account of caring for her mother with dementia was featured on the "One-Minute Memoir" episode of the *Brevity Podcast*.

Yolanda Wiggins is an assistant professor in the Department of Sociology & Interdisciplinary Social Sciences at San José State University. Her scholarly work has been funded by the Russell Sage and National Academy of Education/Spencer Foundations. Wiggins's published articles focus on education, educational policy, race, class, and family and have appeared in *Gender & Society*, *Sociological Perspectives*, *Journal of Black Studies*, and international media outlets, such as the *Los Angeles Times* and *San Francisco Chronicle*.

Madeline Wood holds a Bachelor of Science from West Virginia University and works as a full-time caregiver and coparent in a busy household in Rochester, New York. She finds peace in the quiet apartment she shares with her cat. She is grateful to have coauthored this piece with her dear friend, Rachel, with whom she has been lucky to coparent alongside as well.